Thinking ECOLOGICALLY, Thinking RESPONSIBLY

Andrea, Lorraine, and Nancy at the 2018 Feminist Epistemologies, Methodologies, Metaphysics and Science Studies Conference (FEMMSS) in Eugene, Oregon.

Thinking ECOLOGICALLY, Thinking RESPONSIBLY

The Legacies of Lorraine Code

Edited by

Nancy Arden McHugh and Andrea Doucet

Cover credit: Branch Brook, Rachel Carson National Wildlife Refuge, Maine, USA. By Malachi Jacobs.

Published by State University of New York Press, Albany

© 2021 State University of New York

All rights reserved

Printed in the United States of America

No part of this book may be used or reproduced in any manner whatsoever without written permission. No part of this book may be stored in a retrieval system or transmitted in any form or by any means including electronic, electrostatic, magnetic tape, mechanical, photocopying, recording, or otherwise without the prior permission in writing of the publisher.

For information, contact State University of New York Press, Albany, NY
www.sunypress.edu

Library of Congress Cataloging-in-Publication Data

Names: McHugh, Nancy Arden, editor. | Doucet, Andrea, editor.
Title: Thinking ecologically, thinking responsibly : the legacies of Lorraine Code / [editors] Nancy Arden McHugh, Andrea Doucet.
Description: Albany : State University of New York Press, [2021] | Includes bibliographical references and index.
Identifiers: LCCN 2021006239 | ISBN 9781438486352 (hardcover : alk. paper) | ISBN 9781438486369 (pbk. : alk. paper) | ISBN 9781438486376 (ebook)
Subjects: LCSH: Knowledge, Sociology of. | Environmental responsibility. | Environmental ethics.
Classification: LCC BD175 .L674 2021 | DDC 121—dc23
LC record available at https://lccn.loc.gov/2021006239

10 9 8 7 6 5 4 3 2 1

Contents

ACKNOWLEDGMENTS ix

INTRODUCTION 1
    Nancy Arden McHugh and Andrea Doucet

PART 1
"Knowing Well":
Epistemic Responsibility
and Epistemologies of Ignorance

CHAPTER 1
Ignorance and Responsibility: "Knowledge Didn't Agree with
Slavery," Learning to Read Frances E. W. Harper, 1872   7
    Catherine Villanueva Gardner

CHAPTER 2
Epistemic Ignorance, Epistemic Distortion, and Narrative History
"Thick" and "Thin"   25
    Kamili Posey

CHAPTER 3
Epistemic Deadspaces: Prisons, Politics, and Place   47
    Nancy Arden McHugh

PART 2
"Epistemologies of Everyday Life": Narratives, Stories, Testimonies, and Gossip

CHAPTER 4
Gossip as Ecological Discourse   73
Karen Adkins

CHAPTER 5
A Murex, an Angel Wing, the Wider Shore: An Ecological and Politico-Ethico-Onto-Epistemological Approach to Narratives, Stories, and Testimonies   93
Andrea Doucet

CHAPTER 6
Allowing for the Unexpected: The Thought of Lorraine Code and Mikhail Bakhtin in Conversation   129
Catherine Maloney

PART 3
Reimagining "The Force of Paradigms": Health, Medical, and Scientific Injustice

CHAPTER 7
Institutional Review Boards (IRBs) and Ecological Thinking   149
Carolyn J. Craig

CHAPTER 8
Knowledge Practices as Matters of Care: A Diffractive Dialogue between Lorraine Code's Ecological Thinking and Karen Barad's Agential Realism   175
Émilie Dionne

CHAPTER 9
An Ecological Application to Service-Users in Psychiatry: The Social Imaginary and Ethical, Political, and Epistemological Relationships   193
Nancy Nyquist Potter

PART 4

"Human and Nonhuman Life (and) the Complexity of Interrelationships": Environmental Justice, Climate Change, and Ecological Responsibility

CHAPTER 10
Rethinking Code's Approach of Ecological Thinking from an Indigenous Relational Perspective   219
   Ranjan Datta

CHAPTER 11
How Does the Monoculture Grow? A Temporal Critique of Code's *Ecological Thinking*   243
   Esme G. Murdock

CHAPTER 12
Taking Code to Sea   263
   Susan Reid

CHAPTER 13
Climate Advocacy as a Form of Epistemic Responsibility: A Case Study   285
   Codi Stevens

APPENDIX
"I Am a Part of All That I Have Met": A Conversation with Lorraine Code on "Knowledge Processes and the Responsibilities of Knowing"   303
   Lorraine Code, with Andrea Doucet and Nancy Arden McHugh

LORRAINE CODE'S BODY OF WORK: KEY WORKS, 1973–2021   325

LIST OF CONTRIBUTORS   331

INDEX   335

Acknowledgments

This volume would not have been conceived if it had not been for Lorraine Code's work, which always pushes the boundaries of how to do engaged feminist research. Her ability to think across a range of disciplines has provided a model and a theoretical and epistemological jumping-off point for many feminists in many disciplines. Thus, our deepest gratitude goes to Lorraine for helping us flourish as feminist scholars and for charting new pathways to do this work.

We'd also like to acknowledge our contributors to the volume, who engaged so thoughtfully with Lorraine's work through critique and example building as well by furthering her ideas and applying them in new contexts. We especially appreciate how graciously they took our feedback and developed truly exceptional papers that make a significant contribution to feminist, critical race, and Indigenous theories and epistemologies. By doing so, they honor the legacy of Lorraine's work.

Thank you to all of those who helped to shape this volume, especially Elizabeth Paradis for stellar editing; Kate Paterson for assisting with the Code bibliography and for managing the final stages of manuscript submission; to Jennifer Turner for assisting with correspondence with contributors; to Robyn Braun for the book's Index; and to two anonymous reviewers for their critiques and enthusiasm for this volume. We are grateful to our SUNY editor Rebecca Colesworthy for her patience and sage advice.

We also both want to acknowledge the support of our families, friends, and colleagues throughout this project. Without them we would not be the scholars we are today, nor would we have the energy and strength to see lengthy academic projects such as this one through to their completion. Nancy thanks her family, Patrick and Arden, as well as Nancy Tuana, Shannon Sullivan, and all of the participants in the 2003 National Endowment of the

Humanities Summer Seminar on Feminist Epistemologies. Lorraine was one member of the faculty who led a week-long session during the seminar. It was there that Nancy and Lorraine formed a professional relationship and friendship. Nancy appreciates the years of friendship and mentorship that Lorraine has provided. Andrea thanks her partner, Derek, and her three daughters (Vanessa, Hannah, and Lillian) for their support—and for listening to her talk about Lorraine Code's work for many years. Andrea finally met Lorraine when they traveled together from Toronto to Corvalis, Oregon, to participate in the 2018 FEMMSS 7 conference in Oregon; they have remained in conversation since then. She is grateful to Natasha Mauthner and Carol Gilligan who have both played critical roles in her journey in feminist methodologies, feminist epistemologies, and narrative analysis.

Notes

1. "Knowing Well" is taken from Code's (2006) *Ecological Thinking: The Politics of Epistemic Location* (New York: Oxford University Press), xxxix.
2. "Epistemologies of Everyday Life" is taken from Code's (1995) *Rhetorical Spaces: Essays on Gendered Locations* (New York and London: Routledge), xi.
3. "The Force of Paradigms" is taken from Code's *Ecological Thinking*, 165.
4. "Human and Nonhuman Life (and) the Complexity of Interrelationships" is taken from Code's *Ecological Thinking*, 3.

Introduction

NANCY ARDEN MCHUGH AND ANDREA DOUCET

Thinking Ecologically, Thinking Responsibly: The Legacies of Lorraine Code brings together a transdisciplinary cohort of feminist, critical race, Indigenous, and decolonial scholars who build upon and seek to widen and deepen the legacy and potential of Lorraine Code's work. Since the publication of her 1987 book *Epistemic Responsibility*, which was reissued in 2020 by State University of New York Press, feminist philosopher Lorraine Code has been at the forefront of linking epistemologies, ontologies, ethics, and epistemic injustice to guide critical frameworks for responsible, situated knowing and practices. This volume both enacts and expands Code's theories, epistemologies, and practices. It points to how concepts such as epistemic responsibility and approaches like ecological thinking are not only theoretical and epistemological frameworks for knowing the world; they are also practices and approaches that more and more feminists and critical thinkers are utilizing in their work to think, write, and live critically and responsibly.

In her most recent book, *Manufactured Uncertainty: New Challenges to Epistemic Responsibility* (2020), Code provides us with ways of elucidating the arc and potential of her work and challenges her readers to ask: who do you think you are? This question is not rhetorical: rather it is a significant query that one needs to ponder in order to be an epistemologically responsible ecological citizen and researcher. As *Manufactured Uncertainty* unfolds, Code revisits her former preoccupations—including climate change skepticism, the epistemic virtues necessary for responsible advocacy, the power and particularities of stories and testimonies, knowledge making as collective practices, and ecological social imaginaries of knowledge making and epistemic subjectivities—all with refreshed and incisive analysis.

Our volume, *Thinking Ecologically, Thinking Responsibly: The Legacies of Lorraine Code*, shares terrain with *Manufactured Uncertainty*. Indeed, we were writing and editing this book at the same time that Code was writing hers. We believe that this book is a valuable companion to *Manufactured Uncertainty* as we seek to engage with and widen the many path-breaking themes, issues, methodologies, epistemologies, and problematics to which Code has made major contributions throughout her fecund career of over forty years. This anthology provides critiques of her work, extending some of her arguments to areas Code might not have initially considered. For example, contributors to this volume connect her work with that of other leading thinkers and traditions, including, for example, agential realism, Indigenous and decolonizing epistemologies, narrative thinkers and traditions, epistemic injustice, epistemologies of ignorance, climate change and oceans research, institutional research ethics boards, and philosophies of psychiatry. With humility and diligence, we take up Code's (2008, 76) call to work with ecological thinking as "a way of designating a mode of thought and of philosophical practice," as "a point of entry into an ongoing project, perhaps never to be completed," and as an "ongoing project of constructing this complex conceptual apparatus."

The book is divided into four sections with numerous interconnections between them. Each section's title incorporates a quote from Code's work. The first section, "'Knowing Well': Epistemic Responsibility and Epistemologies of Ignorance,"[1] analyzes and builds upon Code's early arguments for epistemic responsibility, tying these to more recent work by Code and others, such as Charles Mills's (1997) writing on the epistemology of ignorance and epistemic injustice through the lens of literature, narrative history, and US prisons. Epistemologies of ignorance, a termed coined by Charles Mills in *The Racial Contract* (1997), has resulted in a wellspring of analyses of active, intentional unknowing and construction of systems of ignorance that has reshaped the landscape of feminist and critical race theorizing. "'Knowing Well': Epistemic Responsibility and Epistemologies of Ignorance" includes chapters by Catherine Villanueva Gardner (*Ignorance and Responsibility*), Kamili Posey (*Epistemic Ignorance, Epistemic Distortion, and Narrative History of "Thick" and "Thin"*), and Nancy Arden McHugh (*Epistemic Deadspaces: Prisons, Politics, and Place*).

The second section, "'Epistemologies of Everyday Life': Narratives, Stories, Testimonies, and Gossip,"[2] builds on Code's long-standing interest in narratives and social epistemologies as well as her early work on the epistemology of gossip and the gendered nature of knowledge. This section teases out the relationships and distinctions between gossip, narrative, and testimony by putting these concepts into conversation with contemporary concerns, including the relational nature of epistemic responsibility and ecological thinking, as well as ecological and Indigenous approaches to knowledge making. It also draws connections between Code's work and Mikhail Bakhtin's dialogical thinking as well as Margaret Somers's nonrepresentational and onto-epistemological approach to narratives. This section has chapters by three authors: Karen Adkins (*Gossip as Ecological Discourse*), Andrea Doucet (*A Murex, an Angel Wing, the Wider Shore: An Ecological and Politico-Ethico-Onto-Epistemological Approach to Narratives, Stories, and Testimonies*), and Catherine Maloney (*Allowing for the Unexpected: The Thought of Lorraine Code and Mikhail Bakhtin in Conversation*).

The third and fourth sections build upon Code's more recent work in ecological thinking and her critiques of medical and scientific knowledge. Section 3, "Reimagining 'The Force of the Paradigms': Health, Medical, and Scientific Injustices,"[3] reflects Code's view that utilizing feminist epistemologies to develop extended case study examples in science and medicine is a critical tool for seeking justice and virtuous epistemic engagement with the world. These case studies address research on human subjects' research as part of the Institutional Review Board (IRB), intersections between ecological thinking and new feminist materialism, and the value of Code's work for supporting epistemically, ethically, and politically responsible clinical psychiatry. This section includes chapters by Carolyn J. Craig (*Institutional Review Board [IRB] and Ecological Thinking*), Émilie Dionne (*Knowledge Practices as Matters of Care: A Diffractive Dialogue between Lorraine Code's Ecological Thinking and Karen Barad's Agential Realism*), and Nancy Nyquist Potter (*An Ecological Application to Service Users in Psychiatry: The Social Imaginary and Ethical, Political, and Epistemological Relationships*).

Finally, the fourth section, "'Human and Nonhuman Life (and) the Complexity of Interrelationships': Environmental Justice, Climate Change, and Ecological Responsibility"[4] brings together Code's arguments encouraging the use of ecological thinking and promoting epistemic responsibility in order to better understand human intra-action and human responsibilities within nonhuman worlds. The authors in this section present Indigenous Bangladeshi perspectives on environmental justice; reconsider ecological thinking through the lens of Indigenous, Black, and Black feminist thinkers who have provided important critical analyses of Code's work; demonstrate acts of testimony and witness bearing in oceanography; and address climate change advocacy as an epistemic responsibility. Its four chapters are written by Ranjan Datta (*Rethinking Code's Concept of Ecological Thinking from an Indigenous Relational Perspective*), Esme G. Murdock (*How Does the Monoculture Grow? A Temporal Critique of Code's "Ecological Thinking,"*), Susan Reid (*Taking Code to Sea*), and Codi Stevens (*Climate Change Advocacy as a Form of Epistemic Responsibility: A Case Study*).

To conclude the editors of this volume developed a set of interview questions for a wide-ranging conversation with Lorraine Code. That conversation, which Andrea conducted at Lorraine's home in Toronto in winter 2020, provides space to reflect upon and understand Code's career as a feminist epistemologist, how her ecological thinking began and unfolded across time, why she rooted her work in ecologically inspired literatures and metaphors, how it links with other critical creative traditions of knowledge making, and her hopes and dreams for this work as it continues to move into the world. Some of her reflections remind us that Code's (2006, ix) ecological thinking approach grew out of her four-decade long "quest for conceptions of knowledge and subjectivity capable of informing transformative, responsible, and responsive epistemic practices."

As Code writes in *Manufactured Uncertainty*, her newest work takes up four of her long-standing key thematic issues "epistemic vulnerability, incredulity, ignorance, and trust—issues that animate a commitment to crafting principles for constructing ways of knowing/being that foster the democratic, respectful cohabitation that I begin to address in *Epistemic Responsibility* and in *Ecological Thinking*" (2020, 30). Our book seeks to bolster Code's quest and enlarge the scope and impact of her carefully crafted work. Our hope is that this collection, with its contributions from established and new generation scholars, will act as an "extended moment in ongoing conversations and deliberations" (Code 2008, 76) about knowledge-making philosophies and practices and how they might "translate into wider issues of citizenship and politics" in the decades ahead.

PART I

"Knowing Well"

Epistemic Responsibility
and Epistemologies of Ignorance

Chapter 1

Ignorance and Responsibility

"Knowledge Didn't Agree with Slavery," Learning to Read Frances E. W. Harper, 1872

CATHERINE VILLANUEVA GARDNER

> Our masters always tried to hide
> Book learning from our eyes;
> Knowledge didn't agree with slavery—
> 'Twould make us all too wise
>
> —Frances E. W. Harper[1]

In her pathbreaking first monograph, *Epistemic Responsibility* (1987), and in many subsequent publications over the decades, Lorraine Code has argued that orthodox epistemological accounts do not cover all that needs to be said about epistemic responsibility. It is not simply the case, for Code, *that* we know or *what* we know are sufficient epistemic endpoints; rather, *knowing well* is of both ethical and epistemic significance, and "hence, moral issues and questions of 'character' are often integral aspects of epistemic evaluation" (Code 1987, 3). Moreover, according to Code, these aspects bring to our attention the social contexts of knowing. In orthodox accounts of knowledge, the knower is independent and solitary; indeed, such a knower is considered ideal for knowledge acquisition.[2] Given that we know as social beings (we are not independent, solitary knowers), how then do the power structures of our society shape our knowledge, our possibilities for knowledge, and the exercise of our epistemic agency? Moreover, how can we *know well*, in Code's epistemic responsibilist sense, given the interplay of knowledge production and power relations?

In this chapter I explore these questions by framing them within the racial context of nineteenth-century America, in particular under the institution of slavery and in the years following Emancipation. Using Frances E. W. Harper's novel, *Iola Leroy, or Shadows Uplifted*, one of the earliest works by an African American, I will consider how the novel's characters have different epistemic experiences depending on how they are racialized, as well as how Harper's novel can contribute to a discussion of "knowing well" and how to understand cognitive and moral failures within the nineteenth-century American imaginary of white supremacy. Code's work has focused on other historical-cultural positions of privilege, such as the nineteenth-century British class system in "The Power of Ignorance" or South African apartheid in "They Treated Him Well." These epistemic responsibilist analyses can provide a map for examining knowledge of racial inequalities and social difference in nineteenth-century America.[3]

In *Epistemic Responsibility*, Code is not offering a "theory of knowledge in the form of a system of epistemological principles wherein the less general are derived from the more general" (1987, 253). Instead, she proposes "a different way of thinking about epistemological questions, rooted in certain truths about human nature and the structures of human institutions and working toward the development of reflective practice" (253). Of particular interest to my discussion is Code's claim that we can learn about human truths and develop our reflective practice through reading literature: "The development of character can afford a special kind of insight into human endeavors to make sense of the world" (201). Indeed, Code argues, literature *itself* has epistemological value as a "source of knowledge for both writer and reader" (201).

Literature in *Epistemic Responsibility* can be a source of knowledge because an understanding of the particular is valuable; moreover, an understanding of the particular can move beyond this level and offer a more general understanding of human ways of life and social situations. In the case of George Eliot's novels, for example, we understand what it was like to live as a certain type of person in a certain historical-cultural period (Code 1987, 205). A work of literature "opens the way for readers to experience what a situation is like and, hence, makes a difference to their thinking and knowing, if only by putting many of their assumptions in question" (Code 1987, 205). Code is thus arguing that epistemic (in Code's nontraditional sense) and moral knowledge claims can originate from novels; moreover, these claims, no matter how unquantifiable, offer a "degree and depth of understanding" (1987, 214).

In later works, Code nuances her claims about the use of literature. For example, she argues in "They Treated Him Well" (in which Code is thinking through the moral-epistemological issues raised by Nadine Gordimer's novel *July's People*) that knowledge produced by literature is not simply a case of collecting stories to explore humanness; stories do not speak for themselves but are subject to interpretation. Indeed, even the mere act of choosing which stories to collect is a reflection on who we are and our social location and thus a reflection of our relative transparency or opacity to each other. Moreover, Code shows how we can make new sense of human lives (even "if never definitively or completely") through reading literary narratives of different kinds and reimagine "forms of life that cannot have been" ours (2011, 216). Reading literature can challenge our "expectations in matters of recognition and oppression, and can animate strategies of thinking toward a critically creative instituting social imaginary where the occupants of positions of privilege might begin to take responsibility for how that privilege has made them" (2011, 216).

In *Epistemic Responsibility*, according to Christine Koggel, "the idea of the knower as embedded in creative and interactive knowledge-seeking activities in communities plays a key role" and is present throughout Code's work (Koggel 2016, 1). Yet, Koggel adds, "The idea that knowledge seekers are differently situated in terms of relations of power in those very communities" does not explicitly "come to the forefront of Code's work" until Code's 1995 essay collection *Rhetorical Spaces: Essays on Gendered Locations* (1). That being said, there is little doubt that Code's exploration of power relations and knowledge, and thus the close interconnections of epistemological issues and ethical issues, have been pivotal to the development of feminist epistemology, and *from the outset*, as Heidi Grasswick states, Code has offered us ways of reflecting on "our rich and complex interactions with others and taking up the challenges of how to *know well across social divides*" [italics added for emphasis] (Grasswick 2011, xviii).

In "They Treated Him Well," Code offers an examination of white supremacist thinking within apartheid South Africa. Central to this examination is a discussion of the epistemic irresponsibility of a (mistaken) assumption of human sameness on the part of the white folks in order for them to attempt to know people racialized-as-Black and their lived lives. However, in the case of Harper's novel, I would argue that the white characters do not begin from this false moral-epistemic position of seeing the characters racialized-as-Black as sharing the same human characteristics and lived lives. Indeed, without the laws and the whips and chains of slavery to maintain people racialized-as-Black in submission, the white characters of Harper's novel attempt *actively* to employ "mis-knowledge" about people racialized-as-Black to continue the imaginary of white supremacy and the material and social benefits that come from this imaginary for white society.[4]

Harper's character Dr. Latrobe, for example, who we meet at the end of the novel, is a public intellectual. He believes he understands people racialized-as-Black, in brief, they are to be told (by white people) their "place" and kept in it. Dr. Latrobe is concerned that people racialized-as-white should not socialize with Black people, as that "would drag us down . . . our social customs must be kept intact" (Harper 1893, 238). Conveniently, for these views he believes he is able to tell who is genuinely white and who is "passing"; he says his "practiced eye" can see the "tricks of blood" (1893, 229). For the reader's amusement, Harper has Dr. Latrobe pontificate about racial identification and character to another individual who is, in fact, Black but who has decided to hear what Dr. Latrobe would say if he believed he was talking to another white person. Dr. Latrobe leaves in a huff on having his "mis-knowledge" displayed publicly; indeed, the implication is that he may even need to physically exit the room/discussion in order to keep this mis-knowledge intact.

Given the centrality of Code's examination of epistemically irresponsible assumptions of "sameness" to "They Treated Him Well," much of my discussion of *Iola Leroy* will be drawn from Code's "The Power of Ignorance," an article published twenty years after *Epistemic Responsibility*, which is a better fit for an analysis of *Iola Leroy*. In this article, Code analyzes two nineteenth-century texts, George Eliot's *Daniel Deronda* (1876) and James Mill's *The History of British India* (1817), both of which offer examples of epistemological ignorance.[5] Grounded on her initial insights into the value of literature for epistemology, Code explores ignorance, both individual and systematic, and she reads the "darker effects": the "ethico-politically and epistemologically negative dimensions of the power of ignorance, to promote and/or sustain unjust social orders" (2007, 215). In George Eliot's novel *Daniel Deronda*, the character Gwendolen Harlech, Code claims, is ignorant of the daily lives of others and of her own class privilege; she is also ignorant of her ignorance, whereas the real-life philosopher James Mill, author of *The History of British India*, is proud of his ignorance of daily life in India under British colonial rule.[6] Mill and Harlech are not "individual" examples per se; rather, Code holds that they demonstrate a broader point about how epistemic subjects maintain and re/produce systems of ignorance (220).

In exploring the class ignorance and the cultural/racial ignorance of Harlech and Mill, Code invokes analogies with racial (white) ignorance in Charles Mills's *The Racial Contract*, in which he argues that the "social contract" is also a tacit agreement to "*mis*interpret the world" (18). Moreover, the social contract, and therefore what Mills sees as the racial contract, the colonial contract, the slavery contract, etc. "tacitly presuppose[s] an 'epistemological' contract'" (1997, 24–25). The agreement to misinterpret the world blinkers us to evidence that our fundamental beliefs are held in place "by webs of distortion and error—of epistemically careless, irresponsible knowledge construction. Social, sexual, racial contracts require, construct, and condone an epistemology, sustained by and sustaining an ecology of ignorance that comes to be essential to their survival" (Code 2007, 214).

Mill's and Harlech's ignorance are culturally sanctioned, and as such, what Code calls "an ecology of power and privilege" blocks knowledge (2007, 216). So how then are we to think of, or indeed judge, their ignorance? On orthodox epistemology we may expect that their ignorance could be removed with counterevidence, but "because an instituted social imaginary so effectively sustains a self-assured rightness, it may seem impossible even to imagine how an opening could be made for a 'new' conceptual frame to find a point of entry" (224). As Code explains, "Acknowledgment, if it comes, will be gradual, multilayered, persistent, and patient, for webs of belief that hold an entire imaginary together have to be slowly untangled, piece by piece, in a hermeneutics of practice/praxis where it would be implausible to imagine that straightforward true/false—'truth confronting falsity'—could serve as well as many epistemologists have hoped to 'correct' simple individual empirical errors and the damaging moral-political beliefs they generate" (225).

Here Code is explaining that the removal of ignorance, understood on the traditional epistemological view, will fail in this case. Neither Mill nor Harlech is making an "error" that is like, for example, their knowledge of mathematics. In the vast majority of cases of mathematical error, we simply need to walk people through the steps of their reasoning to pinpoint—and then erase—the error. Both the error maker and the teacher share the same conceptual framework. However, Mill and Harlech need to resist somehow the social imaginary that is keeping their false beliefs in place. Their entire conceptual framework about the social world—and thus their supposedly justified place in it—is mutually intersupportive. Each element needs to be untangled in a painstaking and possibly painful process, and Code does not appear overly optimistic that this process will succeed.

I shall offer a similar analysis to Code's analysis in "The Power of Ignorance" of the daily life for women of a certain class in nineteenth-century British society and daily life in India under British colonial rule. Only I will focus on "racialized" ignorance and privilege in nineteenth-century America using *Iola Leroy* as an illustrative example. I will first give an overview and some contextual background to the novel, as it is unlikely to be as well known as *Daniel Deronda* or *July's People*. The narrative outline of Harper's novel is simple (and not uncommon): the central character—Iola Leroy—grows up believing she is white. On her (southern, white, slave-owner) father's death, Iola finds out that she is the daughter of an ex-slave. Iola is tricked into returning to the South and thus into bondage. Unlike most women in her situation, Iola is fortunate to be rescued from slavery during the war and works as a nurse for the Union Army. Here she meets a white doctor, Dr. Gresham, who wants to marry Iola but struggles to come to terms with her racial background when he finds out about it. After the war, Iola goes in search of what remains of her family, and she eventually meets and marries another doctor, who—like Iola—could "pass" for white but refuses to do so.

It is historically evident that ignorance under the system of slavery functioned to maintain the oppression of Americans racialized-as-Black. In other words, ignorance is not always a lack of knowledge; sometimes it was actively produced for the purpose of oppression and exploitation.[7] However, what Harper shows is that this ignorance is not simply a lack of what could be called "white knowledge," such as literacy or financial affairs, it is ignorance of, for example, kinfolk and their whereabouts—what could be called "humanizing knowledge"—including access to knowledge of oneself. Families were sometimes separated when the children were so young that they could not remember the details of how their parents looked, nor could their parents recognize their children fully grown.[8] The central family members of Harper's novel recognize each other through knowledge of half-remembered favorite hymns and facial birthmarks. Iola has a picture of her mother, who she believes is the sister of Robert (the character we meet at the beginning of the novel), but—even with this visual prompt—Robert cannot be certain they are related. Indeed, Harper shows us that slavery can sometimes change characters and bodies so much that family members do not recognize each other even when they finally *are* reunited.[9] Iola's grandmother is reunited with her two children after thirty years, and she exclaims that she would not have recognized her daughter, who has aged prematurely due to her psychological and physical sufferings as a slave.

However, of perhaps more interest to my discussion of Code's work, is the way that the dominant group are ignorant or choose to be ignorant of racism and white supremacy, and, as I shall demonstrate, using Harper's novel, this epistemic stance requires some epistemological contortions. Harper is able to show us how the ignorance of Americans racialized-as-white maintains the slave system and what Code calls the "imaginary" of white supremacy.[10] Code asks in "The Power of Ignorance" how culpability is weighed when ignorance is exposed: Harper offers some epistemologically complex answers to this question through a comparison of the reactions of the central character, Iola Leroy, when she finds out that she is the daughter of an ex-slave (and thus legally Black) and the reactions to this knowledge of a potential suitor, the (white) Dr. Gresham.

Harper's novel has been criticized for its Victorian sentimentality, moreover, on the surface it appears to employ the myth of the "tragic mulatta(o)," a literary trope that is generally acknowledged to have first appeared in Lydia Maria Child's 1842 short story "The Quadroons." Such characters are biracial but often are unaware of their Black ancestry. Upon discovery, the "tragic mulatta" is rejected by white society. Unsure of how to identify racially, and lacking a community, these characters may even commit suicide. An alternative trajectory is where the character cuts him or herself off from their Black family and community completely, while typically living in fear that their "passing" as white will be discovered.

I would argue that such criticisms of sentimentality ultimately *misunderstand* Harper's epistemological ethico-political goals (which I shall demonstrate later). Harper's novel is multilayered. Certainly, it is sentimentalized Victorian fiction, but the form of a novel allows for the depiction of the horrors of the institution of slavery that, frankly, is still a struggle for Americans (both Anglo-American and African American) to accept. Harper *does* use the trope of the tragic mulatta (although Iola does, in fact, rise above her tortured past), but I would claim that the particulars of the novel are so explosive (rape, racial mixing, illegitimacy, lynching), coupled with criticisms of the behaviors and attitudes of white people, that it's as if Harper actively needs the protective cover of literary tropes and the mantle of Victorian sentimentalized fiction.

My argument now shifts to a moral-epistemic analysis of Harper's novel. To recall Code on the epistemological worth of literature, the characters of *Iola Leroy* can give readers insights into how human beings racialized-as-Black made sense of their lives under the system of slavery and how—despite the overwhelming odds—they were able to acquire knowledge. *Iola Leroy* opens with a curious conversation between two enslaved men, Thomas and Robert, ostensibly talking about the freshness of the butter that day. They meet with another man who enthusiastically reports that the fish in the market are fresh, and when they tell a fourth man that the eggs are fresh, he says " 'I thought so; mighty long faces at de pos'-office dis mornin' "[11] (Harper 1893, 8). Harper, using her authorial voice, explains that the enslaved used such conversations to inform each other about the successes of the war for the Union Army ("fresh market produce") or the fears of the white people. Indeed, later in the novel Harper explicitly states that all human faces were the texts that the enslaved read from, faces that could bring clouds or sun in their lives (146).

Here then Harper seems to be indicating that there is a "Black knowledge" that helps the enslaved survive, physically and psychologically. The enslaved characters of the plantations meet in secret regularly for a "church." They pray and sing, but they need to be quiet so as not to get caught. They have a big, cracked pot they use to speak into and tell their information about the success of the war. So here we can see the restrictions on the access to knowledge of the enslaved. They can speak in "market" code about war victories, and they can vocalize into a big pot to tell of their hopes and fears. However, unlike the essentially unlimited freedom of speech and ability to share knowledge in the larger white society, the dimensions and condition of a cracked pot symbolize the limitations on knowledge and communication of people racialized-as-Black.

However, what does Harper say of access to what should perhaps be called "white knowledge"? Historically, it is not the case that *no* enslaved person was literate; literacy laws varied by state and historical period. Some of the enslaved in *Iola Leroy* learn to read, either through their own efforts or because they were taught by their enslavers (primarily for the purpose of helping with simple household tasks). However, Harper makes it clear that literacy frequently brought physical danger, even for those who were taught by their enslavers; for example, Robert tells his army captain that his "owner," Mrs. Johnson, taught him, but when she told her cousin that Robert was literate, the cousin was not pleased to hear this. The cousin said that if Robert had been her slave she would have cut off his thumbs, but the cousin's husband responded that Robert would not have been able to pick cotton if that had happened. Robert comments drily: "As to my poor thumbs, it did not seem to be taken into account what it would cost me to lose them" (Harper 1893, 46). And in these brief comments Harper distills the brutal, intellectually limited life of a slave but also the way Robert uses irony to resist this life as well as to show how this intellectual limitation was ineffectual.

Harper's particular insight into the issue of "white knowledge" is her portrayal of the burning desire of many of the enslaved to learn to read. "Aunt" Linda tells the others at their "prayer meeting" about how whenever she was caught with a book, her fingers were whipped.[12] However, this abuse does not deter her, and it simply leads Linda to ask herself why books are not good for people racialized-as-Black if they are good for people racialized-as-white. Tom's enslaver finds Tom with a book and threatens him with five hundred lashes and additional work if he is caught with a book again. Like Linda, these threats simply encourage Tom to acquire the "forbidden knowledge," and he "thought there must be something good in that book if the white man didn't want him to learn" (Harper 1893, 45). At this point we should ask whether the forbidding of such knowledge is *simply* a case of keeping people racialized-as-Black oppressed and vulnerable to exploitation, or whether the acknowledgment that people racialized-as-Black have the same capacity to learn as people racialized-as-white would *also* disrupt the fabric of the imaginary of white supremacy. Certainly, Mrs. Johnson taught Robert to read, but Harper comments that she did so on the same principle as she would have taught tricks to a favorite dog (16).

In writing about a lack of "white knowledge," Harper does not simply mean knowledge that can be found in books. One of the doctors in the Union soldiers' camp comments that some of the Black soldiers do not know "their right hands from their left, nor their ages, nor even the days of the month" (Harper 1893, 145). It is hard to imagine just how limiting this amount of ignorance would mean for someone's life, but it is easy to see, within a white supremacist world, how vulnerable those racialized-as-Black would have been to oppression and exploitation. Certainly, the enslaved would feign ignorance as a form of resistance, but Harper here is drawing the reader's attention to how controlled slave life was due to actual lack of knowledge. Even if an individual raised the courage to escape, how would it be possible to make their way to the North without an understanding of basic directions (left/right) or the measurement of space and time (miles or months)?

After the war, Iola runs a school for both old and young ex-slaves (and central to Harper's novel is the call for the proper education of freed slaves). One day a "gentleman" (read: white) comes to the school to talk to the pupils "on the achievements of the white race, such as building steamboats and carrying on business . . . he then asks how they did it . . . 'They've got money' said the children . . . when asked how the white people got this money, the children reply, 'They took it from us.'" (147). Harper comments in her authorial voice: "The gentleman was nonplussed; but he could not deny that one of the powers of knowledge is the power of the strong to oppress the weak" (147).

Lack of knowledge controls the reality of the enslaved; for example, they have been told that the Yankees have horns to keep them from running away to the Union Army or helping the soldiers. Robert tells Tom that he (Tom) should not believe what he is told by white men, simply because they are white or that the truth of a man racialized-as-Black means nothing or less when measured against that of a man racialized-as-white, "If ever we get our freedom, we've got to learn to trust each other and stick together if we would be a people" (Harper 1893, 34). This final comment is significant. While Harper shows us a Black world circumscribed by violence and lack of choice, she also shows the reader an alternative world for people racialized-as-Black: in particular, a world of tight-knit families and a respectful community of their own race, in which people like Iola and her future husband will lead their race away from ignorance (and its consequences). In describing such a world, Harper shows the central elements of what could be called "Black knowledge," which is a rejection of any "white knowledge" that contains mis-knowledge of Black people, and a requirement to know well (which includes knowledge of family and taking pride in and trusting their race) that also brings with it a *practical* moral responsibility of raising up the Black community.

Code has been consistently critical of what she calls "S-knows-that-p" epistemology. In the case of ignorance, this epistemological model maintains an ignorance/knowledge binary in place, and this binary contains the assumption that acquisition of knowledge removes ignorance. This assumption certainly works for singly asserted propositions, such as "the car is blue," but it cannot allow for "the complexities—the ecological questions and the responsibility imperatives, both epistemic and moral—invoked by ignorance" (Code 2007, 221). Harper's novel provides a wonderful instance of Code's account of ignorance and epistemic responsibility: we can see not only these complexities but also the moral-epistemological contortions required to maintain white ignorance.

Harper's characters of Iola Leroy and her prospective suitor, Dr. Gresham, provide a fascinating study of epistemic responsibility within a white supremacist imaginary. As I stated earlier, Iola is initially unaware that her mother is an ex-slave, and she grows up believing she is white. Indeed, she believes that the slave system is a benevolent one. She attends a school in the North, and she tells her friends that slavery is not wrong and that her father is a benevolent slave owner and that all their slaves are happy. One of her friends asks if she would not want her freedom if she were a slave: "Oh, the cases are not parallel. Our slaves do not want their freedom. They would not take it if we gave it to them" (Harper 1893, 97–98). Iola has individual ignorance of her own situation, but she also shares in white ignorance when she supports the imaginary of white supremacy and denies the problem of the slave system and its attendant denial of the humanity of those in bondage. Iola's father dies, and Iola is returned to the South as a slave by her father's heir, and she states flatly: "I used to say that slavery is right. *I didn't know what I was talking about*" [italics added for emphasis] (106).[13] At this point in the novel, she learns more about the slave system and the responsibility this knowledge entails through her experience and her epistemic standpoint as a Black enslaved woman.

Once her ignorance is exposed, Iola refuses to "pass" as white and dedicates herself to helping her newfound community and to finding her blood relatives. In Harper's account of Iola's story and her moral and epistemic development, we find a compelling narrative that illustrates Code's account of epistemic responsibility. In moving from ignorance to knowledge of her own situation and that of her community, Iola now has situated knowledge that allows her epistemic privilege, which she uses to serve her new community, primarily as a teacher. This knowledge and the ethico-political action it entails are framed by Harper as what modern readers would conceptualize as "Black privilege." Harper explicitly spells out this form of privilege in a conversation Iola has with Dr. Gresham about Harry, her brother. Harry, Iola states, has greater advantages racialized-as-Black rather than passing as a white man. In Harper's worldview privilege and social advantages are not framed as material advantages; martyrs (not millionaires) are the privileged, as it is they who can lead and inspire others (see Harper 1893, 218–19). Black privilege is not the flip side of the coin to white privilege—it is not social advantage at the expense of others—rather it has epistemic content. Consequently, Iola and Harry (and others like them) have the privilege of serving their community.

Iola's refusal to "pass" comes at significant personal cost, as she struggles to find employment and encounters prejudice even in the supposedly liberal North. Iola meets a white army doctor during the civil war when she is working as a nurse, Dr. Gresham, and he falls in love with her when he believes she is white. To do Dr. Gresham justice, he remains in love with her when he finds out that—according to racial laws—she is categorized as Black, and he still wishes to marry her; however, the marriage would be on the condition that she "passes" as white, and he will "bury her secret in his Northern home, and hide from his aristocratic relations all knowledge of her mournful past" (Harper 1893, 59–60). Dr. Gresham's ignorance is intriguing. He would have been happiest if he had remained ignorant altogether of Iola's racial background. Failing that, he wants to keep his family and community in ignorance of Iola's heritage. Another aspect of his ignorance is his implicit assumption that Iola would actually *want* to be racialized as white, with all its accompanying social and material benefits, even though Iola has explained her views on "Black privilege."

On orthodox epistemological accounts of deception Dr. Gresham intends to get his family and community to believe that p all the while knowing or believing that $\sim p$. However, such accounts do not allow for the sociocultural context in which Dr. Gresham intends to deceive others. In nineteenth-century America, *such deception is, in a sense, necessary*, for transparency (the recognition of a woman of color as equal) would tear at the fabric of the white supremacist imaginary. For Dr. Gresham, the imaginary of white supremacy is so engrained in his conceptual framework that he would actively choose personal ignorance if that were possible and, failing that, deception of others. Despite his personal contribution to the war based on his ideals, he cannot see beyond what we call the social construct of race and the maintenance of white privilege. In short, he fails in his epistemological responsibility in that he fails to *know well*, nor will he even try to know the world as Iola sees it.

Returning to Code's work, in Gwendolen Harlech's case in "The Power of Ignorance," Code argues that ignorance is *not* culpable, for Harlech could not "have known better." Code states that she follows "Michel Foucault in recognizing the impediments to knowing what is not "within the true" (1972, 224), thus within the knowable, within the conceptual framework held in place by an intransigent hegemonic discourse, an instituted social imaginary" (2007, 226). However, Harper's Dr. Gresham is in a different situation as he is *not* being asked to have knowledge completely outside his sociocultural imaginary, and thus—following Code's conceptualization of culpability—his ignorance is culpable. He has at least a partial knowledge of racial equality, demonstrated in his commitment to abolitionist principles, but he fails in his epistemic responsibility to Iola, her community, and the abstract foundational principles he holds for a society of equality and justice.

Even though Harlech's and Gresham's situations are different (hence their culpability), Code's account of epistemic culpability allows us to understand Dr. Gresham's ignorance as well as Harlech's. Dr. Gresham finds it easier to accept a white supremacist world of illusion, a world in which he is the beneficiary. Within this world, he need not struggle with personal doubts; indeed, he believes everything makes conceptual sense, despite the fact that this making sense requires him to hold together disparate evidence. Surely, the fact that he wishes to deceive his family, and the fact that the woman he admires for her moral spirit will not marry him because she wishes to resist a white supremacist imaginary, should be clues that he needs to engage in self-reflection. Returning to a central insight of *Epistemic Responsibility* "intellectual virtue is, primarily, a matter of orientation towards the world and toward oneself as a knowledge-seeker in the world" (Code 1987, 58). Even if Dr. Gresham could not ultimately achieve the sort of racial knowledge and social awareness that Iola possesses, he is a moral failure in that he will not try; he will not, as Wittgenstein said, "go the bloody hard way" (Rhees 1969, 169).[14]

Following Code's question in "The Power of Ignorance," how then do we weigh Dr. Gresham's culpability when his ignorance is exposed? Certainly, he is not responsible for his ignorance of Iola's heritage, but his desire to return to a state of ignorance (if he could) and to keep his family in ignorance reflects badly on his character. Iola and Dr. Gresham have different notions of their responsibility to others. They both have an ethico-political commitment to abolitionism and act upon it, in particular with their contributions to the civil war, but Dr. Gresham does not understand that he is also epistemologically responsible for seeking out further knowledge grounding this commitment. Instead, he believes he is responsible for protecting his family and his community from knowledge of Iola's ancestry (and thus to maintain the imaginary of white supremacy), whereas Iola actively seeks out knowledge about her kinfolk, community, and race once she knows her true heritage. She has the intellectual courage to "know" and live within the ugly and unjust world in which she (and her chosen community) are situated, and it is important to understand that what I am calling here "intellectual courage" is part of Code's framework of epistemic virtue: it is more to do with the way Iola relates to the world, and her self-reflection, than with the "content" of her actions, beliefs, or epistemic claims. Harper makes it clear that Dr. Gresham lacks this kind of intellectual courage, and thus he cannot "know" well or truly appreciate the intellect and character of the woman he believes he loves. If Dr. Gresham had Iola's intellectual courage, he would come to understand (possibly at least in part) the existence of the imaginary of white superiority and how he benefits from it. Epistemic responsibility is both a requirement to *know well* (in the sense of knowing information) but also to *know well* morally. As readers, we judge him and find him lacking (and I believe Harper intends us to) for this character flaw.

Harper makes it clear that despite Gresham's love for Iola and his sentimental ideals that lead him to work for the army, he is not ready to interrogate his own beliefs as they relate to white supremacy. Perhaps the most telling of his many comments reflecting these beliefs is this conversation with other men talking about the "negro question" after the war. "Power," said Dr. Gresham, "naturally gravitates into the strongest hands. The class who have the best brain and most wealth can strike with the heaviest hand. I have too much faith in the inherent power of the white race to dread the competition of any other people under heaven" (Harper 1893, 223). Even though he knows how Iola self-defines, he continues to see her as white, which he sees as paying her a compliment to her intellect, character, and beauty. He thinks Iola's education will be wasted as a teacher in the South; it is not the work as a teacher he objects to but the fact that Iola will be teaching ex-slaves, something he sees as a demeaning role for a woman who appears white. Iola's character shows through her response to Dr. Gresham. Originally, she was the daughter of a rich slave owner, and she says that it was "through their [her father's slaves] unrequited toil that I was educated, while they were compelled to live in ignorance. I am indebted to them for the power I have to serve them" (235).

Can we hold Dr. Gresham responsible for what he "should" know? Following Code, someone like Dr. Gresham is operating within a received social imaginary (see Code 2007, 226). Harper, however, shows us where the imaginary is cracked, and thus he himself has an epistemological split. Dr. Gresham's epistemological split creates a strange kind of "double-think." Combined with his desire to act as if he were ignorant of Iola's heritage, and even to reverse this knowledge (if that were somehow possible), we gain insights into the conscious and subconscious epistemological contortions by white individuals of this era that are required to maintain and accept the system of white supremacy. Unfortunately, we learn from Harper that the contorted nature of white ignorance then means that the system of white supremacy will be hard to dismantle.

As Code argues, and Harper's *Iola Leroy* shows, an investigation into the epistemology of nineteenth-century white ignorance requires the inquirer to peel back layers of racial myths with their interlocking injustices (see

Code 2007, 228). Harper's novel can also be used to show that (as Code argues) an investigation into an epistemology of ignorance is best understood as a "genealogical inquiry into the power relations and structures of power that sustain, condone, or condemn ignorance" and an investigation with "a stronger descriptive-empirical and social-historical component than epistemology in an authorized sense would countenance" (Code 2007, 228).

Notes

1. This poem is in the public domain.

2. Feminist epistemologists, including Code, give epistemic significance to situated knowers—to the historical particulars of knowers, particulars such as gender, race, social status, etc.—and thus these philosophers challenge the ideals and objectives of the traditional epistemological project, with its goal of a universal account of knowledge produced by detached, abstract knowers.

3. Harper was born to free parents in Maryland, but the change in Maryland's law regarding people racialized-as-Black meant that she could not stay there without being legally imprisoned as a runaway and sold into slavery. Although Harper was free, she worked for the Underground Railroad, so it is likely that some of her characters' stories are not pure fiction.

4. Indeed, even Dr. Gresham, the most progressive of the white characters, displays contradictory beliefs about Iola. On the one hand, he would like to marry her, and thus sees her as "morally pure" enough to be with a man racialized-as-white. On the other hand, he (insultingly) sympathizes with Iola for her sufferings under bondage and the fact that she would have been "tempted" to have sexual relations with her owners (Harper 115). Thus, he accepts the stereotype of black women as oversexualized. Thus Dr. Gresham needs to engage in epistemic contortions to put these two conflicting beliefs together.

5. The concept of the epistemology of ignorance was first introduced by Charles Mills. It involves learning to "see the world wrongly, but with the assurances that this set of mistaken perceptions will be validated by white epistemic authority" (Mills 1997, 18).

6. At first Mills's belief that he could offer an epistemologically sound work without knowledge of daily life in colonial India seems almost surreal, but on closer consideration it may be a bizarre manifestation of the need for personal objectivity.

7. See p. 1, introduction to *Race and Epistemologies of Ignorance*.

8. Edward Baptist argues in *The Half Has Never Been Told* that it is a myth that families were only separated in harsh economic times. Instead, the separation of children from parents and husbands from wives was central to the capitalistic slave trade—efficient organization of labor required no attachments.

9. Sometimes children would be separated from their families at such a young age that they would not have recognized them if reunited. Indeed, there are stories of people marrying their own siblings. Whether or not these stories are actually true, the underlying points are that family groups and communities were devastated by the slave system and that this system meant that even knowledge of one's own self was not certain.

10. After the war, people racialized-as-white no longer have the power of naming "their" "boys and girls" and indeed of framing other adult humans as children. Mrs. Johnson, who used to "own" Robert, Iola Leroy's uncle, struggles to address him as "Mr.," and Harper comments in her authorial voice that learning a new social custom at Mrs. Johnson's age would be like learning a new language. In brief, this new language learning would take place within a new conceptual framework or worldview. Harper is offering the reader a powerful image of white social power—the power of naming—as well as the difficulty people racialized-as-white have with learning "new" knowledge of the humanness of people racialized-as-Black (see Harper 1893, 151).

11. Critics have pointed to the fact that Harper's more rustic or uneducated characters tend to be depicted as using stereotypical Black dialect. Given that the point of my overall discussion is racialized ignorance, this use of dialect may not necessarily be problematic and instead serve to make my point.

12. This character may not actually be anyone's aunt. The use of aunt and uncle by white people to address people racialized-as-Black was common.

13. Even though Iola's mother had been manumitted, few judges would have allowed her to inherit.

14. Ludwig Wittgenstein's comment to Rush Rhees. While Code does not make such explicit reference to Wittgenstein in her later work as she does in *Epistemic Responsibility*, the two philosophers share the recognition that doing philosophy—in this case epistemology—is an ethical activity. However, this is, unfortunately, a discussion for another time.

Works Cited

Baptist, Edward E. 2014. *The Half Has Never Been Told: Slavery and the Making of American Capitalism*. New York: Basic Books.

Code, Lorraine. 1987. *Epistemic Responsibility*. Hanover, NH: University Press of New England.

———. 2007. "The Power of Ignorance." In *Race and Epistemologies of Ignorance*, edited by Shannon Sullivan and Nancy Tuana, 213–229. Albany: State University of New York Press.

———. 2011. "'They Treated Him Well': Fact, Fiction, and the Politics of Knowledge." In *Feminist Epistemology and Philosophy of Science: Power in Knowledge*, edited by Heidi Grasswick. Dordrecht, The Netherlands: Springer.

Grasswick, Heidi, ed. 2011. Introduction to *Feminist Epistemology and Philosophy of Science: Power in Knowledge*, i–xxx. Dordrecht, The Netherlands: Springer.
Harper, Frances E. W. 1893. *Iola Leroy, or, Shadows Uplifted*. 2nd ed. Philadelphia: Garrigues Brothers.
Koggel, Christine M. 2016. "The Epistemological and the Moral/Political in Epistemic Responsibility: Beginnings and Reworkings in Lorraine Code's Work." *Feminist Philosophy Quarterly* 2, no. 2: 1–15.
Mills, C. W. 1997. *The Racial Contract*. Ithaca, NY: Cornell University Press.
Rhees, Rush. 1969. *Without Answers*. New York: Schocken.

Chapter 2

Epistemic Ignorance, Epistemic Distortion, and Narrative History "Thick" and "Thin"

Kamili Posey

Traditional analytic epistemology often classifies problems of ignorance as problems of evidence or problems with the objects of belief. In this sense, ignorance is best understood as the absence of knowledge, an absence that can be rectified by probing more deeply into questions of reality, evidence, and justification. But as Charles Mills (1997, 18) so provocatively writes in *The Racial Contract*, there are also "inverted epistemologies"—or epistemologies of ignorance predicated on voluntary misconstrual—and the willingness to engage in self-deceptions that "get the world wrong." In this sense, ignorance is both a belief state and a cognitive tool. It does more than capture lacunae in our knowledge: it has cognitive agency and acts upon other belief states by reordering, rejecting, or reducing the credence of conflicting beliefs. Such cognitive maneuverings are the backbone of the creation of concepts like "whiteness" (Mills 1997, 16–17) and "woman" (Alcoff 1988, 405–406), where active, willful ignorance allows the shaping of identities to appear "natural" or "essential." Traditional analytic epistemology has little conceptual room for analyzing epistemologies of ignorance rooted in the willful *unlearning* of belief for purposes of power and domination (or what I refer to as "epistemic ignorance") (Sullivan and Tuana 2007, 1–2).[1] For that, we would need to turn to the character of epistemic subjects as Lorraine Code did in her groundbreaking work on "epistemic responsibility" (1987, 3).

Code shifted traditional debates in epistemology away from orthodox criteria for knowing "objects of knowledge" ("*S* knows that *p*") to *someone's* objects of knowledge, making both the knower and the known epistemologically significant (Code 1993, 17–18). In Code's revolutionary epistemology, narrow doxastic projects give way to the development of cognitive character and the moral practice of "knowing well" (1987, 29–32). Her view, rooted in neo-Aristotelian virtue ethics, is focused on the cultivation of intellectual virtues. The virtuous knower is an individual who consistently actualizes the intellectual virtues, chief among which is epistemic responsibility. This responsibility entails that the knower has some choice over their "modes of cognitive structuring" and thus must be responsible for their choices as a cognitive agent (Code 1987, 51).

In this chapter, I take a closer look at two of Code's most critical philosophical theses: (i) epistemic responsibility and (ii) the epistemology of ignorance. Code moves away from thinking about knowers in "thin" social contexts, or time slices, i.e., under which conditions can we say that "*S* knows that *p*?" to thinking about the unity of a knower's life in "thick" narrative histories, or how *S* developed into the type of person who either rejects or accepts *p*? (1987, 29). The goal is to incorporate a richer understanding of the agent as well as what is required for her to "know well." The cultivation of cognitive character with its emphasis on intellectual virtue must also be situated in a deeply complex sociopolitical world that uses systematic ignorance as a political and economic tool. For this reason, Code, following Charles Mills, rightfully argues that we need an epistemology of ignorance. This is because failing to investigate ignorance puts us behind an epistemic "veil of ignorance" making us complicit in supporting a range of "colonizing moves" that contribute to the production of socially and politically oppressive beliefs (Code 2007, 219). How can we generate "thick" narrative histories when our beliefs may be distorted by "colonizers" or when we may even be engaged in the act of "colonizing"? That is, how do we protect our narratives from the power of ignorance? Code suggests a genealogical approach to the epistemology of ignorance rooted in a "descriptive-empirical" and "social-historical" inquiry into the institutions and power structures that affirm, condemn, or replicate ignorance (2007, 228). Thus, Code claims, the resolution begins with the process of *uncovering*.

I argue that a descriptive-empirical/sociohistorical analysis of genealogy may ultimately be fruitless. This is because Code's view acknowledges but *underdetermines* the role subjectivity plays in interpreting the relevant factors of genealogical analysis. Linda Martín Alcoff's work on positionality may appear to ameliorate some of these concerns with subjectivity, but I claim that it will fail at the level of structures and institutions—or *systems*—for reasons that Alcoff later highlights. Some power relations are predicated on epistemic ignorance. In these cases, the discursive context of positionality will be overwhelmed by the goals of domination. Secondly, I argue that if the epistemic distortion of some narrative histories by systematic ignorance cannot be resolved by Code's genealogical approach or by positionality then the construction of some "thick" narratives may end up reproducing the ignorance the narrative itself hopes to resolve. This, I argue, will generate substantive problems for Code's imperative of "knowing well." For how can we "know well" when we cannot identify which parts of our narrative history are colonized? Lastly, in line with Code's own question "Who *can* know?," we must address the question of "who *can* be systematically ignorant?" Thinking through Gaile Pohlhaus's concept of "willful hermeneutical injustice," I consider how those with epistemic privilege, a privilege that finds its roots in social and political power, use willful, systematic ignorance to undermine the hermeneutical resources appealed to by marginalized knowers (Pohlhaus 2012, 731).

In the final section, I argue for the existence of both benign and malignant forms of willful hermeneutical ignorance with the former operating as a kind of "not needing to know," or *epistemic laziness*, as discussed by José Medina, while the latter operates as a kind of active disavowal of marginalized knowing full stop (Medina 2013, 34). Malignant willful hermeneutical ignorance, akin to Slavoj Žižek's "fetishist disavowal," is where a dominant knower *knows* the "epistemic terrain" as multivariate and interwoven with specific marginalized experiences but refuses to let the consequences of that knowing bear upon their own dominant beliefs (e.g., "I know very well that most people discriminate against Black males and label them as criminals, but still I believe that most Black males are criminals") (Žižek 1989, 18). In this last section, I ask (1) if willful hermeneutical ignorance will lead to "radical incommensurability" between some dominant and marginalized knowers and (2) if social justice goals in epistemology necessitate charges of epistemic blameworthiness as well as the granting of special epistemic privileges to marginalized knowers, or marginalized communities, in order to rectify to malignant willful hermeneutical ignorance.

Narrative History "Thick" and "Thin"

In *Epistemic Responsibility*, Code proposes a "responsibilist" approach to epistemology where the knower, their environment, and their epistemic communities are all epistemologically significant "constraining factors" in the pursuit and justification of knowledge (Code 1987, 27). To give an account of where a knower succeeds (or fails) in terms of "responsible knowing" one needs a "thickly" descriptive account of the contributing factors to that knower's belief state (Code 1987, 27). We need to know more than the conditions that lead up to a knower either accepting or rejecting a particular belief. We need a richer narrative account of the actions, motives, and behaviors that have shaped a particular knower's life. This is what constitutes Code's concept of "thick" narrative history. The paradigmatic case for Code, both in *Epistemic Responsibility* and "Father and Son: A Case Study in Epistemic Responsibility," is that of nineteenth-century marine zoologist Philip Gosse (Code 1987, 17–36; Code 1983, 268–82). Gosse was a Christian fundamentalist who could not accept theoretical advances in evolutionary theory into his belief system because the advances conflicted with his belief in Creationism. Although a diligent scientist and researcher, Gosse was unable to entertain any views that conflicted with the biblical account of creation.

Code claims that Gosse lacks the virtue of epistemic responsibility. This is not due to Gosse's failure to cede religious beliefs to science but in his failure to account for beliefs in conflict with his own. His dogmatism and, ultimately, his *akrasia* are epistemic vices. We find a contemporary parallel of Gosse's *akrasia* in the example of former Trump administration advisor Myron Ebell. In 2016 Ebell served as the transition leader for the US Environmental Protection Agency with the task of staffing the agency and setting future US climate policy. Ebell also believes that human-generated global warming is a hoax and that the dangers of climate change are overstated to the public by the "expert class" and coastal elites (Carrington 2017). Despite reports by reputable climate scientists and consensus within the scientific community, Ebell, a nonscientist layperson, refuses to accept human-made climate change as anything more than a liberal lobbying agenda (Carrington 2017). Ebell's ability to critically assess new evidence about global warming is compromised by his class-conscious, dogmatic attitudes toward "liberals" and "progressive scientists." As with the Gosse case, Ebell's rejection of human-generated climate change is best explained by looking at a thick description of the contributing factors to his belief state. Ebell's history of hostility toward scientists, his distrust of "urban bicoastal elites," his belief that climate initiatives are part of a liberal agenda, and his proud declaration of being a "climate criminal" are all critical parts of his epistemic character (Boghani 2016). Taking a closer look, we find that Ebell is not unfamiliar with the intricacies of the climate science debate. In fact, it is not *climate science* that Ebell rejects but rather any view supported by climate scientists that contradicts his background belief in the "liberal" control of the climate science debate. This is what prevents Ebell from hearing well.

Ebell's case mirrors Gosse's case in that they both chose to akratically abridge inquiry when it instead demanded the reconsideration of dearly held beliefs. The motivating reasons for their *akrasia* are best understood by unraveling their respective narratives as well as by looking to both men's cognitive characters (Code 1987, 24).[2] There is a correlation between intellectually virtuous characters and epistemic integrity, and that correlation is central to Code's epistemic evaluation. But this does not mean that the possession of an intellectually virtuous character entails the possession of knowledge: it can only point toward the general merit of a claim. As Code explains: "Judging beliefs and knowledge claims from this kind of perspective is like judging the actions of the morally virtuous. It yields no guarantee that an action is right or a claim valid. It can, in light of the quality of character from which actions and knowledge claims originate, give some idea of their worth" (1987, 36). Alongside considerations of whether a knower is intellectually virtuous, it is equally important to ascertain if one is in a *position to know* (Code 1987, 39). Attributions of intellectual virtue are dependent on thick narrative descriptions because how one is shaped as a knower, both dispositionally and in terms of one's epistemic community, impinges upon intellectual development. There are legitimate reasons why a knower's epistemic integrity may be compromised such that they are not (and cannot be) in a position to know. Such cases include knowers with physical and/or cognitive impairments like traumatic brain injury or age-related dementia. Knowers of varied abilities "are capable of intellectual virtue," Code claims, "though there are areas of experience in which they could not claim to be reliable" (1987, 61).

What makes a case one of intellectual *vice*, as with Gosse and Ebell, is that neither agents' epistemic integrity was legitimately compromised: that is, (a) both agents were in a position to know and (b) both agents were capable of assessing and incorporating beliefs that conflicted with their own. These considerations suggest problems of *willful ignorance*. Willful ignorance, or what I call here "epistemic ignorance," facilitates a kind of *unlearning* or *unknowing* of belief that has a symbiotic relationship with systems and structures of power and privilege. What makes the case of Gosse and Ebell problematic is that they are in a position to be beneficiaries of their own epistemic ignorance. This is not the case for all knowers. In the following section, I turn to Code's claim that looking behind the epistemic "veil of ignorance" allows us to see how ignorance operates to reinforce socially and politically oppressive belief systems, or what she calls, "colonizing moves" (2007, 219). I question Code's claim that understanding how power works in the replication of epistemic ignorance is sufficient to combat the colonization of our beliefs by the power structures themselves. That is, how are we to assess intellectual virtue and "knowing responsibly" if we cannot tell whether our beliefs are "colonized" or in the process of "colonizing"? What is more, how we can generate thick narratives—in Code's sense—in the face of such epistemic distortion?

Epistemic Ignorance and Colonizing Moves

Code examines the power of ignorance through the lens of literature, be it Gwendolen Harleth in George Eliot's *Daniel Deronda* or Maureen Smales in Nadine Gordimer's *July's People* (Code 2007, 2011), focusing on the epistemic tension that emerges when the lives of privileged white protagonists run up against the epistemic frameworks that make their privilege possible. This was certainly the case for Gwendolen Harleth in Eliot's final novel when financial ruin threatened to reduce her social status to near servitude. It was equally, if not more so, the case for Gordimer's protagonist in *July's People*, when the novel's postapartheid vision demanded that a middle-class liberal white family take subservient refuge in their former servant's small African village. Gordimer's white protagonists were challenged in the very way they saw themselves, coming face-to-face with their own liberal hypocrisy as they failed repeatedly to conceptualize the lived reality of the Black Africans whose lives were entangled with their own. Their epistemic roadblock came from within the context of their own privilege, a framework that they unquestioningly accepted.

Code uses Gordimer's novel to illustrate how there are "impediments to knowing, from positions of white privilege" what it means to be "othered" in an epistemic framework that presupposes racial inequality (2011, 205). What Code so accurately theorizes through the lens of *July's People* are the ways in which both *colonized* and *colonizer* participate in social epistemic frameworks that reinforce erroneous belief construction. This is the epistemic "veil of ignorance" that allows both oppressor and oppressed to imagine contingent states-of-affairs as necessary conditions: "In the interests of preserving an imagined objectivity, the veil conceals and thus condones an ongoing ignorance of *its own* positionality vis-à-vis people variously Othered by the norms of a liberal-empirical ethical-epistemological imaginary" (Code 2007, 219).

Failures to recognize contingent social epistemic frameworks (e.g., frameworks that reinforce unequal power relations) are really failures of knowing *responsibly*. Code asks us to consider how ignorance of the "contracts that naturalize contingent social orders" rest upon what Charles Mills refers to as "structured blindness" (Code 2007, 214).[3] This blindness "serves to filter out empirical evidence that would unsettle or counter any suspicion that these fundamental beliefs might indeed be held together by webs of distortion and error—of epistemically careless, irresponsible knowledge construction" (Code 2007, 215). While the recognition of structured blindness (as well as other social epistemic impediments to responsible belief construction) might be the first step in identifying critical components of responsible knowledge construction, we still must figure out how to deconstruct our beliefs such that the thick narrative constructions by which we assess epistemic responsibility do not replicate the epistemic distortion in the frameworks themselves. The notion of a social epistemic framework—or social epistemic contract—falls under what Code calls our "dominant social imaginary," and it is from this vantage point that we exist as both knowers and critics of the system itself (Code 2006, 12–13). But the problem here runs deep. Beneficiaries of socially and politically oppressive belief systems may never come to see themselves as illegitimate heirs to beliefs that reinforce their dominance; and obligors, those bound and "othered" by oppressive belief systems, may never be able to destabilize epistemic systems that are dependent upon their oppression. This is what Mills describes as the "naturalization" of oppression where "evasion" and "self-deception" become the "epistemic norm" (Mills 1997, 97).

Consider the following case. In 2014, former Major League Baseball player Doug Glanville was shoveling snow in his driveway in Hartford, Connecticut. A police officer, who worked in the next town over, stopped Glanville and asked if he was trying to make extra money by engaging in illegal for-pay snow-shoveling services. The police officer assumed "that the man shoveling the driveway couldn't possibly be the homeowner" based on his skin color and the respective wealth of the neighborhood (Levin 2015). The police officer's behavior can be explained within a context of systematic epistemic ignorance that presupposes the social, political, and economic inferiority of people of color. The police officer's behavior can also be explained as asserting power in a situation where one's dominance is presumed. As Glanville rightly notes: "It's someone doing [something] simply because they have power or they are trying to assert power" (Levin 2015). Glanville responded by adjusting his tone and trying "to avoid sounding smug even when I was stating the obvious," a compensatory epistemic behavior that Kristie Dotson refers to as "testimonial smothering" (Dotson 2011, 244). The difficulties of trying to construct thick narrative descriptions of the police officer and of Glanville that adequately describe the descriptive-empirical, social-historical apparatus that generated their respective beliefs—that of knowing domination and of knowing oppression—are innumerable. Where would we even begin? How far back through history do we trace the discourse of racial (gender and class) inequality? How do we untangle the descriptive-empirical accounts of both the constructions of race (and gender and class) and the social-historical origins of inequality? And, most importantly, who is the "we" that gets to isolate the pertinent details of analysis?

The process of *uncovering* is deeply subjective. In fact, it is subjective all the way down, explanatorily speaking. A genealogical inquiry may only extend this subjectivity—descriptively—through time and historical imaginaries but will only compound a fundamental problem. Epistemic ignorance is a two-headed beast. Knowers are bound by what Code calls an *instituted social imaginary* that reinforces a kind of perspectival ignorance because knowers are bound by their own subjectivity within the social imaginary (Code 2006, 30–31). For this reason, some knowers might find the Glanville case one of justifiable policing, while others might find it further evidence of unjustifiable police harassment of people of color. It is nearly impossible to destabilize the social imaginary itself via the criticism that some subjective positions are "more true" than others. (This does not discount the project of focusing our epistemic analysis on those typically marginalized, or silenced, in the social-political-epistemic framework. But I will return to this in the next section.) What seems clear is that the dominant social imaginary reinforces socially and politically oppressive beliefs, and our narrative descriptions are built in the background of a dominant social imaginary (or multiple social imaginaries), so our narratives are likely to reinforce socially and politically oppressive beliefs as well. Depending on how we are situated within the dominant social imaginary, our narratives are likely to be colonized or colonizing. One wonders how the police officer (or the system of policing) and Glanville (or those marginalized by systemic oppression) could ever possibly arrive at commensurate narrative descriptions under such circumstances. And some degree of commensurability seems necessary to make meaningful judgments about epistemic responsibility.

Code acknowledges that narratives often track our knowledge as easily as they track our own ignorance because they map both "knowledge-enhancing" and "knowledge-impeding structures and forces" (2014, 20–21). But sussing out conduits and impediments to knowledge would require what Code fundamentally denies: a "view from nowhere" (1993, 16). This epistemic tension is where realism meets what is "within the true" or "within the knowable," or that which is kept in place by "an intransigent hegemonic discourse, an instituted social imaginary" (Code 2007, 226). How, then, do we "get at" epistemic ignorance at all? We might look to broadening our account of the epistemic subject, or the "we" of our genealogical inquiry. Ignorance, Code notes, is often thought to be *somebody's* but most likely belongs to a community or social identity. Attempting a genealogical inquiry where the subject is not a somebody but what Alcoff calls a "visible identity" is a starting point (Alcoff 2006, 6–7).

Alcoff argues for a notion of "subjectivity as positionality" where both subjective experiences and contextual relationships constitute the identity of those occupying racialized and/or gendered bodies (Alcoff 2006, 151). The key supposition is that identity is both a "location for the construction of meaning" as well as a "constantly shifting context" that includes a constellation of factors such as "objective economic conditions, cultural and political institutions and ideologies and so on" (Alcoff 2006, 148). In Alcoff's vision, subjectivity is reimagined as a place, a *location*, for a sociopolitical reimagining of a layered, contextual self. I take up Alcoff's notion of visible identities because it best maps onto Mills's epistemology of ignorance, both of which are characterized by their focus on *marginality*, particularly those who are marginalized by race and gender. The structured blindness Mills claims as informing "inverted epistemology," or an epistemology of ignorance, is not a symmetrical blindness; thus it seems sensible to start with the narratives of those who exist at the margins and upon whom epistemic ignorance is often enacted (Mills 1997, 18). I take this as a kind of ecological location, in Code's sense, but in another important sense it is a *privileged* epistemic location. I come back to the idea of a privileged location later in this chapter.

The issue with subjectivity in constructing and deconstructing narrative descriptions is that "we" as epistemic subjects have blind spots and weaknesses that may prevent us from reading experiences as part of the same narrative continuum (e.g., the police officer versus Doug Glanville). We have problems recognizing our own epistemic ignorance and thus problems making meaningful claims of epistemic irresponsibility about ourselves and others. Subjectivity, in Alcoff's sense, is wedded to a type of self-awareness that may illuminate our epistemic blind spots, both to ourselves and to the larger epistemic communities to which we belong. This ought to make us less susceptible to thinking of our own narratives as belonging to an exclusive "us," or an epistemic vantage point we cannot see beyond. It should reveal the empirical falsehood of a view of subjectivity rooted in immovable, intractable identities (e.g., "African American" or "woman") and allow us to situate ourselves and our narratives within wider networks of relations and affiliations. Identities, as Paula Moya claims, "track social relations" and "are highly contextual and subject to change" (Moya 2011, 80). My hope lies with Alcoff's vision of subjectivity as positionality and its rich epistemological implications, but my worry is that even as "positionalists" our epistemic lenses will be far too myopic. To borrow again from Moya, our identities are "mediated" and interpretative; thus, in many respects, limited (Moya 2011, 80–81). We see what we choose to see, we incorporate what we choose to incorporate, and we omit things from our analyses that are both empirically and psychologically inconvenient.

How far positionality extends is dependent upon how self-aware we are and how far such self-awareness extends. Much like the claim that subjectivity runs all the way down, so does the phenomenology (or the first-person "feels" or "noticing") upon which positionality rests. To see our identities as networked, contextual, and relational leaves room for the structures and institutions that give shape to our identities to use all available tools to promote *system-level* distortion of identity. Consider the economic example of American malt beverage companies from the early to mid-1990s. Companies like St. Ides/McKenzie River Corporation and Pabst Brewing Company promoted cheap alcoholic beverages by appealing to a primarily African American male consumer base through endorsements from hip-hop artists like Ice Cube, Snoop Dogg, Tupac, and the Wu-Tang Clan (Coward 2015). Here the economic structure both appeals to and perverts identity affiliations. At the level of positionality, the messages are mixed. This is because the structures by which we construct our "positional" identities may be predicated on gender and racial disenfranchisement, if not outright oppression, compounding rather than relieving epistemic distortion in identity.[4] There is a sense in which our identities are both locations and *mirrors*; that is, they are generated by voluntary networks and relations while also reflecting the involuntary networks and relations of which we have little control. This will leave us no closer to weeding out epistemic distortion in our narrative histories. At best, it presents another level of serious analysis with which we must contend.

We find a better resolution to the problems introduced by subjectivity by shifting our epistemological focus to social justice methodologies. Social justice methods acknowledge that there are dominant knowers and marginalized knowers within the instituted social imaginary, as well as a full spectrum of knowers and epistemic communities in between. Any remediation of epistemic ignorance cannot be rooted in what any particular knower knows or fails to know, willfully or not. The epistemic distortion that facilitates systemic epistemic ignorance, or *the wholesale colonization of belief*, is predicated on systems of power, privilege, and domination that are beyond the capacity of any individual knower to resolve. Social justice methodologies aid in the remediation of epistemic ignorance by first assessing who can be systemically ignorant and then asking: can we tool our epistemic methods to encourage the decolonization of beliefs?

Marginality and Willful Hermeneutical Ignorance

There is a robust history of social justice methodology in knowledge production with origins in postcolonial, Indigenous, feminist social movements. Although these histories cannot be fully traced here, the work of Sandra Harding on standpoint theory will stand in as both a powerful placeholder *and* torchbearer of such methodologies. A return to Alcoff's notion of visible identities, or those tied to the most visible, racialized, and gendered bodies, is also warranted. As it happens, historically and politically, those with visible identities carry much of the burden of marginalization, and it is here that dominant epistemic groups must turn their lens. However, as Harding and Kathryn Norberg rightly note in their piece: "Dominant groups are especially poorly equipped to identify oppressive features of their own beliefs and practices. . . . Their activities in daily life do not provide them with the intellectual and political resources necessary to detect such values and interests in their own work" (Harding and Norberg 2005, 2010). The reach of their epistemic ignorance is beyond presumptions of neutrality and objectivity, but in how those presumptions of neutrality and objectivity guide epistemological projects that are silencing and exploitative. There are countless examples of how presumed objectivity actively brought about what Boaventura de Sousa Santos calls "epistemicide" or the "murder of knowledge" in conjunction with real, lived violence for marginalized cultures and communities: "Unequal exchanges among cultures have always implied the death of the knowledge of the subordinated culture, hence the death of the social groups that possessed it. In the most extreme cases, such as that of European expansion, epistemicide was one of the conditions of genocide" (De Sousa Santos 2016, 92).

It is from this history of epistemicide that we can read Harding and Norberg's critique of conventional methodology. But social justice methodologies *as* epistemic remediation measures must go hand-in-hand with antiracist, antisexist, anticolonial sociopolitical agendas. Although dominant groups may be "poorly equipped" to see their own beliefs and practices clearly, this is *not* tantamount to claiming its impossibility. It is incumbent upon knowers with relative epistemic privilege to advocate for social justice methodologies and, what Code calls "destabilizing narratives," or narratives that disrupt the dominant social imaginary (Code 2011, 210).[5] Investigating the epistemic tension between collective memory and collective oblivion, between dominance and oppression, and colonizers and colonized, between what one knows and what one *willfully ignores,* are all key parts of decolonizing our own narratives and the narratives of others.

At first glance, social justice–oriented methods appear to reshape and revive our narrative histories through intersubjectivity and the radical retelling, and in some cases, *remaking*, of our collective histories. But there are many complications with this view: (1) epistemically exalting marginalized knowers and marginalized epistemic communities may be too reductionistic and may fail to account for how marginalized knowers often reify their own colonized beliefs; (2) turning our epistemic methodologies into projects of sociohistorical "saints" and "sinners" may result in all dominant knowers being unnecessarily labeled guilty of epistemic crimes; and (3) dominant knowers may resist, in both active and passive ways, analyzing marginalized knowing on its own terms—or using marginalized hermeneutical resources—as a way of either resisting or reasserting challenges to their epistemic dominance. Gaile Pohlhaus and Kristie Dotson conceptualize this last and most critical complication as a revision of and challenge to Miranda Fricker's notion of hermeneutical injustice (Fricker 2007, 155–159). Pohlhaus introduces the notion of willful hermeneutical ignorance as the dominant knowers' dismissal of the epistemic resources of marginalized knowers despite the fact that "that there are whole parts of the world for which dominantly held resources are not very suitable" (Pohlhaus 2012, 720–722). Pohlhaus emphasizes that this dismissal puts the dominant knowers in worse-off epistemic positions regardless of the sociopolitical power differential. This is because being "marginally situated leads not to 'different' knowledge, but, as Harding has argued, to more objective knowledge (Harding 1991, 138–63)" and marginally situated knowers "develop epistemic resources more adequate for making sense of more parts of the experienced world" (Pohlhaus 2012, 720–721).

Consider the main argument of Reni Eddo-Lodge's widely read 2014 blog post and subsequent 2017 book, *Why I'm No Longer Talking to White People about Race*. In Eddo-Lodge's post, as well as in the preface to her book, she describes her experiences talking to white people about race as deeply emotional (for her) but as failed endeavors for most of the white people she engages with. Her discussions of "structural racism" and "white privilege" were met with blank stares, disbelief, and often with outright hostility: "Their eyes glaze over in boredom or widen in indignation. Their mouths start twitching as they get defensive. Their throats open up as they try to interrupt, itching to talk over you but not really listen, because they need to let you know that you've got it wrong" (Eddo-Lodge 2014). Eddo-Lodge charges her white audience with *willful hermeneutical ignorance* as they willfully misunderstand, or fail to hear criticisms of structural racism, whiteness, and white privilege: all concepts that challenge their dominant worldview despite allowing for a better conception of reality *as it is*. She challenges the dominant knower's epistemic intransigence and identifies what is, in many respects, the most difficult part of undercutting the instituted social imaginary with a Codean *instituting* social imaginary. This is what Kristie Dotson, mirroring Charles Mills, aptly describes as "the work required to ever acknowledge its existence" (Dotson 2014, 17–18). Eddo-Lodge's interlocutors stand "itching to talk over you" because they cannot or will not hear how they have "got the world wrong" (Eddo-Lodge 2014).

It might be useful here to make a distinction between magnitudes of the "willfulness" of willful hermeneutical ignorance. We could easily imagine a benign form of willful hermeneutical ignorance that exists somewhere between Miranda Fricker's "epistemic bad luck" and José Medina's "ignorance out of luxury," where a dominant knower *"does not need to know"* and thus *does not know* borne out of a kind of "epistemic laziness" (Medina 2013, 34, italics mine). I would suggest, following Medina, that there is a fine line between "not needing to know" and "needing not to know," with the first case being morally and epistemically permissible and the second case being morally and epistemic impermissible. The moral and epistemic impermissibility of "needing not to know" is rooted in an unearned and rather cynically used epistemic privilege. Medina notes that cases of the second stripe do not constitute areas of epistemic neglect "but areas of an intense but negative cognitive attention, areas of epistemic hiding . . . that require an enormous amount of effort to be hidden and ignored" (Medina

2013, 34). *Needing not to know* also aligns with a form of epistemic injustice described by Dotson as "contributory injustice," where dominant knowers sit comfortably, *willfully*, in their situated ignorance despite the fact that there are alternative hermeneutical resources that they could use in place of "structurally prejudiced hermeneutical resources" (Dotson 2012, 32). This willful hermeneutical ignorance in its malignant form is *active* in its disavowal of marginalized epistemic resources. To borrow from Slavoj Žižek, such disavowal is fetishistic and compulsive in its demand to "know but not know," and can be seen in the myriad ways in which some dominant knowers cognitively maneuver to keep the homogeneity of their worldview intact (Žižek 1989, 18). In some cases, extending credibility to marginalized epistemic resources would generate a worldview so altered and disjointed that any epistemic adjustments would result in a violent cognitive schism. This, I take it, is the epistemic position that generates the most vicious forms of racism, sexism, homophobia, and transphobia. As James Baldwin so aptly describes in *The Fire Next Time*, such knowers are "mad victims of their own brainwashing" (Baldwin 1993, 102).

Malignant willful hermeneutical ignorance also compels us to rethink Lorraine Code's rejection of "radical incommensurability" and Charles Mills's claim that we ought to "avoid the absurd kind of hyperbole" that presupposes such incommensurability (Mills 1998, 28). Code claims, like Mills, that "radical incommensurability" would prevent real knowing and "understanding across differences" and would fail to make sense of our communicative successes (Code 2006, 233). It would also render large parts of our epistemic lives mysterious due to unbridgeable hermeneutical gaps. We would be met too often by the blank stares described by Eddo-Lodge. If radical incommensurability is an untenable thesis, then we can hope that benign willful hermeneutical ignorance is the rule and not the exception. Not needing to know, as opposed to *needing not to know*, would be the default epistemic position of epistemic privilege. It would describe the dominant knower who is socially, politically, and epistemically comfortable, as a knower who is epistemically incurious but not epistemically vicious. Consider the white, heterosexual male CEO who is surprised to learn of hiring discrimination with regard to LGBTQAI+ applicants in his company but is not curious enough to learn about heteronormative biases in hiring and workplace discrimination. He is not hiding from himself, epistemically speaking, yet he remains untroubled and incurious about the lives of marginalized others. Is he epistemically culpable? Would he be receptive to narrative histories of others? Would he be willing to engage in the *project* of epistemic responsibility? In the final section below,

I conclude with two worries about benign willful hermeneutical ignorance and the possibility of decolonizing our narrative histories. The first worry is that we may be too optimistic about the possibility of "understanding across difference" and the impossibility of radical incommensurability. The second and related worry is that we may be too reluctant to find dominant knowers epistemically culpable for their benign willful hermeneutical ignorance. Absent claims of epistemic culpability, how should we ground social justice methodologies that privilege marginalized knowers? We may achieve better objectivity, yes; we may advance marginalized epistemic resources that are "more adequate for making sense" of the world (Pohlhaus 2012, 720–721). But that is only part of the story. We generate better objectivity because we have identified and seek to correct a faulty epistemic landscape. We seek to correct *knowing gone wrong*.

Culpable Ignorance and Social Justice Methodologies

To begin with the second worry: without a doubt there is a conceptual link between how ignorant a dominant group can be about the world "as it is," so to speak, and how that ignorance maps onto the use of dominant and/or marginalized hermeneutical resources. At the farthest end of this mapping, I think you find the fetishism and the cognitive compulsion of the explicit racist, sexist, and so on, or those holding worldviews at the opposite extreme of those held by marginalized or oppressed peoples. Here also I think you find real radical incommensurability in the hermeneutical resources relied upon by dominant knowers versus those relied on by marginalized knowers. (This may account for the incommensurability of narratives in the case of Doug Glanville and the police officer.) This is not because marginalized knowers fail to understand the hermeneutical resources of, say, racists or sexists but because radical incommensurability does not require symmetricality. A dominant knower who violently refuses marginalized knowing maintains such a strongly prejudicial worldview as to render both marginalized knowers *and* marginalized epistemic resources invalid. In my view, dominant knowers of this type are epistemically culpable. We ought to blame them for their epistemic ignorance or what they willfully fail to know about the world. However, this is the easy case. It is easy to blame the racist or sexist. But what about our "benign" CEO?

One may argue, as Lorraine Code does, for a kind of due caution when levying charges of moral and epistemic blame. Code warns us via her example of Gwendolen Harleth in *Daniel Deronda* that charges of the form, "She should have known better!" ring hollow because "She *could not* have known otherwise" in the Foucauldian sense that Code adopts (Code 2007, 226). Her claim is this: there are "impediments to knowing what is not 'within the true' (1972, 224), thus within the knowable, within the conceptual framework held in place by an intransigent hegemonic discourse, an instituted social imaginary" (Code 2007, 226). We can neither indict the dominant knower for what was not known nor claim our own epistemic innocence. There is no "innocent position from which 'we' could level charges of culpability, for often, in the 'normal' course of events, we cannot, by definition, know of the ignorance from which *we* speak" (Code 2007, 226). There is a welcome theoretical humility to these claims. If the CEO is guilty, then what prevents the indictment of *all* dominant knowers? And who are *we* to be leveling such charges?

I suggest that epistemic justice requires claims of *epistemic blame*. This is, in part, because the social justice methodologies described by Harding and Norberg rely on this critical fact: marginalized knowing has been polluted by social and political violence and oppression. The marginalized knower has been wronged. To borrow from Moya, for marginalized knowers, this "wronging" is as much a part of the place "from where we speak" as any other specificity of our epistemic location (Moya 2011, 81–82). If social justice methodologies are to destabilize the dominant epistemic landscape, to generate what Code calls an *instituting social imaginary*, then it will exist in the places where dominant knowers are capable of doing the soul-searching, empathetic epistemic work of understanding the wrongs of dominant knowing as well as they understand the benefits that dominant knowing affords. It will exist in places where knowers can take advantage of what José Medina refers to as "beneficial epistemic friction," or places to be "self-critical, to compare and contrast one's beliefs, to meet justificatory demands, to recognize cognitive gaps, and so on" (Medina 2013, 50). Epistemic blame need not render a dominant knower inactive; instead, it can mobilize dominant knowers toward engaging in better collective knowledge making. These are the places where thick narrative histories may reveal their true epistemic import because these are the places where dominant knowers may be able to truly "hear well."

Lastly, I worry that avoiding claims of epistemic blame may forestall another kind of epistemic justice. It is the epistemic justice a marginalized knower seeks by exclaiming, "They should have known better!" to a dominant knower whose epistemic intransigence is rooted in either benign or malignant hermeneutical ignorance. Claims that rely on the impossibility of "epistemic innocence" render this aspect of epistemic justice inert. There is an operating assumption that epistemic power and privilege inversion look the same on both sides of the hermeneutical gap. If epistemic privilege is admitted and epistemic blame assigned, then marginalized knowing will be unjustly exalted. And how can this be epistemically responsible? Perhaps power inversion does, in fact, work this way. But perhaps holding fast to the claim that it *must* work this way prevents a different future from being realized. When I consider Eddo-Lodge's frustration with discussions of structural racism and white privilege, what stands out are the missed opportunities—the missed moments of engagement when those with epistemic privilege refused to cultivate the "ecological sensitivity" to see the world as interconnected and made of many meanings (Code 1995, 184). One of those meanings, I would argue, is that the future looks different from different vantage points. There is no need to double down on the ignorance and oppression that has dictated so much of the past by delimiting the possibilities of the future.

Notes

1. Here I use the term "epistemic ignorance" as shorthand for Shannon Sullivan and Nancy Tuana's description of epistemologies of ignorance, or "unknowledges," that are "actively produced for purposes of domination and exploitation" (2007, 1). I take these terms as interchangeable in the same sense that one might use "mathematic" to denote a state, quality, or property of something *or* as having to do with the study of mathematics. That is, the meaning of the term is ambiguous and will depend almost exclusively on a clarification of its contextual usage. I clarify my own usage here in order to avoid the charge that I am conflating terms that definitively refer to two different things. See Shannon Sullivan and Nancy Tuana, "Introduction," in *Race and Epistemologies of Ignorance*, 1–2. Albany: State University of New York Press, 2007).

2. See also Amélie Rorty, "Akratic Believers." *American Philosophical Association Quarterly* 20, no. 2 (1983): 179 and Ernest Sosa, "How Do You Know?," *American Philosophical Quarterly* 11, no. 2 (1974): 113–122. It is important to note, as Code mentions, there need not be an "outright intention to be irresponsible" to be epistemically culpable; instead, the akratic knower pursues knowledge in a way that is "wholly antithetical to the development of an exemplary intellectual character" (Code 1987, 91).

3. Shelley Tremain argues that the epistemic injustice and epistemological ignorance literature often uses ableist metaphors like "epistemic blindness," "epistemic deafness," "meta-blindness," "gender-blind," and "silenced" despite the work done by disability theorists to highlight the problematic nature of the language (2017, 348–349). Charles Mills's term, "structured blindness," trades in ableist language,

and so I use it here with some serious reservations. In this chapter, I use Mills's term for purposes of clarity and continuity to preserve the meaning from his work to my own, but I agree that we need new and better ways of talking about prejudicial deficits in understanding and/or inquiry that do not rely on the dubious equation of deficit with disability. As Tremain goes on to argue, using ableist metaphors without addressing the framework, or social apparatus, of disability as well as the theoretical insights of disability theorists may itself be a form of epistemic injustice (Tremain 2017, 349).

4. In 1991, the opinion of the New York state attorney was that St. Ides/McKenzie River Corporation was in fact guilty of disempowering communities of color by targeting young African American and Hispanic men with its advertising efforts. Although the suit was settled out of court, it successfully rattled St. Ides/McKenzie River Corporation and mobilized communities of color in New York City to fight to remove the racist advertising. In 1999 New York City Councilman Bill Perkins was quoted in a *New York Times* article expressing outrage over St. Ides/McKenzie River Corporation's racist targeting of young African Americans: "These guys seem to market to my community and the African-American community in general in that perverse sexual way that they wouldn't dare do in a white community . . . When you raise it to them they say it's a joke, but it's a joke on us, and in my opinion it's a racist joke." See: Nina Siegal, "NEIGHBORHOOD REPORT: HARLEM; Councilman Condemns Beer Ads as Crude, Racist," *New York Times*, February 21, 1999. https://www.nytimes.com/1999/02/21/nyregion/neighborhood-report-harlem-councilman-condemns-beer-ads-as-crude-racist.html.

5. Code claims that we must draw upon different skills in order to disrupt "dominant social imaginaries." Such skills require the juxtaposition of the dominant social imaginary against alternative possibilities that can "interrogate the social structure to destabilize its pretensions to 'naturalness' and 'wholeness' " (Code 2011, 210). We do this, she claims, through supporting socially challenging narratives, like Susan Brison's powerful recounting of her own rape and the rebuilding of self in "Surviving Sexual Violence: A Philosophical Perspective" and later in *Aftermath: Violence and the Remaking of a Self*.

Works Cited

Alcoff, Linda. 1988. "Cultural Feminism Versus Post-Structuralism: The Identity Crisis in Feminist Theory." *Signs: Journal of Women in Culture and Society* 13, no. 3: 405–436.

———. 2006. *Visible Identities: Race, Gender, and the Self*. Oxford: Oxford University Press.

———. 2007. "Epistemologies of Ignorance: Three Types." In *Race and Epistemologies of Ignorance*, edited by Shannon Sullivan and Nancy Tuana, 39–57. Albany: State University of New York Press.

Baldwin, James. 1993. *The Fire Next Time*. New York: Vintage International.
Boghani, Priyanka. 2016. "Meet Myron Ebell, the Climate Contrarian Leading Trump's EPA Transition." *Frontline*, November 14. https://www.pbs.org/wgbh/frontline/article/meet-myron-ebell-the-climate-contrarian-leading-trumps-epa-transition/.
Brison, Susan. 1993. "Surviving Sexual Violence: A Philosophical Perspective." *Journal of Social Philosophy* 24, no. 1: 5–22.
———. 2002. *Aftermath: Violence and the Remaking of a Self*. Princeton, NJ: Princeton University Press.
Card, Claudia. 1991. "Removing Veils of Ignorance." *Journal of Social Philosophy* 22, no. 1: 155–161.
Carrington, Damian. 2017. "Green Movement 'Greatest Threat to Freedom,' Says Trump Advisor." *Guardian*, January 30. https://www.theguardian.com/environment/2017/jan/30/green-movement-greatest-threat-freedom-says-trump-advisor-myron-ebell.
Code, Lorraine. 1983. "Father and Son: A Case Study in Epistemic Responsibility." *Monist* 66, no. 2: 268–82.
———. 1984. "Toward a 'Responsibilist' Epistemology." *Philosophy and Phenomenological Research* 45, no. 1: 29–50.
———. 1987. *Epistemic Responsibility*. Hanover, NH: University Press of New England.
———. 1993. "Taking Subjectivity Into Account." In *Feminist Epistemologies*, edited by Linda Alcoff and Elizabeth Potter, 15–48. New York: Routledge.
———. 1995. *Rhetorical Spaces: Essays On Gendered Locations*. New York: Routledge.
———. 2001. "Rational Imaginings, Responsible Knowings: How Far Can You See From Here?" In *Engendering Rationalities*, edited by Nancy Tuana and Sandra Morgen, 261–282. New York: State University of New York Press.
———. 2006. *Ecological Thinking: The Politics of Epistemic Location*. Oxford: Oxford University Press.
———. 2007. "The Power of Ignorance." In *Race and Epistemologies of Ignorance*, edited by Shannon Sullivan and Nancy Tuana, 213–229. Albany: State University of New York Press.
———. 2011. "'They Treated Him Well': Fact, Fiction, and the Politics of Knowledge." In *Feminist Epistemology and the Philosophy of Science: Power in Knowledge*, edited by Heidi Grasswick, 205–222. New York: Springer.
———. 2014. "Feminist Epistemology and the Politics of Knowledge: Questions of Marginality." In *The SAGE Handbook of Feminist Theory*, edited by Mary Evans, Clare Hemmings, Marsha Henry, Hazel Johnstone, Sumi Madhok, Ania Plomien, and Sadie Wearing, 9–25. London: SAGE.
Coward, Kyle. 2015. "When Hip-Hop First Went Corporate." *Atlantic*, April 21. https://www.theatlantic.com/business/archive/2015/04/breaking-ad-when-hip-hop-first-went-corporate/390930/.
De Sousa Santos, Boaventura. 2016. *Epistemologies of the South: Justice against Epistemicide*. New York: Routledge.

Dotson, Kristie. 2012. "A Cautionary Tale: On Limited Epistemic Oppression." *Frontiers: A Journal of Women Studies* 33, no. 1: 24–47.
Dotson, Kristie. 2014. "Conceptualizing Epistemic Oppression." *Social Epistemology: A Journal of Knowledge, Culture, and Policy* 28, no. 2: 115–138.
Dotson, Kristie. 2011. "Tracking Epistemic Violence, Tracking Practices of Silencing." *Hypatia: A Journal of Feminist Philosophy* 26, no. 2: 236–57.
Eddo-Lodge, Reni. 2014. "Why I'm No Longer Talking to White People About Race." *Reni-Eddo Lodge*. February 22. http://renieddolodge.co.uk/why-im-no-longer-talking-to-white-people-about-race/.
Fricker, Miranda. 2007. *Epistemic Injustice: Power and the Ethics of Knowing*. Oxford: Oxford University Press.
Glanville, Doug. 2014. "I Was Racially Profiled in My Own Driveway." *Atlantic*, April 14. https://www.theatlantic.com/national/archive/2014/04/i-was-racially-profile-in-my-own driveway/360615/.
Gordimer, Nadine. 1981. *July's People*. London: Bloomsbury.
Harding, Sandra. 2015. *Objectivity and Diversity: Another Logic of Scientific Research*. Chicago: University of Chicago Press.
Harding, Sandra. 1991. *Whose Science? Whose Knowledge? Thinking From Women's Lives*. Ithaca, NY: Cornell University Press.
Harding, Sandra, and Kathryn Norberg. 2005. "New Feminist Approaches to Social Science Methodologies: An Introduction." *Signs: Journal of Women in Culture and Society* 30, no. 4: 2009–15.
Levin, Michael. 2015. "Shoveling While Black." *Politico Magazine*, April 14. https://www.politico.com/magazine/story/2015/04/doug-glanville-racial-profiling-116969.
Medina, José. 2013. *The Epistemology of Resistance: Gender and Racial Oppression, Epistemic Injustice, and Resistant Imaginations*. Oxford: Oxford University Press.
Mills, Charles. 1997. *The Racial Contract*. Ithaca, NY: Cornell University Press.
———. 1998. *Blackness Visible: Essays on Philosophy and Race*. Ithaca, NY: Cornell University Press.
Moya, Paula. 2011. "Who We Are and from Where We Speak." *Transmodernity: Journal of Peripheral Cultural Production of the Luso-Hispanic World* 1, no. 2: 79–94.
Pohlhaus, Gaile, Jr. 2012. "Relational Knowing and Epistemic Injustice: Toward a Theory of Willful Hermeneutical Ignorance." *Hypatia: A Journal of Feminist Philosophy* 27, no. 4: 715–35.
Rorty, Amélie. 1983. "Akratic Believers." *American Philosophical Association Quarterly* 20, no. 2: 175–83.
Siegal, Nina. 1999. "NEIGHBORHOOD REPORT: HARLEM; Councilman Condemns Beer Ads as Crude, Racist." *New York Times*, February 21. https://www.nytimes.com/1999/02/21/nyregion/neighborhood-report-harlem-councilman-condemns-beer-ads-as-crude-racist.html.

Sosa, Ernest. 1974. "How Do You Know?" *American Philosophical Quarterly* 11, no. 2: 113–122.
Sullivan, Shannon, and Nancy Tuana. 2007. "Introduction." In *Race and Epistemologies of Ignorance*, edited by Shannon Sullivan and Nancy Tuana, 1–2. Albany: State University of New York Press.
Tremain, Shelley. 2017. "Knowing Disability, Differently." In *Routledge Handbook of Epistemic Injustice,* edited by Ian James Kidd, José Medina, and Gaile Pohlhaus Jr., 348–349. New York: Routledge. PDF ebook.
Žižek, Slavoj. 1989. *The Sublime Object of Ideology*. New York: Verso.

Chapter 3

Epistemic Deadspaces

Prisons, Politics, and Place

Nancy Arden McHugh

An oubliette is an intentionally dark, narrow, confining underground dungeon built to inflict maximum psychological damage. Oubliettes were used to primarily contain/detain political prisoners. The term is derived from the French verb *oublier*, which means "to forget." The forgetting was twofold. The oubliette was designed to shut political prisoners off from the outside world and ensure that they were forgotten and thus not a source of political interest, social awareness, or discomfort. Moreover, the design of the oubliette, built to inflict psychological trauma, was constructed to shut down the epistemic efficacy of the prisoner through a simultaneous teasing hint of possible escape via a narrow ladder or a rope, which was hung too high for the prisoner to reach, and the utter physical and sensory control of confinement itself. Escape, the outside world, and the promise that these held were meant to be a continual taunt to the prisoner whose whole world was shaped by the confines of the oubliette and the sole guard, who provided minimal subsistence to ensure nothing more than the survival of the political prisoner.

The design of the oubliette was constructed to occlude a prisoner's view of the outside world, to generate feelings of helplessness and dependency, and shape an epistemic state that calls into question the prisoner's knowledge of the external world and their own epistemic agency and efficacy. Eventually, prisoners shut down, lose touch with reality, and are forgotten by those who knew them. Along with the forgetting of the political prisoner was also frequently the forgetting of the conditions that led to their confinement and torture. Thus, as a political subject, both via their ability to act as an epistemic agent and to be known on the outside as a political subject, the prisoner has forgotten the outside world and is in turn forgotten by society.[1]

In the twenty-first century the United States has its own version of the oubliette: these are habitats designed to displace, confine, hide, and shut down epistemic efficacy. I call these "epistemic deadspaces."[2] This chapter begins by laying out the initial framework for the significance of epistemic location building to Lorraine Code's work on ecological thinking and located knowing. It goes on to show how this can help us understand the inverse of ecological thinking: epistemic deadspaces. Like the oubliette, epistemic deadspaces are spaces that make us politically and socially uncomfortable, and in many ways those confined in these spaces are *political prisoners:* people who are incarcerated, immigrants, Indigenous people, and people whose existence causes a level of social, psychological, and epistemological discomfort to those on the outside. This project is geared toward revealing what has been kept hidden by deadspacing and breaking the epistemic deadspace by making people and places visible. In my development of epistemic deadspaces, I lay out a series of interrelated deadspace features, developing an understanding through specific examples from one of the most overt and destructive enactments of epistemic deadspaces: US prisons.

Habitats to Know and Know From

Lorraine Code has long described her approach as one that engages "an epistemology of everyday life" (1995, xi). There is nothing more "everyday" than habitats, the physical spaces that we live within and through, physically and socially. Code asks her readers to think about how habitats are also epistemological spaces—ones that in living in and through, we are also thinking in and through. As Code and many other feminists working from a situated knowledges perspective have argued, location/habitat shapes epistemic engagements on multiple levels, including what we know and what we count as knowledge (e.g., Code, Collins, Haraway, Harding, Lugones, Sandoval, Narayan). In *Ecological Thinking* Code made salient the nature of epistemic location through arguing for the physical nature of epistemic location, tying it intimately to habitat. In short, Code argues that habitats are also places to know and to interrogate in their physical and social manifestations (2007,

25). Understanding habitat in this sense of a materiality that "demands" to be interrogated (2007, 100), Code argues, is critical for ecological thinking (2007, 37). Ecological thinking for Code, even as she frames it in earlier work, is a critically located, embodied, responsible epistemic engagement with the material and social world, one that both "examines the potential of epistemic and ethico-political practices to produce 'habitats' where people live well together, locally and globally, and respectfully within the physical/natural world" (1999, 65) and works to create ameliorative conditions to foster living well (2007, 19). Thus, ecological thinking is both descriptive and prescriptive.

Code frames the antithesis of ecological thinking with the logic of "masterful way of autonomous man" (1995, 65) and his "hegemonic discourses of mastery and domination" (2007, 19). These nonecological practices are epistemically irresponsible, precluding the ability to "live well together" (2007, 20)—that is, cohabitate in the fullest sense of the word (2007, 24)—are built on the "assumption that he can be master of all he surveys allows surveying to substitute for engaged participation, and mastery to suppress diversity for the sake of instrumental simplicity" (Code 1999, 65). This logic of mastery is framed through what Cornelius Castoriadis calls an "instituted social imaginary" (2007, 30–31). Instituted social imaginaries are our habits of living and knowing that are "instituted" into humans through a range of normative social practices. These habits and ways of being range from actual institutions, such as courts of law or medical organizations to moral, aesthetic, and social values and practices that provide the "grooves" that we live within and shape what we hope for in the future and how we read the past. The logic of mastery as instituted social imaginaries, Code argues, "extends across the ethos and expectations of the affluent white western world that sees no limits to human possibilities of mastering and controlling the world's resources-animal (both human and nonhuman), vegetable, and mineral—no reason to contest the rightness of man's claims to dominion over all the earth, and no reason to take issue with the generic concept of man's exclusionary referential scope" (2007, 31).

While *instituted social imaginaries* are regulative, the *instituting social imaginaries* are "vehicle[s] for radical social critique" that call into question the normative structures and practices of the instituted social imaginary (2007, 33). They are place based (i.e., shaped and located within habitats), providing a radical, responsible reconfiguration of "knowledge, subjectivity, responsibility, and agency" (2007, 33) that "denaturalize[s] the instituted imaginary of mastery" (2007, 51). José Medina builds on Code's work on social imaginaries, pointing out that Code is a "notable exception" in her work in feminist standpoint theories and social imaginaries in understanding how spaces can be simultaneously knowable and unknowable (Medina 2013, 293–294). Medina argues that imaginaries are relational in that they work in tandem, clash with each other, and provide resistance that requires one to question and critique dominant systems and to explore the possibilities for alternative systems and routes. Thus, Medina argues that the relational nature of instituting social imaginaries allows for resistant imaginations, or those that are "ready to confront relational possibilities that have been lost, ignored or that remain to be discovered or invented" (Medina 2013, 299).

This relational understanding shapes understanding of ecological thinking and how *instituting* social imaginaries intimately relate to each other. Code argues, "An ecologically modeled conception of knowledge and subjectivity thus initiates an *instituting* epistemic-moral-political imaginary in which these three conjoined modes of inquiry work reciprocally, intra-actively together" (1987, 36). Thus, ecologically modeled epistemologies are those that are capable of launching instituting social imaginaries that radically and substantially subvert current normative, regulative structures that obscure social, institutional, and cultural dysfunctions by not only providing clarity regarding these structures and their dysfunctions but also by providing avenues, practices, and directions for social change (i.e., for substantive changes in habitat in a manner that can result in thorough remapping at multiple levels).

Are all *instituted* social imaginaries and their accompanying habitats malleable and susceptible to the sort of corrective that ecological thinking can provide? Or are there some structures, physical and social, that are highly resistant to ecological thinking and *instituting social imaginaries*, making them *almost* impermeable to radical change and through their very structures are self-sustaining and enabling of densely epistemically irresponsible behavior? In other words, are some structures and spaces more heavily weighted toward pressing *unknowability* than knowability? I am suggesting that there are such structures that function through a physical and social habitat, much like the oubliette in my opening, that are structurally designed to shut down epistemic agency and efficacy, to result in the forgetting by those and of those on the inside of these structures and to facilitate *instituted* social imaginaries that enable dominant, oppressive social institutions.

These are spaces I am calling "epistemic deadspaces." Epistemic deadspaces are those spaces that are intentionally co-construc*ting physically* and *epistemically* to be the exact opposite of ecological thinking and are habitats designed to shut down knowing. Like the oubliette, they house people who are politically and socially troubling to the general public—people incarcerated for crimes, immigrants, free people of color, people who have mental health illness—away from the public eye and by design establish conditions to disrupt and terminate knowing on multiple levels. They also house habits and practices of privilege and domination and obscure the actors and actions of material and epistemic domination: much like the "inclusivity" of predominantly white colleges and universities obscures the epistemic violence inflicted upon Black students.[3] Epistemic deadspaces are the physical spaces, the habitats, that house (and are dependent on) epistemic ignorance, epistemic injustice, gaslighting, and epistemic violence for its functioning and maintenance. It creates these dysfunctional epistemic structures and is created by them as a product of broader dysfunctional social structures.

Operational Features Epistemic Deadspaces

Epistemic deadspaces operate through a series of features that maximize their effectiveness. Other oppressive structures/experiences share some of these features. Instead, it is the way these features converge, overlap, and sustain each other that organizes epistemic deadspaces.[4]

Habitats and Habits of Unknowing

First, epistemic deadspaces consist of physical spaces (habitats) that are intended to close or keep others out and hold others in, with or without force, such as prisons (state, federal, and for-profit) and detention centers (immigrant detention, juvenile detention, prisoner combatant detention, such as Guantanamo Bay), Native American reservations, gated communities, and (under the right conditions) churches, medical wards, and predominantly white colleges and universities.

Prison walls keep people out just as effectively as they keep people in. Thus, epistemic deadspaces are frequently built structures, much like the oubliette, intentionally constructed to preclude outside observation and critique at the same time that it keeps its inhabitants in. It is a habitat designed to contain and hide; in many ways, it functions as a world within itself. In most cases there is little to no inside view from the outside into the epistemic deadspaces or no unobscured view of the outside. Within these spaces there are physical and social structures that are obscured or allow for obscuring of actors and actions, and these structures are active in their work to suppress epistemic agency of those inside the structure and the ability of people on the outside of the structure to know what is happening inside. And, as I will highlight, in many cases deadspacing is part of the structural violence individuals and groups experience.

Arbitrariness in Everyday Rules

Epistemic deadspaces function through a combination of formal and informal rules that make it *appear* as if the system has a level of predictable and rational function. Foucault maps this out in *Discipline and Punish* with a daily schedule that is predictable, routinized, and embodied to the point at which the formal and informal rules are no longer thought about by those inhabiting epistemic deadspaces. These spaces are self-regulated by docile bodies, those that are trained or conditioned to be rule following without having to reflect upon (or sometimes even understand) the rules of a particular structure. For example, in prison everyone needs to be back in their "dorm"[5] at regular intervals for count (i.e., for the number of people who are incarcerated in the prison to be counted and all bodies accounted for). Failure to appear for count can result in anything from a "ticket"[6] to time in solitary confinement. This would be the example of a formal rule in prison. An informal rule would be avoiding eye contact with anyone you don't know reasonably well to avoid anything that might be taken as a challenge and result in significant violence.[7] For what it is worth, in some state systems eye contact is a semiformal rule and "reckless eyeballing" can result in a ticket (Shapiro 2018). A recent study found that incarcerated women are "ticketed," frequently resulting in solitary confinement, for reckless eyeballing and other minor "disciplinary infractions": these infractions are cited at a greater rate than among men (Shapiro 2018), thus pointing to the gendered nature of prison rules.

The system is also designed to be arbitrary, unpredictable, inconsistent, and opaque on multiple levels. It is designed to keep one wondering what might happen next and what those consequences might be. People who are incarcerated have numerous examples of the arbitrary enforcement of rules, many of which are low stakes but whose pervasive nature shapes daily life.

In prisons, rules and practices regarding food provide an enlightening example of the arbitrary application of rules and power and its effect on daily life. In her 2006 article "Food for Thought: An Analysis of Power and Identity in Prison Food Narratives" Rebecca Godderis analyzes the overt and covert application of institutional power in prisons through the controlling and monitoring of food and prisoners' consumption of food. Prison narratives, including those of people interviewed by Godderis, make apparent the importance of food in prison culture. Food holds an important place in prisons for many reasons, but the four reasons that are most salient are the relationship of food to home and comfort, the relationship of food and food choice to autonomy, the lack of appetizing and healthy food in prisons, and finally that food is used as a form of punishment in prison.[8] The first two reasons highlight the relationship of food to identity, the third to a physical desire to survive in prison, while the fourth highlights the way in which a person's nutritional sustenance can be used as a tool against them. Because food is so heavily weighted in prison, people who are incarcerated often find ways to make their own food in their cells or dorms.

In terms of food and an arbitrary application of rules, Godderis, in her interviews, provides the example of an inmate who would routinely take a small container of sugar out of the prison cafeteria to use for coffee in his cell. Most of the time this was acceptable, in part because sugar was also available at the commissary and not a banned item. However, certain COs would force him to dump the sugar out as he was leaving the cafeteria, citing "security concerns about the possibility of prisoners making 'brew' with it" (Godderis 2006, 66) ("Brew" refers to prison-made alcohol.) However, as was pointed out by the person being interviewed, since any person who is incarcerated could buy sugar from the commissary, and this person was taking small amounts, "the dumping of sugar was a symbolic exhibition of the guard's power [rather] than a response to a security matter" (Godderis 2006, 66). Although this might seem like a minute example of an arbitrary exercise of power, it is one of numerous examples that occur in the daily lives of people who are incarcerated. As the LoCI-Wittenberg University Writing Group[9] points out in the article "An Epistemology of Incarceration: Constructing Knowing on the Inside" (LoCI-Wittenberg University Writing Group 2016) and Godderis asserts in her article, the arbitrary application of rules and power generates an environment in which people who are incarcerated feel helpless. This arbitrariness contributes to an instability in which decision making and autonomy become increasingly compromised (Godderis 2006, 69).

Arbitrary Application of Governmental Rules

On the outside, many people, especially those who are privileged, assume that laws are consistently applied and provide protection to enable one's ability to live and function well. In prison even the rules and policies mandated by states and the federal government are opportunities for epistemic deadspacing, opportunities facilitated by the physical and bureaucratic structure of prisons. There are numerous examples of the capricious, dangerous, and dehumanizing ignoring of rules by prison staff I could point to, but the two I am going to focus on are sexual victimization of trans women and control of their access to information.

All prison personnel in the United States are required to be PREA (Prison Rape Elimination Act) trained and to follow PREA guidelines for interaction with people who are incarcerated.[10] Not only is inappropriate sexual contact explicitly illegal under PREA, PREA guidelines refer specifically to trans women and men as an especially vulnerable population. A 2014 report by the Department of Justice "Sexual Victimization in Prisons and Jails Reported by Inmates, 2011–2012" states that 39.9 percent of trans people in state and federal prisons reported being sexually victimized (Beck 2014, 1). Like all types of sexual victimization, this number likely represents an underreported number of victims. 15.2 percent of all trans people in state and federal prisons reported prison staff being the victimizer, with 85.1 percent of victims reporting that these were nonconsensual sex acts; 51.1 percent reported force being used, and 66.1 percent reported being pressured (Beck 2014, 2). Thus, even though there are explicit rules that make sexual contact with people who are incarcerated illegal, there are incidents of prison staff assaulting trans men and women who are in their custodial care.

Doe v. Massachusetts Department of Corrections demonstrates the ease with which COs can sexually victimize trans people. This is especially the case with trans people of color who are arrested and incarcerated at a higher rate than white trans people, with 47 percent of Black trans people having been being arrested one or more times (Grant et al. 2011, 163). The legal suit file by GLAD on behalf of Jane Doe states that she is housed inappropriately in a men's prison. Having transitioned to living as a woman forty years ago and identifying as female, Doe has received a three- to four-year sentence for a nonviolent drug offense. "She is regularly subjected to strip searches by male correctional officers, who routinely grope her breasts in the process" (*Doe v. Massachusetts Department of Corrections* 2018). PREA mandates that female inmates are strip searched by female COs and that male inmates are searched by male COs. In the case of trans women and men, PREA also provides guidelines if an exception must be made. It is worth noting that many men's prisons have female COs, which would thus allow them to follow items (a) and (b) below, thus making following cross-gender searches of nonbinary people, (f), a rare need (i.e., a nonbinary person can be searched by COs who share the same gender identification). Federal PREA rules state the following:

> Paragraph 115.315 Limits to cross-gender viewing and searches (a) The facility shall not conduct cross-gender strip searches or cross-gender visual body cavity searches (meaning a search of the anal or genital opening) except in exigent circumstances or when performed by medical practitioners. (b) The agency shall not conduct cross-gender pat-down searches except in exigent circumstances.
>
> (f) The agency shall train security staff in how to conduct cross-gender pat-down searches, and searches of transgender and intersex residents, in a professional and respectful manner, and in the least intrusive manner possible, consistent with security needs. (PREA n.d.)

Note that even *if* there are circumstances in which a trans person may need to be searched by a CO whose gender she or he does not identify with, PREA mandates that this happens in a "professional and respectful manner, and in the least intrusive manner possible" (PREA n.d.). Given that Jane Doe's breasts are being groped and that she is subject to routine strip searches by male COs (which should be a rarity, not the norm), it is pretty clear that PREA guidelines and Jane Doe's rights are being violated on a regular basis by the COs and prison officials who have a custodial duty and federal mandate to not violate her rights.

Furthermore, Jane Doe "is forced to shower in view of male prisoners who inappropriately comment on her body and otherwise harass her" (*Doe v. Massachusetts Department of Corrections* 2018). Again, PREA guidelines state the following in section 115.42(f): "Transgender and intersex inmates shall be given the opportunity to shower separately from other inmates" (PREA n.d.). Although there may be some interpretative leeway in what "showering separately" may mean, clearly it is not intended to involve trans women and men being required to shower in areas visible to those of a different gender. Again, COs and prison officials who are responsible for Jane Doe's care, safety, and rights, which are explicitly protected by PREA, appear to be purposefully and actively violating state and federal prison laws and compromising her safety, health (mental and physical), and her rights.

Finally, there is the question as to where Jane Doe should be housed. Currently she is serving her term in a men's prison. PREA guidelines state the following:

> (c) In deciding whether to assign a transgender or intersex inmate to a facility for male or female inmates, and in making other housing and programming assignments, the agency shall consider on a case-by-case basis whether a placement would ensure the inmate's health and safety, and whether the placement would present management or security problems.
>
> (e) A transgender or intersex inmate's own views with respect to his or her own safety shall be given serious consideration. (PREA n.d.)

Thus, since Jane Doe was arrested for a nonviolent drug offense it would be hard to classify her as a security risk in a women's prison, and it is quite obvious how her safety would be and has been extremely compromised in a men's prison, especially given not only the numerous personal testimonies by trans women regarding their safety in prisons but also the significant body of data gathered regarding trans people and sexual victimization in prison. Thus, guideline 115.42(c) is being violated. Jane Doe has clearly stated that she is unsafe in her current situation, has demonstrated that she is being harmed, and has stated her preference to be sentenced to a women's prison. Thus, with guideline 115.42(e), which does create some leeway with the language of "*given serious consideration*," it does not appear that *serious consideration* was given. Furthermore, the federally funded website, the PREA Resource Center, in response to the question of whether a policy that "houses transgender or intersex inmates *based exclusively* on external genital anatomy violates Standard 115.42(c) & (e)" (my emphasis) states "yes" (PREA 2016). Since Jane Doe does not present a security risk, is clearly in danger, is currently being sexually victimized, and has stated a clear preference for being housed in a women's prison, federal guidelines are again being violated.

In a preliminary injunction in March 2018 a federal court issued an order granting temporary relief until the case went to trial to resolve the constitutional issues of Jane Doe's rights. The temporary relief involved an order that female COs search her, that she be housed in her own cell, and that she showers separately from men and that they are precluded from observing her by positioning a CO to prevent men from entering the shower. However, the court decided that it "is premature and should await the resolution of the constitutional issue" instead of also granting temporary relief for her housing (*Doe v. Massachusetts Department of Corrections* 2018). This injunction is particularly illustrative of deadspacing in that it demonstrates that instead of seeing the violation of Jane Doe's rights as the deployment of the conditions set up and intended to be facilitated by the habitat (the men's prison), it treats them as ancillary issues that can be resolved on their own with strategically placed prison personnel and an individual cell. In other words, instead of changing Jane Doe's conditions by moving her to a women's prison, which would give her significantly more safety and freedom of movement, the "remedy" is providing more of the same structures already present. Epistemic deadspacing is so powerful because the structures of habitat are self-regulative and self-norming, such that appeals to more of the same are the only reasonable responses. This is especially curious given that PREA provides a ready means to approach this situation, one that would not present a "premature" resolution and would also allow for an environment that can meet Jane Doe's safety needs and her desire to be housed in a women's prison in a way that meets federal and state guidelines.

Control of access to knowledge, especially legal knowledge, via the arbitrary application of rules is another strategy of epistemic deadspaces. This violation is utterly predictable given the ways in which epistemic deadspacing both replicates rule manipulation that ensures it continuation and actively works to occlude knowledge production by its inhabitants.

Again, this can readily be seen in the treatment of trans women in prison. Lesley Webster, a Black trans woman, was incarcerated in a men's prison in Georgia and was eventually sent to a male probation center where she was placed in solitary confinement and reported being denied access to the detention law library. She was seeking legal information so that she could file a legal suit on her behalf to be released from solitary and moved to a women's facility. Webster argues that only trans women were denied their legally entitled access to legal information in the law library.[11] She did file a claim against the facility, but it was thrown out in court for lack of sufficient information and legal argumentation. Thus, Webster could not act as an epistemic agent on her behalf, experiencing what Kristie Dotson aptly describes as epistemic silencing: that is, predictably, given the structural norms of prisons that have built-in epistemic violence (Dotson 2011), her ability to act as an epistemic agent was intentionally blocked by the prison.

Thus, prison rules and their arbitrary enforcement ensure the replication of the system and are enabled by its physical and bureaucratic structure. At the same time, their ability to capriciously choose whether to follow federal and state guidelines has devastating and destabilizing effects on the lives of people who are incarcerated, especially those that are already exceedingly oppressed and endangered in the prison system, inflicting and replicating violence systemically through physical, emotional, and epistemic pathways.

Weaponized Evidence

Evidence holds a special place in the academy with many of our disciplines dependent upon empirical evidence and/or argumentative evidence as a framework for our work. In many of our fields the proper use and generation of evidence is something that is inculcated into us at the earliest stages of our career.[12] At best, in epistemic deadspaces evidence is like the use of formal and informal rules previously mentioned: slippery, contingent, and arbitrarily applied to benefit those with the most power. At its worst, in epistemic deadspaces evidence is weaponized and used as a manipulative tool by the powerful against the disempowered. In these cases, the "evidence" does not have to meet any of the justificatory standards that academics in various disciplines assume that it should have. The justificatory standards are determined and shaped by those who have control and whose power and positioning allows them to coalesce around the justificatory standards and evidence in a way that precludes outside analysis, critique, and intervention.[13] Ironically, the justificatory standards tend to be very low, whereas the outcomes and consequences are quite high.

One can think of weaponized evidence as a little like a parent telling a child "because I said so." The evidential standard is the one determined by the parent, which in this case is just their authority or word. There is a radical power asymmetry. The only other appeal is potentially to another parent, who is likely to feel like they have to support the initial parent's decision (i.e., they coalesce around what counts as evidence). Finally the goal of the initial parent is clearly to shut down dialogue and preclude opposition, which considering the amount of control parents can have, especially over young children, is rather effective. The child walks off realizing there is no point in arguing because no matter what they say (i.e., what evidence or argumentation they muster) it will not matter because the parent's control of the evidence is high. Further, their need to justify it is low because of how parent and child relationships are asymmetrically shaped, and there is no real ability to appeal to outside authority for analysis or critique because the other parent who has the ability to provide these is part of the power structure. In many ways this is a type of testimonial smothering in which one suppresses their testimony because they know they will not be heard (Dotson 2011): this gets replicated on a regular basis in parent-child relationships.

In epistemic deadspaces one sees a similar phenomenon, and some habitats are incredibly conducive to it. Again, criminal justice provides a telling example. In the case of Walter McMillian, chronicled by Bryan Stevenson in *Just Mercy*, who served six years on death row in Alabama for a crime he did not commit, "evidence" by white officers, white "witnesses," and Black "witnesses" who were paid/incentivized by the white officers, was viewed as reliable, irrefutable evidence. Whereas evidence from the many family members who were with Mr. McMillian the day and time the murder was committed did not meet the standards of evidence demanded by the white polity simply because it was evidence provided by people who are Black and not at the prompting of people who are white (i.e., their evidence was nonevidence). In subsequent attempts to get a retrial, the evidence of the state was routinely held to low standards or no standards by judges, and evidence that called into question Mr. McMillian's guilt was not allowed to be admitted (i.e., it was not even allowed to count as evidence). This radical imbalance in justificatory standards is fully predicted by the epistemology of the racial contract as described by Charles Mills in which the white polity constructs epistemic practices and standards that benefit the maintaining of the racial contract and are so fully ensconced in and enabling of the white polity that they do not even notice their existence (Mills 1997). They take their manipulation as a fact of whiteness.

Epistemically Suspicious

The asymmetries in power discussed above enable epistemic deadspaces as habitats in which radical epistemic suspicion is rife and is contingent upon power asymmetries. People who are housed or contained within these habitats are always viewed as epistemically suspect and not only as epistemically deficient but also as epistemically manipulative, unreliable, and untrustworthy. There is perhaps an irony that one can be seen as epistemically deficient and yet also be epistemically proficient enough to manipulate a system or individuals. However, this contradiction does not seem to be a concern or even noted. Perhaps it is because those who have power in these asymmetrical relationships are viewed as the epistemic authorities, and they can either afford to not notice the contradiction or are epistemically precluded from noting it (i.e., epistemically ignorant). Nevertheless, the outcome seems to be the same: the disempowered group ends up in an epistemically compromised position in terms of chronically being viewed as epistemically suspicious and thus a compromised epistemic agent regardless of countervailing evidence.[14]

Epistemic relations in prison provide an apt example of the generation of epistemic suspicion. If you are a free person entering a prison you hear repeatedly that people who are incarcerated are manipulative, not to be trusted, and that they lie. In their work on penal harm nursing (what I refer to as "health harm") (McHugh 2018), M. Katherine Maeve and Michael S. Vaughn make clear how this epistemic suspicion even shapes the care of ill prisoners through the enculturation of prison nurses. They state that

> upon employment in correctional facilities, nurses are taught not to hold conversations with prisoners, that "empathy [with prisoners] will be your downfall." . . . Training films warn new employees that inmate politeness should always be viewed as a form of manipulation. (Maeve 2001, 59)

People who are incarcerated are also put in a position where they are institutionalized to distrust their own epistemic efficacy. In other words, they become epistemically self-suspicious. Not only is it clearly communicated to them that they are perceived to be untruthful and manipulative, but they are clearly shaped and institutionalized to doubt themselves. This results in a loss of epistemic agency and epistemic efficacy. Medina describes this as a type of epistemic ego skepticism, an overgrowth of epistemic humility, which Code and Medina argue is an epistemic virtue. Ego skepticism develops to the point that it is becoming a vice and consists of "[a]n internalized lack of appreciation and a constant self-questioning . . . [as well as] poor self-esteem, a lack of self-confidence, and even an inferiority complex" (Medina 2013, 42). It is not only epistemically debilitating but practically debilitating and can lead to other types of epistemic vices, such as close-mindedness: this is because someone was in so much self-doubt that they become afraid to trust their judgment with other activities or challenges. In doing so it shares many of the psychological and epistemic features of gaslighting (McKinnon 2017). The LoCI-Wittenberg University Writing Group articulates how this plays out in a carceral setting.

> In prison this is most likely to develop into the epistemic vice of closed-mindedness such that an inmate is unwilling, or perhaps unable, to be open to "experiences and viewpoints that can destabilize (or create trouble for) one's own perspective" (Medina 2013, 35). Thus, epistemic closed-mindedness in prison can lead to inmates not viewing themselves as benefitting from and/or worthy or capable of taking the GED or enrolling in college-level or trade courses, or participating in programming that might challenge their point of view and lead them in new directions. (LoCI-Wittenberg University Writing Group 2016, 14–15)

In many ways this loss of epistemic efficacy serves the needs of the prison well because it prevents people who are incarcerated from developing a critical epistemic lens. This is what the LoCI-Wittenberg University Writing Group refers to as an "epistemology of incarceration," which is an epistemic state actively practiced by inmates to understand, assess, critique, and productively resist the dehumanizing structures of prison. Epistemically shut down prisoners are much easier to manage and maintain than those who are epistemically astute and epistemically rebellious. Foucault made this critically clear in his articulation of the concept of docile bodies: bodies that are shaped, trained, and managed by institutions such that they become self-monitoring and self-managing in ways that fit institutional needs and goals (Foucault 1977).

Inflicted Embodiment of Epistemic Deadspaces

The epistemology of deadspace shapes an ontology, a way of being in the physical structure. The embodiment of epistemic deadspaces can be indelibly inked upon bodies because with *intent* it reshapes body-mind habits and the corporeal body.

Epistemic deadspaces become embodied in several different ways, with these interacting and coproducing each other and furthering the goals of epistemic deadspaces.

The first of these modes of embodiment is contingent upon two factors: the physicality of epistemic deadspaces and the asymmetrical power relationship that exists within and outside of the structures. The physicality of epistemic deadspaces precludes those on the outside from seeing in, whereas the asymmetrical power relationships set up the conditions that the authoritative and physical structures of the space/habitat preclude people who are harmed from reporting the harm. Examples of this are rife, such as sexual assault in a range of cloistered spaces, such as Catholic churches, health-care offices,[15] and prisons.

In prison this combination facilitates prison administration and staff to act toward people who are incarcerated in ways that further the harm mentality of incarceration, what is known as "penal harm" (Clear 1994). When these harms occur in medical settings, I refer to them as "health harm." Many of these types of harms, such as penal and health harm, are gender-based or sexual-based harms, such as the forced sterilization of women, the shackling of pregnant women in labor, and prison sexual violence, which is a threat to everyone who is incarcerated, particularly for cisgender women and those within the LGBTQI communities.

For example, in 2013 the ramifications of epistemic deadspace and the way it facilitates health harm gravely came to light when the Center for Investigative Reporting in California uncovered that 144 women incarcerated in two California women's prisons were sterilized by prison doctors, primarily through double tubal ligations. An audit of the prisons stated: "The unauthorized sterilization of women in prison was facilitated . . . by a combination of inhumane practices, overcrowding, bureaucratic inconsistencies, and medical neglect" (Stearn 2013). At least 116 of the women were sterilized via tubal ligation during labor and delivery and typically were never told why the procedure was being performed. As Nikki Montano, one woman who was given a tubal ligation, stated about the doctor, "He never told me nothing about nothing" (Johnson 2013).

In addition to not receiving information, other women reported being prompted to sign consent forms while under sedation, one on her way into a C-section delivery. Kimberly Jeffrey stated: "He said, 'So we're going to be doing this tubal ligation, right?' I'm like, 'Tubal ligation? What are you talking about? I don't want any procedure. I just want to have my baby.' I went into a straight panic" (Red Phoenix). Jeffrey states that the destabilizing effect of having one's body violated and utterly altered in such a gendered, racist, and classist way by medical personnel whose responsibility was to care for her and protect her health "produced in me a despair" (Shapiro 2018). As she argues: state prison officials "are the real repeat offenders" (Shapiro 2018).

Several other women in the same prisons were manipulated into having hysterectomies after receiving a false diagnosis of cervical cancer. They were not presented with alternate options for treatment and did not receive care after the hysterectomy, nor did they have cancer. What they had was a uterus that the state wanted to remove. Many of the women had several children and multiple convictions. And although the audit does not give demographic details, all the women interviewed by the Center for Investigative Reporting were women of color. Crystal Nguyen, a woman who had been incarcerated at Valley State Prison, California, and worked in the infirmary, stated: "I was like, 'Oh my God, that's not right.' . . . Do they think they're animals, and they don't want them to breed anymore?"

The Center for Investigative Reporting states that many of the women who underwent forced sterilization did not want to talk about it at least in part because of the "shame and trauma from the surgery" (Johnson 2013). Thus, in this example, epistemic deadspace is incredibly effective. It allows for egregious acts of medical violence against women's bodies, especially women of color, via the mechanism of incarceration, and it prevents them telling anyone about it because of a lack of access to outside advocates and the way the health harm has shamed and traumatized them. The false diagnosis of cancer is an incredibly manipulative lie because the women are not in a position to question the diagnosis by receiving a second opinion. The "safe" option, the one that appears least likely to lead to death, is trusting medical personnel. (Note that many of these women have children to care for upon their release.) This is a physical and epistemic violence that results in trauma and shame. It is also a powerful example of testimonial smothering (Dotson 2011). These women know that speaking up on their own behalf is likely to be ineffective because they are viewed with epistemic suspicion due to their status as felons and because the prison medical staff is doubly empowered, protected, and authoritative as medical professionals and prison staff.

A second way that epistemic deadspaces become embodied is through institutional mechanisms that become habituated and wear on the body. We experience these in the outside world all the time, and in many ways these kinds of habits allow us to function well. For example, the use of red, yellow, and green lights is an institutional (federal and state) mechanism that allows for the effective and safe flow of traffic. Experienced drivers automatically brake at red lights. Inexperienced drivers have to think about braking.

In epistemic deadspaces these institutional mechanisms function just as effectively and are just as intentional in their shaping of bodies and habits, but they inherently damage and wear away emotionally, epistemically, and physically those who experience them. There are numerous examples of these in prison, some quite overt, such as the ways solitary confinement damages inmates' epistemological and ontological conception of space such that they start self-battering against the sides of their seven-by-nine-foot cells, in what Lisa Gunther describes as "cellular embodiment" (Guenther 2013). A more subtle type of body-mind habit reshaping is the obsessive compartmentalization of personal belongings that many people who are incarcerated engage in. This is such a common aspect of long-term institutionalization in prison that when younger inmates see older inmates acting this way, they excuse the behavior by saying she or he "has been down awhile" (LoCI-Wittenberg University Writing Group 2016). In other words, the person has served many years in prison and is thus "institutionalized," a phrase used by incarcerated people to describe the dysfunctional habits of body-mind that become ensconced after years of incarceration.

Finally, there is the embodiment of epistemic deadspaces that are the result of those in power embodying epistemically misaligned roles that result in the physical and psychological damage of those who are disempowered. This is replicated over and over again by people who abuse positions of institutional power that place them in a care role and instead come to embody a harm and/or predatory role. Examples of this are rife and immediately obvious. The physical and emotional abuse of children in immigration detention by their "caregivers," the abuse of children by Catholic priests and their subsequent treatment by the Catholic Church, the abuse of athletes by their coaches or health-care providers are all enabled by the physical, social, and institutional structures of epistemic deadspaces.

Examples of this abound in prison, especially when it comes to health-care workers in prison. As I argued above, health-care workers take on the penal harm mentality of the prison and engage in health harm when they should be providing health care for their patients. They thus embody the harm role of other prison staff, such as COs. This is one of the prime reasons why people are afraid to die in prison (Cleveland 2020, McHugh 2018). They know that in their most vulnerable moments they are going to be treated by those responsible for their care as prisoners, not patients.

Intimately Linked to Other Types of Injustices

Finally, epistemic deadspaces are almost always dependent on and enabling of other types of injustices, such as health injustice, environmental injustice, mass incarceration, immigration injustice, and injustice related to ability/disability. The building of prisons over EPA Superfund sites and the subsequent health outcomes for people who are incarcerated combine many of these types of injustice—health injustice, environmental injustice, and mass incarceration. A total of 134 prisons are located within one mile of an EPA Superfund site. Other prisons are built over old unused mines or on top of former landfills, places that in many cases are considered to be uninhabitable for most people but deemed suitable for those who are incarcerated (Bernd et al.). Furthermore, even though the US EPA has environmental justice guidelines requiring that climate impact be particularly scrutinized when it affects people of color, people who are incarcerated and who are disproportionately people of color are not included in these considerations.

Conclusion: Habits and Habitats

The breadth and depth of Code's work in epistemology provide language for shaping projects that allow her readers to do more than just see more clearly the epistemic habits and habitats that shape knowing and unknowing. Her work also provides avenues for critiquing broad systems, institutions, and locations that have been enabled by pervasive epistemic habits and by our lack of collective will, collective imagination, and collective compassion to rethink and repair these systems that appear to be broken by design. Furthermore, it allows for the launching of new epistemic frameworks such as epistemic deadspace, which allows for the explaining and critiquing of dominant systems of oppression in ways that couldn't have been furthered by what Code repeatedly refers to as "S knows that p" epistemologies (Code 1987, 1995, 2021). Code's project has been and continues to be one of calling on us to not only recognize the effects of our epistemic habits on how we live but also to cooperatively reshape our epistemic habits and habitats to live well in this world together.

Notes

1. I want to thank Devora Shapiro who, after my FEMMSS 2018 presentation of epistemic deadspaces, suggested the analogy of the oubliette to visual epistemic deadspace.

2. Epistemic deadspaces exist globally. For the purposes of this paper, I am specifically analyzing the US context in terms of examples. As I point out, there are many spaces through which one could study epistemic deadspaces, including many exclusionary sites of privilege. However, my approach is more modest here: to develop the concept of epistemic deadspaces through looking at the prison system.

3. Thank you to ShaDawn Battle who in conversation with me about epistemic deadspace helped to articulate the deadspacing of predominately white colleges and universities.

4. Rereading Patricia Hill Collins's *Black Feminist Thought*: her description of Black feminist thought helped me to articulate this language of "convergence." See Collins (2000, 22).

5. The use of "dorm" to describe the space that prisoners sleep and keep their belongings is an interesting "softening" of the reality of prison. This term romanticizes prison life to make it seem like a prisoner is in a dorm like a college student. Yet most college dorms or dorm rooms are not routinely shaken down in an attempt to look for contraband with students' pictures of their families torn up while the students lay on the floor in a "checked" position in their underwear, hands behind their backs, legs crossed, chin on the ground, and their allowed personal items destroyed and their beds flipped over. Nor do most college dorms have a mandatory "lights out" time nor a mandatory wake-up time. Nor do they have cameras overlooking beds or lights at perpetual twilight. And, for the most part, they don't have to worry about being killed or assaulted while they are sleeping and vulnerable.

6. A ticket is a write up for an infraction or a perceived infraction that usually adds time on to an inmate's minimum sentence, sometimes weeks or months, potentially years if there are many of them. Tickets can also result in a prisoner being reassigned to a higher security floor or prison or to solitary confinement.

7. See Shaka Senghor's book for the critical importance of appropriate eye contact to survive in prison.

8. One common theme in my discussions with my students who are incarcerated is the lack of fresh food, like produce, and that poor-quality food is used as a form of punishment in prison. For example, there is the infamous "prison loaf," officially known as "Nutraloaf," which is served as a form of punishment to inmates who have broken rules. It is described by prisons as a "behavioral management tool." See for example https://www.miamiherald.com/news/nation-world/national/article129786704.html.

9. The LoCI-Wittenberg University Writing Group, of which I was a member, was made up of ten people who are/were incarcerated and four people who are free. We wrote collaboratively inside of a men's level 2 prison.

10. There are numerous problems with PREA. See, for example, Palacious (2017) and Gilna (2017).

11. It might be tempting to question Webster's assertion and argue that she is mistaken, but gaslighting her in such a way when she has significant epistemic access to how trans women are treated in prison would be a further epistemic injustice. See McKinnon "Allies Behaving Badly."

12. This is not to say that the nature of evidence isn't contested in the academy. For example, Mills's work as well as that of Alcoff, Code, Collins, Dotson, and Tuana and all make clear the need to contest what counts as evidence in the academy.

13. Foucault makes this point via his genealogical approach to numerous subjects including incarceration.

14. Dotson's 2012 critique of Code's work on epistemic injustice provides useful language for framing how individuals react to epistemic violence or are affected by epistemic violence. Oppressed subjects react to this type of epistemic asymmetry by self-censoring one's own testimony, which Dotson refers to as "testimonial smothering" or the "failure of the listeners to recognize the marginalized speaker as an epistemic authority, testimonial quieting."

15. The sexual assault of female and male athletes by coaches, trainers, and team doctors falls into this category.

Works Cited

Alcoff, Linda Martín. 2009. "Epistemologies of Ignorance: Three Types." In *Race and Epistemologies of Ignorance*, edited by Shannon Sullivan and Nancy Tuana, 39–58. Albany: State University of New York Press.

Beck, Allen. 2014. *Sexual Victimization in Prisons and Jails Reported by Inmates, 2011–2012*. Washington, DC: US Department of Justice.

Bernd, Candice, Zoe Loftus-Farren, and Maureen Nandini Mitra. 2017. "America's Toxic Prisons." *Earth Island Journal*. https://www.earthisland.org/journal/americas-toxic-prisons/.

Castoriadis, Cornelius. 1981. *Philosophy, Politics, Autonomy: Essays in Political Philosophy*. Edited by David Ames Curtis. Oxford: Oxford University Press.

Chase, Randall. 2017. "'Baked Slop': Prison Loaf Served to Unruly Inmates Is Called Cruel, Unusual by Some." *Miami Herald*, January 31. https://www.miamiherald.com/news/nation-world/national/article129786704.html.

Clear, Todd. 1994. *Harm in American Penology: Offenders, Victims, and Their Communities*. Albany: State University of New York Press.

Cleveland, Corina, and Nancy McHugh. forthcoming. "Sentenced to Death: Incarceration, Healthharm, and Institutional Epistemic Injustice." In *Applying Nonideal Theory to Bioethics: Living and Dying in a Nonideal World*, edited by E. Victor and L. Guidry-Grimes. New York: Springer.

Code, Lorraine. 1987. *Epistemic Responsibility*. Hanover, NH: University Press of New England.

———. 1995. *Rhetorical Spaces*. New York: Routledge.

———. 1999. "Flourishing." *Ethics and the Environment* 4, no. 1.

———. 2007. *Ecological Thinking: The Politics of Epistemic Location*. New York: Oxford University Press.

———. 2021. "The Power and Perils of Examples: 'Literizing is not Theorizing.'" In *Making the Case: Feminist and Critical Race Philosophers Engaging Case Studies*, edited by Heidi Grasswick and Nancy McHugh. Albany: State University of New York Press.

Collins, Patricia Hill. 1990/2000. *Black Feminist Thought: Knowledge, Consciousness, and the Politics of Empowerment*. 2nd ed. New York: Routledge.
Doe v. Massachusetts Department of Corrections. 2018. Civil Action No. 17-12255-RGS. United States District Court of Massachusetts, March 5. https://www.leagle.com/decision/infdco20180306d26.
Dotson, Kristie. 2008. "In Search of Tanzania: Are Effective Epistemic Practices Sufficient for Just Epistemic Practices?" *Southern Journal of Philosophy* 46: 52–64.
———. 2011. "Tracking Epistemic Violence, Tracking Practices of Silencing." *Hypatia* 26, no. 2 (Spring): 236–57.
Foucault, Michel. 1977. *Discipline and Punish*. New York: Vintage.
Gilna, Derek. 2017. "Five Years after Implementation, PREA Standards Remain Inadequate." *Prison Legal News*, November 8. https://www.prisonlegalnews.org/news/2017/nov/8/five-years-after-implementation-prea-standards-remain-inadequate/.
Godderis, Rebecca. 2006. "Food for Thought: An Analysis of Power and Identity in Prison Food Narratives." *Berkeley Journal of Sociology* 50: 61–75.
Grant, Jaime M., Lisa A. Mottet, Justin Tanis, Jack Harrison, Jody L. Herman, and Mara Keisling. 2011. *Injustice at Every Turn: A Report of the National Transgender Discrimination Survey*. Washington, DC: National Center for Transgender Equality and National Gay and Lesbian Task Force.
Guenther, Lisa. 2013. *Solitary Confinement: Social Death and its Afterlives*. Minneapolis: University of Minnesota Press.
Johnson, Corey. 2013. "California Was Sterilizing Its Female Prisoners as Late as 2010." *The Guardian*, November 8. https://www.theguardian.com/commentisfree/2013/nov/08/california-female-prisoner-sterilization.
LoCI-Wittenberg University Writing Group. 2016. "An Epistemology of Incarceration: Constructing Knowing on the Inside." *philoSOPHIA* 6: 9–26.
Maeve, Katherine M., and Michael Vaughn. 2001. "Nursing with Prisoners: The Practice of Caring, Forensic Nursing, or Penal Harm Nursing?" *Advances in Nursing Science* 24: 47–64.
McHugh, Nancy. 2018. "Ending Life: Incarceration, Health and Epistemic Injustice." *Public Philosophy Journal* 1.
———. 2015. *The Limits of Knowledge: Generating Feminist Pragmatist Cases for Situated Knowing*. Albany: State University of New York Press.
McHugh, Nancy. 2018. "Ending Life: Incarceration, Health and Epistemic Injustice." *Public Philosophy Journal* 1.
McKinnon, Rachel. 2017. "Allies Behaving Badly: Gaslighting as Epistemic Injustice." In *Routledge Handbook to Epistemic Injustice*, edited by José Medina, Gaile Pohlhaus, and Ian James Kidd, 167–74. London: Routledge.
Medina, José. 2013. *The Epistemology of Resistance*. New York: Oxford University Press.
Mills, Charles. 1997. *The Racial Contract*. Ithaca, NY: Cornell University Press.

Palacios, Lena. 2017. "The Prison Rape Elimination Act and the Limits of Liberal Reform." *The Gender Policy Report* (University of Minnesota). https://genderpolicyreport. umn.edu/the-prison-rape-elimination-act-and-the-limits-of-liberal-reform/.

PREA. n.d. "115.315 Limits to cross-gender viewing and searches." *National PREA Resource Center.* PREA. https://www.prearesourcecenter.org/ec-item/1175/11515-limits-to-cross-gender-viewing-and-searches.

———. n.d. "115.42 Use of Screening Information." *National PREA Resource Center.* https://www.prearesourcecenter.org/ec-item/1190/11542-use-of-screening-information.

———. 2016. "Does a policy that houses transgender or intersex inmates based exclusively on external genital anatomy violate Standard 115.42(c) & (e)?" March 24. https://www.prearesourcecenter.org/node/3927.

Red Phoenix. 2013. "California prisons sterilized female inmates without permission" https://theredphoenixapl.org/2013/07/09/california-prisons-sterilized-female-inmates-without-permission/.

Senghor, Shaka. 2016. *Writing My Wrongs.* New York: Convergent.

Shapiro, Joseph. 2018. "In Prison, Discipline Comes Down Hardest On Women." *All Things Considered*, October 15. https://www.npr.org/2018/10/15/647874342/in-prison-discipline-comes-down-hardest-on-women.

Stearn, Alex. 2013. "Sterilization Abuse in State Prisons: Time to Break With California's Long Eugenic Patterns." *Huffington Post*, July 23. https://www.huffpost.com/entry/sterilization-california-prisons_b_3631287.

Stevenson, Bryan. 2014. *Just Mercy: A Story of Justice and Redemption.* New York: Spiegel & Grau.

Tuana, Nancy. 2013. "Embedding Philosophers in the Practices of Science: Bringing Humanities to the Sciences." *Synthese* 190, no. 11: 1955–73.

PART 2

"Epistemologies of Everyday Life"

Narratives, Stories, Testimonies, and Gossip

Chapter 4

Gossip as Ecological Discourse

KAREN ADKINS

In the middle of her impressive professorial career, Lorraine Code wrote a brief article on gossip ("In Praise of Gossip") that appeared in her book *Rhetorical Spaces* (1995). Compared to the rest of her professional output, which is substantial and deeply interrelated, this article seems like a one-off; she makes a case for the epistemic value of gossip, but even in *Rhetorical Spaces* itself, gossip gets only one brief mention outside its chapter of focus (158). This reflects the general status of gossip in academia; while any working academic knows that the practice of gossip is a useful tool for professional survival, gossip as a subject of scholarship is still largely degraded within academic philosophy. Code herself has suggested that she would like to return to the subject of gossip;[1] here I take up the task of demonstrating the way in which her work on gossip is deeply connected to her more long-standing project on ecological thinking. In particular, the markers she identifies as distinctively ecological—ideas emerging within habitats or context, advocacy as an epistemically valuable practice, and the need to sacrifice perfect logical consistency in favor of productive dynamism—are present in her work on gossip. But more saliently, the fact that Code's work on gossip gets comparatively less academic attention outside gossip scholarship to me speaks to the role of discourse in ecological knowing; the discourse in which our ideas emerge must have enough "presentability" for the ideas to be recognized and received. In other words, an ecological theory must be attentive to the ways in which marginalized discourse can excessively limit possibilities of knowledge making.

I want to illustrate the risks of overemphasizing critical rather than constructive practices of knowledge. Code describes ecological thinking as "both conflicted and unstable . . . capable of infiltrating gaps in the discourses of mastery . . . demonstrating how those discourses sit in the wider world" (2006, 7). On a surface level, these markers apply equally to gossip as discourse, as she demonstrates in her own analysis of gossip (1995). Both gossip and ecological thinking are interested, engaged, speculative practices that uncover gaps between received knowledge and alternative visions. But in scholarly discussions gossip tends to get segmented off as an additive to received or conventionally authoritative knowledge. It offers pieces of information or specific interpretations of events, personalities, or decisions that challenge and destabilize our conventional ways of knowing. Code herself acknowledges this when she describes gossip as "produc[ing] knowledge so valuable that *it can contest* the paradigm status of scientific method as the only reliable means of establishing truth" (1995, 150, emphasis added). Contestation is not a constructive activity but a skeptical one. Standard philosophic defenses of gossip, even those as innovative as Code's, often position gossip as functioning in a separate-but-equal domain to scientific truth. Gossip runs alongside authoritative knowledge (or ahead of it in a red dress, as Liz Smith famously said), but its epistemic path too rarely intersects with more received knowledge. This positioning of gossip limits its impact; given the overwhelming social, political, and economic status of authoritative knowledge systems like science, gossip can be acknowledged but does not have to be taken seriously.

By contrast, Code's own analysis of how ecological thinking functions (2006, 2008) can be extended fruitfully to gossip, to demonstrate the ways in which gossip is more present and more potent than typically acknowledged. Gossip isn't simply alternative data points or alternative interpretations. Gossip is often embedded *within* conventional systems of discourse and knowledge making. The oral, fragmented, meandering traits that mark gossip function in the sorts of ecological ways Code describes in *Ecological Thinking*, for example. Code ascribes greater responsibility to ecological thinking; its location and contextuality make its claims more reliable than the ostensibly neutral claims of propositional epistemology. Connecting these lines of argument reminds us of the importance that discourse practices play in affecting the content of our discussion and that the assumed clear distinction between rational and orderly rhetoric/knowledge and irrational and disorderly rhetoric/knowledge is in part based on selective attention. This analysis reveals not merely an instability to these more authoritative knowledge systems but at least some ways in which they are always already partly ecological.

Let me frame this discussion with some conceptual clarity. Definitions of gossip vary substantially, not least because some scholars focus more on the *what* of gossip: the subject of the conversation. This is best illustrated by W. H. Auden's description of gossip being about only three topics: "love, crime, and money" (1938, 534). Others focus more on the *how* of gossip: the social conditions of the conversation and its means of fermentation, as exemplified by Max Gluckman's characterization of gossip as an expression of norms and fissures within communities and subgroups (1963, 313). Code identifies some rhetorical markers of gossip (1995, 146): it is interested or speculative talk that does not follow conventional expectations of rational orderliness. I will use a definition that is roughly compatible with Code's approach and focuses more on the *how* than the *what* of gossip: gossip is loose, evaluative talk that emerges from intimacy.[2] This definition, which is consistent with other scholars' approaches, also fits well with the fictional example Code analyzes.[3] To extend her analysis, I will add a few examples of workplace gossip that while still fitting this definition also demonstrate the more public reach of gossip.

The Role of Context

Conventional analytic epistemology is propositional in nature; "S knows that p" is the paradigm within which knowledge questions are considered. Code's attention to context in both her ecological and gossip-focused work reminds us that propositional claims do not emerge in vacuums. In ecological terms, "context" means something like habitat; as Code describes it, habitats are locations *both* physical and social (2006, 25); they are neither purely natural (and thus tempting for reductive, propositional approaches to knowledge as simple description of the world), nor purely social. The natural and the social are always already intertwined. Ideas, information, and arguments aren't voiced in neutral space but in often deeply contested backdrops of power.[4] Attempts to understand and sort out what we know and why we know that discard these contextual factors present a denuded and inadequate knowledge. By contrast, Code calls for us to pay attention to the context in which claims are made: patterns of who speaks where and against what racial, social, economic, and political backdrop means that we are rarely passive receivers of data but more or less discerning judges of the quality and value of what we are hearing (2006, 110–112).

The ways in which social and political power correlate with reputational credibility are a crucial feature of Code's understanding of context: we are predisposed to take more seriously testimony that comes from publicly credentialed speakers (which is often justified) and predisposed to dismiss testimony that emerges from uncredentialed speakers who nonetheless directly participate in or are affected by the question or act under assessment (which is less well justified). Her ecological analysis of testimony regularly employs examples that conform to her work on gossip; she notes that decontextualized work in medicine will dismiss the testimony of patients (in her example, female patients suffering symptoms of fibromyalgia) as "hysterical, overreactive, irrational" (2006, 113). These two features—dismissing testimony from those without credentials, and dismissing it as emotional and irrational—are precisely the dismissals the testimony of gossip gets when we ignore the context in which it emerges.

By contrast, when we think about what people may say to each other when they trust each other and speak freely, we can see examples of gossip that offers crucial context to otherwise thin narratives of officialese. In the source material Code considers in developing her account of gossip (Susan Glaspell's story "A Jury of Her Peers"), two women articulate a plausible theory for why a third woman (the ironically named Mrs. Wright) killed her husband in his sleep. Their attention to household details, which the investigating sheriff considers trivial, aids them; they recognize the significance that abandoned domestic tasks and a broken birdcage may have for the isolated inhabitants of a rural farmhouse. Context isn't merely spatial but temporal and relational: one of the women has known Mrs. Wright for a full twenty years and remembers the joyful and exuberant girl she was. She contrasts it with the silent and tense woman who lives with a silent and dour husband (1995, 145). That dramatic difference is a rupture that requires explaining; it may not be noticed by detectives simply reviewing a scene. While Code's example is primarily domestic and intimate, the contextual lessons of gossip can be extended outward. Chris Wickham gives a Wittgensteinian spin on this idea when he describes how inadequate it would be to write a history of a university using only its official minutes, syllabi, and reports, while ignoring the years of faculty, staff, and student lounge gossip (Wickham 1998). Most people (even university leaders) don't bother reading the official rules of the university iterated in such documents, he notes; rather, the habitat of the university is contextual, improvised, often implicit, revised, and present in the realm of gossip (1998, 17). In other words, the official language of aspirational academia is often belied by the habitat of the actual universities in which people work.

While Wickham's observation is offered wryly if sincerely, the stakes of what he's describing are substantial. The discipline of philosophy is just one of the many academic specialties that has been publicly criticized, for good reason, for indifferent and complicit responses to sexism and sexual harassment. The challenge is long-standing; the American Philosophical Association created its Committee on the Status of Women in 1969, and progress has been marginally detectable in the intervening five decades. However, the recent public eruption of anger over these long-standing issues in the profession overlooks the way in which women philosophers have long talked informally among themselves both about the problems of sexism and sexual harassment in philosophy and the ways in which their professional commitments and achievements were judged against this context of sexism. Many feminist philosophers recount stories in which their professional work in feminist philosophy is dismissed as not "real" philosophy.[5] The blog *What Is It Like to Be a Woman in Philosophy*, which has published anonymous accounts of women's experiences in academic philosophy since 2010, demonstrates the wide and troubling range of too many women's experiences in the profession, ranging from subtle degradation or insults, objectification, financial or professional discrimination, to sexual harassment and even assault. In particular, the blog has an entire category of submissions devoted to colleagues making assumptions that any woman professor of philosophy was simultaneously a scholar of feminist philosophy ("But Surely You Do Feminist Philosophy"). These data points, as a group, speak to the way in which sexism in philosophy is rarely purely personal or professional; it is generally an overlapping relationship between the two realms. Feminist philosophers are often diminished or undermined as philosophers (their work is assumed to be less than legitimate or done out of purely personal motives or agendas); they have fewer colleagues to draw upon as collegial allies; and their bodies may be scrutinized. These kinds of backdrop patterns of diminishment are relevant context; as Code phrases it, they negotiate the terms on which we come to knowledge (2006, 5). Demystifying this context—making it plain and public—makes it possible for it to be remedied (we can assess the terms of knowledge making with an eye toward epistemic justice). In situations where professional stakes are high—making accusations of sexism against a colleague, supervisor, or dissertation chair can be fatal to an academic career, particularly if the accuser is a graduate student or early career professional—this contextual work happens behind the scenes via unofficial channels like gossip. For women, blogs and gossip networks function to reveal to each other the fraught circumstances in which they often do their philosophical work so they are better able to resist them. In Wickham's terms, they would not be part of any official history of philosophy, and the absence of this story would make such a history gravely incomplete.

The Value of Advocacy

Infusing a fuller sense of context into knowledge invites us to revisit the role and purpose of knowledge inquiry. Enlightenment-era values of self-governance and inquiry presuppose a kind of neutrality to the speaker and the posing of questions, and work to occlude the knowledge and power systems that produce or privilege certain speakers and statements over others (Code 2006, 164–65). By contrast, Code contends that in ecological thinking, these values are in productive tension with those of advocacy. The practices of advocacy—arguing or acting on another person or group's behalf—go beyond the demands of mere context as described in the previous section. They both presuppose a specific perspective and thus function to connect pieces of information into a synthetic viewpoint, and a recognition that this perspective is underrepresented or -regarded by more recognized lines of authority (Code 2006, 169). The criteria of contextualization are skeptical requirements that we need to look more closely at what we think we know. Practices of advocacy outright contest conventional perspectives as all too often only feigning a neutrality that in fact erases or minimizes relevant perspectives. In their place, advocacy practices offer counterperspectives, or outright demands for alternative courses of action. Advocating for an unpopular perspective is challenging and can meet with real resistance. But effective advocacy's result, Code suggests, can be a fuller and more responsible sense of epistemic autonomy that actually reflects the breadth and diversity of the lived local community (2006, 181).

What Code describes as the practices and values of advocacy is instantiated in her prior work on gossip. Code describes gossip as "interested" or "engaged," by which she means something similar to an effect of advocacy (1995, 146). The women in "A Jury of Her Peers" are gossiping about why the seemingly ordinary Mrs. Wright would have killed her husband for no good reason. (Mr. Wright is described as hardworking and responsible in his personal habits and with his money.) They are drawn to the gossip because the facts don't cohere; there is an initially incoherent or incomplete narrative. The story they construct is a story of advocacy. Their collectively assembled story of the murder rests upon Mrs. Wright's long-suppressed rage at her husband. The rage is distinctly feminist: she has been consistently diminished and disrespected, having had her most precious values and connections undermined and eliminated. The "on behalf" nature of advocacy is fully present in this story. Mrs. Wright's advocates can hear or see facts that a general audience may miss or connect facts that may appear to be unrelated to people who are absent or unrepresented. Mrs. Wright is in jail for the duration of the story, and what we hear about her (secondhand, via the sheriff) are dismissive and condescending quotes that reduce her to an irrational and unthinking woman. Against this backdrop of erasure, the women's gossip aims for subversive sense making.

Code's point is that people gossip; and contrary to historical reputation, gossip is engaged in not merely out of idleness but as a way of answering a question or resolving a tension. Colleen Mills's analysis of workplace gossip around CEO succession—a clear instance of an organizational lacuna that would provoke intense anxiety around people's status—identifies advocacy patterns to the gossip at different stages. Code identifies a feature of advocacy as its deemphasis on the individual knower; *we* advocate, not *I*. Advocacy often "makes knowledge possible" because groups articulate a viewpoint or perspective that is unrecognized by authoritative speakers.[6] In short, advocacy practices can actually broaden the realm of ideas and perspectives discussed. In Mills's analysis, advocacy patterns are present in both the recruitment process of a new CEO, and in response to the new CEO (2010, 223–225). During the recruitment process, workers traded stories about potential members of the shortlist and their weaknesses in terms of leadership of the organization (224). Gossip again heightened with the new CEO because employees were anxious to ascertain to what extent the new CEO represented a change or threat to their work or future (225). The "on-behalf" quality in this gossip is employees gossiping about their own status as a collective, expressing anxiety about the way in which their professional well-being may be insufficiently attended to in a search process driven by a board of directors. The earliest gossip reflected anxiety about the old CEO's departure and the extent to which it was engineered by the board of directors (224). In other words, a major thread of employee gossip around this transition was the extent to which this transition reflected their shared concerns and status, and the persistence of the gossip suggests an ongoing anxiety over an absence of this perspective's recognition.

Code's promotion of advocacy practices and values raises an inevitable objection, one that regularly gets extended to gossip as well. Promoting advocacy as an epistemic value supports the closing (rather than the opening) of epistemic doors. In other words, skeptics would argue that the broadening of discourse doesn't happen in a vacuum but as a zero-sum game: perspectives or positions get added to an epistemological mix explicitly in opposition to other viewpoints, which are presumably discredited as a result. Moreover, isn't it possible that an admittedly interested inquirer has already forgone epistemic neutrality; wouldn't her mind be so effectively made up in the direction of her favored narrative that she will simply cherry-pick examples and evidence to support her claim? Advocacy, by this view, isn't merely telling an epistemic story that lacks deserved epistemic attention but dishonestly exaggerating or misrepresenting ideas to color what would be an otherwise impartial discussion of evidence. The strategic or political goal, in other words, has overwhelmed the epistemic discussion. This objection to advocacy, which Code considers (2006, 174–175) is also regularly used to undermine the value of gossip; gossip is simply the trading of negative stories about another by people with axes to grind.[7] Gossips are determined to ruin a reputation or create dissension and will exaggerate—if not misrepresent—evidence to achieve the goal.

Code's response to this critique of advocacy is helpful and can be extended to gossip itself. She does not discount that advocacy practices are premised upon the closing of some epistemic doors but encourages us not to take the worst violation of this closure for the bearing of the standard (2006, 175). More relevantly, she reminds us to look to the particular conditions surrounding the work of advocacy for criteria of responsibility. Good advocacy takes many details into account, not simply a few highly lurid ones; it functions dialogically, engaging with multiple stakeholders in a situation and emerges from relationships of trust (2006, 176). Code's indicator of healthy advocacy is ecological in nature: it should cohabit or coexist with values and practices around autonomy. Her analysis of effective advocacy within health-care practices, for instance, does not eliminate goals of epistemic resolution or self-governance but situates them within a diverse discourse community. The result will clearly not be a single conclusion but more likely a series of renegotiated conclusions and practices (2006, 206).

This is, of course, an uncomfortable conclusion for many policymakers (let alone for epistemologists); it suggests that clarity and certainty of conclusions is perennially up for grabs and renegotiable. This is why, for instance, Code's ecological analysis often gets applied to issues of policy and health care, in Code's own work and in others (e.g., Shotwell 2016). When current practices and standards in policy areas seem to result in injustices, we should consider the means by which we draw our conclusions and formulate our policies: maybe, ecological thinkers contend, we aren't listening to enough people and attending to enough needs. (We may be the sheriff or the attorney in Glaspell's story.) While this is uncomfortable, Code's reminder to us is that the validating of clarity in conventional analytic epistemology often comes at the cost of relevance. The Gettier problem, which considers the burning question for two interlocutors of whether or not a third person owns a Ford or a Chevy, is representative. While this is technically a problem of testimony (and thus has some formal similarity to the workings of gossip—A tells B something she believes about C), the dullness of the statement in question means that little appears to hinge on its resolution. Its use is merely formal. Obviously, the concern with an advocacy-oriented epistemology is that the advocacy obfuscates rather than clarifies the analysis; advocates, by definition, are interested in results and thus may be more likely to observe some facts at the expense of others, or privilege certain perspectives. Shotwell allows for this danger when she reminds us that "life was quite literally at stake" in questions about AIDS policy in Canada (2016, 2) and that successfully navigating the epistemic questions "make[s] it possible to live" (2016, 3). Code both acknowledges this challenge and indicates a path forward when she reminds us that advances in knowledge in fraught fields like medicine often come about because of advocacy. Code contends that advocacy must be combined with an atmosphere of trust and recognition (2006, 190–196)—but the implication of this discussion is that advocacy is often the sine qua non of advances. Absent a perspectival recognition of incompleteness or inaccuracy in a diagnosis or treatment pattern, and absent a continual commitment to its resolution, it is simply too easy for the gaps to go unrecognized. This two-sided observation is helpful for thinking about gossip's troubled reputation. Gossip often functions as a form of advocacy. Gossip networks around sexual harassment in professions clearly function as a way of helping other professionals see a larger context for their predicament, to register that women philosophers are not responsible for their situation, and to help them negotiate paths for professional fulfillment. Yet gossip can only succeed in provoking new approaches and ideas if it spreads in an atmosphere of trust and recognition. When gossip meets resistance and skepticism, widespread improvements are deferred if not defused.[8]

One of the ways in which contemporary gossip scholarship has extended Code's analysis is to take the idea of advocacy gossip further into the public realm than her own analysis does. Code's references to gossip do not explicitly challenge its reputation as primarily trivial (1991, 195, 308; 1995, 145). While it is clear that she sees a public role for gossip—she makes a passing reference to gossip in the workplace, and gossip about politicians' extramarital affairs (1995, 152–153)—these possibilities go unexplored in her analysis. Given that her case for gossip largely confines its conclusions to discovering "corrigible, renegotiable truths . . . about people" (1995, 147), it is hard to see an expansive role for public gossip within those limits. By contrast, workplace or institutional gossip is often centered on questions that have a larger social impact than the personal gossip at the heart of Glaspell's story; questions around organizational direction, patterns of discrimination and harassment, possible mass layoffs, and similar events affect entire groups of people, including those far removed from the institutions at hand. The idea of gossip as institutional or political advocacy or subversion has been fruitfully developed in recent years.

Dynamism and Contestation as Epistemically Productive Values

Subversion is an intrinsically destabilizing force, and indeed, one of the more trenchant aspects of both ecological thinking and theories of gossip is their embrace of destabilization as not automatically destructive. Theories of ecology often point to equilibrium as a model; species functioning and persisting in relationships of tension and variance but with ultimate balance. And yet, the reality of ecology is a constant multivocal pressure of countervailing forces; examined in detail, the balance is hard to see and only visible when large patterns are examined and assessed. As we have just seen, in epistemology this myth versus reality is even starker. Conventional viewpoints on epistemology are predicated on assumptions of methodological and logical coherence and consistency within and between statements: these views can result in a thin description of reality. Frege puzzles, for instance, focus on logical paradoxes between propositions that contain multiple referents, and debate has been vigorous about potential solutions to them since their inception in 1892 to the present day, focused mostly on ways to resolve the paradoxes to achieve consistency.[9] (Code herself critiques Fregean epistemological assumptions in "The Knowing Subject," 1984.) But by contrast, an ecological theory like Code's presents a challenging soundscape of multiple and cacophonous voices, singular and collective, often speaking in tension if not outright antagonism or contradiction.

Code's summary of the dynamism of ecological thinking sounds daunting: "Every cognitive act takes place at a point of intersection of innumerable relations, events, circumstances, and histories that make the knower and the known what they are, at that time" (1991, 269). This stark iteration of a constant interchange between innumerable relationships, locations, and past events and circumstances can urge the skeptical reader back to the simplicity of "S knows that p"; certainty, on this ecological model, seems impossible. How could we observe or make sense of these infinite relationships, acts, and locations? Code immediately offers pragmatism: because we can't, we focus on some cognitive events more than others and put only some of the context in the foreground (1991, 269). Code herself offers a caveat against an overly simplistic approach to ecology. If we simply think of the ecology of knowledge as requiring us to focus on the background context of speakers and ideas, we are not departing enough from a conventional approach. Instead, we are merely adding contextual "color" to fundamentally propositional approaches. Code's key insight for ecology is its *dynamism*; ecological systems feature forces working symbiotically, in tension, procreatively, and generatively. As such, text and context must be considered "reciprocally constitutive" (2006, 5). This sort of system thinking is challenging, not least because it cannot lead to stable resolutions; it is "conflicted and unstable" (2006, 7). More worrying is that ecosystems' prioritization of balance and the health of the community can lead to the possibility of suppression of "dangerous" elements (1991, 275). When a priority is the health of the whole, silencing more singular outliers is a persistent temptation.

Code's work reminds us of the way in which posing stability as a value can often do dangerous epistemological rescue work; it "cleans up" inconsistencies that actually reflect deeper disputes about meaning and interpretation that often track along power disparities. Voices that go unrecognized in conversations interpret data and policies differently than the more homogeneous voices that produce this information. The subjects and proliferation of gossip often tidily track these power disparities and the temptations. Where gossip proliferates is often where an official narrative of meaning only holds weight with a certain prominent segment of the population: a whisper network may exist that contests and undermines publicly stated values. The recently revealed scandals of persistent sexual harassment in a panoply of industries (Silicon Valley, Hollywood, news media, the academy, US Congress, state legislatures, and others) indicates this stark divide of knowledge based upon access. Sexual harassment is described as an "open secret" in many of these industries but a protected one nevertheless. For instance, the legal and financial structures developed to protect Hollywood producer and serial sexual harasser Harvey Weinstein are perhaps extreme but also speak to the ways in which entrenched power structures can go to great lengths to ensure their continued and unchallenged existence (Farrow 2017). More recently, some companies' practices that work against employee continuity and conversation, like increased casualization of the workforce or expansive and unjustified use of nondisclosure agreements for departing employees who have no meaningful proprietary information, function only to increase the power disparity between employer and employee: as a result, worker solidarity and activism become legally and personally perilous (Adkins 2017, 252–254). When companies resort to these measures, absent any evidence of widespread or nefarious employee practices that might justify them, it consolidates the power of decision making and critique in too few (and too removed) hands. It is the opposite of the kind of dynamism and contestation that Code contends ultimately leads to healthier knowledge and policy practice. While such top-heavy and coercive practices may ensure an official, enforced narrative of company practices and values, they may also lead to other kinds of instability. Waddington's contention that good managers should want to be aware of the gossip at work—and that gossip often serves as an early warning alert for problems at the workplace—speaks to this danger (2012, 133). Limiting employees' ability to assess and critique their work lives together may stave off criticism in the short run but demonstrates a fundamental lack of confidence in and respect for employees that can lead to more systemic long-term problems. Healthy workplaces should value this kind of dynamism.

If anything, Code's characterization of gossip overstates its dynamism in comparison to her later work on ecological thinking. The subtitle of her chapter "In Praise of Chaos" alludes not just to contestation but incoherence. Her later descriptions of gossip as "random" and "disorderly" (1995, 146, 150) reaffirm rather than resist this narrative of gossip. There is no discussion of patterns within gossip as there is within ecological thinking (or systems of assessment) even though in the Glaspell short story it's clear that conclusions are drawn on a version of deductive thinking. The women know what their lives and their friends' lives are like and what the rhythms and patterns of female domestic lives are like in their small, rural community. They recognize a multitude of ways in which Mrs. Wright's life departs from theirs, rendering her more isolated and more damaged. Despite the textured analysis Code gives to fictional gossip, her emphasis on gossip's absence of method undermines its potential for meaningful contestation of received narratives, let alone the construction of fuller epistemic narratives. Perhaps unwittingly, her emphasis on chaos plays into the hands of critics of gossip. Gossip in this sense becomes meandering trivia that cannot reliably track or report patterns in thinking and observation to fruitful epistemic good.

Knowledge Making as Social Activity

Dynamism is a fruitful epistemic practice in part because it replaces individual actors with networks of interaction. Similarly, gossip is by definition social: I cannot gossip to myself. Gossiping requires interlocutors (whether in person or virtually). But Code rightly notes that we persistently undervalue the conclusions drawn from such a social process (1995, 149). Throughout her career, Code has defended sociality in knowledge; examining our knowledge from others' points of view and interrogating our own previously strongly held conclusions about what we know led to more responsible knowing (1987, 10, 60). Both gossip and ecological thinking depend on recognizing the ways in which, depending on the question at hand, traditionally disempowered (or underempowered) speakers can have credible and relevant information, ideas, and perspectives. Code reminds us that conventional views of epistemology often prioritize knowledge over experience. Calling something "knowledge" credits a statement with a neutrality and objectivity that is by definition denied to experience—always personal, localized, subjective. But Code complicates this picture by reminding us that this objectivity relies on an erasure of experiences that don't fit a dominant narrative (1991, 250–258). In her analysis of the failure of a Tanzanian health-care model driven by Western NGOs, and her offering up of a more just alternative, she directs much of her analysis at the importance of valuing native Tanzanians as coequal participants in constructing and directing resources for health care, particularly by valuing their testimony (2008, 45–47).[10]

Part of what makes the ecological model so appealing for thinking about knowledge is that it recognizes the absence of sharp borders between individuals and communities in knowledge and experience: racial, economic, gender, political barriers are permeable. Gossip, as a means of transmission, is intrinsically transgressive and relies upon relationships of trust, which while often co-located in relationships of identity, aren't necessarily so. Gossip has a long history as a resource for marginalized communities to counter prevailing viewpoints of them or as a means of fomenting resistance (Scott 1987). Indeed, gossip that spreads gains force because it is relevant and comprehensible beyond a small community. One of the conventional assumptions about gossip (as with ecological thinking as social activity) is that it is less reliable or trustworthy because of its sociality. If barriers to entry are low (you can speak freely to any colleague you trust), if formal or informal assessments of credibility don't occur, and if the talk is loose or playful, the results must be less reliable.[11]

And yet examples of workplace gossip demonstrate the ways in which it is often ahead of the official reporting line—and accurately so (Smeltzer and Zener 1992). Gossip scholarship indicates that the accuracy of gossip is often connected to its social features—its reliance on trust and confidentiality means that people risk their reputations by gossiping and thus typically don't engage in high-stakes gossip unless they have real certainty about their ideas. Because gossip is usually person to person, we are able to assess and rely on credibility. (Someone who has lied to me or spread wildly exaggerated gossip to me before is not someone whose word I'll take as gossip gospel.) In other words, the myth of gossip as unreliable typically relies too strongly on popular images of its chaotic nature and disregards some ways in which its chaotic appearance actually rests on well-developed and well-maintained social networks of trust and reliance. These instances of workplace gossip, along with some of the subversive uses of resistance gossip, remind us that folk collectives have the potential to destabilize even well-established hegemonies.

The Epistemic Siloing of Gossip

One of the implicit points of Code's analysis of gossip demonstrated in other gossip-related work is that how we talk frames and conditions not just what we talk about but what and how we think. Gossip's domain of intimacy, trust, and informality leads to different and more creative ways of connecting ideas and information that can augment knowledge, not degrade it. The sociality of gossip also leads to certain conclusions about its tone and tenor. It is regularly described in the scholarly literature not just as loose or disorderly but with metaphorical elements of play: it is playful, unruly, or whimsical, and the figure of the gossipmonger is sometimes compared to the trickster of folklore. These aspects of play and whimsy are ill-suited to the worlds of propositional epistemology or public policymaking. Code herself makes this connection in her ecological work; she notes that it is the space of friendship, with its reliance on trust and respect, that foments ecological thinking (1991, 278). These threads of symmetry and symbiosis, of play and whimsy, should invite connections between Code's work on gossip and her work on ecological thinking. And yet the reception of Code's work is typically bifurcated. Despite the thematic connections between her work on gossip and her work on ecology, scholarship on Code's epistemology typically does not reference her gossip work. Likewise, gossip scholars who routinely cite Code's analysis on gossip typically do not put it in the context of her other work on epistemology.[12]

I think that this gap in citation is more than simply a by-product of a hyperspecialized academy. Rather, I think it demonstrates the way in which even contextual, dynamic, and ecological discussions of knowledge still want to situate some contexts as beyond the domain of the epistemically respectable. Not all aspects of an ecosystem deserve equal hearing. For gossip to be epistemically successful, it must be receivable; that is, it must be recognizable as valuable. It is here that not only the power dynamics within gossip but also its social siloing have their most devastating effect. In the Glaspell story, it is relevant that the gossip ultimately goes unreported. The women's explanation for why Mrs. Wright kills her husband would guarantee her guilty verdict; the attorney persistently reminds us that he needs a motive to ensure a guilty verdict; the fact that one woman is married to the sheriff should give her more, not less, incentive to report incriminating evidence and theories. But the male characters in this story consistently overlook or mock the very disparities in Mrs. Wright's kitchen that lead the women to piece together a motive and theory for the case. Thus the women keep their thoughts to themselves for two related reasons. First, they have sympathy for Mrs. Wright's rage (one character compares her own youthful rage at a boy's cruelty to Mrs. Wright's toward her husband). Second, the male characters' persistent mockery of the women's interest in kitchen "trifles" makes it clear that their story would get a skeptical reception: "Wouldn't they *laugh*," Mrs. Peters says about telling the story to the attorney and the sheriff. In other words, both their initial gossip to assemble the story *and* their ultimate holding back of the gossip are strategic. They seek to understand why Mrs. Wright would kill her husband and stay silent: because the gossip, if believed, would further damage a woman they clearly see as already victimized and unlikely to be believed (thus marginalizing her further). Gossip is only valuable when it has ready and receptive auditors. All too often, gossip stays underground, and its lessons are disregarded by those with authority.

This is no mere fictional tableau. The panoply of stories about sexism and sexual harassment in a wide variety of professions and industries makes it clear that women and men have been talking off the record about problematic people and practices for years (if not decades) and at times paying costly settlements to silence accusers and thus perpetuate cycles of abuse.[13] Such long-standing and shared strands of gossip that undermine public narratives in ways that should be morally if not legally problematic should be an epistemic crisis for many communities: How could we have missed this? How could we have ignored these voices and this pain for so long? And yet the tendency to segregate off-the-record or embodied thought from more regimented and systematic thought is present even in sympathetic accounts of feminist epistemology. For instance, Vrinda Dabmiya and Linda Alcoff's (1993) discussion of old wives' tales explicitly positions the knowledge of midwives as constructed, perpetuated, and transmitted in ways qualitatively different than that of doctors. To be clear, Dabmiya and Alcoff make the point that historical midwives were often *more* effective than their medically trained counterparts at successful childbirth and maternal health techniques (223). Medical knowledge is "institutional," "codified," and "objective," whereas midwifery knowledge is "embodied," "empathic," and "first-person"(-al) (225). Dabmiya and Alcoff's discussion of these two traditions of medical care indicates the ways in which they run along parallel epistemological tracks: the two communities of knowledge don't consult one another, and Dabmiya and Alcoff make clear that the medical community does not recognize midwifery as legitimate knowledge—it does not meet medical standards of justification. Dabmiya and Alcoff are surely correct to challenge that historical judgment (embodied and empathically attained midwifery knowledge can be described, and subject to assessment, judgment, and critique, as can other forms of knowledge [1993, 237]). Additionally, extending this historical discussion to feminist epistemology is fruitful, and Dabmiya and Alcoff conclude this discussion with an explicit call for epistemology to be more integrative in its approach and methodology. In this conclusion, they reflect other feminist work on epistemology, which recognizes subversive ways that women come to knowledge, its degraded status, and call for integration.

The siloing of gossip as irresponsible and off the record is itself both epistemically and morally irresponsible. Code's ecological approach reminds us that looking at a phenomenon in its habitat, its dynamism, and its sociality requires integration right from the start; we must attend to sometimes hard-to-detect patterns as well as voices of dissent. This is mirrored in scholarship on gossip; as Mills concludes in her analysis of workplace gossip around CEO transition, gossip is often "embedded . . . in other forms of both formal and informal communication" (234). Thus, contrary to the idea that interlocutors are either working officially or unofficially, epistemic borders are often already being crossed in how we talk and think. Our discourse is ecological, as is our thinking. We simply fail to acknowledge it.

Notes

1. Personal conversation with author, NASSP conference, July 2015.
2. For a fuller discussion of this definition of gossip, see Adkins 2017, 7–11.
3. See Waddington (2012, 25), and Kurland and Pelled (2000, 429).
4. This is why Code's use of context as ecological goes well beyond conventional understandings of it as "separately given" (2006, 7).
5. For examples, see the narratives in Linda Martin Alcoff, ed., *Singing in the Fire: Stories of Women in Philosophy* (Lanham, MD: Rowman & Littlefield, 1993). Sally Haslanger provides empirical support for this by documenting the dearth of feminist philosophy in prestigious philosophy journals in "Changing the Ideology and Culture of Philosophy: Not By Reason (Alone)," *Hypatia* 23, no. 2 (2008): 210–223.
6. Indeed, Code explicitly considers advocacy as an antipodal concept to autonomy, which emphasizes an individual, self-sufficient knower (2006, 163–165).
7. Mills reinforces this concern by noting that a nontrivial portion of the gossip around the CEO transition consisted of "scaremongering" (225).
8. The public discussion of a hostile climate for women in Anglophone philosophy indeed met with vigorous and widespread resistance; unsurprisingly, improvements for women philosophers did not occur until years after the initial public eruption. For discussion, see Adkins (2017): 88–92, 98–99.
9. For recent discussion of Frege puzzles from a variety of philosophical orientations, see Millar (2016), Pickel and Rabern (2017), and Soames (2013).
10. Kristie Dotson challenges this reading, observing that the mere presence of Tanzanian testimony only indicates their usage as sources of information, not fully credited interlocutors (2008, 59–60).
11. The assumption that gossip tends toward the unreliable, incidentally, is not systematically demonstrated throughout the literature. See Adkins (2017, 43–44, 250) for discussion.

12. Unsurprisingly, this observation does not apply to Code herself; her article on gossip explicitly connects her analysis to some of her earlier work on context in knowledge and interpersonal paths to knowledge (1995, 147, fn 5). But interestingly, her later work on ecological thinking does not contain references to her work on gossip; in other words, she cites her earlier work on epistemology as a way of locating and grounding her work on gossip but does not cite her work on gossip later when she writes on ecology, despite the significant points of overlap.

13. As several commentators have noticed, the overwhelming majority of reports of sexual harassment and assault have been by white women and in high-income and high-status fields. This unfortunately reproduces and reinforces the racism of mainstream feminism and reminds us of the dual burden of gossip within multiply marginalized communities.

Works Cited

Adkins, Karen. 2017. *Gossip, Epistemology, and Power: Knowledge Underground*. New York: Palgrave Macmillan.

Auden, W. H. 1938. "In Defense of Gossip." *The Living Age*, February 1, 534–538.

Code, Lorraine. 1984. "The Knowing Subject." *Idealistic Studies* 14, no. 2: 109–126.

———. 1987. *Epistemic Responsibility*. Hanover, NH: University Press of New England.

———. 1991. *What Can She Know? Feminist Theory and the Construction of Knowledge*. Ithaca, NY: Cornell University Press.

———. 1995. *Rhetorical Spaces: Essays in Gendered Locations*. New York: Routledge.

———. 2006. *Ecological Thinking: The Politics of Epistemic Location*. Oxford: Oxford University Press.

———. 2008. "Advocacy, Negotiation, and the Politics of Unknowing." *Southern Journal of Philosophy* 66: 32–51.

Dabmiya, Vrinda, and Linda Alcoff. 1993. "Are 'Old Wives' Tales' Justified?" In *Feminist Epistemologies*, edited by Linda Alcoff and Elizabeth Potter. New York: Routledge.

Dotson, Kristie. 2008. "In Search of Tanzania: Are Effective Epistemic Practices Sufficient for Just Epistemic Practices?" *Southern Journal of Philosophy* 66: 52–64.

Farrow, Ronan. 2017. "Harvey Weinstein's Army of Spies." *New Yorker*, November 6. https://www.newyorker.com/news/news-desk/harvey-weinsteins-army-of-spies.

Gettier, Edmund L. 1963. "Is Justified True Belief Knowledge?" *Analysis* 23:121–123.

Gluckman, Max. 1963. "Gossip and Scandal." *Current Anthropology* 4, no. 3: 307–316.

Kurland, Nancy, and Lisa Hope Pelled. 2000. "Passing the Word: Toward a Model of Gossip and Power in the Workplace." *Academy of Management Review* 25, no. 2: 428–438.

Millar, Boyd. 2016. "Frege's Puzzle for Perception." *Philosophy and Phenomenological Research* 43, no. 2:368–392.
Mills, Colleen. 2010. "Experiencing Gossip: The Foundations for a Theory of Embedded Organizational Gossip." *Group & Organization Management* 35, no. 2: 213–237.
Pickel, Bryan, and Rabern, Brian. 2017. "Does Semantic Relationism Solve Frege's Puzzle?" *Journal of Philosophical Logic* 46: 97–118.
Scott, James. 1987. *Weapons of the Weak: Everyday Forms of Peasant Resistance*. New Haven, CT: Yale University Press.
Shotwell, Alexis. 2016. "Fierce Love: What We Can Learn About Epistemic Responsibility from Histories of AIDS Advocacy." *Feminist Philosophy Quarterly* 2, no. 2 (Fall), article 8.
Smeltzer, Larry R., and Marie F. Zener. 1992. "Development of a Model for Announcing Major Layoffs." *Group & Organization Management* 17, no. 4: 446.
Soames, Scott. 2013. "Cognitive Propositions." *Philosophical Perspectives* 27: 480–501.
Waddington, Kathryn. 2012. *Gossip and Organizations*. New York: Routledge.
Wickham, Chris. 1998. "Gossip and Resistance among the Medieval Peasantry." *Past and Present* 160: 3–24.

Chapter 5

A Murex, an Angel Wing, the Wider Shore

An Ecological and Politico-Ethico-Onto-Epistemological Approach to Narratives, Stories, and Testimonies

Andrea Doucet

Introduction: Knowledge and Subjectivity

Just over 43 years ago, in 1978, Lorraine Code completed and defended her doctoral dissertation at the University of Guelph in Ontario, Canada. Her thesis was simply titled "Knowledge and Subjectivity."[1] In a 2015 talk at her alma mater, where she received an honorary doctorate, Code reflected that it was an "odd project then" (in the late 1970s) as "the idea that questions about subjectivity might figure in thinking and writing about knowledge was outrageous to many philosophers." She also admitted that "it may seem I have spent the almost forty intervening years writing and rewriting that dissertation," revealing how questions about knowledge and subjectivity have remained at the heart of her work "albeit in different guises" (Code 2015, 1).

Concepts, practices, and "different guises" of knowledge and subjectivity have undergone seismic shifts in the past few decades, not only in Code's work but across expansive multidisciplinary fields that highlight intraconnections between epistemology, ontology, and ethics—or, in Karen Barad's (2007, 185) terms, "ethico-onto-epistemological" entanglements. On this terrain of constantly changing turns (i.e., new materialist,[2] postconstructionist,[3] posthumanist,[4] performative posthumanist,[5] and ontological,[6] among others)—a varied landscape Patti Lather (2013, 634) calls one of "posts, post-posts and neo-posts"—there has been an explosion of new thinking on knowledge making and subjectivities. Broadly speaking, knowledge is now approached less as a product and more as unfolding processes of knowledge making that are performative, nonrepresentational, and ontologically relational. The "knowing subject," which was once central to feminist theoretical and methodological work and was initially reconceptualized through poststructuralist interventions (see, e.g., Butler 1995) and through critiques of Cartesian-informed notions of subjectivity, has now been further reshaped into a subject that knows and is known within assemblages, in dynamic intra-relations and "intra-action" (Barad 2007, 33) and through relational ontologies. As Karen Barad (2007, 394) writes, "There is no 'I' separate from the intra-active becoming of the world." She explains that "in contrast to the usual 'interaction,'" which assumes that there are separate individual agencies that precede their interaction, the notion of intra-action recognizes that distinct agencies emerge through their intra-action and *are only distinct in relation to their mutual entanglement; they don't exist as individual elements*" (Barad 2007, 33).

These interventions about relational and intra-active knowledge making and revisioned conceptions of subjectivity (both researcher and researched subjectivities) have generated massive theoretical, methodological, and epistemological excitement and have led to the development of new research approaches across incredibly wide, deep, and diverse transdisciplinary and scholarly fields. Yet they have also raised—or resurrected—unsettling questions about the processes of knowing human subjects, especially marginalized, vulnerable, or suffering subjects. As feminist postqualitative (and new materialist) methodological writers Lather and Elizabeth St. Pierre (2013, 63) note, there is "the big, risky, question": "Dare we give up that 'I,' that fiction—the doer before the deed? How are we anyway in entanglement? How might we become in becoming?"

Concerns about knowing others and how to theorize and work with the human "I" in narratives, stories, and testimonies are especially urgent now that testimonial "voice," long under attack by poststructural thinking, is reappearing in public and academic discourses. For example, testimonies and narratives about sexual violence and human suffering experienced by people across the globe have long formed an integral part of feminist research, including research that grapples with how to recognize and honor stories and experiences while simultaneously critiquing, contextualizing, and reconfiguring concepts of experience, voice, or stories (e.g., Alcoff 2011; Bartky 1990, 2002; Kruks 2001, Oskala 2014). In Canada, this tension also appears in two national inquiries that describe the "cultural genocide" of Canadian Indigenous peoples (The National Inquiry into Missing and Murdered Indigenous Women and Girls 2019a, 2019b; The Truth and Reconciliation Commission 2015a). The Report of the Truth and Reconciliation Commission (TRC) (2015, 2), based on the testimonies of over six thousand Indigenous Canadians "who had been taken from their families as children, forcibly if necessary, and placed for much of their childhoods in residential schools," is a harrowing account of more than a century of physical and sexual abuses experienced by many Indigenous children (First Nations, Métis, and Inuit) in church- and state-run schools. A few years later, women's voices, stories, and testimonies were central to the National Inquiry into Missing and Murdered Indigenous Women and Girls' (MMIWG 2019a, 2019b) research process, report, dissemination, and media coverage. Indeed, the MMIWG Report (2019a 2019b, 64) stated: "In sharing their truths with the National Inquiry, family members and survivors told not only stories about violence but also stories about the relationships through which violence takes place." MMIWS's "truth sharing podcasts" revolved around women's experiences, stories, voices, and voice-giving in addition to "truth gathering" (www.sacredmmiwg) and "gathering truth" (MMIWG 2019a, 60).

Set against a burgeoning scholarly landscape of nonrepresentational, processual, relational, and performative thinking, these inquiries and the continued calls for research that focuses on voice, truth, stories, and testimonies seem to bolster and return us to representational conceptions of knowledge making and subjectivities. They raise concerns about how to work with what Code calls "vexed questions" (Code 2006, 205) of knowing others as well as questions about how scholars working on the edges of the these "posts, post-posts and neo-posts" can approach knowledge making that is rooted in stories and testimonies. As Code (2006, 52) herself writes, this issue of "reposition(ing) and revalor(izing) experiential evidence"—including stories and testimonies that are told from that experiential evidence—is "currently alive and urgent in feminist, antiracist, and other postcolonial theories of knowledge."

On my reading, the various "turns" previously mentioned share a focus on historical epistemologies, relational ontologies, multiple ontologies, knowledge making as both ethical and political, a reconfigured view of what it is that *we are actually doing* as researchers and knowledge makers, and a dissolution of long-standing distinctions between epistemology, methodology, ontology, and ethics. One turn that is less visible in these approaches, however, is the *narrative turn*.[7] In its varied forms and iterations, the narrative turn builds on decades of extensive critiques of the individual, male, liberal,

Cartesian subject and reworks connections between embodied and relational human subjectivities, human-nonhuman entanglements, testimonial evidence, storytelling, temporality, ethics, critical humanism (e.g., Arendt 1958/1998; Plummer 1983, 2000; Ricoeur 1991a, 1991b, 1992; Simpson 2011, 2017), and critical posthumanism (Braidotti 2016, 2018). Yet very few key theorists who utilize ethico-onto-epistemologies attend to the possibilities and challenges of working with human storytelling and with narratives, stories, and testimonies. I argue that, in this respect, Code is a rare exception.

This chapter begins to develop what I am calling an *ecological and politico-ethico-onto-epistemological approach* to narratives, stories, and testimonies, as well as the beginnings of an ecological approach to narrative methodologies and narrative analysis. Working across the varied influences that coalesce within Code's approach to ecological imaginaries, I argue that in addition to the many weavings of knowledge and subjectivity that have been central to her work, there has been a less visible but equally compelling and important focus on *narrative*. This is partly because ecological thinking is a project that attends to the challenges of "knowing people in complex, elaborated, and often extraordinary situations" (Code 2006, 225). Code (2006, 210–11) argues that "responsible knowing makes a difference—often a vital difference—to people's lives" and that "knowing well is a matter both of moral-political and of epistemic concern" (1991, 72).

I begin with one important point that both motivates and frames the writing of this chapter: in the wide cross-disciplinary fields of narrative studies and social epistemologies, narratives, stories, and testimonies are often treated as *similar and interchangeable* units of analysis. Counter to this, I argue that Narratives (distinguished here by a capital letter) are the broader "relationality of parts" (Somers 1994, 616) that comprise all narrative dimensions and forms, including stories and testimonies, which are similar in what they *do* despite their different contextual characteristics. As I will argue, stories and testimonies are specific narrative forms, namely *ontological narratives* (Somers, 1992, 1994), and they form part of the wider category of Narratives.

This chapter is organized as follows: I first lay out my reading of what Code refers to as dominant *instituted* social imaginaries of knowledge making and subjectivity. Second, I explore what Code refers to as instituting imaginaries, noting, as she does, that ecological imaginaries are just one of many evolving *instituting* social imaginaries that seek to reconfigure how we approach knowledge making and subjectivities (i.e., research subjects and their stories and testimonies, and ourselves, in our roles as epistemic subjects and, indeed, what Code [2006, 2020a] calls "ecological subjects"). Third, I explore the unique strengths of ecological imaginaries for research focused on Narratives, stories, and testimonies, especially when these fall broadly within the domains of social justice, human rights, and human suffering.

Finally, I think through one way of translating ecological imaginaries into an ecological and politico-ethico-onto-epistemological approach to narratives and to narrative methodologies. This is a small part of a work in progress that builds on Code's long-standing and ongoing excavations of narrative resources, including her forays into existential phenomenology, hermeneutic-phenomenology (e.g., Bartky 1990, 2002; Kruks 2001), narrative hermeneutics (e.g., Ricoeur 1991a, 1991b, 1992), and writing about first-, second-, and third-person narratives (e.g., Cavarero 2002, 2005). Seeking to translate ecological imaginaries into narrative practices, I also engage in a unique pairing of Code's work with that of Margaret Somers, an American historical sociologist who is well known for her reshaping of narrative theory in ways that emphasize epistemologies, ontologies, ethics, and nonrepresentational analyses (e.g., Somers 1992, 1994, 1996, 1998, 2008). I argue that Code's ecological imaginaries create fruitful pathways for navigating the challenges and possibilities of working with narrative and that combining her extensive work on these matters with that of other narrative thinkers can help us contend with central tensions that emerge when we attempt to know others through their stories and/or testimonies.

I write this chapter as a feminist, qualitative, postqualitative, and narrative researcher whose work has been mainly informed by feminist, transdisciplinary, and social science debates on epistemologies and methodologies. With over three decades of research centered on listening to people's stories and constructing knowledges with and from them, especially through adapting and developing the Listening Guide approach to narrative analysis (e.g., Brown and Gilligan 1993; Doucet 2018b; Doucet and Mauthner 2008; Mauthner and Doucet 2003), I take up Code's call for researchers to engage with what it means to put ecological imaginaries into practice.[8] My connection to her work partly stems from my deep respect for Code's (2006, xi) slow and sustained four-decade "quest for conceptions of knowledge and subjectivity capable of informing transformative, responsible, and responsive epistemic practices." I read her work, not only as an ethico-onto-epistemological approach to knowledge making and subjectivities but as a *politico*-ethico-onto-epistemological approach to knowledge making, subjectivity, and narratives.

It is important to say at the outset that I am not presenting ecological thinking per se but my diffractive engagement with it and with the varied scholarly resources that I bring into conversation with Code's approach to knowledge making, subjectivities, and narratives. My engagement with Code and the other authors mentioned in this chapter is thus guided by a method of reading that embodies some of the elements of an ecological approach to knowledge making. Rather than relying on "a top-down, aloof, and interchangeable spectator model" (Code 2006, 285), I use an intra-active, relational, engaged, and constantly unfolding approach to working with authors, one that Karen Barad (2007) calls "diffractive readings." This diffractive reading approach is partly based on Donna Haraway's (1991, 273) concept of diffraction, which is "about heterogeneous history, not about originals." As Barad (2007, 30) notes,

> Diffraction does not fix what is the object and what is the subject in advance, and so, unlike methods of reading one text or set of ideas against another where one serves as a fixed frame of reference, diffraction involves reading insights through one another in ways that help illuminate differences as they emerge: how different differences get made, what gets excluded, and how those exclusions matter.

I thus engage in diffractive readings as "respectful, detailed, ethical engagements" (Barad 2007, 30). To read diffractively is to read generously and "to read through, not against; it means reading texts intra-actively though one another, enacting new patterns of engagement" (Barad 2009, 14; see also Code 2006; Mauthner 2015).

Instituted Social Imaginaries

In varied publications spanning the decade since *Ecological Thinking* was published in 2006, Code has written about both *instituted* and *instituting* imaginaries of knowledge making. Guided by a larger discussion of social imaginaries (Castoriadis 1998; Le Doeuff 1989) and her long-standing contributions to the field of naturalized epistemologies[9] (1981, 1987, 1991, 1995, 1996, 2006), Code approaches epistemologies and knowledge making practices as objects of investigation (see also Hacking 2002; Law 2004). As she explains, she began to examine

> how *instituted social imaginaries* work to shape and govern possibilities of being, thinking, acting; how they legitimate or preclude certain epistemic and other human relations, to one another and to the physical/natural/conceptual world; how philosophical systems reflect and reinforce these imaginaries. (Code 2006, 7)

Instituted imaginaries of knowledge making are described by Code (2006, 9) as being associated with an "exaggerated ideal of scientific knowledge making." They are the "social imaginary of the affluent liberal western world" and "the epistemic imaginary inherited from analytic philosophy" (2006, 213)—in other words, "empiricist, positivist and rationalist theories of knowledge" (1995, 190) that broadly reflect and support positivism, modernity, and colonialism. Instituted imaginaries of knowledge making, Code (1995, 24) explains, are, "dominant epistemologies of modernity, with their Enlightenment legacy and later infusion with positivist-empiricist principles" (see also Tuhiwai Smith 2012). This illusion of scientific objectivity forms the basis for what Haraway (1988, 589) and others (e.g., Nagel 1986) have called "the view from nowhere"; it establishes a concept of knowledge making premised on enduring binaries: nature/culture, nature/social, subject/object, "matters of fact and matters of concern" (Latour 2004, 231), and science as separate from its social contexts. Rouse (2009, 24) provides a good description of this instituted social imaginary when he writes that there is "a separation between knowers and known, a spectatorial conception of knowing, a contrast of the unity of the object to the multiplicity of standpoints, and a static and perhaps mostly retrospective understanding of epistemic normativity" (see also Verran 2001).

Hegemonic instituted imaginaries also hold a fairly consistent view of the researcher's role: researchers are scientists who let "the facts speak for themselves" (Law 2004, 120). Within these "spectator epistemologies," the knower "stands as a shadow figure invisibly and indifferently apart from discrete objects of knowledge" and objects supposedly "remain inert in and unaffected by the knowing process" (Code 2006, 41). All the while, these knowers often proclaim " 'the surveys show' and 'experts have proved' " (Code 2006, 97) or "science has proved" (244), obscuring two decades of feminist methodological and epistemological work that questions how it is possible for knowers to "bring no affective, personal historical, or idiosyncratic baggage to 'the epistemological project' . . . neither deriving from nor serving particular interests or motivations nor allowing enthusiasms or aversions to divert its rational course" (Code 2006, 17).

Instituting Social Imaginaries

In spite of the weight, hegemony, and longevity of the dominant social imaginary of knowledge making, Code (2006, 32) argues that other imaginaries of knowledge making are possible and, indeed, are continually emerging as forms of "radical social critique." She draws again on Castoriadis and his idea of a juxtaposing "instituting" imaginary, which she describes as "the critical-creative activity of a society" through which "imaginatively initiated counter-possibilities interrogate the social structure to destabilize its pretensions to 'naturalness' and 'wholeness,' thus initiating a new making (a *poiesis*)" (Code 2006, 31). As she puts it, *instituting social imaginaries* supersede some of the limitations of instituted social imaginaries. That is, they provide "a cluster of subversive and productive practices, metaphors, images—capable, with persistent effort, of shaking epistemology free from the monocultural/monological hold of the imaginary that has kept standard theories of knowledge isolated from the very knowledge they have sought to explicate" (33).

Ecological imaginaries are just one form of the many radical instituting social imaginaries of knowledge making and subjectivities that are unfolding across the Global North and Global South from a highly diverse array of thinkers influenced by the multiple social theory "turns" mentioned in the introduction to this chapter. Some of these instituting social imaginaries include, for example, new materialist feminisms (e.g., Alaimo and Hekman 2008; Coole and Frost 2010), transcorporeal feminism (Alaimo 2008, 2010), viscous porosity (Tuana 2008, 2014), agential realism (Barad 2003, 2007), relational empiricism and "ecologies of emergence" (Verran 2001, 2002, 2013), and decolonizing epistemologies (Kovach 2010; Santos 2014; Savransky 2017; Tuhiwai Smith 2012).

On my reading, all of these approaches—in ways that are similar or distinct depending on their scholarly roots and aims—are concerned with (i) historical epistemologies, (ii) relational ontologies, (iii) multiple ontologies, (iv) knowledge making as both ethical and political, (v) a reconfigured view of what it is that *we are actually doing* as researchers and knowledge makers, and (vi) with breaking down the distinctions between epistemology, ontology, and ethics. I will elaborate on five of these points generally, across several approaches, with some specific examples related to ecological thinking.

First, and briefly, historical epistemologies focus on "practices in a performative rather than a representationalist mode" (Barad 2007, 88), which translates into a view of knowledge making practices as *objects of investigation* rather than as tools to facilitate or engender representation. Code arrived at a similar perspective through her long-standing contributions to the field of naturalized epistemologies (1981, 1987, 1991, 1995, 1996, 2006).

Second, relational ontologies are at the heart of a broad range of instituting social imaginaries of knowledge making. The concept of intra-action, derived from Karen Barad's (2007) agential realism approach, for example, refers to how entities come into being through relationships with human and other bodies (see also Dionne, this volume). Deepening the relational concept of interaction, which infers relationships between preexisting entities, this position constitutes a radically different understanding of relationality; it challenges the view of the dominating Euro-Western epistemology, representationalism, "that the world is composed of individual entities with separately determinate properties" (Barad 2007, 55; see also Haraway 1997, 2008, 2016; Scheman 2014; Tuana 2008).

A third central aspect of ethico-onto-epistemological approaches is that they engage with multiple ontologies and their varied articulations, including ontological multiplicity, ontological alterity, "enactments of worlds" (Blaser 2010, 3), and multiple worlds, rather than assuming that ours is a "one-world world" (Law 2015; see Blaser 2014; Verran 2001). As Mario Blaser (2014) writes, such an approach points broadly to "ethnographic descriptions of the many-fold shapes of the otherwise, an injunction not to explain too much or try to actualize the possibilities immanent to others' thoughts but rather to sustain them as possibilities; and, as a corollary, a politics that initially hinges upon the hope of making the otherwise visible so that it becomes viable as a real alternative."

If multiple worlds or wordlings are possible, then the researchers' role is not to *represent*, but to contribute to bringing new stories, relationships, and worlds into being. This task, a fourth significant dimension of a broad range of instituting social imaginaries of knowledge making, including ecological imaginaries, moves us toward thinking very differently about our positioning as researchers who are responsive to and responsible for their participation in and accounting of unfolding worlds and relationally constituted knowledges. Broadly put, this shifts our roles from data gathering, "collecting stories" (Code 2011, 217), and representing data to "intervening" in (Hacking 2002; Verran 2002, 2013) and "intra-act[ing]" (Barad 2007) with data and with research subjects and their worlds. Instituting social imaginaries of knowledge making signal a move away from "spectator epistemologies" (Code 2006, 2015) toward knowing as nonrepresentational, performative, interventionist, and entangled—not "from standing at a distance and representing but rather from a *direct material engagement with the world*" (Barad 2007, 49).

A fifth important element of ethico-onto-epistemological approaches is that in addition to revisioning our understandings of *what* we are doing as researchers, they rearticulate our epistemic responsibilities as researchers. Knowledge making cannot be neutral; we must take responsibility for what we bring into being. The kind of engagement and commitment where one puts their "subjectivity . . . on the line, and [assumes] responsibility for what and how he/she claims to know" (Code 2006, 275) is one of Code's seminal contributions to reconfigured social imaginaries of knowledge making. I am referring here to her forty-year (e.g., Code 1983, 1987, 1991, 2006, 2015) evolving approach to epistemic responsibilities, which recognizes that knowledge making is an intervention that always has consequences.

Code's (2015, 2) concept of epistemic responsibility was, as she has acknowledged, "something of a sleeper" and was "subject to vicious attacks at philosophy conferences and in reviews" when she first introduced it in the late 1980s. She recently confirmed, however, that "the concept and the practices it signals are acquiring new respect" (Code 2015, 2). Over the past decade, epistemic responsibilities and sister concepts, such as "ontological politics" (Mol 1999, 2002) or "accountability" (Barad 2007; Kenney 2015; Verran 2001), are receiving growing positive attention. Barad (2007, 37) writes that questions of accountability, responsibility, and realism are "not about representations of an independent reality but about the real consequences, interventions, creative possibilities, and responsibilities of intra-acting within and as part of the world." Researchers understand that they work with a "politics of possibilities" (Barad 2007, 46) rather than with representations and they do so in specific sets of relations and conditions of possibilities.

As I detail in this chapter, this sense of politics extends through Code's ecological metaphors to political habitats. In her terms, researchers, as knowers, must "learn how to acknowledge and take responsibility for the implications and effects of situation, to recognize the impossibility of an innocent positioning, while striving to achieve a politically-epistemically responsible one" (Code 2006, 219). Put differently, epistemic responsibilities are based on "an understanding of responsibility that is as epistemological as it is ethical and political" (Code 2006, ix). This strand of thinking has been present across Code's entire writing career, but as I detail below, its political urgency has increased over time and her arguments are especially compelling in her most recent book, *Manufactured Uncertainty New Challenges to Epistemic Responsibility.*

What Is Unique about Ecological Imaginaries as an Instituting Social Imaginary of Knowledge and Ethico-Onto-Epistemic Subjectivities?

Like many of the instituting social imaginaries of knowledge-making practices and subjectivities, *ecological imaginaries* challenge hegemonic "epistemologies of mastery" steeped in Cartesian and neo-Kantian philosophies. They reconfigure a wide series of relationships: epistemological, ontological, ethical, scientific, and political relationships, as well as those between and among living beings and between human and nonhuman subjects and worlds.

Ecological thinking also takes what Code (2011, 218) calls a "scavenger approach to epistemic resources," utilizing an incredibly wide array of epistemological and theoretical resources; these include, among others, feminist epistemologies, naturalized epistemologies, social epistemologies, virtue epistemologies, epistemologies of ignorance, philosophical pragmatism, postcolonial and antiracist epistemologies, and hermeneutic-phenomenological resources, as well as a broad range of ecological theories (from the natural and social sciences). Each of these resources plays its own part, bringing different influences and foci to this evolving approach to knowledge making and subjectivities.

Reading diffractively across Code's writing, I can identify at least five key influences that work together in ecological thinking and that make it particularly apt for thinking through the political, ethical, ontological, and epistemological challenges of working with narratives and with narrative resources. First, from feminist epistemologies, a field to which she has made major contributions, Code draws on enduring issues of power and knowledge. She engages with how to know marginalized people and asks, "Whose knowledge are we talking about?" (Code 2006, 21). Code focuses on "situated knowledges" (Haraway 1988) and "situated knowing," which Heidi Grassick (2011, xvi) recently called "the single most influential concept to come out of feminist epistemology." Second, ecological thinking is influenced by Code's deep immersion in phenomenologically and/or hermeneutic-phenomenologically informed thinkers—an interest in subjectivities, experiences, interpretation, and narratives that may have taken root during her studies at the University of Guelph in the 1970s and her MA thesis on phenomenology and language (entitled "Three Philosophies of Language: Wittgenstein, Heidegger, and Merleau-Ponty"). Across time, this influence has deepened through her continuing engagement with phenomenological and hermeneutic resources (e.g., Code 1995, 2003, 2006, 2020a). Third, Code (2010, 30) has drawn on and contributed to social epistemologies, noting "the centrality [they accord] to testimony and to knowledge-conveying exchanges in the real world." Fourth, Code has been influenced by ecological theories and philosophies, including the work and research practices of the late American ecologist Rachel Carson. Finally, the increasingly urgent political aspect of ecological imaginaries that appears in Code's work derives from her creative and eclectic writing about and from epistemologies of ignorance, postcolonial epistemologies, philosophical pragmatism, and epistemic injustice (e.g., Fricker 2007; Sullivan and Tuana 2007).

I maintain that these multiple influences have characterized ecological imaginaries with four unique features that translate into particular ways of working with narratives. An ecological imaginary (i) widens relational ontologies to articulate a specifically *ecological* approach to relational ontologies, (ii) adheres to the political view that epistemic communities are not innocent nor "benign" (Code 2006, vii) and that this matters to how we approach knowledge-making practices and our responsibilities as researchers, (iii) contends that knowledge making has to be *negotiated* and that "*advocacy* often makes knowledge possible" (Code 2006, 23), and (iv) pragmatically and strategically recognizes the need to sometimes cross social imaginaries of knowledge making. I briefly address each of these points below.

ECOLOGICAL RELATIONAL ONTOLOGIES

Code's thoughts on ecological relational ontologies are a central aspect of ecological imaginaries. Here she draws on two powerful influences: Deleuzian ethology and a broad range of ecological resources, including ecological philosophies and theories from the natural and social sciences, from environmental studies, and eco-feminism. From Gilles Deleuze (1988, 125–26), Code borrows the view that "the capacities for affecting and being affected that characterize each thing," which means that we do not study individual entities, objects, or stories but rather "the compositions of relations or capacities between different things" as "a matter of sociabilities and communities." Ethology is about mapping relations between people and between people and their multilayered locations and habitats; always attending to "physicality, sociality, place, cultural institutions, materiality, corporeality . . . where neither 'worlds,' 'beings,' nor 'relations' can be presumed before the fact to be static, unchanging" (Code 2008, 3).

From ecological theories (e.g., Plumwood 1993; Shiva 1989), philosophies of ecological science (e.g., Shrader-Frechette 2002), and ecological science in practice (see Code 2006, 2008, 2015), Code (1996, 13) aims to achieve "an appropriate balance between literal and metaphorical readings of the governing concept—ecology." Throughout *Ecological Thinking*, she uses extensive literal and metaphoric examples (e.g., seashells and shorelines, seeds, Japanese beetles) "to indicate the pertinence—and power—of ecological thinking" and "how this epistemological imaginary is translatable, with refinements and variations of substance and detail, across other parts of the epistemic terrain, other lives and situations" (Code 2006, 47). A concrete explication of this approach is found in her case study of Rachel Carson. Best-selling and award-winning author of three books about the sea—*Under the Sea Wind* (1941), *The Sea Around Us* (1951), and *The Edge of the Sea* (1955)—and her infamous *Silent Spring* (1962), which launched her as one of the founders of the American environmental movement that challenged pesticide companies and the use of DDT in crop spraying, Carson is presented by Code (2006, 38, 36) "as exemplary for ecological knowing" and as a "pathbreaking practitioner of twentieth-century ecological thinking and practice."

I develop two points here from Code's case study of Carson. The first point, made by Code as well as by two of Carson's biographers, is that it was only with her third book, *The Edge of the* Sea (1955/1998), that Carson's work became distinctly ecological (Lear 1997; Souder 2012). This was vividly apparent in the book's preface, where Carson made it clear that an object can only be known in its temporal, spatial, relational, historical, and unfolding habitats. She wrote that

> to understand the shore, it is not enough to catalogue its life. Understanding comes only when, standing on a beach, we can sense the long rhythms of earth and sea that sculptured its land forms and produced the rock and sand of which it is composed; when we can sense with the eye and ear of the mind the surge of life beating always at its shores—blindly, inexorably pressing for a foothold. *To understand the life of the shore, it is not enough to pick up an empty shell and say "This is a murex," or "That is an angel wing." True understanding demands intuitive comprehension of the whole life of the creature that once inhabited this empty shell*: how it survived amid surf and storms, what were its enemies, how it found food and reproduced its kind, what were its relations to the particular sea world in which it lived. (Carson 1955/1998, 3; emphasis added)

Code draws from this example, using the relation between an empty shell and the larger shoreline to discuss how we come to know and classify objects and to illustrate the complexity of naming and constructing taxonomies and categories. She explains that "entities, organisms, and events do not fall naturally into categories and kinds"; rather, "classifications are multiply contestable" partly because *what something is*—including, as I detail below, a story or testimony—depends on "the habitats, patterns, or processes in which seemingly distinct organisms and entities interact" (Code 2006, 50). In light of what Deleuze (1988, 125–26) claims about "the capacities for affecting and being affected that characterize each thing," a murex or an angel wing—what they *are* and what they *do*—are different depending on their specific temporal, spatial, and relational habitats. Code (2006, 50) argues that instead of working to "achieve, create, or impose a certain order," ecological thinking "maps it differently." This mapping "requires understanding how those *specificities work together*" and addressing "the explanatory power of an attentive concentration on local particulars [and] specificities," while also seeking to "*generate responsible remappings* [emphasis added] across wider, heterogeneous epistemic terrains" (Code 2006, 50).

Code takes this further, noting that these mappings and remappings are not neutral; we see from where we are and in accordance with how we believe the world is and *should be* constituted. In this way, Code's work resonates with that of Joseph Rouse (2016, emphasis added), who reminds us that "conceptual understanding and ethical accountability are always entangled" and that our wider responsibility as researchers "also establishes an accountability for *what we become and how we live*" (see also Barad 2007; Haraway 1991, 1997; Rouse 2015). As Code (2006, 93) puts it: "Ecological naturalism establishes such a moral stance at the core of its deliberations, insisting on obligations to answer for oneself/ourselves, to maintain skepticism in the face of overweening authority, and to work toward ways of ensuring better, justice-honoring cohabitability." Her rationale for this is partly evident in her view that habitats are not only the wide social and natural worlds within which all objects are located and unfold but also epistemic communities, with their political and ethical concerns.

Epistemic Communities Are Not Benign

On my reading, one intriguing part of *Ecological Thinking* is when Code reflects on a key change in her work and acknowledges that she had previously relied on an "excessively benign conception of community" (Code 2006, v). Extending the insights of feminist empiricism (Longino 1990; Nelson 1993), wherein knowers are not individuals but rather "individuals-in-communities" (Grasswick 2004, 98), Code contends that indeed many communities are implicated in knowledge making and its possibilities, reception, and effects.

Her attention to the explicitly political character of epistemic communities and their very real everyday effects has increased over time. In *Ecological Thinking*, Code (2006, viii) noted that tensions within epistemic communities introduce new or reconfigured understandings of responsibility and accountability in "the production, circulation, and acknowledgment of claims to know" and that this results in a wider sense of sociopolitical responsibilities. Consequently, "epistemic responsibilities have to be negotiated" in order to "counter the excesses of demonstrably unjust social-political-epistemic orders" (Code 2006, vii).

Using detailed case studies,[10] including her central study of Rachel Carson, Code highlights potential and sometimes inevitable epistemic tensions between researchers and their varied epistemic communities comprising funders, invested parties, and research communities, each with its entrenched methods, concepts, interests, and aims. Arguing that "ecological thinking is distantly related to a radicalized rereading of the 'strong objectivity' associated with standpoint epistemology" (Code 2006, 62), she writes that a key advantage of her approach

> derives not from cleansing inquiry of interests, materialities, presuppositions, or the constitutive effects of situation and place, but from analyzing these as fully as it analyzes traditionally conceived "objects of knowledge" and from its self-reflexive commitment constantly to monitor its processes of inquiry.

In *Ecological Thinking*, Code (2006, 24) argues that thinking ecologically is not just about doing research but about how this research could "translate into wider issues of citizenship and politics" so that the entire endeavor is "about imagining, crafting, articulating, and endeavouring to enact principles of ideal cohabitation" (24). In the years since *Ecological Thinking* was published, this aim has deepened, and the ecological research that she envisions is tied even more to thinking about how it could generate "innovative, revisionary knowledge projects with the social-political transformations, renewals, and disruptions they may animate" (Code 2011, 209).

In her newest book, *Manufactured Uncertainty*, Code (2020a, 3) takes this even further, arguing that researchers must address "the effects—the consequences—be they positive or negative, of 'our' ways of living." She posits that "social justice is an overarching issue" and that the framing of ecological imaginaries is indeed "ethical-epistemological-ontological-political" (3). This extension of Code's work draws a great deal from Naomi Oreskes and Eric Conway's 2010 book *Merchants of Doubt*; she joins them in their "challenge to socially embedded assumptions about the taken for granted 'certainty'—the rarely contested 'reliability'—of publicly announced and analysed scientific findings" (Code 2020a, 1). As she puts it: "People will argue for—advocate for—what they care about and/or fear to lose: both the deniers and the convinced engage in such practices" (2020a, 96). This idea is connected to another central and unique aspect of ecological thinking: a focus on advocacy.

Advocacy Makes Knowledge Possible

In connection with her point above and the need to negotiate knowledge making, Code (2006, 23) posits that even though it is a "contentious claim," she holds to the view that "advocacy is often what makes knowledge possible." Advocating for others is "both an epistemic and an ethico-political issue" (193), and she is careful to explain that it is not meant to be a patronizing activity whereby one speaks for others (see also Alcoff 1991). Code concurs with Haraway (2000, 167), quoting her assertion that knowing "is always an interpretive, engaged, contingent, fallible engagement"; implicitly or explicitly, we make choices about what narratives we will bring attention to, stand with, and fight for, thereby "casting our lot with some ways of life and not others" (Haraway 1997, 36).

Code makes this point in *Ecological Thinking*, but as with her expanding interest in the political dimensions of inquiry, over time, advocacy has become a more pressing and political concern. What is needed now, Code writes (2020a, 96), is for us "to—advocate-debate responsibly, knowledgeably, and *humbly*—paradoxical as this need may be—in the minutely informed and ethically/politically respectful way," and this means that we must "recognize how zealously the deniers seek to defend places and putative values that are, quite simply, unsustainable."

Methodological Pluralism and Pragmatism: Crossing Social Imaginaries

Code argues that it was in the writing and reception of Carson's fourth and final book, *Silent Spring*, that Carson effectively, pragmatically, and strategically worked between and across instituted and instituting social imaginaries of knowledge making in order to have her work taken seriously by diverse epistemic communities and audiences. This was especially critical because she was unexpectedly caught up in a battle for public legitimacy as the pesticides industry mounted a massive campaign to discredit her work. Before the book was released, Carson's publisher, Houghton Mifflin, was being sued by chemical, pesticide, and pharmaceutical companies, who depicted Carson as a "hysterical female" and a "communist" (Code 2006, 58). The FBI even opened up a file on her (Souder 2012). As Souder (2012, 12) writes in his biography of Carson, her "detractors imagined her in league with a lunatic fringe that included food faddists, anti-fluoridationists, organic farmers, and soft-headed nature lovers. . . . [and] a front for 'sinister influences' in the Soviet Union and its Eastern European satellites." In response to all of this negative attention, she remained pragmatic, not denouncing pesticides outright but arguing that they should be more thoroughly studied and more prudently used, sometimes advocating "waiting an extra season or two" (Carson 1962, 98) to study crop and pesticide patterns and effects rather than relying on a "quick (chemical) fix" (Code 2006, 46).

Carson applied this same pragmatism to her research process, using multiple methodologies to obtain and analyze her data. As Code (2006, 40) describes it, Carson mapped out diverse readings of different kinds of evidence, "charting, bringing together, and moving back and forth between/among quite different subject areas" and "various kinds of knowledge with widely differing histories, methods, and assumptions." For Code (2006, 44), Carson needed to be

> multilingual and multiply literate: to speak the language of laboratory science, wildlife organizations, government agencies, chemical-producing companies, secular nature lovers, and many others; to understand the detail of scientific documents and the force of experiential reports; to work back and forth between an *imaginary of mastery and of ecology*. (emphasis added)

Carson's epistemic practices, Code (2006, 43) maintains, were situated on "a middle path, working back and forth" between instituted and instituting social imaginaries. This is an important point that connects to the arguments I make below about strategically moving between representational and non-representational ways of working with narratives, stories, and testimonies. Operating within and sometimes against a variety of epistemic communities, researchers must negotiate instituted and instituting social imaginaries in order to maximize the possibilities for ethical knowing and intervention. This point underlines Code's commitment to the feminist epistemological principle of attending to power in knowledge making and to how different forms of negotiated evidence can challenge power-infused epistemic practices, institutions, and effects. For Code, the relationship between instituted and instituting imaginaries is not oppositional, fixed, or linear, nor can one replace the other. Rather, the "instituted imaginary is never seamless or static . . . it is always in motion" and its "gaps . . . open up spaces for the work of the instituting imaginary" (Code 2006, 33).

Ecological Imaginaries and Narratives, Stories, and Testimonies

Code has worked on the edges of the narrative turn for several decades. In her book *Rhetorical Spaces: Essays on Gendered Locations* (1995), she articulated her desire to develop an "epistemology of everyday life" (Code 1995, xi) and "a 'storied epistemology' . . . that grants epistemic force to narratives that tell of the construction of knowledge, of theories of knowledge, and of subjectivities, stories which are specifically contextualized within and located in relation to human lives" (xvi). In her subsequent writing, she has continued to reflect on the complex relations between first-, second-, and third-person narratives (Code 1995, 2006) and how narrative fiction helps to develop moral epistemologies aimed at knowing people across differences (Code 2011). Over twenty years ago, in 1998, one of the world's most prolific narratologists, Mieke Bal (1993, 299), argued that "Code even makes narrative the core of her 'epistemic responsibility.'" Specifically, Ball drew from Code's *What Can She Know*, where Code (1991, 170) argued that "once epistemologists recognize the locatedness of all cognitive activity in the projects and constructions of specifically positioned subjects, then the relevance of narrative will be apparent as an epistemological resource."

Reading Code's work diffractively from within many of the new social theory turns laid out at the beginning of this chapter, it is clear that she treats narratives as *much more than* epistemological; indeed, as her concern with narratives has developed across time, I believe that Code has increasingly approached them as *politico-ethico-onto-epistemological* resources. In *Rhetorical Spaces* (1995) and in *Ecological Thinking* (2006), she reflected on the challenges of listening, the tensions of working between representational and nonrepresentational approaches to narratives, and the imperfect-yet-strategic value of dialogic narrative approaches. Code's (2006, 225) aim to bring full attention to "situations where knowing people in complex, elaborated, and often extraordinary situations is the issue" is extended even further in her new book, *Manufactured Uncertainty* (2020a), in which she elaborates on the importance of balancing particularity and specificity in stories and testimonies while maintaining a vigilant eye on "the *politics* of testimony" (Code 2020a, 36). More recently, Code draws on Oreskes and Conway (2010) to deepen her argument that epistemic communities are not "benign" (Code 2006, vii), that particular stories and testimonies can be constrained or go unheard because of "credentialed epistemic communit(ies)" such as 'the tobacco industry, pharmaceutical companies, and climate change deniers,'" whose power and "opaque structures of vested interest" (Code 2020a, 52) have burgeoned since her case study of Rachel Carson.

When thinking about how ecological imaginaries might help to frame or guide research that is focused on stories, testimonies, and narrative, it is important to say at the outset that ecological thinking, partly because of its ecological relational ontologies, cannot be mapped in any one way. Yet Code's work on ecological imaginaries can provide useful stepping-stones for researchers who are attempting to conceptualize and analyze stories, testimonies, or narratives in their fieldwork and data analysis research practices. To chart potential pathways, I bring Code into conversation with Somers and with a small selection of resources from the narrative turn in order to think through how ecological imaginaries might guide or intra-act with narrative research and narrative analysis.

In the following, I connect the unique qualities of ecological instituting social imaginaries of knowledge making and subjectivities to narrative resources, exploring how to generally apply these imaginaries to projects that include narrative and narrative analysis. Although it is a very expansive field in the social sciences and in qualitative methodologies, on my reading, the field of narrative and narrative analysis remains dominated by two tendencies. The first, as Somers noted over twenty years ago, is that most narrative analysis approaches treat narratives as representational objects and as matters of epistemology; that is, narratives are seen to reflect, represent, or impose a narrative structure on experiences, life stories, or realities. Building from resources similar to those used by Code, notably the work of Paul Ricoeur, Somers (1994, 607) calls for an approach that defines "narrative and narrativity as concepts of *social epistemology* and *social ontology.*"

The second strong tendency in narrative studies, as well as in social epistemologies, is to view Narratives, stories, and testimonies as synonymous, interchangeable, undifferentiated. I make this argument based on my diffractive reading of Somers, Code, and other narrative resources, while also using it as a strategic opening for thinking about Narratives as a wider category that includes stories, and testimonies as well as multiple narrative dimensions and forms.

Ecological Relational Ontologies: Narratives as a "Relationality of Parts" (that Straddle First-, Second-, and Third-Person Narratives)

Somers offers a rich and multilayered approach to Narrative that includes at least four *kinds* of nested narratives, each of which exhibits four dimensions or more. The four types of narrative forms are (i) ontological narratives (which I view as stories or testimonies), (ii) social, public, and cultural narratives, (iii) metanarratives, and (iv) conceptual narratives; the four narrative *dimensions* are "1) relationality of parts, 2) causal emplotment, 3) selective appropriation, and 4) temporality, sequence, and place" (Somers 1994, 616). Put differently, all Narratives "are constellations of relationships (connected parts) embedded in time and *space*, constituted by what [she calls] *causal emplotment*" (Somers 1992, 601) (for more details, see Doucet 2018a, 2018b).

Somers's approach to Narrative offers a potential counterpoint to the dominant conceptualization of Narratives, stories, and testimonies as interchangeable, particularly on my reading, which aligns it with Code's ecological relational ontologies. The ecological character of Narratives means that the differences between types of narratives will depend on their habitats.[11] For example, I would argue that Code's work widens Somers's (1994, 618) description of "social, public and cultural narratives" as "intersubjective webs of relationality [that] sustain and transform narratives over time" and as "attached to cultural and institutional formations larger than the single individual, to intersubjective networks or institutions, however local or grand." On my reading, Code adds a significant and explicitly *political* dimension (in the sense that Oreske and Conway's work signifies *political*) to social, public, and cultural narratives.

When we speak about Narratives I believe that we are necessarily referring to the different narrative forms and dimensions. *Narratives also contain a combination of first-, second-, and third-person narratives.*

First-Person Narratives: Stories and Testimonies as Ontological Narratives

Ontological narratives are the stories and/or testimonies that people tell, "the stories that social actors use to make sense of—indeed, to act in—their lives" (Somers 1994, 618). Drawing on Somers and other resources, I argue that their ontological nature differentiates stories and testimonies from Narratives—as the latter encompasses a broader array of narrative types and their "relationality of parts" (Somers 1994, 616). It is important, however, to recognize that there are also differences between stories (which are told in interview settings or informal settings) and testimonies (which are more connected to people's accounts of particular political, legal, and historical events, often as part of large-scale testimony projects) (see High 2014, 2015; Regan 2010; Shaffer and Smith 2004).

Ontological narratives (which I will refer to as "stories" or "testimonies" in the remainder of this chapter) have several key features. They are not representations per se; rather, they are agential, performative, and generative. They make identities and worlds and have the "capacity to re-present the world in ways that are generative for the people and practices that the narratives stories are about, as well as for the authors and their academic collectives" (Winthereik and Verran 2012, 37). Stories and testimonies "act" and "do things" (Frank 2010, 43); they create new relationships, materialities, and social realities (Frank 2010; Haraway 2008; Law 2015).

Stories and testimonies also make and remake "narrative identities" (Somers 1994; Ricoeur 1992). Indeed, an ontological (and performative) approach to narratives and narrative identities intersects with decades of recurring poststructuralist critiques about identities and subjectivities. As Somers argues, "it is through narratives and narrativity that we come to know, understand, and make sense of the social world and it is through narratives and narrativity that we constitute our social identities" (Somers 1994, 606; see also Ricoeur 1992; Taylor 1989). Code (2006, 59) makes a similar point in her characterization of "bioregional narratives," quoting Jim Cheney (1989, 126), who weaves together Indigenous (Native American) myths and postmodern environmental ethics and who views narrative identities as "narrative grounded in geography rather than in a linear, essentialized narrative self."

Whether one is referring to stories or to testimonies, ontological narratives are performative and worldmaking. This point is well expressed in the work of Indigenous scholars. As Leanne Betamosake Simpson (2011, 33) argues, "Storytelling is at its core decolonizing, because it is a process of remembering, visioning and creating a just reality"; storytelling becomes a way to "envision our way out of cognitive imperialism, where we can create models and mirrors where none existed and where we can experience the spaces of freedom and justice" (see also Tuhiwai Smith 2012).

Finally, stories and testimonies focus on the inseparability of tellers, listeners, and their varied communities and on the *dialogic intra-action* between them. Put differently, they are told to specific others such that "the telling performs an action that presupposes an Other" (Butler 2005, 81; see also Code 2006) and the "narrative self" is always constituted in relation to others (Ricoeur 1984). Code's (1991, 87) contribution to thinking about narratives and narrative identities as dialogic is rooted in her long trajectory (1987, 1991, 1995, 2006) of using the concept of "second personhood" (building on Annette Baier's [1995] concept) to describe "relational and historical being(s)." That is, most narratives are told and analyzed in the first or third person although, as Code (2006, 229) maintains, "both forms of speaking have been fraught with difficulties." She thus advocates the recognition of second-person narratives that do not seek a "detached assent to an indifferent truth," but rather "a second-person acknowledgment from and of (an)other(s)" (229). This leads to my next point about Narratives, stories, testimonies, and second persons.

SECOND PERSONS, "ACKNOWLEDGEMENT AND ADVOCACY"

The "acknowledgement" of a story or testimony from an engaged listener and community—a second person—is what "make[s] knowing possible," Code (2006, 229) writes. To press this point, I draw on Code's (2006) reading of Paul Ricoeur's work, and especially his (1993) speech to Amnesty International on how to make sense of stories, testimonies, and narratives in the midst of postmodern arguments on fragmented subjectivities. She writes how

> in response to Amnesty's question, Ricoeur proposes a revisioned, addressive-dialogic selfhood *enacted* in an ability to take present, and future, responsibility for its thoughts and deeds. This is a subject for which *recognition* is constitutive of both the self and his/her other; thus a subject open to first- and third-person narratives from which people often learn as much about themselves as about the other-as-narrator; and, perhaps most significantly, a subject not complete onto itself but one that requires interlocutors, listeners sensitive to the modalities and nuances of the tellings. (Code 2006, 212)

Code's choice of this example is noteworthy as it reinforces that political habitats and contexts matter. Code is deeply attuned to stories and testimonies of trauma, especially those of rape and human rights abuses, and to sociopolitical crises, including climate change crises (see Code 2014, 2020a). Stories from people with little sociopolitical power who address or attempt to expose enormous financial and political issues in research, like Rachel Carson did, are compelling because they deliberately interrogate "whose experiences count and why on an epistemic terrain where credibility is unevenly distributed and testimony often discounted or denigrated on the basis of whose it is" (Code 2006, 51; see also Fricker 2007).

Code's (2006, 102) arguments about second-person narratives and acknowledgment are closely linked, on my reading, to her concerns about advocacy, "negotiating empiricism," and crossing social imaginaries of knowledge making.

CROSSING SOCIAL IMAGINARIES

A key tension that plagues researchers who work with stories and testimonies, on the one hand, and Narratives, on the other, is figuring out how we might still hold on to the *representational* dimensions of stories when we move toward nonrepresentational ways of knowing. Can we have representation without representationalism? (Neimanus 2015). As these concerns are part of a massive theoretical and epistemological terrain, I will develop five subpoints to map out my arguments.

First, as indicated above, I am approaching Narratives as ecological relational ontologies, as "constellations of relationships (connected parts)" (Somers 1992, 601), and as relationalit[ies] of many different narrative dimensions and forms. At the same time—and this is my second point—although nonrepresentational approaches to Narrative entail a shift from the noun "plot" to the verb "emplot," and take into account how emplotments occur within specific sets of resources and relationships and through processes of *"selective appropriation"* (Somers 1994, 617), they do not completely dispense with plot. On my reading, both Code and Somers are attentive to the *particularities* and *specificities* of the plots of stories and testimonies and how they are told. Bal (2009, 5) describes such specificities as part of a story's *fabula*, or the "material content that is worked into a story," including a series of "logically and chronologically related events that are caused by or experienced by actors." Somers (1992, 604) agrees, writing that "a plot must be thematic." Code (2006, 52) argues that ecological thinking "repositions and revalorizes experiential evidence" from a strategic "ethico-political" and pragmatic position and that "experiential, testimonial reports claim an enhanced, if not uncontested, credibility and authority in this approach to knowledge" (23). Working with ecological metaphors, Code (2006, 17–18) states that an ecological approach to Narratives

> require[s] sensitivity to detail, to minutiae, to what precisely—however apparently small—distinguishes this woman, this contestable practice, this social intervention, this place, this problem of knowledge, this injustice, this locality from that—just as biologically based ecologists distinguish this plant, this species, this rock pool from that one.

My third point is that Code deepens this attention to specificity in her latest book, *Manufactured Uncertainty*. Working especially with narrative theorist Adriane Cavarero, and engaging in another version of crossing social imaginaries of knowledge making, she recognizes that "an epistemological turn toward particularity evokes certain caveats," including the view that conceptually and ontologically, its "purpose is not to reclaim the individualism against which feminist, post-colonial, anti-racist moral-political-epistemological critique has, appropriately, been directed" (Code 2020a, 30). Rather, consonant with arguments made by human rights scholars and those who have written about Canada's two national inquiries on Indigenous histories, "engagement with the specificities of agency, detail, and situation is of vital significance in drawing attention to the omissions endemic to universalist analyses" (31).

Fourth, Code, like Somers, draws on feminist and hermeneutic-phenomenological resources, including Ricoeur's (1992) writing on dialogic narrativity and his view that neither storytelling nor Narratives are ethically or politically neutral. They are also influenced by Gadamer's "hermeneutic circle," with its "dialectical relationships between, on the one hand, sociohistorical and political contexts and conceptual frameworks, and, on the other hand, a particular object of investigation" (Code 2003, 12). Code also looks to feminist existential phenomenologist Sonia Kruks's (2001, 18) work on narrative identity as rooted in "concepts of a subject that is neither reduced to pure freedom nor is the passive plaything of social and discursive forces."

I end this section on crossing social imaginaries with Kruks (who is featured in Code's two most recent books) (2006, 2020a), reading diffractively between Kruks's (2001) *Retrieving Experience* and Code's analysis of that text. Specifically, I point to how Kruks (2001) reworks Joan Scott's (1992, 26) highly cited piece, "Experience," in which Scott contests foundationalism as "some primary premises, categories, or presumptions" and argues for "historicism," which "takes all categories of analysis as contextual, contested and contingent." Kruks disagrees with Scott's (1992) position that experience is not the root of our analysis but something to be explained. Rather, she maintains—and I agree with her—that Scott is presenting "a false antithesis" (Kruks 2001, 138). She argues that

> experience can serve as a point of origin for an explanation *and* as the object of an explanation. Whether one chooses to explore it as one or the other—or indeed as both—is a choice that should not be foreclosed a priori. For one's method of investigation may well depend on the reasons *why* one is undertaking a particular study. (Kruks 2001, 138; emphasis added)

If we substitute *story* or *testimony* here for experience, there is a parallel point to be made. Here I am advocating a politico-ethico-onto-epistemological approach to Narrative that attends to the general and the specific, the context and the content, "particularity and wholeness" (Code 2020a, 175), and "whole-part" relations (Verran 2001), one that also addresses the plot lines and "fabula" of a wide range of ontological narratives (stories and testimonies) as well as narrative analysis and the selective and purposeful emplotment of narratives. This approach is especially critical when listening to stories or testimonies of trauma, violence, genocide, rape, and other human rights abuses. As Code (2020a, 16) writes:

> It is vital, then, to the achievement and maintenance of social justice broadly conceived, for would-be knowers to work, collaboratively and singly, toward developing an apt measure of *hermeneutic* understanding with respect to negotiating knowledgeably, and empathically with one another across diverse situations, "identities," and circumstances.

We must, she asserts, "endeavor to do just that, if never perfectly to achieve it" (Code 2020a, 16).

The *purpose* of our research thus matters in our attempts, flawed as they are, to take on this work within specific sociocultural, historical, and political habitats. As researchers, we selectively emplot particular scholarly narratives, and these emplotments vary "depending on whether one poses the question as one of primarily socio-historical interests or else with a political agenda for effective intervention in mind" (Kruks 2001, 138).

On my reading, Code supports this view. Referencing Kruks (2001) in her recent book, Code (2020a, 16) maintains that we need to articulate a "'healthy skepticism' about the reach of the aggregated first-person plural pronoun—'we'—and about the extent and the quality of 'our' epistemic and affective capacities to understand one another, whether 'personally' or 'situationally,' across stark otherness." She asserts that we must try to "engage *listening* as a central modality of epistemic practice" and as "a fundamental human capacity to open oneself to the world" (19). We must also "honour 'our' opacity to one another," which "requires listening and negotiating across differences, even if these negotiations generate deeper commitments to preserving silence: 'to holding open a space for not knowing'" (175). Code (39) states that there are no "simple either/or choices: thinking well about them produces more questions than answers."

I end with the idea that ecological imaginaries are deeply political and ethical. They do not focus on knowledge products per se but are committed to "constructing knowledge that fosters democratic, respectful cohabitation and interaction" (Code 2020a, 144). They break down divisions "between epistemology and ethics-politics" and acknowledge "the urgency of epistemic responsibility as an intellectual *and* ethical value and commitment" (97). I would take this even further, following the logic of Code's analysis, to view epistemic responsibilities and approaches to Narratives as matters of politico-ethico-onto-epistemology. My position extends her earlier work on habitability as embracing "ontological questions about who 'we' are and how 'we' can live responsibly, together and separately, in the human, natural, and social-political world" (2).

Conclusion

In her third book, *The Edge of the Sea*, Rachel Carson (1955/1998) was keen to have her writing reach multiple epistemic communities, but she recognized that some people might indeed want to be able to name ocean specimens (i.e., *"This is a murex,"* or *"That is an angel wing"*). Thus, in the same preface where she laid out her ecological approach to analyzing the "the seashores of the world" with their "rugged shores of rock, the sand beaches, and the coral reefs and all their associated features," each with "its typical community of plants and animals" (Carson 1995/1988, 3), she also revealed her awareness that not all audiences would appreciate or even understand her ecological perspective. Carson knew that people might need to identify an object without attending to broader ecological concerns about what it does, how it intra-acts, and the dependency of its becoming on its constitutive relational ontologies and habitats (regardless of that object's identification in multiple sites as, for example, a murex or an angel wing). She wrote:

> For the convenience of those who like to pigeonhole their findings neatly in the classification schemes the human mind has devised, an appendix presents the conventional groups, or phyla, of plants and animals and describes typical examples. Each form mentioned in the book itself is listed under its Latin as well as its common name in the index. (Carson 1955/1998, 3)

Here I want to make a conceptual and metaphorical leap to argue that for narrative researchers, familiar plot lines can sometimes appear alongside a multitude of possible emplotments and multiple ontologies. I mentioned in the introduction, for example, two commissions that relied on the stories of Indigenous Canadians. In spite of differences between the sociopolitical, cultural, temporal, and spatial contexts, conditions, and habitats in which these events were experienced and narrated, many who listened to and analyzed these testimonies argued that they could identify common themes and narratives of suffering, cross-generational trauma, and cultural genocide (see, e.g., Aboriginal Healing Foundation 2012; Fontaine, Craft, and the Truth and Reconciliation Commission of Canada 2015a, 2015b; High 2014, 2015; Regan 2010; The National Inquiry into Missing and Murdered Indigenous Women and Girls 2019a, 2019b). These themes are the identifiable patterns and objects—Carson's murexes and angel wings—that nevertheless come into being only within and as shaped by the particularities (specific emplotments) of the wider Narrative shores (tellers, listeners, narrative identities, narrative contexts, and constitutive habitats) that make and remake those symbolic murexes and angel wings.

I am arguing here, working from my diffractive reading of Code's writing on ecological imaginaries, that researchers must recognize and accept the paradoxical existence of both particularity and specificity in stories and testimonies; they must contend, however imperfectly and inconclusively, with the potentially recognizable themes within and across epistemic communities, as well as the wider Narratives, and the relationalities of parts that contextualize and trouble any specific reading or analysis of stories and testimonies. As Kruks (2001, 139) asks: "Can we both value differences and pursue broader political agendas for human emancipation that transcend differences?" Like Code, she recognizes the dangers of dwelling too much on specificity and of focusing too much on people's narrated experiences; at the same time, she suggests that "there needs to a be a division of theoretical labour, in which *not all* feminist theory devotes itself to the potentially interminable deconstruction of concepts and categories" (Kruks 2001, 139, emphasis added). Particular stories and testimonies must be given space in order to continue "to develop explanatory frameworks, or a kind of theoretical paralysis threatens to set in" (Kruks 2001, 139–140). Influenced by Haraway, Kruks (2001, 128) posits a conception of situated objectivity partly defined as shared norms within epistemic communities, arguing that "knowledge must be both practical and situated" (see also Code 2006; McHugh 2015).

Drawing a great deal on Kruks and Haraway (and extending their work), Code argues that ecological imaginaries can reshape how we approach knowledge making and subjectivities. In this chapter, I have diffractively traced the tremendous potential of Code's ecological approach for working with Narratives, stories, and testimonies, which is derived from the rich and diverse resources that inform it: a broad range of epistemological traditions (notably, naturalized, social, and feminist), her long-standing interest in narratives and hermeneutic resources, as well as her more than forty years of work on knowledge making, subjectivities, and "vexed questions" of knowing others. To conclude with a nod to Carson (1955/1998, 3), the approach I have laid out signals our need, as researchers, to identify recognizable patterns and objects—for example, "this is a murex" and "this is an angel wing"—while also metaphorically "standing on a beach" and "sens(ing) the long rhythms of earth and sea that sculpted its land forms," thereby "gaining an intuitive comprehension of the whole life" and the relationalities and creative potentialities of any object, story, or testimony.

Notes

1. I would like to thank Janna Klostermann and Nancy McHugh for their insightful comments on this chapter.

2. See, for example, Alaimo and Hekman (2008); Barad (2003, 2007); Coole and Frost (2010); Hekman (2010).

3. See, for example, Lam (2015); Lykke (2010).

4. See, for example, Braidotti (2016, 2018).

5. See, for example, Barad (2003, 2007); Mauthner (2015, 2018).

6. See, for example, Barad (2007); Blaser (2014); Cooke and Frost (2011); Hacking (2002).

7. Like all social theory and philosophical turns, the narrative turn has unfolded in varied and multiple articulations since the 1960s, across many scholarly fields in the humanities and the social sciences, such as philosophy, social epistemologies, oral history, narrative fiction, narratology, and narrative theories, with influences of phenomenology, hermeneutics, phenomenological-hermeneutic combinations, poststructuralism, narrative psychology, and narrative sociology (e.g., Andrews 2014; Frank 2010; Hinchman and Hinchman 2001; Hyvärinen 2010; Meretoja 2014, 2018; Riessman 2008).

8. I first began working with Code's philosophical insights in the early 2000s, recognizing her as a rare feminist philosopher and epistemologist who was attempting to translate these insights into methodological practices (e.g., Burt and Code 1995) (see Doucet and Mauthner 2002/2012). After being out of print for many years, a new edition of *Epistemic Responsibility* was reissued by State University of New York Press in 2020.

9. Code's 1996 article on naturalized epistemologies, which builds partly on W. V. O. Quine's work, argues, for example: "Naturalistic projects can contribute to emancipatory epistemological agendas to the extent that they are prepared to examine the constructed dimensions both of nature and of scientific knowledge, and to assess the ecological effects of those constructs. Hence, they need to engage questions of historical, cultural, gendered epistemic specificity as constitutive features of 'science as an institution or process in the world'" (Code 1996, 16, citing Quine 1969, 26).

10. Code (2006) also develops a case study of Nancy Olivieri, a Canadian medical doctor who blew the whistle on the pharmaceutical industry's role in science practices.

11. For example, as Watts (2013) highlights in her writing on indigenous narratives, specifically Anishinaabe and/or Haudenosaunee Canadian First Nations cosmologies, "place-thought" narratives that give weight to nonhuman narratives could be another kind of narrative layer in some contexts.

Works Cited

Aboriginal Healing Foundation. 2012. *Reflections on Reconciliation and Residential School.* Ottawa: Aboriginal Healing Foundation. http://projectofheart.ca/wp-content/uploads/2012/08/Speaking-My-Truth.pdf.

Alaimo, Stacy, and Susan Hekman, eds. 2008. *Material Feminisms.* Bloomington: Indiana University Press.

Alcoff, Linda. 1991. "The Problem of Speaking for Others." *Cultural Critique* 20: 5–32.

Alcoff, Linda Martín. 2011. "Experience and Knowledge: The Case of Sexual Abuse Memories." In *Feminist Metaphysics*, edited by C. Witt, 209–223. New York: Springer.

Andrews, Molly. 2014. *Narrative Imagination and Everyday Life*. New York: Oxford University Press.

Arendt, Hannah. 1958/1998. *The Human Condition*. 2nd ed. Chicago: University of Chicago Press.

Baier, Annette C. 1995. "A Note on Justice, Care, and Immigration Policy." *Hypatia* 10: 150–152.

Bal, Mieke. 1993. "First Person, Second Person, Same Person: Narrative as Epistemology." *New Literary History* 2: 293.

———. 2009. *Narratology: Introduction to the Theory of Narrative*. Toronto: University of Toronto Press.

Barad, Karen. 2003. "Posthumanist Performativity: Toward an Understanding of How Matter Comes to Matter." *Journal of Women in Culture and Society* 28: 801–831.

———. 2007. *Meeting the Universe Halfway: Quantum Physics and the Entanglement of Matter and Meaning*. Durham, NC: Duke University Press.

———. 2009. " 'Matter Feels, Converses, Suffers, Desires, Yearns and Remembers': Interview with Karen Barad." In *New Materialism: Interviews & Cartographies*, edited by Rick Dolphijn and Iris van der Tuin, 48–70. London: Open Humanities.

Bartky, Sandra Lee. 1990. *Femininity and Domination: Studies in the Phenomenology of Oppression*. London: Routledge.

Bartky, Sandra Lee. 2002. *Sympathy and Solidarity and Other Essays*. Lanham, MD: Rowman and Littlefield.

Blaser, Mario. 2014. "The Political Ontology of Doing Difference . . . and Sameness: Theorizing the Contemporary." *Cultural Anthropology*, January 13. https://culanth.org/fieldsights/the-political-ontology-of-doing-difference-and-sameness.

Braidotti, Rosi. 2016a. *The Posthuman*. London: Polity.

———. 2018. "A Theoretical Framework for the Critical Posthumanities." *Theory, Culture & Society* 36: 31–61.

Brown, L. M., and Gilligan, C. 1992. *Meeting at the Crossroads: Women's Psychology and Girls' Development*. Cambridge, MA: Harvard University Press.

Butler, Judith. 1995. "Contingent Foundations." In *Feminist Contentions: A Philosophical Exchange*, edited by Seyla Benhabib, Judith Butler, Drucilla Cornell, and Nancy Fraser. New York and London: Routledge.

———. 2005. *Giving an Account of Oneself*. New York: Fordham University Press.

Burt, Sandra D., and Lorraine Code. 1995. *Changing Methods: Feminists Transforming Practice*. Peterborough, ON: Broadview.

Carson, Rachel. 1941. *Under the Sea—Wind*. New York: Penguin.

———. 1951. *The Sea around Us*. Oxford: Oxford University Press.

———. 1955/1998. *The Edge of the Sea*. Boston: Houghton Mifflin Harcourt.

———. 1962. *Silent Spring*. Boston: Houghton Mifflin Harcourt.
Castoriadis, Cornelius. 1998. *The Imaginary Institution of Society*. Translated by Kathleen Blamey. Cambridge, UK: MIT Press.
Cavarero, Adriana. 2002. *Relating Narratives: Storytelling and Selfhood*. London: Routledge.
Cavarero, Adriana. 2005. *For More Than One Voice: Toward a Philosophy of Vocal Expression*. Palo Alto, CA: Stanford University Press.
Cheney, Jim. 1989. "Postmodern Environmental Ethics: Ethics as Bioregional Narrative." *Environmental Ethics* 11: 117–34.
Code, Lorraine. 1981. "Is the Sex of the Knower Epistemologically Significant?" *Metaphilosophy* 12: 267–276.
———. 1983. "Responsibility and the Epistemic Community: Women's Place." *Social Research* 50: 537–555.
———. 1984. "Toward a 'Responsibilist' Epistemology." *Philosophy and Phenomenological Research* 45: 29–50.
———. 1987. *Epistemic Responsibility*. Hanover, NH: University Press of New England.
———. 1988. "Experience, Knowledge and Responsibility." In *Feminist Perspectives in Philosophy*, edited by M. Griffiths and M. Whitford, 187–204. Bloomington: Indiana University Press.
———. 1991. *What Can She Know? Feminist Theory and the Construction of Knowledge*. Ithaca, NY: Cornell University Press.
———. 1995. *Rhetorical Spaces: Essays on Gendered Locations*. New York and London: Routledge.
———. 1996. "What is Natural about Epistemology Naturalized?" *American Philosophical Quarterly* 33:1–22.
———, ed. 2003. *Feminist Interpretations of Hans-Georg Gadamer*. University Park: Pennsylvania State University Press.
———. 2006. *Ecological Thinking: The Politics of Epistemic Location*. New York: Oxford University Press.
———. 2008. "Thinking Ecologically about Biology." *Insights* 1: 2–17.
———. 2010. "Testimony, Advocacy, Ignorance: Thinking Ecologically about Social Knowledge." In *Social Epistemology*, edited by Adrian Haddock and Alan Millar, 29–50. Oxford: Oxford University Press.
———. 2011. "Self, Subjectivity, and the Instituted Social Imaginary." In *The Oxford Handbook of the Self*, edited by Shaun Gallagher, 713–736. Oxford: Oxford University Press.
———. 2014. "Culpable Ignorance?" *Hypatia* 29: 670–676.
———. 2015. "Knowledge and Subjectivity." Guelph Philosophy at 50, Guelph: University of Guelph.
———. 2020a. *Manufactured Uncertainty New Challenges to Epistemic Responsibility*. Albany: State University of New York Press.

———. 2020b. *Epistemic Responsibility.* 2nd ed. Albany: State University of New York Press.
Code, Lorraine, Maureen Ford, Kathleen Martindale, Susan Sherwin, and Debra Shogan. 1991. *Is Feminist Ethics Possible?* Ottawa: Crlaw/lCreF.
Coole, Diana, and Samantha Frost. 2010. "Introducing the New Materialisms." In *New Materialisms: Ontology, Agency, and Politics,* edited by D. Coole and S. Frost, 1–43. Durham, NC: Duke University Press.
Deleuze, Gilles. 1988. *Spinoza: Practical Philosophy.* San Francisco: City Lights Books.
Doucet, Andrea. 2018a. "Decolonizing Family photographs: Ecological Imaginaries and Nonrepresentational Ethnographies." *Journal of Contemporary Ethnography* 47: 729–757.
Doucet, Andrea. 2018b. "Revisiting and Remaking the Listening Guide: An Ecological and Ontological Narrativity Approach to Analyzing Fathering Narratives." In *How Qualitative Data Analysis Happens, Moving Beyond "Themes Emerged,"* edited by Aine Humble and Elise Radina, 80–96. London: Taylor and Francis.
Doucet, Andrea, and Natasha Mauthner. 2002/2012. "Knowing Responsibly: Ethics, Feminist Epistemologies and Methodologies." In *Ethics in Qualitative Research,* edited by M. Mauthner, M. Birch, J. Jessop, and T. Miller, 123–145. London: SAGE.
———. 2008. "What Can be Known and How? Narrated Subjects and the Listening Guide." *Qualitative Research* 8: 399–409.
Fontaine, Phil, Aimée Craft, and Truth and Reconciliation Commission of Canada. 2015. *A Knock on the Door: The Essential History of Residential Schools from the Truth and Reconciliation Commission of Canada.* Manitoba: University of Manitoba Press.
Frank, Arthur W. 2010. *Letting Stories Breathe: A Socio-Narratology.* Chicago: University of Chicago Press.
Fricker, Miranda. 2007. *Epistemic Injustice: Power and the Ethics of Knowing.* Oxford: Oxford University Press.
Deleuze, Gilles. 1988. *Spinoza: Practical Philosophy.* San Francisco: City Lights.
Grasswick, Heidi E. 2004. "Individuals-in-Communities: The Search for a Feminist Model of Epistemic Subjects." *Hypatia* 19: 85–120.
———. 2011. "Introduction: Feminist Epistemology and Philosophy of Science in the Twenty-First Century." In *Feminist Epistemology and Philosophy of Science: Power in Knowledge,* edited by Heidi E. Grasswick, 205–222. New York: Springer.
Hacking, Ian. 2002. *Historical Ontology.* Cambridge, MA: Harvard University Press.
Haraway, Donna 1988. "Situated Knowledges: The Science Question in Feminism and the Privilege of Partial Perspective." *Feminist Studies* 14: 575–599.
———. 1991. "Situated Knowledges: The Science Question in Feminism and the Privilege of Partial Perspective." In *Simians, Cyborgs and Women: The Reinvention of Nature,* edited by Donna Haraway, 183–201. London: Free Association.

———. 1997. *Modest-Witness@Second-Millennium.Femaleman-Meets-Oncomouse: Feminism and Technoscience*. New York: Routledge.
———. 2000. *How Like a Leaf: An Interview with Thyrza Nichols Goodeve*. New York: Routledge.
———. 2008. "Otherworldy Conversations, Terrain Topics, Local Terms." In *Material Feminisms*, edited by Stacy Alaimo and Susan Hekman, 157–187. Bloomington and Indianapolis: Indiana University Press.
———. 2016. *Staying with the Trouble: Making Kin in the Chthulucene*. Durham, NC: Duke University Press.
Hekman, Susan. 2010. *The Material of Knowledge: Feminist Disclosures*. Bloomington: Indiana University Press.
High, Steven. 2014. *Oral History at the Crossroads: Sharing Life Stories of Survival and Displacement*. Vancouver and Toronto: University of British Columbia Press.
———. 2015. *Beyond Testimony and Trauma: Oral History in the Aftermath of Mass Violence*. Vancouver and Toronto: University of British Columbia Press.
Hinchman, Lewis P., and Sandra K. Hinchman. 1997. *Memory, Identity, Community: The Idea of Narrative in the Human Sciences*. Albany: State University of New York Press.
Hyvärinen, Matti. 2010. "Revisiting the Narrative Turns." *Life Writing* 7: 69–82.
Kenney, Martha. 2015. "Counting, Accounting, and Accountability: Helen Verran's Relational Empiricism." *Social Studies of Science* 45: 749–71.
Kovach, Margaret Elizabeth. 2010. *Indigenous Methodologies: Characteristics, Conversations, and Contexts*. Toronto: University of Toronto Press.
Kruks, Sonia. 2001. *Retrieving Experience: Subjectivity and Recognition in Feminist Politics*. Ithaca, NY: Cornell University Press.
Lam, Carla. 2015. *New Reproductive Technologies and Disembodiment: Feminist and Material Resolutions*. Farnham, UK: Ashgate.
Lather, Patti. 2013. "Methodology-21: What Do We Do in the Afterward?" *International Journal of Qualitative Studies in Education* 26: 634–645.
Lather, Patti, and Elizabeth A. St. Pierre. 2013. "Post-Qualitative Research." *International Journal of Qualitative Studies in Education* 26: 629–633.
Latour, Bruno. 2004. "Why Has Critique Run Out of Steam? From Matters of Fact to Matters of Concern." *Critical Inquiry* 30: 225–248.
Law, John. 2004. *After Method: Mess in Social Science Research*. London: Routledge.
———. 2015. "What's Wrong with a One-World World?" *Distinktion: Journal of Social Theory* 16: 126–139.
Le Doeuff, Michèle. 1989. *The Philosophical Imaginary*. Translated by Colin Gordon. Stanford, CA: Stanford University Press.
Lear, Linda. 1977. *Rachel Carson: Witness for Nature*. London: Penguin.
Longino, Helen E. 1990. *Science as Social Knowledge: Values and Objectivity in Scientific Inquiry*. Princeton, NJ: Princeton University Press.

Lykke, Nina. 2010. "The Timeliness of Post-Constructionism." *NORA—Nordic Journal of Feminist and Gender Research* 18: 131–136.

Mauthner, Natasha S. 2015. "'The Past Was Never Simply There to Begin with and the Future Is Not Simply What Will Unfold': A Posthumanist Performative Approach to Qualitative Longitudinal Research." *International Journal of Social Research Methodology* 18: 321–336.

———. 2018. "A Posthumanist Ethics of Mattering: New Materialisms and the Ethical Practice of Inquiry." In *The Sage Handbook of Qualitative Research Ethics*, edited by R. Iphofen and M. Tolich. 51–72, London: SAGE.

Mauthner, Natasha S., and Andrea Doucet. 2003. "Reflexive Accounts and Accounts of Reflexivity in Qualitative Data Analysis." *Sociology* 37: 413–431. https://doi.org/10.1177/00380385030373002.

McHugh, Nancy Arden. 2015. *Limits of Knowledge: Generating Pragmatist Feminist Cases for Situated Knowing*. Albany: State University of New York Press.

Meretoja, Hanna. 2014. *The Narrative Turn in Fiction and Theory: The Crisis and Return of Storytelling from Robbe-Grillet to Tournier*. Basingstoke, UK: Palgrave Macmillan.

Meretoja, Hanna. 2018. *The Ethics of Story Telling: Narrative Hermeneutics, History, and the Possible*. New York: Oxford University Press.

Mol, Annemarie. 1999. "Ontological Politics. A Word and Some Questions." In *Actor Network Theory and After*, edited by John Law and J. Hassard, 74–89. Oxford: Wiley-Blackwell.

———. 2002. *The Body Multiple: Ontology in Medical Practice*. Durham, NC: Duke University Press.

National Inquiry into Missing and Murdered Indigenous Women and Girls. 2019a. "Reclaiming Power and Place: The Final Report of the National Inquiry Into Missing and Murdered Indigenous Women and Girls." Volume 1a.

———. 2019b. "A Legal Analysis of Genocide." *Supplementary Report of the National Inquiry into Missing and Murdered Indigenous Women and Girls*.

Neimanis, Astrida. 2015. "No Representation without Colonisation? (Or, Nature Represents Itself)." *Somatechnics* 5: 135–53.

Nagel, Thomas. 1986. *The View from Nowhere*. New York: Oxford University Press.

Oreskes, Naomi, and Erik M. Conway. 2010. *Merchants of Doubt: How a Handful of Scientists Obscured the Truth on Issues from Tobacco Smoke to Global Warming*. New York: Bloomsbury.

Oksala, Joanna. 2011. "Sexual Experience: Foucault, Phenomenology, and Feminist Theory." *Hypatia* 26: 207–23.

Plummer, Ken. 1983. *Documents of Life: An Introduction to the Problems and Literature of a Humanistic Method*. London: Urwin.

———. 2000. *Documents of Life 2: An Invitation to a Critical Humanism*. London: SAGE.

Plumwood, Val. 1993. *Feminism and the Mystery of Nature*. London: Routledge.

Quine, W. V. O. 1969. "Epistemology Naturalized." In *Ontological Relativity and Other Essays*, edited by W. V. O. Quine. New York: Columbia University Press.

Regan, Paulette. 2010. *Unsettling the Settler Within Indian Residential Schools, Truth Telling, and Reconciliation in Canada.* Vancouver: UBC Press.

Ricoeur, Paul. 1983. *Time and Narrative.* Trans. Kathleen McLaughlin and David Pellauer. Vol. 1. Chicago: University of Chicago Press

———. 1991a. *From Text to Action: Essays in Hermeneutics II.* Translated by Kathleen Blamey and John Thompson. Evanston, IL: Northwestern University Press.

———. 1991b. "Life: A Story of Search of a Narrator." In *A Ricoeur Reader: Reflection and Imagination*, edited by Mario Valdés. New York: Harvester Wheatsheaf.

———. 1991c. "The Creativity of Language." In *Reflection and Imagination*, edited by Mario Valdés. New York: Harvester Wheatsheaf.

———. 1992. *Oneself as Another (1990).* Translated by Kathleen Blamey. Chicago: University of Chicago Press.

———, 1993. "Self as Ipse." In *Freedom and Interpretation: The Oxford Amnesty Lectures,* edited by Barbara Johnson, 103–119. New York: Basic Books.

Riessman, Catherine 2008. *Narrative Methods for the Human Sciences.* Los Angeles: SAGE.

Rouse, Joseph. 2015. *Articulating the World: Conceptual Understanding and the Scientific Image.* Chicago: University of Chicago Press.

———. 2016. "The Conceptual and Ethical Normativity of Intra-active Phenomena." *Rhizomes: Cultural Studies in Emerging Knowledge* 30. http://www.rhizomes.net/issue30/rouse.html.

Santos, Boaventura de Sousa. 2014. *Epistemologies of the South: Justice Against Epistemicide.* Boulder, CO: Paradigm.

Savransky, Martin. 2017. "A Decolonial Imagination: Sociology, Anthropology and the Politics of Reality." *Sociology* 51: 11–26.

Schaffer, Kay, and Smith, Sidonie. 2004. *Human Rights and Narrated Lives: The Ethics of Recognition.* New York: Palgrave Macmillan.

Scheman, Naomi. 2014. "Empowering Canaries: Sustainability, Vulnerability, and the Ethics of Epistemology." *International Journal of Feminist Approaches to Bioethics* 7: 169–191.

Scott, Joan W. 1992. "Experience." In *Feminists Theorize the Political*, edited by J. Butler and J. W. Scott, 22–40. London: Routledge.

Shiva, Vandana. 1989. *Staying Alive: Women, Ecology and Development.* London: Zed.

Shrader-Frechette, Kristin. 2002. *Environmental Justice: Creative Equality, Reclaiming Democracy.* Oxford: Oxford University Press.

Simpson, Leanne B. 2011. *Dancing on Our Turtle's Back: Stories of Nishnaabeg Re-Creation, Resurgence, and a New Emergence.* Winnipeg: Arbeiter Ring.

Simpson, Leanne B. 2017. *As We Have Always Done: Indigenous Freedom through Radical Resistance.* Minnesota: University of Minnesota Press.

Somers, Margaret R. 1992. "Narrativity, Narrative Identity, and Social Action: Rethinking English Working-Class Formation." *Social Science History* 16: 591–630.

———. 1994. "The Narrative Constitution of Identity: A Relational and Network Approach." *Theory and Society* 23: 605–649.

———. 1996. "Where Is Sociology after the Historic Turn? Knowledge Cultures, Narrativity and Historical Epistemologies." In *The Historic Turn in the Human Sciences*, edited by Terrence J. McDonald, 53–89. Ann Arbor: University of Michigan Press.

———. 1998. "'We're No Angels': Rational Choice, and Relationality in Social Science." *Journal of Sociology* 104: 722–784.

———. 2008. *Genealogies of Citizenship: Markets, Statelessness and the Right to Have Rights*. Cambridge, UK: Cambridge University Press.

Souder, William. 2012. *On a Father Shore: The Life and Legacy of Rachel Carson*. New York: Random House.

Sullivan, Shannon, and Nancy Tuana, ed. 2007. *Race and Epistemologies of Ignorance*. Albany: State University of New York Press.

Taylor, Charles. 1989. *Sources of the Self*. Cambridge, MA: Harvard University Press.

Truth and Reconciliation Commission of Canada. 2015a. *Honouring the Truth, Reconciling for the Future: Summary of the Final Report of the Truth and Reconciliation Commission of Canada*. Winnipeg: Truth and Reconciliation Commission of Canada.

Tuana Nancy. 2008. "Viscous Porosity: Witnessing Katrina." In *Material Feminisms*, edited by Stacy Alaimo and Susan Hekman, 188–213. Bloomington: Indiana University Press.

———. 2014. "Being Affected by Climate Change: The Anthropocene and the Body of Ethics." In *Ethics and the Anthropocene*, edited by Kenneth Shockley and Andrew Light. Cambridge, MA: MIT Press.

Tuhiwai Smith, Linda, ed. 2012. *Decolonizing Methodologies: Research and Indigenous Peoples*. 2nd ed. London: Zed.

Verran, H. 2001. *Science and an African logic*. Chicago: University of Chicago Press.

———. 2002. "A Postcolonial Moment in Science Studies: Alternative Firing Regimes of Environmental Scientists and Aboriginal Landowners." *Social Studies of Science* 32: 729–762.

Verran, Helen. 2013. "Engagements between Disparate Knowledge Traditions: Toward Doing Difference Generatively and in Good Faith." In *Contested Ecologies: Dialogues in the South on Nature and Knowledge*, edited by Lesley Green. Cape Town, South Africa: HSRC.

Watts, Vanessa. 2013. "Indigenous Place-Thought & Agency amongst Humans and Non-Humans (First Woman and Sky Woman go on a European World Tour!)." *Decolonization: Indigeneity, Education & Society* 2: 20–34.

Winthereik, B. R., and H. Verran. 2012. "Ethnographic Stories as Generalizations that Intervene." *Science Studies* 25: 37–51.

Chapter 6

Allowing for the Unexpected

The Thought of Lorraine Code and Mikhail Bakhtin in Conversation

CATHERINE MALONEY

Epistemological modes that allow for new and unexpected ways of thinking and understanding are essential for underpinning action that is both socially and politically responsible. Without such modes, dominant ways of being and doing in the world ride roughshod over others. The work of Lorraine Code and Mikhail Bakhtin both provide epistemologies that are sensitive to nuance and as such are responsible to the knowers with whom they engage; in fact, their work shares many characteristics. Both consider meaning making to be situated and relational; both identify the stabilizing and destabilizing forces at work in dominant expressions of meaning making (instituted and instituting imaginaries for Code and centripetal and centrifugal forces for Bakhtin); and both are concerned with how new or "unexpected" meaning can enter into current discourses. However, while Code and Bakhtin share a dialogic impulse, there are also some significant differences in approach. Whereas Code grounds her work in real-world examples and cases, Bakhtin looks to certain kinds of artistic forms as singularly able to permit "content to be found for the first time" (1999, 43). Whereas Code keeps the perils of and structural inhospitableness to dialogic thinking explicit and at the front of mind, Bakhtin, whose extant writing is often only fragmentary, gives these challenges only passing mention if any at all. This chapter explores points of convergence and divergence in Code and Bakhtin's thought, particularly in relation to the ways in which Code's development of advocacy practices and Bahktin's use of *creative understanding* allow for new or unexpected knowledges.

In their work, Code and Bakhtin are both engaged in "claiming discursive space" (Code 2006, 176) that allows new or previously hidden ways of thinking to emerge. Their dialogical epistemic frameworks open up possibilities for meaning making and understanding, while simultaneously exposing pitfalls to knowing well. I will argue that Code and Bakhtin's approaches are mutually enriching and that both point to the central role of self-understanding for understanding across differences. Further, I will argue that considering their work in parallel allows nuances of thought to be foregrounded, which leads to a deeper understanding of each author's work and of the possibilities for knowing responsibly that are inherent to dialogical thinking. The chapter will take the following trajectory: I will begin by looking briefly at similarities in the early work of both Code and Bakhtin, namely an early influence from Kant, a partial rejection of Kant along similar lines, and finally an appeal to responsibility. I will then proceed to outline some of the basic concepts of their later dialogical/ecological work. I will conclude with a discussion of what their work offers to projects of understanding across difference and where their works might be complementary or at odds.

Early Work: Code and Bakhtin on Kant

In their early work, Lorraine Code and Mikhail Bakhtin both clearly engaged with the work of Immanuel Kant. In her first book-length work, *Epistemic Responsibility*, Code writes that the theoretical basis of part of her argument in that work is "broadly Kantian in outline and orientation" (99). She states: "I take the Kantian conception of a creative synthesis of the imagination to be one of the most important innovations in the history of philosophy" (9) and further that the "Kantian characterization of knowledge as the product of a *creative synthesis of the imagination* places the epistemological subject at the centre of the cognitive process. This characterization is wholly revolutionary in the history of epistemology" (99). It is possible to see this Kantian orientation strongly in evidence in *Epistemic Responsibility*. In that work Code's central claim is that "knowers, or would-be knowers, come to bear as much of the onus of credibility as 'the known'" (1987, 8–9). This claim follows from the shift she effects in this work away from the predominant epistemological tradition's focus on "products [or] end-states of cognition" (1987, 8) and toward the *act* of knowing or "cognitive activity." The actors, that is the knower(s) and the known, can be held accountable for their contribution toward the activity of knowing. However, even in her earliest work, Code does not accept Kant's thinking without reservation; she writes: "For all its revolutionary character, however, the concept of the creative synthesis falls short of providing an adequate context to explain how individual human knowers, as organic creatures, create the products we call knowledge" (99). For Code, the contexts of knowledge creation include epistemic communities. In *Epistemic Responsibility*, the structure of community is a combined forms of life/contract/practices model (1987, 188) in which one knowing subject has more or less the same access to the resources of the community as another, although they may bring disparate perspectives to the table. By the time she wrote *Ecological Thinking*, the structure of epistemic community as the context in which cognitive activity takes place, has become fully ecological; that is, it is a relational space governed by social imaginaries in which "epistemic responsibilities have to be negotiated, much more arduously" (2006, viii) than she had previously assumed.

Code makes some specific statements about the places she departs from Kant's thinking. First, she writes that "Unlike Kant, I do not think there is an a priori element in knowledge; but I do not reject the a priori in favour of something resembling a tabula rasa view of human cognitive capacity" (1987, 103). Code maintains throughout her corpus, a sense of the interplay between knower and known. Knowledge is situated, but still constrained by reality. As Christine Koggel writes in her 2008 essay on *Ecological Thinking*, Code is able to "reveal the spaces between realism and relativism" (178) and in this way allows access to previously discounted knowledges without losing the ability to make judgments about the quality of what is known.

Code's second point of departure from Kant, is her rejection of his assumption that there is a universal or standard knower:

> Kant was, admittedly, less concerned about the individuality of particular knowers than about formulating general principles of knowledge and understanding, valid for all subjects in all cognitive circumstances. There is, in Kantian epistemology, the assumption that there is a "standard knower": one might even suggest that he takes the cognitive processes of an intelligent, forty-year-old Konigsberg bachelor as constitutive of the norm

> for human knowledge in general. A recognition of individual differences among knowers would not destroy his theory, however, and would indeed enhance it. . . . Kant's doctrine of the transcendental unity of apperception must be re-cast. For Kant, the possibility of an identical "I think" accompanying all representations is a necessary precondition of experience, without which the empirically given manifold of sense perception is incapable of being thought and, so, of becoming knowledge. (1987, 110–111)

While the nuances of the epistemically responsible knower at the heart of cognitive activity evolved over the course of Code's writing, even in *Epistemic Responsibility* Code states that "Knowledge is always acquired from a certain perspective" (112). By the time she published *What Can She Know?* (1991) the harm resulting from assumptions of standard knowers or value-neutral knowing had moved to the foreground.

Code's third point of departure from Kant, which is also entwined with the first two, is the transcendental nature of his argument. She writes:

> Finally, the very term "transcendental" connotes the complete separation of knowers from the known so that reciprocity characteristic of cognitive processes cannot adequately be taken into account. . . . This involvement results in a continuous, reciprocal structuring of both knower and known. In a genuine sense, I am not the same person I was before I learned not to fear the dark; and the dark is something different for me now that I no longer fear it. (1987, 112)

This last point of departure from Kant emanates from the core of Code's central argument that knowers are responsible for what and how they know. The active nature of knowledge creation requires the participation of both the knower and the known; this situated interaction can never occur "transcendentally" or prior to the interplay that constitutes knowledge creation.

Despite her serious reservations about elements of Kantian thought, however, Code does see strengths in Kant's epistemological approach. She retains some of his insights into the nature of human knowers while broadening other aspects (1987, 123); she follows Piaget in maintaining an "attunement" with Kant while rejecting some of the specifics of his arguments (1987, 104).

Bakhtin also engaged deeply with Kantian philosophy, and this was perhaps inevitable. The academic environment from which he emerged was steeped in German philosophy and neo-Kantianism in particular. During his secondary level education at gymnasiums in Vilnius and Odessa he read systematic and existentialist German philosophers (Holquist 2002, 2). Additionally, although he studied Greek and Latin classics at university, German philosophy and specifically neo-Kantianism was especially "well entrenched at Petersburg University" where he studied (Clark and Holquist 1984, 57). In fact one of his professors emphasized philosophy as integral to understanding "the complete spectrum of classical civilization" (Holquist 2002, 2). Upon finishing university in 1918 and in the wake of the October Revolution, Bakhtin went to the countryside (as did many other young people at that time) and began an engagement with a circle of scholars who studied and debated work in philosophy, particularly the neo-Kantianism of Hermann Cohen and the Marburg school (Holquist 2002, 2–4). Indeed, Sergeiy Sandler writes that what "we now call 'The Bakhtin Circle' started off as a 'Kant seminar'" (2015, 166). It was during this time of deep engagement with Kant, that Bakhtin was writing his earliest works (1919–1924)—the larger project that is now collected in English as *Art and Answerability* and the smaller work which exists as the fragment, *Towards a Philosophy of the Act*.

Bakhtin's relationship to Kantian thought runs in a parallel path to that of Code's. His early work shows both his reverence for the magnitude of the overall shift affected by Kant's "Copernican Turn," as well as the many ways in which Bakhtin assessed Kant as having fallen short of the mark. Akin to Code's praise for the "creative synthesis of the imagination," Bakhtin picked up on what he "would come to interpret" as "the dialogue . . . between mind and world" (Holquist 2002, 4). This influence is apparent in much of Bakhtin's early work, for example in "Art and Answerability" where he writes: "The three domains of human culture—science, art, and life—gain unity only in the individual person who integrates them into his own unity." (1990, 1). In *Towards a Philosophy of the Act*, however, one begins to see Bakhtin's ambivalence toward Kantianism and neo-Kantianism. Here he writes that "one can and should acknowledge that in the domain of the special tasks it sets itself modern philosophy (and neo-Kantianism in particular) has obviously attained great heights." (Bakhtin 1993, 19). In the very same passage, however, he continues "But this scientific philosophy can only be a specialized philosophy, i.e., a philosophy of the various domains of culture and their unity in the form of a theoretical transcription from within the objects of cultural creation and the immanent law of their development.

And that is why this theoretical philosophy cannot pretend to being a first philosophy" (Bakhtin 1993, 19). The tarring of neo-Kantianism as *theoretical* philosophy points to the core of Bakhtin's divergence from the Marburg neo-Kantians and Kantianism in general. Sergeiy Sandler suggests that the whole of (the extant fragment) of *Towards a Philosophy of the Act* "is concerned with refuting the fundamental tenets of neo-Kantianism" (2015, 168).

Bakhtin reacts to three elements of Kantianism that parallel Code's critique; these are the preeminence of the a priori, the presumption that knowing can be universal, and the transcendental nature of knowledge. Bakhtin's disparagement of neo-Kantianism as "theoretical" philosophy signals his deemphasizing of the a priori. He writes that "all attempts to force one's way from inside the theoretical world and into actual Being-as-event are quite hopeless" (1993, 12). Such attempts merely recreate "one theory . . . into a moment of another theory" (1993, 12). Knowing must always be achieved; it occurs as the "act or deed that I perform" (1993, 2) as the site where world and mind converge. As is the case with Code, however, he does not posit that relativism is the outcome of his rejection of what he calls *theoreticism* (1993, 9). He acknowledges a similar in-between space to the one Christine Koggel notes that Code maintains. Using an example from physics he explains that while Newton's laws were valid before Newton discovered them, they did not "exist as *cognized* truths" (1993, 10). It is the performed act of cognizing that is key.

Bakhtin also rejects the idea of a universal knower at the center of "the act" of knowing. The act or deed that constitutes knowing happens in a highly localized way. Holquist writes that Bakhtin seeks a return to the local, from Kant's "highly abstract" system; Bakhtin wants a return to "the naked immediacy of experience" (Holquist in Bakhtin 1993, x). He describes a world in which a unique "I" exists that is both concrete and pluripotent:

> The world is given to me, from my unique place in Being, as a world that is concrete and unique. . . . In correlation with my unique place of active issuing-from-within-myself in that world, all thinkable spatial and temporal relations gain a value-centre around which they arrange themselves into a certain stable, concrete architectonic whole, and this possible unity becomes actual uniqueness. My active unique place is not just an abstract geometrical centre, but constitutes an answerable, emotional-volitional, concrete centre of the concrete manifoldness of the world. (1993, 57)

Bakhtin is asserting that an individual's particular location is perspectival, shaped by the lenses of her particular space and her particular time. Each person is obligated to shape the world through her active engagement with its possibilities and her own situatedness. Bakhtin clarifies what he means by the "architectonic disposition of the world" (1993, 65) through a consideration of a Pushkin poem in which two lovers are separating. There are two people in the poem and thus "two value-contexts" and "two concrete reference points" (Bakhtin 1993, 66). The place from which the female person leaves is a foreign land to her and the place to which she is going is a homeland. For the male lyrical hero of the poem, it is the opposite. For him she is leaving, and for her she is returning (Bakhtin 1993, 67). Bakhtin gives the poem an extended and rich treatment, but for this purpose it will suffice to say that despite the one concrete, objective, circumstance of the parting, the experience of the two lovers is subjectively distinct; thus, the meaning they make of it, although perhaps overlapping in parts, is unique.

Implicated in his critique of universal knowing, is Bakhtin's desire to "detranscendentalize Kant" (Holquist in Bakhtin 1993, ix), a point that marked a separation between Bakhtin and Cohen and the Marburg neo-Kantians (Holquist 2002, 6). Far from separating knowers from the known, Bakhtin posited the concept of the "non-alibi," or the lack of an excuse for not acting. He writes that "*my non-alibi in Being*" is a "fact" which "underlies . . . the answerably performed act" (1993, 40). The knower has a responsibility to act, and that action is performed by a unitary or unique knower in a unique circumstance (Bakhtin 1993, 56). An answerable act is "precisely that act which is performed on the basis of an acknowledgement of my obligative (ought-to-be) uniqueness. . . . It is only my non-alibi in Being that transforms an empty possibility into an actual answerable act or deed (through an emotional-volitional referral to myself as the one who is active) (Bakhtin 1993, 42). A knower can of course escape this obligation but only at the cost of pretending to be someone else (Bakhtin 1993, 42). Had, for example, the female lover in the Pushkin poem tried to repress her feelings of joy at her return to her homeland, she could have more closely approximated her lover's experience of their separation—but only at the cost of abdicating her own experience.

It seems clear that Code and Bakhtin's early writing reveals a remarkably similar relationship to Kant's thought. What this means for their later works is less clear. Writing about Bakhtin, Michael Holquist claims that "the philosophical underpinnings of the work he would do for the rest of his life were established during these crucial [early] years" (2002, 7). Emerson and

Morson, however, see Bakhtin's early work as "very much the product of influences Bakhtin soon outgrew" and suggest that reading him as Holquist does can occur "only at the expense of blunting [the early manuscripts'] most interesting and radical points" (1990, 7). Certainly there are substantive differences between the early and late work of both Code and Bakhtin; however, there are themes that do seem to remain. Both Code and Bakhtin retain an emphasis on the situatedness of knowing. Code also retains the related idea that a knower is responsible for what she knows, although what this entails does become more complex in *Ecological Thinking*. She even references the importance of Kant's Copernican revolution in the opening paragraph of *Ecological Thinking* before continuing on to remind the reader of Kantianism's "parochial" nature (2006, 3). For Bakhtin, the active nature of knowing remains, but the concomitant language of responsibility (i.e., nonalibi, answerability) that was present in the early work drops away in his later work. I contend that while their philosophical thinking certainly evolves over time, the basic themes that Code and Bakhtin explore in their early work set them up to develop—in different ways—the dialogical nature of their later work.

Later Work, Part I: The Dialogical in Code's Concept of "Ecological Thinking" and Bakhtin's Use of Genre and His Theory of the Novel

Turning now to the later work, I will anchor the discussion around Code's concept of *ecological thinking* and Bakhtin's concept of genre, as well as other concepts from his theory of the novel, to expose the dialogical nature of their later work. In a broad sense, a dialogic approach to understanding is characterized by dialogue or conversation in which meaning is created by the interaction and responsiveness of the various viewpoints expressed. It is a relational process that is sensitive to context. While Code does not explicitly label her work as dialogical, her ecological approach is a dialogical one. Ecological thinking, as Code develops it, draws analogically on the relational web of interdependence that marks an ecosystem and relocates it to the epistemic realm:

> Ecology (metaphorically) draws the conclusions of situated inquiries together, maps their interrelations, consonances, and contrasts, their impoverishing or mutually sustaining consequences, from

a commitment to generating a creatively interrogative, instituting social imaginary to denaturalise the instituted imaginary of mastery that represents itself as "the [only] natural way" of being and knowing. (2006, 51)

There are several noteworthy and connected components of ecological thinking as articulated here: the embedded and situated nature of knowledge, the mapping of a variety of complementary and contrasting situated knowledges, and the creativity and reflexivity required for decentering an instituted social imaginary. Ecological thinking metaphorically embeds a knower in a system of meaning making that is at once general and specific. That is, knowers can see themselves as generally ecological beings and also as part of a specific ecosystem. The former gets at the relational aspect of meaning making and the latter at the situated nature of knowing. Meaning is made through the particular ecosystem, or epistemic community, in which an individual thinks and exists. Ecology then provides a model to begin conversations about social imaginaries, both instituted and instituting (i.e., both stabilizing and destabilizing or in Bakhtinian language centripetal and centrifugal).

In his later work Bakhtin does explicitly embrace and use the term *dialogical*. The relational and situated nature of meaning making is expressed through his use of *genre*, which comes up in Bakhtin's work in two ways: one, as speech genres, which describe the situated spheres in which meaning is created and two, as a particular and privileged genre, the dialogical novel, which functions as a model and means of allowing unexpected or new meanings to emerge and more fully illustrates the relational nature of meaning creation. In his late essay, "The Problem of Speech Genres," Bakhtin defines a speech genre as a "sphere in which language is used" and which has developed "its own relatively stable types of . . . utterances"; utterances in turn have three aspects: content, style, and structure (1986, 60). As such, speech genres encompass situated communities of meaning making. Within a given genre, individuals understand implicitly how things mean; that is, how a given symbol would usually be interpreted or what common phraseology is appropriate for a particular situation. Bakhtin stresses that the three aspects of an utterance are integral to its overall meaning and that style, in particular, cannot be separated from the utterance without fundamentally changing its meaning. In an earlier work, Bakhtin wrote that "artistic form, correctly understood, does not shape already prepared and found content, but rather permits content to be found and seen for the first time" (1984, 43). Indeed, Bakhtin contends that the genres most conducive to expressing individuality "are those of artistic literature," whereas the genres least conducive to such unique expression are those that "require a standard form" (1986, 63).

The privileged genre that Bakhtin described in his theory of the novel was articulated over several pieces of writing. In *Problems of Dostoevsky's Poetics*, Bakhtin introduces the concept of *polyphony*. He contends that Dostoevsky is the author of "a new type of artistic thinking," possibly even "a new artistic model of the world" (Bakhtin 1984, 3). He uses the analogy of the musical concept polyphony to illustrate the uniqueness of Dostoevsky's poetics. In polyphonic music, the different voices maintain their independent and distinct lines while coming together to form something new in the harmonies they create. Bakhtin writes that the "fundamental event" (Bakhtin 1984, 7) of a Dostoevskian novel is not captured at the level of plot but is the result of the interaction of the voices of the characters. This is the dialogical novel par excellence: a relational space in which the voices and worldviews of different characters come together in tension to create and support something new, which is the whole of the novel. In a slightly later piece, "Discourse in the Novel," Bakhtin has dropped the language of polyphony but maintains the basic idea that the novel is fundamentally about an interacting diversity of voices:

> The novel can be defined as a diversity of social speech types (sometimes even diversity of languages) and a diversity of individual voices, artistically organized. . . . The novel orchestrates all its themes, the totality of the world of objects and ideas depicted and expressed in it, by means of the social diversity of speech types and by the differing individual voices that flourish under such conditions. Authorial speech, the speeches of narrators, inserted genres, the speech of characters are merely those fundamental compositional unities with whose help heteroglossia can enter the novel; each of them permits a multiplicity of social voices and a wide variety of their links and interrelationships (always more or less dialogized). These distinctive links and interrelationships between utterances and languages, this movement of the theme through different languages and speech types, its dispersion into the rivulets and droplets of social heteroglossia, its dialogization—this is the basic distinguishing feature of the stylistics of the novel. (1981, 262–263)

There is much packed into this one passage. I will focus on heteroglossia, dialogization, and some comparisons to ecological thinking.

Later Work, Part II: Heteroglossia, Dialogization, and Ecological Thinking

Heteroglossia as Bakhtin uses it in "Discourse in the Novel" is not equivalent to his earlier term *polyphony*. It maintains the sense of plurality that polyphony carries but is more complex in that it also contains a sense of the disruption caused by constantly introducing newness and difference into established speech genres. Heteroglossia is opposed to "unitary language," which Bakhtin writes is not "given but is always in essence posited" (1981, 270). By posited he means that it takes an effort to standardize language; it is a task that dictionary writers and grammarists take up (Morson and Emerson 1990, 140) against the "realities of heteroglossia" (Bakhtin 1981, 270), which is always embedded in a specific time and place and introduces difference. Certainly, when Bakhtin writes about *language* he is not speaking simply of a particular codification of speech: he is speaking of "language conceived as ideologically saturated, language as a world view" (1981, 271). Taken together with his concept of speech genres, we start to get something similar to Code's social imaginary as an "effective system of images, meanings, metaphors, and interlocking explanations-expectations within which people, in specific time periods and geographical-cultural climates enact their knowledges and subjectivities and craft their self-understandings" (2006, 29), although without the explicit discussion of power as it plays out in these spheres of meaning.

Within a sphere of language, Bakhtin identifies centering and decentering forces at work. The forces that keep unitary language whole are what Bakhtin calls "centripetal" forces, whereas heteroglossia, the natural entropic state of language, he calls a "centrifugal" force. These conflicting forces "intersect in the utterance" (Bakhtin 1981, 272). A parallel can be drawn here to Code's use of instituted imaginaries as maintaining "normative social meanings" (2006, 30) and instituting imaginaries as the "critical-creative activity of a society that . . . put[s] itself in question" (2006, 31). Bakhtin maintains that the novel, "plasticity itself . . . a genre that is always questing, ever examining itself and subjecting its established forms to review" (1981, 39) formed under the influence of centrifugal forces, while poetry developed under the influence of centralizing, centripetal forces "of verbal-ideological life" (1981, 272–273).

Dialogism is, in essence, the act of putting into conversation various voices or subjectivities in which the whole is not the simple sum of its parts. It arises for Bakhtin, at least in part, out of an impulse to push back against the monologic method of the "exact sciences" in which he says "the intellect contemplates a *thing* and expounds upon it" (1986, 161). Bakhtin is interested in understanding human subjectivities and as such must proceed dialogically, giving voice to the involved subjects: "A subject as such cannot be perceived and studied as a thing, for as a subject it cannot, while remaining a subject, become voiceless, and, consequently, cognition of it can only be dialogic" (1986, 161). As the model of dialogism, Bakhtin is able to say that "when the novel becomes the dominant genre, epistemology becomes the dominant discipline."

Since the Dosteovskian novel is the paragon of a dialogical novel for Bakhtin, a quick look at *The Brothers Karamazov* will help to illustrate the point. Looking just at the three brothers of the title, the reader finds three individuals with radically different points of view; Ivan is a man of reason, Dimitri a romantic and irrationalist, and Alyosha a man of faith. Each of these three characters are fully valid and free within the novel. They are not caricatures; they are what E. M. Forster called "round characters" (1990, 73).[1] The world is presented to the reader in a focalized way through each brother. In this respect, there is no objective world, and the action of the novel is free to roam between these various spheres. Bakhtin is quick to point out that Dostoevsky's novel is not dialectical in its whole. If it were, there would be a merging of voices, and the novel would ultimately be monological. Instead of the work progressing linearly toward a single consensus, the heroes' worlds interact by means of the "event" (i.e., the emplotment of the narrative). The interaction and interdependence of the various voices is what is important in Dostoevsky's work. It is "dialogized heteroglossia" in which individual meanings enter a conversation as utterances "filled with specific content and accented as an individual utterance" (Bakhtin 1981, 272). I suggest that Bakhtin sees in the event of the dialogical novel—which the Dostoevskian novel is a prime example—a heuristic narrative method[2] for engaging with otherness. The positions of the three main characters in the novel hold incommensurable positions, and the event of the novel takes place within that tension. The reader is not led to a meaning but is left to engage in the conversation of the characters and to make sense of the whole. A dialogical novel then can both introduce new ideas to the reader and help a reader develop the dialogical muscle necessary for engaging with difference in the real world.

Once again it is possible to see a parallel between Code and Bakhtin. At the beginning of *Ecological Thinking* Code writes that her "overriding thesis is that the dominant model of knowledge and epistemology in Anglo-American philosophy produces an *epistemological monoculture* . . . whose consequences are to suppress and choke out ways of knowing that depart from the stringent dictates of an exaggerated ideal of scientific knowledge making" (8–9). Ecological thinking is a means of counteracting the unifying effect of epistemology's mainstream. Code does not use the terms dialogical and monological, and very rarely uses even the more common term *dialogue*, but the relationality of knowers in her ecological model of knowing works in the same way as Bakhtin's dialogism to counteract homogenization of thought and further to allow access to new or otherwise suppressed ideas.

At the end of her 1991 book, *What Can She Know?*, where Code first announces her preliminary thoughts on an ecological epistemology, she writes that "an ecological model can shift epistemological inquiry away from autonomy obsession toward an analysis explicitly cognizant of the fact that every cognitive act takes place at a point of intersection of innumerable relations, events, circumstances, and histories that make the knower and the known what they are, at that time" (269). Both Bakhtin and Code retain this thread from their early work: that knowing happens in a context, by a particular thinking individual within a complex of values and experiences that constitute her perspective and in relation to all the other complex thinking individuals she comes into contact with. The context in which knowing happens is both specific in time and place and part of an intersubjective web of meaning: what Code calls a "habitat, as a place to know" (2006, 36) and what Bakhtin would call a chronotope that expresses itself as an emplotted event.

The Role of Community in Accessing Unexpected Knowledges

The relational or intersubjective nature of ecological/dialogical thinking means that community is necessarily a part of the epistemic equation for both Code and Bakhtin, and it is precisely this connection with community that allows the decentring/centrifugal forces of an instituting imaginary to come together and give access to new or unexpected ways of knowing.

Code and Bakhtin exhibit a similar impulse in regard to the necessity of community for knowing responsibly or well, but their work also displays a significant difference. Both Code and Bakhtin recognize the need for reflexivity in social understanding, both acknowledge the necessity of and also the difficulty inherent in empathy as a tool for understanding another person, and both recognize that epistemological projects are always unfinished projects that can never be whole. The main point of divergence in their theories, however, is in the acknowledgment (or lack thereof) of the role of the sociopolitical aspect of spheres of meaning; that is the role that power plays in understanding. Looking at Code's invocation of advocacy practices as a means of "developing an *instituting* social imaginary" (2006, 170) and Bakhtin's use of creative understanding as a model for understanding across difference, it will be possible to see more sharply the consonances and contrasts between these two thinkers.

In *Ecological Thinking*, Code looks to advocacy as "integral to the very possibility of developing an *instituting* social imaginary" (169–170), which can unsettle entrenched modes of thinking and allow access to the unexpected. Because societal imbalances of power dictate *whose* voice is credible and whose is not within an instituted imaginary, advocacy of a certain type can work to counteract that imbalance. Community is both necessary for knowing well and an obstacle to it. Code's invocation of advocacy practices is a direct result of the sociopolitical element of knowing of which she is so conscious. Code writes that

> advocacy practices work to get at truths operating imperceptibly, implicitly, below the surface of the assumed self-transparency of evidence. They can be strategically effective in claiming discursive space for 'subjugated knowledges,' putting such knowledge into circulation where it can claim acknowledgement, working to ensure informed, emancipatory moral-political effects. (2006, 176)

An advocate can use her greater credibility to lend weight to a particular perspective, to push against "intransigent imaginaries" (Code 2006, 178).[3] Aware of the pitfalls of advocacy, particularly paternalistic advocacy and naïve monologic attempts at advocacy, she suggests that an epistemically responsible advocacy would yield "an autonomy remodelled" (2006, 195) in which formerly silenced voices might become audible for the first time. Advocacy of this sort must be informed by careful listening and "imaginative empathy" (2006, 231) and motivated by a desire ultimately to allow formerly silenced voices to be heard on their own terms. Advocacy that leads to remodeled autonomy increases the autonomy of an individual by allowing her "to claim the autonomy of acknowledged knowledgeability" (2006, 180). Advocacy of this type is a necessary part of responsible knowing and is the means by which new knowledge (new, at least, to the greater community) enters into the social imaginary.

Working from a similar impulse for hospitality to newness Bakhtin articulates a concept he calls *creative understanding*. Creative understanding is a mode of understanding that requires the knower to remain both rooted in her epistemic position and to gain *outsideness*, or an outside view of herself. This seemingly paradoxical approach to understanding, as Bakhtin develops it, allows for both a deeper understanding of self and the possibility of understanding across difference. It occurs through a dialogic engagement with an other in which the interlocutors do not attempt to adopt each other's viewpoint but rather acknowledge their own locations and are willing to have their meanings transformed. In contrast to the explicitly political and power-infused overtones of Code's *advocacy*, Bakhtin's *creative understanding*, while acknowledging hurdles to understanding well, does not explicitly address the issue of power. Creative understanding as a concept is explicated briefly in Bakhtin's late essay "A Response to a Question from *Novy Mir*." This is a short piece but an interesting one: because in the few pages where he addresses creative understanding he is employing dialogical methods outside of the context of the novel. He writes that

> a meaning only reveals its depths once it has encountered and come into contact with another, foreign meaning: they engage in a kind of dialogue, which surmounts the closedness and onesidedness of these particular meanings, these cultures. We raise new questions for a foreign culture, ones that it did not raise itself; we seek answers to our own questions in it; and the foreign culture responds to us by revealing to us its new aspects and new semantic depths. Without one's own questions one cannot creatively understand anything other or foreign. . . . Such a dialogic encounter of two cultures does not result in merging or mixing. Each retains its own unity and open totality, but they are mutually enriched. (1986, 7)

Creative understanding itself is the work an individual does when engaging in dialogue with an other or others. It leads by turns both to greater self-understanding and to greater understanding of and for the other(s). It emphasizes the need for an epistemic community, for without the dialogical back and forth of interlocutors, understanding would be severely limited as meaning would remain hidden. This conception of epistemic community shares a great deal with Code's ecological thinking, although it does seem like a "benign" (2006, vii) concept of community—to use the term Code herself uses for her later view on her own development of community in *Epistemic Responsibility*—in that there is no sense that understanding may be impacted by differences of power or privilege between interlocutors. It seems fitting, however, especially when discussing a piece of writing that deals with meaning as connected to its time and place, or epoch (as this essay by Bakhtin does) to consider that this particular difference in Code and Bakhtin's writing might have something to do with the very different moments of their writing. In this same essay Bakhtin himself writes that "Semantic phenomena can exist in concealed form, potentially, and be revealed only in semantic cultural contexts of subsequent epochs that are favourable for such disclosure" (5). Bakhtin's work is full of allusions to the machinations of power in moments of meaning making, yet it is never explicitly articulated. Perhaps reading him in the early twenty-first century, and together with Code's work, uncovers these new layers of meaning.

Concluding Thoughts

The ecological work of Lorraine Code and the dialogical work of Mikhail Bakhtin teem with parallels. Both thinkers exhibit similar philosophical impulses—from their relationship to Kantian thought to their later relational/conversational theories of understanding—as well as a preoccupation with how new or unexpected ideas enter into the common discourse but do so in very different contexts: a feminist exploration of power relations in epistemic practices on the one hand and a dialogism rooted in a theory of the novel on the other. Despite these different contexts, they exhibit many of the same concerns: a wariness of empathy as a tool for understanding others, an explicit commitment to the unfinalizability of their epistemic projects, and a sense that tensions and discomforts are part of the epistemic process.

One significant way in which their work differs is in the way they engage the concept of community. In both cases *community* is the ground of possibility for new ideas and understandings; it is the mechanism by which reflexivity becomes possible. However, Code's epistemically responsible advocacy, which both requires community and is a precursor to epistemic community, works to expand social understanding, while Bakhtin's creative understanding is focused on the individual and her interlocutor coming to greater understanding of themselves and each other but never deals with transmitting that understanding out into the larger world. The end goals are differently focused. The two conceptions of community are complementary in that the reflexivity provoked in the knower through creatively understanding in a Bakhtinian sense amplifies the type of epistemic posture that Code describes as necessary for advocacy, but without Code's development of advocacy practices, the new understandings uncovered through creative understanding would not find their way to the sociopolitical realm and into society at large. It may be argued, however, that the heuristic potential that Bakhtin identifies in the dialogical novel could act as a type of training for the work that is required of the advocate in Code's responsible advocacy practices. While Code's ecological thinking is necessary to enact the latent sociopolitical potential of dialogical thinking and therefore to become a fully responsible mode of understanding, reading the work of Code and Bakhtin in parallel, dialogically/ ecologically, helps to pull out the nuances of meaning in each of their work and bolster the overall effort of understanding well.

Notes

1. Forster makes a distinction between flat and round characters. Flat characters "are constructed round a single idea or quality" (1990, 73), and the character gains curvature with each new factor or element. The flat character is "not changed by circumstances" (1990, 74), whereas the round character is amenable to change. In short, round characters are more human.

2. In my master's thesis I suggested that Bakhtin's concept of the "polyphonic novel" identified a "heuristic narrative ethics" in the Dostoevskian form of the novel.

3. As an example of this type of advocacy working to destabilize an instituted imaginary, Code cites an example of the *Harvard Women's Health Watch*. When it published an article corroborating the experiences of women with Syndrome X, the credibility of the testimony of people with this illness increased (2006, 193).

Works Cited

Bakhtin, Mikhail. 1990. *Art and Answerability*. Edited by Michael Holquist and Vadim Liapunov. Translated by Vadim Liapunov. Austin: University of Texas Press.

———. 1981. *The Dialogic Imagination*. Edited by Michael Holquist. Translated by Caryl Emerson and Michael Holquist. Austin: University of Texas Press.

———. 1984. *Problems of Dostoevsky's Poetics*. Edited and Translated by Caryl Emerson. Minneapolis: University of Minnesota Press.

———. 1986. *Speech Genres and Other Late Essays*. Edited by Caryl Emerson and Michael Holquist.Translated by Vern W. McGee. Austin: University of Texas Press.

———. 1993. *Toward a Philosophy of the Act*. Edited by Vadim Liapunov and Michael Holquist.Translated by Vadim Liapunov. Austin: University of Texas Press.

Clark, Katerina, and Michael Holquist. 1984. *Mikhail Bakhtin*. Cambridge Massachusetts: The Belknap Press of Harvard University Press.

Code, Lorraine. 2006. *Ecological Thinking: The Politics of Epistemic Location*. New York: Oxford University Press.

———. 1987. *Epistemic Responsibility*. Hanover, NH: University Press of New England.

———. 1991. *What Can She Know: Feminist Theory and the Construction of Knowledge*. Ithaca, NY: Cornell University Press.

Forster, E. M. 1990. *Aspects of the Novel*. London: Penguin.

Holquist, Michael. 2002. *Dialogism: Bakhtin and His World*. 2nd ed. New York: Routledge.

Koggel, Christine. 2008. "Ecological Thinking and Epistemic Location: The Local and the Global." *Hypatia* 23, 1: 177–186.

Maloney, Catherine. "The Crooked Wood: Dostoevsky's Response to Utilitarianism and Moral Relativism." Master's thesis, University College Dublin, 2001.

Morson, Gary Saul, and Caryl Emerson. 1990. *Mikhail Bakhtin: Creation of a Prosaics*. Stanford, CA: Stanford University Press.

Sandler, Sergeiy. 2015. "A Strange Kind of Kantian: Bakhtin's Reinterpretation of Kant and the Marburg School." *Studies in East European Thought* 67, 3–4: 165–182.

PART 3

Reimagining "The Force of Paradigms"

Health, Medical, and Scientific Injustice

Chapter 7

Institutional Review Boards (IRBs) and Ecological Thinking

Carolyn J. Craig

This chapter explores the possibilities and limitations of American Institutional Review Boards (IRBs) for advancing Lorraine Code's vision for ecological thinking. American IRBs are mandated by the 1974 National Research Act, which established the first nationwide set of protections for individuals who participate in (and whose information is used for) biomedical or behavioral research. The federal law and the regulations that emerged from it provide a standard framework for human subjects protections, yet one that permits significant variation among IRBs and their operations. Additionally, the law and regulations have contributed to the development of networks between IRB members, administrative staff, regulators and policymakers, researchers, and individual and community participants in research. Today, IRBs are situated within a dynamic landscape of international, national, and local laws, regulations, policies, and norms that shape how human subject research and science are conducted. IRBs and the contexts in which they operate are therefore crucial sites for the critical investigation and transformation of knowledge production practices. In many ways, the IRB framework has created conditions for the epistemic orientations and engagement of ecological thinking Code has proposed. At the same time, Code's critiques of contemporary science and prevailing epistemological paradigms speak directly to the limitations of the regulatory framework that governs research with human subjects in the United States today.

In *Ecological Thinking: The Politics of Epistemic Location*, Code critiques dominant sociopolitical imaginaries for their "putatively universal, a priori theories of knowledge and action" and offers "a revisioned mode of engagement with knowledge, subjectivity, politics, ethics, science, citizenship, and agency that pervades and reconfigures theory and practice" (Code 2006, 4–5). The text is an extension of Code's previous work, and it also furthers feminist scholarship on epistemology and research ethics (Doucet 2018). Code is concerned not only with expanding our ideas about what can be known and how we can know it but also the implications of knowledge-seeking and knowledge-making precepts and practices for individuals as constituents of ecological systems. And Code's work demonstrates how advancing justice through any course of research must recognize and address the relationship between ideas and practices attendant to knowledge production and their roles in constituting power and privilege. This chapter examines the extent to which key elements of Code's revisioned mode of engagement can be found in or pursued through contemporary human subject research paradigms, institutions, and IRB practices.

Examining the review board landscape with the insights of Code's ecological thinking, this chapter seeks to understand how IRBs and the broader institutions that support them foster or foreclose an ethics of research dedicated to interrogating truth and power; equipped for transforming ideas, institutions, and practices; and capable of advancing well-being for those regularly exploited, excluded, marginalized, erased and otherwise harmed by dominant social, political, and economic systems. More specifically, and directly related to key themes in Code's large body of work—and *Ecological Thinking* in particular—this chapter focuses on the IRB framework's prospects for promoting reflexive and relational research, disrupting notions of mastery that support and reproduce inequities and injustice, and reorienting ideas about what counts as research and researcher. In this way it explores the IRB framework's capacity to facilitate "inquiry 'down on the ground' where knowledge is made, negotiated, circulated; and where the nature and conditions of the particular 'ground,' the situations and circumstances of specific knowers, their interdependence and their negotiations, have claims to critical epistemic scrutiny equivalent to those of allegedly isolated, discrete propositional knowledge claims" (Code 2006, 6). This chapter's explicit examination of the IRB framework—as well as ideas and practices that have emerged from and interact with it—through the lens of ecological thinking is thus animated by the premise that ecological thinking represents a research ethics that expands access to and accountability for knowledge production and praxis in ways necessary for a more just research enterprise.

The chapter maintains that the IRBs in the United States—individually, and as part of formal and informal networks—have and can continue to encourage ecologically oriented research. At the same time, the chapter highlights limitations of the IRB framework and offers three critiques of it related to the themes in Code's work previously identified. First, although the IRB framework reflects a widespread understanding that social context matters and research design should, as much as possible, minimize harms to individuals and communities, by no means does it demand reflexivity or an accounting of researcher subjectivity. Second, embedded within the regulations is a privileging of expert knowledge and expertise that allows researchers and IRBs to ignore, diminish, or foreclose the inclusion of outsider and local knowledge, judgment, capacities, and concerns related to the design and implementation of a research agenda. Finally, the IRB regulations impose a distinction between research, on the one hand, and everything else (e.g., education, evaluation, journalism, etc.) on the other; this distinction denies and undermines their mutuality, valorizes particular research norms, and reinforces myths about research as a realm of activity distant from so many others in our daily lives. In these ways the regulatory framework undermines the potential of IRBs to advance the forms of advocacy practices Code argues are attendant to ecological thinking—practices that address hierarchies of power and privilege, include the contributions of nonexperts, accept interdependence as a fundamental human and ecological condition, and emerge from and regenerate trust between advocates and those they claim to represent. This is not to say that the IRB framework does not allow IRBs or anyone engaged in research endeavors to adopt or enact this orientation, but rather, formidable impediments to it emerge from the regulations themselves.

I have written this chapter from the perspective of an IRB insider, someone with over eight years of experience with and versed in various aspects of the IRB review and approval process at a large public research university. Employed as a compliance administrator whose job involves supporting my institution's IRB, and as an alternate voting member of that IRB, I have a vested interest in an institutional framework that both contributes to my financial well-being and a sense that my work contributes to the well-being of others. At the same time, I feel the need to be critical of the regulations and features of the landscape in which I work: not only because critique is welcome there but also because I have a range of personal privileges that offer me options for alternative sources of income and work I find meaningful. Additionally, I feel both a personal and professional obligation to offer critique with thoughtfulness, a commitment to action, and regard for the influence that accompanies the positions I hold. As an IRB insider, being an ecological subject requires that I "own and take responsibility for [my] epistemic-moral-political activity" (Code 2006, 5) through deepening my understanding of the IRB landscape within the context of a spectrum of critical and laudatory assertions made about it and working with others to improve it. Indeed, I am not a researcher who conducts human subject research, so I cannot write from a researcher's perspective. And I am even further removed from the perspective of someone participating in research as a research subject.

Despite being removed from research "on the ground," my positions have exposed me to a wide range of approaches to the design and implementation of research, researchers' ideas about their relationships to participants and the context of their research, attitudes toward institutions that regulate research, and participant concerns about the conduct of research. I have heard firsthand many critiques of IRBs, including that they are bureaucratic, paternalistic, overreaching, rigid, and ineffective regulatory bodies that function primarily as obstacles to research in general and creative research in particular.[1] My positions afford me the opportunity to understand precisely why IRBs are perceived in such ways and how their performance could generate such perceptions. At the same time, I have learned of their capacities to facilitate ethical research and transform ideas about research and research practices. My experience has also taught me that they maximize such capacities when called upon to do so by board members, members of the research community, research participants, and the public at large. It is these lessons about transformation that inform my perspective in this chapter on the possibilities for ecological thinking within and among IRBs.

The chapter begins with a brief history of the IRB regulatory framework in the United States. The chapter then examines the features of the framework that create the conditions for situated and reflexive knowledge production, as well as the inherent limitations of that framework. These features include the ethical principles advanced in concert with the federal regulations, as well as regulatory imperatives related to requirements of IRB approval and oversight, board membership, and the definition of *human subject research*. The chapter then summarizes key features of recent revisions to and delayed implementation of the federal human subjects protection regulations. Ultimately, the chapter points to the need for continued transformation of the IRB regulations, institutional expectations, and norms in order for individual IRBs and the larger networks they constitute to fulfill their potential to advance ecological thinking and praxis as fundamental to research ethics committed to justice and well-being.

Brief History of American IRBs

The story of the emergence of the IRB regulatory framework in the United States commonly told among IRB practitioners usually begins with a discussion of the Nuremberg Code (1948) and the Declaration of Helsinki (1964); the US National Institutes of Health (NIH) policy (1966) requiring all Public Health Service research to be reviewed by an ethics committee; and passage of the National Research Act (1974) in the United States (Amdur and Bankert 2011). These codes and the many policies and laws that have followed them—in Western countries, and increasingly worldwide[2]—have contributed to a vast network of legal and normative institutions mandating that certain activities involving living individuals (or their private identifiable information) and carried out for research purposes undergo review by a committee, or a member thereof, and require that body's stamp of approval before research activities commence and before changes to the research are implemented. IRBs (or "ethics boards") therefore have significant power and authority over what and how research can be conducted.

The Nuremberg Code and the Declaration of Helsinki reflected an international shift in public understanding of and attitudes about individual rights and the proper limits of authority at a time when Western governments were emboldened to create institutions that advanced liberal commitments to these rights. The Nuremberg Code, an artifact of the post–World War II Nuremberg trials of Nazi war criminals, articulated a universal human rights paradigm that includes an individual's right to choose whether or not they want to participate in research, which in turn requires an informed consent process and provisions for permitting the subject to withdraw from research participation at any time. Moreover, the code established a requirement that there be a favorable benefit-to-risk ratio. The World Medical Association's Declaration of Helsinki further articulated a set of principles spelling out patients' rights and the ethical obligations of medical practitioners in the conduct of medicine and medical research; since 1964 the declaration has been amended seven times, clarifying and expanding the scope of ethical standards and responsibilities to which medical practitioners are accountable. Today, the WMA is only one of many organizations that provide international guidelines and otherwise support and promote continued discussion of the ethics of research within and across national boundaries.[3]

In the United States, the proliferation of IRBs can be traced directly to the passage of the 1974 National Research Act, which stipulates that institutions receiving federal funding and conducting human subject research establish an IRB for review of such research. This legislation emerged from increasing awareness—within the scientific community,[4] among the general public, and in Congress—that even when motivated by benevolent intentions, research and researchers require some kind of external review. The need for research oversight was made abundantly clear through the US Public Health Service's Tuskegee syphilis study (1932–1972), a federally funded study that exploited poor Black men in order to study the untreated progression of syphilis, even after treatment was available. The call for research review requirements was not directed at biomedical research alone. Social behavioral studies like Stanley Milgram's study of authority and obedience (1963), and Philip Zimbardo's Stanford prison experiment (1971) raised concerns for woefully inadequate consent processes and for disregarding participants' clear discomfort and desire to cease study participation (Amdur and Bankert 2011). In addition to requiring IRB oversight of any federally sponsored research, the National Research Act established the National Commission for the Protection of Human Subjects of Biomedical and Behavioral Research to articulate the principles that should guide IRBs' review and approval of the research. This commission produced the Belmont Report (1978), which emphasizes respect for persons, beneficence, and justice. The report's prescriptions have been translated into actionable items and regulatory criteria but mostly function to orient researchers and IRBs to one set of considerations for evaluating what constitutes ethical research.

This commonly told origin story of IRBs in the United States is thus a story of a collective awakening, followed by action taken, to ensure the protection of people or their data from harm at the hands of malevolent or ignorant researchers. Certainly, this is not the only story one has told or could tell about how an enormous bureaucracy—and attendant industry—for the protection of human research subjects emerged (see, e.g., Heimer and Petty 2010; Schneider 2015). Nevertheless, the IRB framework does reflect a skepticism of researchers as impartial, infallible, and all knowing—godlike. Moreover, the regulatory framework and many of the professional norms and practices that have emerged alongside it are attuned to the power dynamics inherent in research and the consequences of research activities for individuals and communities situated differently within them. In these ways, the very existence of the IRB framework aligns with Code's critiques of understandings of science that attribute both a capacity for and value to human detachment among scientists and their subjects of study. Furthermore, the contemporary IRB framework creates possibilities for ecological thinking and practice by demanding that members of the research community continually revisit the principles of beneficence and justice, inviting engagement with the norms and values embedded within particular research projects as well the research enterprise in general, and other social, political, and economic structures within which it operates. The sections that follow examine the federal regulations closely to illuminate the tensions among the ideas and ideals embodied in the regulations; the ways in which contemporary practices that accompany IRB review conform to or depart from its formative ideas and ideals; and the extent to which prevalent norms and practices associated with implementing the regulations invite or inhibit ecological thinking.

Board Membership and Criteria for Approval: Opportunities and Limitations

The title of the regulations that provide the foundation for the IRB system—*Federal Policy for the Protection of Human Subjects* (hereafter, 45 CFR 46)[5]—belies a radical departure from many of the conventions of Western science. However, the regulations are built upon the recognition that research is social, context based, and value laden and were drafted to allow for significant diversity in research design and implementation—orientations to knowledge production that are essential to ecological thinking and praxis. Many critiques of IRBs can be traced to a regulatory framework that on the one hand demands research review and, on the other, permits boards significant latitude in the review because that latitude enables boards to engage in what some believe are excessive and stifling policing of the creative research process (Van den Hoonaard and Hamilton 2016; Schneider 2015). However, ecological thinking is possible precisely because the regulatory framework acknowledges the situated nature of research and diversity among peoples, shifts some authority over research to community members, and allows for adaptability in the application of the regulatory criteria. That IRBs may be poised to advance ecological thinking is by no means a guarantee that they will, however. The primary critique advanced later in this section is that the regulations retain vestiges of notions of objectivity and homogeneity across human experience that limit IRBs' capacities for ecological practices of "placing respect above mastery, preservation before control, understanding for what is and has been before predictions of what might be" (Code 2006, 32). This section illuminates the role of the regulations in advancing or undermining ecological thinking through a close examination of the regulatory requirements of board membership and criteria for IRB approval of research.

Opportunities

The regulatory criteria for IRB membership set the stage for diverse perspectives and dialogue in the review of research. It demands that every IRB be diverse in terms of "race, gender, and cultural backgrounds," include at least five members, have at least one scientist and one nonscientist, have at least one member not affiliated with the institution (including through immediate family), and have members who are knowledgeable about and experienced in working with members of subject populations considered vulnerable (45 CFR 46.107). This composition is intended to promote dialogue among individuals who can offer a variety of perspectives, as well as ensure the board can adequately represent and advocate on behalf of participants. Finally, the regulations encourage IRBs to consult outside experts when reviewing a project that is beyond the board's represented areas of expertise. In these ways IRBs can engage in advocacy practices as conceived by Code, and they are poised to challenge universalizing tendencies of positivist epistemologies by decentering the authority of the "objective" scientist and detachment in the research enterprise. The attention to diversity and representation on IRBs creates an opening for the type of advocacy needed to "(re)enfranchise epistemically disadvantaged, marginalized, disenfranchised Others" (Code 2006, 165).

In practice, many IRBs have more than five members, and depending upon the types of research commonly conducted by agents of the institution, boards may have significant representation from or for vulnerable populations, in addition to the diversity required for adequate representation of "community attitudes" (45 CFR 46.107). The requirement that boards offer at least a modicum of diversity has created opportunities for and expectations that institutions ensure multiple perspectives are enlisted during the review and approval of human subjects research, particularly research with risks beyond what most community (or participant population) members experience in daily life. The diversity within and across boards reflects a shared understanding of the IRB's role in helping facilitate an advocacy essential to ecological thinking: one that recognizes the structures of oppression, the historical marginalization, and the dislocation of individuals promised autonomy and enfranchisement by liberal societies unable or unwilling to fully deliver on such promises.

The regulatory criteria for IRB approval invite a range of interpretations of the regulations; again, this flexibility is essential to setting the stage for the situated epistemological praxis Code argues for. The regulations do not provide formulas nor any type of scientific method for the review and approval of research. Even when criteria for regulatory approval can be converted into a checklist, assessing whether criteria have been satisfied is largely subjective. The principles articulated in the Belmont Report, local institutional knowledge and culture, norms and "best practices" shared (and reified) across the profession, and individual staff and IRB members' experiences guide evaluations of proposed research.

The criteria for approval (45 CFR 46.111) include seven conditions that must be considered for all proposed research; items 4 and 5 can also be waived by the IRB under specific circumstances. The criteria are described briefly as follows:

1. Risks to subjects are minimized.

2. Risks to subjects are reasonable in relation to anticipated benefits, if any, to subjects, and the importance of the knowledge that may reasonably be expected to result.

3. Selection of subjects is equitable.

4. Informed consent will be sought from each prospective subject or the subject's legally authorized representative.

5. Informed consent will be appropriately documented.

6. When appropriate, the research plan makes adequate provision for monitoring the data collected to ensure the safety of subjects.

7. When appropriate, there are adequate provisions to protect the privacy of subjects and to maintain the confidentiality of data.

The revised regulations added an eighth condition making secondary use of private identifiable data subject to specific consent requirements; this new "broad consent" provision is largely redundant in the context of the other provisions but does clarify the regulatory commitment to consent considerations for long-term and unforeseen uses of personal data, even when the researcher does not have identifiable participant information recorded with the data or access to identifiers.

This section on criteria for approval further specifies that "when some or all of the subjects are likely to be vulnerable to coercion or undue influence, such as children, prisoners, individuals with impaired decision-making capacity, or economically or educationally disadvantaged persons, additional safeguards have been included in the study to protect the rights and welfare of these subjects" (45 CFR 46.111). Here again the regulations represent an implicit rejection of the elements of universalism Code has critiqued and creates space for a social imaginary that situates epistemic practices. The regulations recognize that not all participants in research are the same and that their diversity may be measured by degrees of power. The regulations advance an understanding of "human interventions throughout the world, both physical and social, as requiring sensitivity to, and responsibility in relation to, specificities of diversity and detail" (Code 2006, 32). Certainly, the regulatory categories of vulnerable populations can be critiqued for a different form of essentializing along one axis of experience. And the regulations do not preclude paternalism, particularly given assumptions of mastery encoded in the regulations (and discussed further later in this chapter). However, the flexibility afforded researchers and IRBs creates possibilities for a dynamism in research that is fundamental to ecologically oriented epistemic practice.

Any one of the regulatory criteria for approval can become the subject of extensive discussion, debate, and discord. And even in the few places where the regulations elaborate briefly on how the criteria should be evaluated, the regulations permit a range of interpretations. For example, the direction embedded in the first criteria, that risks be minimized, specifies that risks can be minimized "by using procedures which are consistent with sound research design and which do not unnecessarily expose subjects to risk" (45 CFR 46.111). What is "sound research design" to one investigator (or IRB member) may not be considered as such by another. For IRBs charged with reviewing a great deal of social, educational, and behavioral research, and research designed and implemented by students (undergraduate and graduate), the concept of sound research design is generally much broader, allowing for a range of methods and projects with much less scientific justification than biomedical research.

As previously mentioned, detractors of IRBs find much to criticize about a system that gives boards significant latitude in review and approval processes. At the same time, Code discusses methodological pluralism as essential for advancing ecological thinking, allowing for recognition of situations as not merely backdrops for experience but *constitutive of* them (Code 2006, 19). Similarly, the definition of "minimal risk" provided in the regulations is open to vast interpretation: "*minimal risk* means that the probability and magnitude of harm or discomfort anticipated in the research are not greater in and of themselves than those ordinarily encountered in daily life or during the performance of routine physical or psychological examinations or tests" (45 CFR 46.102 [j]). Ultimately, the assessment of risk, particularly for social, behavioral, and educational research, generally occurs without reliance upon empirical studies and is largely shaped by the expertise of IRB members, their professional staff, and researchers; personal experiences of IRB staff and IRB members and sometimes participants in research studies; and input from advocacy organizations. The requirements for diversity and representation,—particularly of historically marginalized groups,—infuse the mandate to evaluate appropriateness of design and risk with both the exercise of and expected attention to conceptions of subjectivity that are fundamental to ecological thinking and praxis.

The informed consent process is another area where the regulations invite a wide range of interpretations and applications. Even though the regulations specify general requirements and contain nine "basic elements" of informed consent (45 CFR 46.116), those elements, like the criteria for approval, can be satisfied by many different consent processes. Additionally, under certain conditions the regulations permit the alteration or waiver of specific elements, or the waiver of the entire consent process. The conditions are framed in terms as follows: "The waiver or alteration will not adversely affect the rights and welfare of the subjects"; "The research could not practicably be carried out without the waiver or alteration"; and "Whenever appropriate, the subjects will be provided with additional pertinent information after participation" (45 CFR 46.116). These phrases have allowed a wide range of consent processes to be used, particularly for research that is considered no greater than minimal risk. Additionally, the regulations allow for a waiver of the requirement that researchers obtain documentation of consent (45 CFR 46.117), an option frequently approved by IRBs when seeking a signed form would be maladaptive to the local customs, even offensive, and when seeking the signature could increase the potential for harm to the participant, as might be the case for undocumented immigrants or participants in studies on stigmatized medical conditions, domestic violence or workplace harassment, or illegal/illicit behaviors.

The regulatory requirements related to board membership, risk assessment, and the consent process are just a few examples of many areas within the regulations that reflect regulatory criteria established precisely to accommodate a range of research designs, methods, and cultural contexts. The flexibility of the regulations reflects a shared understanding that research is a social activity, firmly rooted in systems of power, and can have consequences unrelated to the researcher's research agenda. Flexibility also permits IRBs to adopt practices that respond to instances or patterns of unethical research and shifts in norms. For example, US nontribal researchers' egregious exploitation of Indigenous peoples and their communities for research purposes has led many nontribal IRBs in the United States to require their researchers working within American Native communities to demonstrate consultation with and approval from tribal authorities prior to conducting the research. While the regulations acknowledge tribal sovereignty (45 CFR 46.101), many individual nontribal IRBs take additional steps for research on or with tribes—including developing policies or research agreements with tribes in their region—to ensure researchers engage with tribal representatives before proceeding with research, including for human subject research that is exempt from the federal regulations. Moreover, the regulations are clear that the single IRB requirement for collaborative research shall not preclude tribes from retaining oversight of research with or in their communities (45 CFR 46.114). While this regulatory flexibility does not guarantee engagement with ecological thinking, it demonstrates an understanding that research circumstances and locations are not interchangeable, evincing a break from the universalism of positivism and inviting ecological thinking.

In sum, the IRB's charge is based on beliefs that members of the research community have an obligation to seek to understand the social context of research and the power relationships within it, to imagine the consequences of the research with these in mind, and to protect those most vulnerable and likely to be impacted by the research. It is important to note that the federal regulations specify that certain types of research are exempt[6] from IRB review and approval, and they specify which types of research may be reviewed via an expedited review process that involves review by a person or persons designated by the IRB chairperson to conduct such reviews. Nevertheless, the IRB is the body charged with the responsibility of ensuring that human subject research is reviewed in accordance with the federal regulations and attendant ethical principles.

Code's analyses of advocacy practices, particularly in the context of oppressive structures, reveal many problematics associated with "speaking for" others, and IRBs can certainly misappropriate their role as representatives of others. While IRBs can function to reproduce the status quo, many institutions and the professions that have emerged to support IRBs have embraced their regulatory charge as an opportunity to question, challenge, and transform ideas about research and how it is practiced. Consequently, many aspects of research—from the questions asked, to the methods used to investigate them, to the subject population invited to participate in the research—are interrogated on a regular basis at board meetings, conferences, and in online fora where board members, researchers, and IRB staff present and respond to procedural and ethical issues.

LIMITATIONS

Despite their contributions to the disruption of dominant themes across our epistemic imaginary,[7] the regulations themselves can work in service to them. Even the more transformative elements of the framework are imbued with assumptions about the researcher, the research, and the researched and ideas about the relationships between them that privileges the knowledge of the investigator, the IRB, and the staff supporting the board. Endowing a board of mostly "experts" far removed from the actual research with the authority to approve the research based on their assessment of its protection of "subjects" inhibits (in terms of vision and practice) other arrangements through which responsible research could be pursued. Moreover, the regulations presume an approach to research that follows the Western scientific method and its commitment to the ideal of an objective researcher, even if that researcher is to be "checked" by the IRB. As a result, the opening to dialogue and constant scrutiny of research discussed here is often exclusionary.

The exclusionary tendencies stem from several features of the IRB framework at both the organizational (e.g., university) and the US federal level. First, as just discussed, the board requirements favor credentialed experts, and the regulatory framework does not establish any requirements that research participants be part of the dialogue about the need for the research, or the means and methods by which knowledge will be produced and reproduced. While the regulations do require that informed consent be obtained from individual subjects, rarely are research subjects afforded an opportunity to participate in the design and implementation of the research, the analysis of the findings, or the production and dissemination of reports (or other products) of the research. Thus, while on a study-by-study basis the regulations invite a consideration of the participants' experiences and evaluation of risks associated with the research given the social context, the failure of the regulations to confer equal status to, or easily accommodate the contributions of nonprofessional or student researchers, inhibits or impedes the reflexive and responsible engagement with the world necessary for ecological thinking and practice. In this way, the regulations fail to match their contributions toward "materially situated subjectivity" (discussed in the preceding section) with the "deliberative interdependence" fundamental to ecological thinking (Code 2006, 200).

Second, IRBs generally accept applications for research led only by someone formally affiliated with the institution, and the person identified as the principal investigator on a study must meet institutional criteria for permission to serve as such. The regulations are built on a model of research with clear lines between the subjects of the research and the primary investigator: the physician, faculty member, or institutional employee who proposes the research as an agent of their institution. The regulations and guidance also call for the investigator to demonstrate that they have sufficient education, training, or other expertise to lead and carry out the research. Moreover, all researchers must be identified as such on IRB application submissions and provide documentation of their training in human research subject protections in order to be approved to conduct human subject research. In these ways the regulations continue to support a model of research that privileges the knowledge of the expert scientist over direct experience.

Regulations and guidance assume that investigators commence engagement with a clear research question and/or set of hypotheses and a detailed plan for investigating the questions/testing the hypothesis. All activities that human subjects will be involved in must be described in detail, from the point of recruitment to the disposition of the research records. Moreover, under the current regulations and as a matter of common practice across most institutions, once researchers have an IRB-approved protocol, they must seek and obtain IRB approval for any changes to the protocol: from the addition of research assistants, funding, and minor changes to recruitment flyers, to an increase in participant numbers, research locations, and the addition of research instruments.[8] Any change to any described aspect of the research or any materials provided to participants (e.g., recruitment scripts, consent materials, research instruments) must be submitted to the

IRB via the amendment process and receive IRB approval before it can be implemented. This not only creates time-consuming work for investigators, IRB staff, and the IRB, it inhibits (if not outright prevents) dynamic research projects where researchers can readily adapt their research to new insights or imperatives and where community members can act as researchers.

Community-based participatory research (CBPR) and participatory action research (PAR) represent precisely the kind of dynamic research one might expect from ecological thinking and that proves challenging for IRBs and the application of the regulations. Such research "resists practices, common in science-venerating cultures, of superimposing a grid upon events, experiences, and situations" (Code 2006, 280). In CBPR, PAR, and similar types of research, community members take an active role, including leadership, in all aspects of the research, from identification of the research need or question to the design of the research, data collection, analysis, and presentation and dissemination of research findings (Hacker 2013; Ross et al. 2010; Zavala 2013). This approach is challenging for IRBs (and researchers wanting to embrace it) not only because community members assume the roles and responsibilities once thought appropriate only for trained expert researchers, but the approach diverges from the model of science and research that undergirds the federal regulations.[9] In CBPR and PAR, which presume that the subjects are experts and where success is measured in terms of its meaning to them and the improvement of their well-being, research roles and practices cannot be so neatly determined and controlled as the federal regulations presume it should be. Particularly when the subject population may be considered vulnerable, given their socioeconomic status—people without secure housing, migrants, incarcerated persons, etc.—concerns among researchers about the imposition of unreasonable requirements of a community and action-oriented research design can quash innovative and collaborative approaches at the point of conception.

The IRB system is fundamentally not well suited for knowledge production practices that do not retain clear demarcations between researcher and the researched—those individuals who will provide the investigator with information as the subject of their research. This may be due not only to philosophical commitments to objectivity and mastery but also to the logistical challenges of protecting or advocating for those who are vulnerable. Fundamental to ecological thinking is "an *imaginative-interpretive* [sic] attentive-ness to human and locational specificities and commonalities as essential for knowing people well enough to act responsibly and respectfully with them, toward them, and for them" (Code 2006, 211). This knowing requires active engagement: "The required sensitivity enjoins circumspect negotiation between subjects-to-be known and putative knowers, in the interest of achieving reasonable understandings across experiences and situations far less knowable either instantaneously or from surface readings than simple observational givens are imagined to be" (Code 2006, 211). Such engagement demands that community members and their researcher partners, along with IRBs and their staff, continue to search for and find creative ways to advance research that challenges a model of science detached from experience and imbued with notions of mastery. The emergence of CBPR decades before it was first explicitly recognized in a National Institutes of Health (NIH) study in 1995 (Felix 2007) and the growth of community engagement in research demonstrate that the regulatory framework can adapt to research practices that directly challenge its presumptions about how research is or ought to be conducted. Similarly, the rise of "citizen science,"—where members of the public contribute to data collection and even initiate research projects,—exemplifies an alternative to the model of research that envisions the researcher as a highly educated professional or expert (Buchan 2016). And increasing interest among IRBs, IRB professionals, researchers, and research participants in establishing participant review boards (Bozeman and Hirsch 2005) provide further evidence that community members, students, and professional researchers are finding ways to overcome the shortcomings of the federal regulations and the systems and norms that support it. Such efforts are necessary for overcoming the limitations of the regulatory framework and advancing ecological thinking and practice.

What Counts as Research and a Human Subject

Ideas about what counts as *research* and a *human subject* drive engagement of IRBs in any institutional effort to evaluate, alter, and oversee any human subject research: only proposed activities that meet the regulatory definitions of these words are subject to IRB review. The definitions provided by the regulations reflect and reproduce many of the dominant epistemological assumptions critiqued by Code.

The regulatory definition of *research* is the starting point for determining whether any proposed activity is subject to IRB review. Within the federal regulations, *research* is defined as "a systematic investigation, including research development, testing, and evaluation, designed to develop or contribute to generalizable knowledge" (45 CFR 46.102(d)). This definition invokes the

Western scientific method, whereby a researcher identifies a problem or puzzle, delineates the scope of analysis or the relevant constellation of variables for examination, identifies the number of subjects necessary to generate valid findings for the purpose of generalization, and then applies as consistently as possible the same treatment to the subjects in a manner that could be replicated, even if only in an approximated fashion.

Despite their fuzzy boundaries, concepts like "systematic investigation" and "generalizable knowledge" attribute value and ethical scrutiny to some knowledge production activities but not others. The regulations' limits for advancing ecological thinking are starkest here, for they foreclose the agency and deliberative process Code's ecological subjects need to determine for themselves what are legitimate paths to knowledge. One effect of this is the elision of many research practices. For example, the conception of participants as interchangeable data points (within the parameters attributed to the necessary features of the unit of analysis) and the ultimate goal of producing results deemed representative of a larger population are not prerequisites of much research in disciplines such as the arts and humanities, nor are they necessary for the use of many interpretive methods. Institutions must have their purview, purpose, and functions clearly defined in order to be effective. Yet the narrowly conceived definition of research advanced by the regulations illuminates the harms presented by the regulatory system itself: the creation of classes of subjects worthy of protection and knowledge production practices worthy of institutional investment. To fully embody an ecological approach to research, the regulations would embrace a different understanding of *research*—one in which perceptions about what counts as involvement in a research agenda and the researcher's and institution's obligation to act according to a commonly shared set of principles are not determined by whether or not the researcher proclaims their findings can be applied to a larger population or not.

As with the definition of *research*, the definition of *human subject* has emerged from and reinforces an epistemic imaginary of research about people that conforms to the ideas about distinction and detachment that animate the Western scientific method. According to the federal regulations, "human subject" "means a living individual about whom an investigator (whether professional or student) conducting research: (1) obtains information or biospecimens through intervention or interaction with the individual, and uses, studies, or analyzes the information; or (2) obtains, uses, studies, analyzes, or generates identifiable private information or identifiable specimens" (45 CFR 46.102 (e)(1). This definition perpetuates a conceptualization of subjects in

"Anglo-American theories of knowledge [where] the liberal self appears as a standardized but barely acknowledged epistemic subject: a subject . . . who is everyone and no one" (Code 2006, 207). Within the definition we also see a "hybrid, depersonalized objectivism . . . continue to exert a pull" where "the orthodox epistemic subject is a plausible figure . . . within a reductively homogeneous everydayness represented as the experiential, circumstantial norm and masquerading as 'the human condition'" (Code 2006, 210–211).

The definition also conveys a relationship of mastery, whereby the researcher/scientist does something to a person serving as their research subject. The positioning of researcher-as-expert alongside the subject-without-agency reproduces the relationship between knower and those to be known that ecological thinking seeks to transform. While many within and outside the research enterprise have attempted to address this presentation of the researcher/researched by referring to research subjects as "participants" or even "volunteers,"[10] the regulations are not premised upon expectations of parity between the researcher and those who are the subject of the research within the research context. As previously explained, subjects/participants/volunteers typically gain access to research participation solely at the discretion of the expert researcher and are permitted to do so only if determined to be a sufficiently representative case of whatever is being evaluated.

Moreover, the regulatory emphasis on *individual* subjects diverts attention away from the interconnections among people and people and their environment (Beever and Morar 2016). The emphasis on the individual is closely associated with the Belmont Report's principle of respect for persons, which in turn is premised upon the ethical convictions that "individuals should be treated as autonomous agents."[11] Much of Code's work has advanced a critique of conceptions of individuals as independent from the systems around them: liberalism's veneration of an individuated existence, and the idea that each individual embodies an idealized discrete living organism, has produced political institutions, policies, and scientific practices organized around service to these beings with harmful consequences for the individuals and communities writ large. As Code explains, "Social scientific adherents must restrict their observations to separate, discrete behaviors and overt utterances of people extracted from the circumstances that generate those behaviors and made them possible, appropriate, and meaningful" (Code 2006, 160). This conception of an individuated orientation therefore reproduces inequities and injustices predicated on that paradigm and precludes a depth of knowledge that could be gained from a different orientation to research.

The emphasis on the individual within the regulations therefore presents one of the greatest barriers to ecological thinking.

Ecological thinking demands conceptions of *research* and *human subject* that are different from those on offer by the regulatory framework. While the definitions serve the necessary function of establishing boundaries for the application of the regulations, they ignore the relational aspects of research and reproduce existing power structures that reward experts and privileged members of society. IRBs, however, can play a role in advancing and institutionalizing new ways of thinking about and practicing research and education. Institutions and researchers have successfully engaged in and continue to offer creative and collaborative approaches to knowledge production that diverges from the Western scientific model. As with many aspects of the regulatory framework discussed in this chapter, these definitions can be expected to continue to inspire discussion and debate not only among IRBs and their staff but across the institution and research enterprise.

Politics of Regulatory Change

On January 19, 2017, the US Department of Health and Human Services (HHS) and fifteen other federal departments and agencies issued a final rule revising the federal human subject protection regulations.[12] The final rule does not alter the fundamental framework or orientation of the regulations, but it does change several key aspects of the existing regulations and represents the most significant and wide-ranging activity impacting IRBs in over two decades. Even though the federal government introduced its intent to revise the regulations in 2011, the final rule contained new terms, provisions, and expectations most IRBs and their institutions were not prepared to fully understand and implement within one year, particularly since many provisions in the final rule differed from those advanced in the proposed rule. The requirement of compliance within one year sent the IRB world reeling. The revisions contained only several major departures from the existing rule, but some, such as the elimination of the requirement that IRBs review all approved research at least annually, would require institutions to overhaul their compliance systems (e.g., databases, forms, standard operating policies and procedures, websites, etc.) and educate and train researchers, IRB members, faculty, and staff across departments and at all levels of the organization. At the eleventh hour, and in direct response to pressure from institutions, advocacy organizations, and the HHS Secretary's own Advisory Committee on Human Research Protections (SACHRP), the federal government issued an interim rule delaying implementation of the revised regulations for at least six months, if not longer. Indeed, six months after issuing the last-minute delay, HHS issued another six-month delay, putting off implementation of the revised regulations until January 21, 2019 (the revised regulations are referred to as the "2018 Requirements," based on the final rule's initial compliance date).

These events provide some insight into the nature and significance of IRBs today. First, at the most basic level, they represent the institutionalization of research norms and practices founded upon the idea that individuals are the source of valuable information and that access to their information generally should be accompanied by individuals' informed and voluntary consent. As previously discussed, how individuals are invited to share their information and access to their bodies, and the roles and authority afforded them, is often highly problematic; however, a shared commitment to protections of individually identifiable private information is evident in the revised rule. In the context of debates over researcher responsibilities to share their data (Mauthner 2016), the revised rule occupies a middle ground: the preamble to the revised rule acknowledges trends in data sharing, but the regulations do not require it. Instead, amid increasing calls—even mandates—for data sharing by funders, journals, academic associations, and research programs across the United States, the regulations anticipate more data sharing by researchers and address this through enhanced participant consent provisions. The revised regulations stipulate that data sharing and future use of data, even for de-identified data, requires consent; otherwise, researchers must explicitly inform participants that their private information or biospecimens will not be used or distributed for future research, even if identifiers are removed. The regulations thus retain a commitment to participant privacy and informed consent, in spite of predominant presumptions that data sharing is a paramount social good and the attendant pressures among academic and scientific circles for researchers to publicize their participants' information.

Second, the long period of development leading to the revised rule and the government's extension of the mandated implementation date reflect the formidably complex nature of the institutions that have emerged in service to the protection of human research participants. The requests for the delay by institutions (ranging from small liberal arts colleges to large universities, medical schools, and research institutes) related largely to the challenges of rewriting internal policies and procedures and changing electronic systems to accommodate the revisions. Even interpreting what the revised regulations mean, or developing a shared understanding of them at the institutional level, would take more than the time provided. The social and highly contextual development, maintenance, and evolution of institutions established for one aspect of the research enterprise demonstrate significant diversity and divergences in ideas about and capacities for the conduct of research today.

Finally, the dialogue and events preceding, surrounding, and following publication of the revised rule indicate that the regulatory framework behind IRBs is not likely to fundamentally change anytime soon, yet regulating agencies are in fact responsive to the research community and change more generally. Relative to some issues—such as the proposal to forbid any secondary use of information without specific consent for that use—the final rule varied considerably from the proposed rule. Additionally, the final rule includes new provisions that require its adoptive agencies to reexamine definitions of "identifiable private information" and "identifiable biospecimen" at least every four years to ensure they are adequate given any advances in techniques and technologies during that period. Given that the regulations will most likely remain with us well into the future and play an important role in knowledge production, the responsiveness of actors at all levels of the IRB system can serve ecological thinking when viewed as invitations for further inquiry, contestation, and creativity.

Conclusion

An interrogation of the IRB regulatory framework guided by Code's insights into the inadequacies, inequities, and injustices inherent in particular approaches to science and knowledge production practices reveals opportunities for, and persistent barriers to, ecological thinking and other epistemological possibilities for human subject research. The elements of ecological thinking examined closely here are necessary for advancing a research ethics committed to preventing or reducing harm, promoting individual and collective well-being, and advancing justice. On the one hand, the IRB regulatory framework retains vestiges of the "instrumental rationality, abstract individualism, reductionism, and exploitation of people and places that traditional epistemologies have consistently legitimated" (Code 2012, 87). On the other hand, the IRB regulatory framework has created sites for "generating reconfigured modalities of knowing whose regulative principles are responsive and responsible to the specificities of local knowledge-making in the natural and social world, both found and made, of western-northern twenty-first-century societies" (87).

The IRB framework's attention to the local context and researcher responsibilities toward it have created space for further examination of the assumptions underlying dominant scientific practices and alternatives to it. Increased awareness of and efforts to incorporate community-based and participatory-action research, citizen research, and participant review boards (PRBs) are some examples. While not enshrined in the "old" or recently revised regulations (and perhaps because of it), these practices permit and proliferate radically different processes of knowledge production. The fact that they are not encoded in the regulations means that at the very least there shall remain significant tension between IRBs and their attendant institutions, and researchers seeking to overcome and eliminate the barriers they present to reflexive, dialectic, situated research. These tensions can serve to encourage ecological thinking advanced by Code by keeping on the table conversations that examine, question, and envision new avenues for what research is conducted, how research is conducted, and ultimately the knowledge to be claimed about ourselves, our communities, and the larger worlds around us.

Notes

1. Van den Hoonaard and Hamilton's edited volume (2016) offers a range of critiques and alternatives to the model of ethics review institutionalized in both Canada and the United States.

2. The US Federal Office for Human Resource Protections (OHRP) publishes on an annual basis the *International Compilation of Human Research Standards*. This is a collection of laws, regulations, and guidelines governing human subject research protections in 130 countries.

3. In addition to the WMA, organizations working for international harmonization include the Council for International Organizations of Medical Sciences (CIOMS), and the International Council for Harmonisation of Technical Requirements for Pharmaceuticals for Human Use. There are no comprehensive guidelines for international social behavioral research.

4. Henry Beecher's (1966) survey of egregious research practices is often cited as especially influential in galvanizing support for regulations to prevent abuses of research participants at the hands of doctors and scientists.

5. Throughout this chapter, references to the federal human subjects protection regulations refer primarily to *Title 45 Code of Federal Regulation Part 46: Protection*

of Human Subjects, Subpart A—Basic HHS Policy for Protection of Human Research Subjects, which establishes the bulk of the requirements related to IRB review. By 1991 Subpart A, also known as the Common Rule, had been adopted by fifteen federal departments and agencies. For ease of quick reference, the regulations are typically referred to as 45 CFR 46. The text of the revised Common Rule is the source of any regulatory citations in this chapter.

      6. Institutions can exercise considerable discretion regarding what information must be presented to the institution in order for it to make the exempt determination and what researchers are required to do in order to receive an official exempt determination. As a result, exempt research at some institutions is not subject to any IRB oversight, while at others, such research is expected to meet all or most of the regulatory requirements for expedited research.

      7. I owe the use of "epistemic imaginary" in this chapter to Code's application of the concept of social imaginaries in her critiques of postpositivist epistemology, as well as her discussion of the transformative nature of ecological thinking (Code 2006).

      8. Institutions can exercise considerable discretion regarding what information must be presented to the institution at the time of amendment.

      9. This is not to suggest that conventional scientific methods are not employed in CBPR but rather that CBPR invites a variety of research methods across research questions and contexts.

      10. While the revised regulations continue to refer to research subjects, the OHRP has established a research participants' resource page on its website that uses the term "volunteer" for participants in research.

      11. As an extension of this, the Belmont Report stipulates "that persons with diminished autonomy are entitled to protection"; the regulations incorporate this principle through several provisions: for example, they include special protections for children and mandate the use of a legally authorized representative for those unable to consent for themselves.

      12. The other departments include: Department of Homeland Security, Department of Agriculture; Department of Energy, National Aeronautics and Space Administration, Department of Commerce, Social Security Administration, Agency for International Development, Department of Housing and Urban Development, Department of Labor, Department of Defense, Department of Education, Department of Veterans Affairs, Environmental Protection Agency, National Science Foundation, and Department of Transportation.

Works Cited

Amdur, Robert, and Elizabeth A. Bankert. 2011. "Institutional Review Board Member Handbook." Sudbury, UK: Jones and Bartlett.

Beecher, H. K. 1966. "Ethics and Clinical Research." *New England Journal of Medicine* 274, no. 24: 1354–60.

Beever, Jonathan, and Nicolae Morar. 2016. "The Porosity of Autonomy: Social and Biological Constitution of the Patient in Biomedicine." *American Journal of Bioethics* 16, no. 2: 34–45.

Bozeman, Barry, and Paul Hirsch. 2005. "Science Ethics as a Bureaucratic Problem: IRBs, Rules, and Failures of Control." *Policy Sciences* 38, no. 4: 269–291.

Buchan, Kit. 2016. "Citizen Science: How the Net is Changing the Role of Amateur Researchers." *Guardian*, July 3. https://www.theguardian.com/science/2016/jul/03/citizen-science-how-internet-changing-amateur-research.

Code, Lorraine. 1987. *Epistemic Responsibility*. Hanover, NH: University Press of New England.

———. 1991. *What Can She Know? Feminist Theory and the Construction of Knowledge*. Ithaca, NY: Cornell University Press.

———. 1995. *Rhetorical Spaces: Essays on Gendered Locations*. New York: Routledge.

———. 2006. *Ecological Thinking: The Politics of Epistemic Location*. Studies in Feminist Philosophy. Oxford: Oxford University Press.

———. 2012. "Ecological Responsibilities: Which Trees? Where? Why?" *Journal of Human Rights and the Environment* 3: 84–99.

———. 2016. "The Myth of the Individual." *American Journal of Bioethics* 16, no. 2: 59–60.

Doucet, Andrea. 2018. "Feminist Epistemologies and Ethics: Ecological Thinking, Situated Knowledges, Epistemic Responsibilities." In *Sage Handbook of Qualitative Research Ethics*, edited by Ron Iphofen and Martin Tolich, 73–88. London: SAGE.

Felix, Holly C. 2007. "The Rise of the Community-based Participatory Research Initiative at the National Institute for Environmental Health Sciences: An Historical Analysis Using the Policy Streams Model." *Progress in Community Health Partnerships: Research, Education, and Action* 1, no. 1: 31–39.

Hacker, Karen. 2013. *Community-based Participatory Research*. Thousand Oaks, CA: SAGE.

Heimer, Carol A., and JuLeigh Petty. 2010. "Bureaucratic Ethics: IRBs and the Legal Regulation of Human Subjects Research." *Annual Review of Law and Social Science* 6:601–26.

Klitzman, R. L. 2015. *The Ethics Police? The Struggle to Make Human Research Safe*. New York: Oxford University Press.

Mauthner, Natasha S. 2016. "Should Data Sharing Be Regulated?" In *The Ethics Rupture: Exploring Alternatives to Formal Research Ethics Review*, edited by Will C. Van Den Hoonaard and Ann Hamilton, 206–229. Toronto: University of Toronto Press.

Michelson, Melissa. 2016. "The Risk of Over-Reliance on the Institutional Review Board: An Approved Project Is Not Always an Ethical Project." *PS, Political Science & Politics* 49, no. 2: 299–303.

Minkler, Meredith, and Wallerstein, Nina, eds. 2008. *Community-Based Participatory Research for Health: From Process to Outcomes.* Hoboken, NJ: John Wiley.

National Commission for the Protection of Human Subjects of Biomedical and Behavioral Research. 1979. *The Belmont Report: Ethical Principles and Guidelines for the Protection of Human Subjects of Research.* Washington, DC: US Department of Health and Human Services.

Ross, Lainie Friedman, Allan Loup, Robert M. Nelson, Jeffrey R. Botkin, Rhonda Kost, George R. Smith Jr., and Sarah Gehlert. 2010. "Human Subjects Protections in Community-Engaged Research: A Research Ethics Framework." *Journal of Empirical Research on Human Research Ethics: An International Journal* 5, no. 1: 5–18.

Schneider, Carl. 2015. *The Censor's Hand: The Misregulation of Human-Subject Research.* Basic Bioethics. Cambridge, MA: MIT Press.

Van den Hoonaard, Will C., and Ann Hamilton, eds. 2016. *The Ethics Rupture: Exploring Alternatives to Formal Research Ethics Review.* Toronto: University of Toronto Press.

Zavala, Miguel. 2013. "What Do We Mean By Decolonizing Research Strategies? Lessons from Decolonizing, Indigenous Research Projects in New Zealand and Latin America," *Decolonization: Indigeneity, Education & Society* 2, no. 1: 55–71.

Chapter 8

Knowledge Practices as Matters of Care

A Diffractive Dialogue between Lorraine Code's Ecological Thinking and Karen Barad's Agential Realism

Émilie Dionne

Introduction

Around the same time that Lorraine Code's *Ecological Thinking* found its way onto our bookshelves, feminist new materialism (FNM), feminist sciences studies (FSS), and feminist sciences and technology studies (FSTS) were making contributions of their own to thinking anew the making, doing, and effects of epistemology, ontology, ethics, and politics in scientific endeavors. Code shares similar preoccupations with these thinkers, and their respective works encourage the creation and exploration of pathways leading to innovative and positive apparatuses of thought and imagination. Yet there has been little discussion within scholarly literatures of the connections between Code's ecological thinking, FNM, FSS, and FSTS. It is my aim in this chapter to bring into conversation these areas of feminist thought by focusing on Karen Barad's contribution to FNM, FSS, and FSTS (2007, 2010) and how it fits with the feminist/social epistemology advanced by Lorraine Code (1987, 1991, 2006). Both authors offer complementary parts of the complex puzzle that is "knowing responsibly" (response-*ably*, i.e., enabling the ability to respond) in shared, dynamic, open, and damaged worlds (Code 2006). This chapter will show how both thinkers are committed to presenting ethical ways of knowing and acknowledge and embrace the dynamic relationship that configures knowers and what is known, thereby rejecting strict boundaries between ontology, epistemology, ethics, and politics.

FNM (including FSS and FSTS) rework the notions and practices of epistemology and ontology by focusing on their relationship to the ethical concept of responsibility, which has all too often been left unacknowledged by traditional approaches to these branches of human inquiry. Both the role advocacy plays in knowing well, as Code describes it in *Ecological Thinking*, and the importance placed on the identity of the knower (as she argues in *What Can She Know*) are actually integral to FNM, FSS, and FSTS but are rarely presented as such. I will explore this connection, arguing that Code's work on the importance of advocacy, the validity of testimony, and the relationship between communities and knowledges/knowers can (and should) be woven into FNM's manifold narratives to better connect the contributions of FNM to politics, implementation sciences, and the more concrete and ongoing interactions (or rather, *intra*-actions) between politics and the sciences. To this day, while FNM does engage with politics in thinking through the implications of its work for our everyday lives, this conversation remains marginal and has yet to find its way into daily conversations among scientists, the politicians who regulate or motivate their practices, and the journalists who report on them. Code's work contributes to the emergence of new imaginative possibilities of knowing. Her notions of *testimony, trust, cognitive interdependence, imaginative epistemology, imaginative empathy,* and *advocacy* provide us tools to "make a difference" (Barad 2007, 36, 72; Code 2006, 121), discursively and materially, to what counts as knowledge and knowledge practices. Although rarely addressed in FNM work, ecological thinking compliments FNM; when interlinked, they provide a stronger *ethico*-onto-epistemology, a more responsive and responsible way of understanding how we are in and of the world, and are more apt to "make differences" in the mainstream spaces where politics and science meet, allowing FNM ideas to take root.

In their own unique ways, Code and Barad provide nonfeminist scientists as well as nonscientist feminists with tools that enable them to develop better knowledges, where "better" is meant in both an epistemological and ethical sense. In *Ecological Thinking*, Code emphasizes the importance of the community to knowledge, that cognition is "interdependent" (Code 2006, 173). It is through dialogue that meaning reveals itself (Code 176; see also Maloney 2016, 12). *Ecological Thinking* embraces and illustrates the *relational framework* needed for knowledge and knowing and gives an important role to dialogue for its ability to open up the space to think creatively together

(Godard 1989). This chapter lays the foundation for the *entanglement* of both of their contributions into one approach by creating a conversation between their dense conceptual apparatuses; this provides feminist thinkers operationalizable tools for engaging with matters of science and politics in everyday life. I was inspired to craft this chapter as a meeting place where some of these dialogic possibilities can take place. To this end, I begin with an account of Barad's concept of *agential realism*, then I move on to Code's innovative *ecological thinking* approach and her conceptual work about the idea of "person" in knowing. Using a joint, *intra-active* reading, I then explore the contributions they make to methodology through their respective deployments of *diffraction*—a concept proposed by Donna Haraway in *Situated Knowledges*. I conclude by arguing that Code's concepts (specifically her retention of a focus on persons) do not only contribute critically to agential realism but may just be what is needed to make FNM more politically effective, both in how sciences are done and how they are socially and politically received.

Agential Realism: Rethinking How Matter *Matters*

Agential realism rejects the putative dichotomy between classical (or naïve) realism and social constructivism by showing that these two approaches share an assumption regarding the "nature" of nature: namely, that it is made of a matter that remains fixed and endures regardless of time and space. In this picture, matter can thus be known or not, where knowledge is understood as producing accurate *pictures* or representations of the object of its study. This identity is conceived as unique, isolated, and isolate-able from other things. For Barad, the disagreement between classic realism and social constructivism pertains solely to the *methods* available or not to represent a nature that *is*. The social constructivists argue that human knowledge is bound to include culture in knowledge endeavors; it cannot extricate itself from context. Barad's (2007) agential realism, her contra classical realism approach, reveals the complex processes by which "the real" is not given but made (or, to use her terminology, "configured"). Here it is the nature of matter and of the real that is put into doubt. Rather than assumed as *fixed* conception of matter and the real, endowed with transcendent, timeless and spaceless identities, agential realism holds that matter is *performative* (Barad 2007; see also Butler 1980). This means that its "identity" or "essence" is always transformed and made through material practices; there is no transcendence, only immanence. And in opposition to social constructivism, agential realism insists that although the real is knowable through the scientific method, it is not real as the classical realists depict it. But the methods matter: there is no knowledge that is detached from the emergence of an object of study. Knowledge is achieved and is possible *because* knowledge practices are *intervening* practices, intimately involving themselves in the *mattering processes*, the perpetual (re)configuration process that is matter.

For agential realists, the real is dynamic and always "in-the-making"; it is real only by virtue of being made and remade on an ongoing basis. Matter does not sit still in the process of materialization; it actively participates in its own making. Therefore, acquiring knowledge means taking part in this ongoing process of knowledge making through practices as well as through theories of knowledge.

What Is Matter? Indeterminacy as (the) Matter

What, then, is matter if it lacks an essence, and how can we know it without being able to identify it? Agential realism maintains that there are things that can be known but that to know a thing requires an understanding and an account of co-constitutiveness: that is, the relations a thing has with other things are part of its identity. Inspired by quantum physicist Niels Bohr, Barad insists that matter is indeterminate without context (i.e., the web of its co-constitutive relationships). Matter can, however, be known scientifically; this is done by intervening in matter to temporarily stabilize that which is ontologically dynamic and indeterminate. Such "interventions," where matter materializes, can only occur in a complex situation to which its identity is irrevocably entangled. For knowledge practices, this means that to know *this* object, one must also account for its context of emergence and its relation to the many other things that either participate in its emergence or that also emerge as a constitutive other. In addition, for Barad, matter is neither completely material nor completely discursive, and, as such, agential realism retains aspects of both classic realism and social constructivism. It rejects the suspect ideology of representationalism as the hegemonic way through which knowledge is (to be) acquired yet respects the materiality of matter in a way social constructivists have not.

Agential realism is groundbreaking for its proposal that one can develop better knowledge about matter by knowing *with* matter: for example, by knowing what it "is" by doing what matter does. Agential realism understands matter as an ongoing process of "differential becoming" (Barad 2007,

353); matter is constantly in-the-making, yet it does not remain made. It also *unmakes* (it)self, or rather, *self*-ness. According to Barad's reading of Bohr, matter is ontologically indeterminate when without context and only materializes in context (as material-discursive entanglements and in relational webs); it also ontologically tends *toward indeterminacy*, meaning that *agential* matter undoes what has been done. Yet science works because it involves processes of stabilization where matter is temporarily and locally (in context) stabilized and, as such, can be known. However, stabilization is made possible solely by stabilizing other things as well, which become integral to knowing that "object" (which Barad refers to as "agencies of observation" [Barad 2007, 114–5]). This is "configured matter" rather than *enduring* matter. For agential realism, configured matter is the achievement of this stability, but this stability is only temporary.

The configuration of matter that makes scientific knowledge possible is a process of materialization that leaves marks on matter, even agential/indeterminate ones. These marks (or scars), for Barad, can be seen as coming together to form a "lively fabric," a lively (dynamic, changing, *agential*) embodied memory of matter.[1] All matter remains caught in processes of ongoing *mattering*, which entangles both meaning and matter. These processes are neither infinite in number nor reversible. Past enactments/configurations can never be erased, but they are not determined, fixed, or immutable. Processes of *mattering* are material (and ought to count) because of the traces they leave. In part, these traces are necessary for the reproducibility of scientific findings, and while the process of ongoing *mattering* continues to *enfold*, the trajectory of future materialization retains the traces and marks of all past enactments. These do not determine the matter of the future; they do, however, inform the trajectory of its possible (and impossible) materializations.

"To know" not only means to identify the ongoing configuring processes of materialization (*mattering*) that matter is/does, but it also involves partaking in them. Knowledge practices are thus irrevocably entangled in ethics. As ontology-making projects, they necessarily have consequences that can only be responded to and never erased. This is why, for Barad, knowledge practices should not keep the ontological separate from the epistemological and the ethical and why her agential realism is best regarded as an *ethico-onto-epistemology* that entangles each of these fields of inquiry. This is needed because with her agential realist conception of matter, Barad shows that there is no other way to know than to interact with matter and that this interaction produces its own ontological effects for which knowledge producers ought to be held responsible. In this sense, she shows that knowledge practices are always "playing with" the fabric of the world. In other words, the process of knowing proceeds by way of opening up and foreclosing, at once, the actualization or virtualization of the trajectories of what is and is not possible within new "configurings" of the real. These practices have real material consequences that can affect all bodies. Knowledge practices are therefore always and already "caught" in the responsibility of what emerges, and therefore practitioners need to be held accountable for their actions and to abide by an ethic of knowing.

What Is the Knower? Rethinking Knower as *Agencies of Observation*

Traditionally, however, practitioners of science have maintained a certain distance from their objects of study, something believed to be necessary to achieve the objectivity that has characterized good science. Consider the case of the Stern-Gerlach experiment Barad provides in *Meeting the Universe Halfway*. This experiment, which demonstrates space quantization,[2] is used by Barad (2007, 165) to illustrate, first, how the knower materializes as a singular phenomenon and, second, just how complex and manifold the assemblage that constitutes the agencies of observation is, compared to the former notion of the subject.[3] Otto Stern, a leading scientist for the experiment, used to smoke a specific brand of cheap cigars. The composition of this type of cigar is what allowed him (and his fellow scientists) to witness a particular result and thereby make a significant contribution to science.

> Stern held the plates in his hands and studied them at a distance close enough so that the plates could absorb the fumes of Stern's sulfuric breath, turning the faint, nearly invisible, silver traces into jet black silver sulfide traces. . . . The reproducibility of the experiment depends on the cigar's presence. Not any old cigar will do: the high sulfur content of a cheap cigar is crucial. (Barad 2007, 165)

In this example, we witness how embodiment and context (gender, race, class, etc.) entangle to make particular scientific findings possible. Barad explains that the reasons why Stern smoked *this* cigar and not another kind depended on his situation. "Class, nationalism, gender, and the politics of nationalism, among other variables, are all part of this apparatus (which is

Knowledge Practices as Matters of Care / 181

not to say that all relevant factors figure in the same way or with the same weight)" (Barad 2007, 165). To ignore some parts of this apparatus amounts to failing to grasp precisely *what* the instruments of measure are. Smoking *this* cigar is what brought about the ontological change that would not have happened otherwise. It was part of the reason why the "Stern-Gerlach" experiment was a success. But the contributions of class, gender, nationalism, etc., fail to be accounted for. From the point of view of science, they are immaterial; but for Barad and feminist new materialists, it does matter—in both senses of the word.

This distance and the erasure of the personal lends credibility to the idea that science at its heart is apolitical. Scientists themselves have maintained something of a distance from the political and have insisted on the apolitical nature of their practices. Barad exposes the fallacy of this position, but it is through Code's contribution that one can more clearly understand the sociopolitical ethical concerns of supposedly innocent, detached, and neutral scientific or knowledge practices. One of the main effects of this is to situate ethical considerations at the heart of scientific endeavors.

Ecological Response-*ability*: Ecological Thinking, Knowing Ethically, and Relational Subjectivity

Code's ecological thinking is a reimagined *imaginative* epistemology designed to reconfigure the "social imaginary." In so doing, ecological thinking is able to provide knowers from all fields with practical conceptual tools to engage in scientific practices ethically, or responsibly and well, as Code (2006, 35) puts it. Concerned with transforming the imaginative capacity that permeates the current "instituted" and "instituting imaginaries,"[4] Code's approach takes inspiration from the concept of ecology as a way to instill care and carefulness in knowing and to expose the inherent relationality and interdependency between human existence and epistemic capacity.

Her ecological thinking revises and produces new "modes of engagement with knowledge, subjectivity, politics, ethics, science, citizenship, and agency" (Code 2006, 24). To do this, Code highlights the role, significance, and reach of the concept of *place* in relation to knowing well. She argues that thinking requires not only thinking *about* and *with* places but also thinking *from* places: that is, to recognize that places become part of the "subject" of knowing and that when we know, we always know from somewhere. She is inspired, in part, by Donna Haraway's notion of *situation*. In *Situated Knowledges*, Haraway (1997) argues that knowledge(s) and knowledge practices are always and necessarily situated in a locality *and* intertwined with history, culture, economics, politics, class, gender, sex, sexuality, race, ethnicity, ability, and so forth. The notion of *situated knowledges* emphasizes how all these features take part in the making of knowledge (Code 2006, 121). Knowers/would-be knowers always stand in networks of relations that are not only physical but also social, political, economic, historical, psychological, ideological, and so on.

The approach of ecological thinking enables a different *mattering* of "places" as more than just acknowledging their physicality, regarding them as "actants" (Latour 2009, 75) that demand unique responses. In Code's (2006, 100) words, "situation becomes a place to know in two broad senses: as a place where epistemic activity occurs, and as a place that itself demands to be known in those of its aspects that facilitate or thwart knowing responsibly and well."

Using the lens of environmental ethics, ecological thinking enables knowers and would-be knowers to care (and care *well*) for the fragility of certain physical places by recognizing that they are complex entanglements of relationships constitutive of subjectivity and active as forces also involved in knowledge practices. In Code's (2006, xi, 4, 6, 20–1, 37) account, places become "fleshed out," complex. Inspired by Barad's concepts, physical places are intricate parts of agencies of observation and not just objects of observation.

Ecology in Ecological Thinking

> Focus on habitat as a place to know is central to ecological thinking . . . in its more metaphorical applications . . . social political, cultural, and psychological elements figure alongside physical and (other) environmental contributors to the "nature" of a habitat and its inhabitants, at any historical moment.
>
> —Lorraine Code, *Ecological Thinking*

Ecology is the study of the rich complexity of places known as habitats. Attending well to this complexity requires care and responsiveness because we are entangled in the world of which we are *and* with which we inhabit. This is why our care for (response to) a place requires our careful attention to and articulation of details and differences—to ensure our ethical and sustainable cohabitation with the world and with others (Code 2006, 53).

Ecological thinking is also about fostering ways to become available, sensible to the "detail and larger patternings of human and 'natural' diversity" (47).

Code takes her ecological inspiration from the environmental ethicist Verena Conley, who perceives ecology as a "way of inhabiting the world" (as cited in Code 2006, 7). The term "ecology" is derived from the concept of home (the prefix *eco* coming from the ancient Greek word *oikos*, which refers to three related but distinct concepts: the family, the property of the family, and the home). Habitation and cohabitation are concepts central to Code's new epistemology. For her, a person inhabits the world by weaving herself through and with the world, as "she" simultaneously articulates herself as "her" and as a "self" with the world. Code's (2006, 100) ecological thinking offers a new mode of "cohabitation," a more ethical, positive way of inhabiting the world that allows one to dwell *and* know together, ethically *and* responsively.

Knowing as One Knows a Person

Ecological thinking fosters a form of knowing similar to that of meeting and coming to know *a person*. Building from her previous work on epistemic capacity and responsibility, Code suggests that more responsible, responsive, and caring ways of knowing in all knowledge practices, including the sciences, may well involve learning anew how to know "things" as we know persons. Knowing as one knows a person is a process that is at odds with the strong objectivism adopted in positivist sciences. To know something well in the positivist sense is to know its essence—to know what it *really* is and not how it appears to us in our particularity. Take a "simple" perceptual example as the one Code offers in *What Can She Know?* At first glance, knowing that a cat is on the mat does not seem to require knowing anything more than the bare facts: x is a cat, y is a mat, and x and y stand in an "on" relationship. We need not feel one way or another about the cat to know that it is on the mat. Yet once a knower/would-be knower attempts to know something as complex as a person, the failings of the positivist approach become evident; it is impossible to know a person without engaging deeply with them at a level that transgresses the detached objectivity demanded by the positivist sciences. Knowing a person is more than knowing that a particular body exists at a particular point in space and time. The person one comes to know exists in networks of relations with others, including relations to histories, practices, and values that inevitably exceed the mere descriptive data of this living, breathing "object" of knowledge. Knowing *this* person is always and necessarily a much more complex, dynamic, and *involved* process of knowing than the conventional example of knowing the cat is on the mat makes it seem.

But this complexity is not only due to the complexity of this "object" but to the complexity of the knower as well. Knowing that the cat is on the mat is a classic example of the "*S* knows that *p*" locution of traditional epistemology, where the identity of *S* is irrelevant to the content of *p*. In *What Can She Know?*, Code makes the case that it *always* matters who the *S* is and that attempts to neutralize the situatedness of *S* amount to an application of the institution of epistemologies of mastery.[5] Code illustrates how mundane examples of traditional epistemology that treat the particularities of the knower as irrelevant to knowledge mask the significance of greater involvement in knowing. She fleshes out a case where a cat is seen on a mat, not by a disembodied rationality represented by *S* but by a real person named Sara. Sara's circumstances are such that her claims are challenged by her community, and her very epistemic capacity is called into question by others, who deny that there is a cat on the mat. Whether or not there is a cat on the mat, Code asks us to consider how this situation would affect Sara's life. Given that her perception of a cat on a mat is as real to her as any other, Code explains, she would likely come to doubt her own observations and Sara's friends and family would lose trust in her. This maddening experience, argues Code (1991, 216–17), "is not so fanciful [but rather] generalizes readily to women's epistemic lives per se . . . [as] women are often, both metaphorically and literally, driven crazy by their incapacity to gain any greater acknowledgement for their knowledge." This is so because "it is easy to argue that both women and men see cats on mats pretty much indistinguishably in similar circumstances, it appears to be nonsensical to suggest that women's knowledge claims are frequently suppressed for want of acknowledgement" (Code 1991, 216–17).

With *Ecological Thinking*, Code further pushes the epistemic responsibility that knowers/would-be knowers have toward those whose claims find little to no resonance within *instituted* knowledge practices. For Code, knowing a person does not simply reveal that in knowing practices, a knower is much more involved and entangled with the objects she aims to know (i.e., what Barad qualifies as "material-discursive" practices that can involve, e.g., affect and emotions); it also reveals the ethical concerns that live at the heart of what it means to know. In coming to know a person, one inevitably comes to care for *the* person by developing an affective capacity and a certain generosity that entails making oneself vulnerable. Only then will the advocacy necessary for giving a voice to nonlegitimized, unconventional epistemic possibilities and testimonies silenced by epistemologies of mastery become possible. For Code, there are certain things we cannot know unless we develop generosity and emotional vulnerability. Therefore, any knowledge making practice that does not recognize these capacities will be incomplete and poorly equipped to provide us with the knowledge we need to live and act in the world as best we can:

> Practices of advocacy often make knowledge possible within hierarchical distributions of autonomy and authority and in institutional divisions of intellectual labor in western societies, where those lacking the autonomy that social and economic self-sufficiency provides tend in consequence to be excluded from the epistemic autonomy that would ensure and secure their recognition as knowers whose claims to know are to be taken seriously. Advocacy, in such situations, performs a liberatory function. (Code 2006, 165)

Always Second Person First

The ecological thinking approach embeds relationality into the very heart of ontological matters. Thinking and knowing are fundamentally communal—there is no knowledge without the active involvement of a community (Code 2006, 42). Code even speaks of the knower *as* community, an idea that can be explored through the notion of "second person."

In *What Can She Know?* Code (1991) argues that epistemic agency is constituted largely by a primal epistemic *interdependency*. Here, Code is influenced by Annette Baier's development of the notion of "second person" in her work with children. Baier concludes that, ontologically speaking, *any* person becomes *a person* by being first a *second* person. From the moment of birth, a person emulates others and thus learns to be in the world, eventually also becoming her own person, a *first* person, but only insofar as she was initially (and continues to be) a second person (Code 1991, 218–20). That we are second persons first shows how interdependence and autonomy are not mutually exclusive or even dichotomous concepts, contrary to much of the literature exploring human psychology and identity (Code 1991, 74). This is the case because although for Code the person emerges only "out of interdependence" (82), she also does so as a constantly renewed "integration of autonomy and solidarity" (74). "Second persons" are tied to their "first persons"; they continuously "turn back . . . for affirmation and continuation" (82). To become a person, one requires a community: one becomes a person by knowing another person. The notion of the "second person" is therefore central in a responsible and responsive epistemology.

This idea radically transforms the concepts of the individual and of autonomy because at the core of personhood is a complex "relational subjectivity" that determines which knowledge practices can emerge. Code (1991, 83) writes that "personal knowledge depends on common knowledge," such as the "ability to change one's mind." *Cognitive interdependence* and the *imaginative community* are essential to knowing well; a community of exchange makes constant questioning possible, providing "dissensus," disagreement, or *diffraction,* which is essential for working toward ameliorating knowledge-making practices.

Making a Difference by Making Difference Matter: Barad and Code on a Diffractive Methodology

The concept of diffraction employed by Code stems from the influential work of Donna Haraway, who reimagines diffraction as an alternative to reflection, which she argues has been given unjustified preferential treatment by scientific and knowledge endeavors still operating under the ideology of representationalism. Barad also relies on the physical phenomenon of diffraction. As opposed to reflection, which is interested in similarities, in physics, diffraction focuses on differences—the differential *patterns* that "emerge within phenomena" (Code 1991, 89), for example. It is about knowing matter through the differences one witnesses and by making differences matter. A diffractive methodology enables scientists to study what matter does rather than what it "is." With regard to phenomena in physics, both Haraway and Code recognize that reflection corresponds to the idea of something being "displace[d] . . . elsewhere" yet as "*the same,*" whereas diffraction aims to "make a difference in the world" (Code 2006, 121, cited in text).

For Code, knowers, especially those with power and access to resources, have a responsibility to allow other knowledges and ways of *knowing*—those that do not matter (have not materialized or are not valued) in current configurations of the real—to emerge. Making a difference in the world, she argues, is about being concerned with how knowers *ought to care* when observing "differences-making patterning": the differences that come to exist and the manner(s) in which they do.

Diffraction thus accounts for the "heterogeneous histories" within "matters" (Code 1991, 121). For Code, differences are important, and they ought to matter in knowing. One has to be careful about the desire to draw generalizations. This is not to say that analogies cannot be explored—they can and should. But Code insists that *analogism* should always be "carefully balanced" with *disanalogism* (281). It is through this attention to *diffraction*—the differences that matter, the heterogeneity—that ecological thinking (re-)introduces "movement in thought," participating in the creation of a new *instituting* social imaginary whereby new imaginative possibilities—new ways of perceiving and knowing—can arise, and, in Code's words and hopes, can bring about more ethical ways of inhabiting the world (280).

To this end, Barad's (2007, 181) agential realism pushes Haraway's usage of the concept further by revealing difference as a fundamental feature of reality (a differential ontology). She deploys diffraction as a methodology, a way through which matter can be known *and* do what it does. That is, diffraction, like matter, creates differences and does so by way of *marking matter* (i.e., whereby matter is conceived as a lively [alive, agential] "memory" that constantly remakes itself), and this making has both material and discursive dimensions. In Barad's (2007, 137) words, "Mattering is differentiating." Barad's diffractive methodology retains the ability to know that is required for the practice of science but sees matter as known without essential, unchangeable qualities but rather as something fundamentally lacking a foundation. To know matter is to know it through the uniqueness of its dynamism, that is, its "differential becoming," whereby differences that matter are made.

By contrast, Code's mobilization of diffraction explores how advocacy encourages unique and otherwise unavailable knowledge and epistemic capacities to emerge, resulting in different ways of knowing, different knowers, and different knowledges that matter. As I have mentioned, this is done in part through care, attentiveness, and the affective capacity of embodiment, which makes us available to situations, people, and places. Committed to "differences that matter" (Code 2006, 133), *Ecological Thinking* is a critique of what Code coins the "epistemologies of mastery." These epistemologies regard objectivity as the measure of knowledge, rejecting all that is subjective, contextual, or indeterminate. In this sense, the epistemologies of mastery are informed by the same ontological and epistemological biases of representationalism. Code exposes how the scientific method aims to distance the researcher from the object of study; it removes or downplays the role of affect in knowing and searches for similarities, drawing generalizations that obscure or ignore important differences and that change *how* these differences *matter* (41). The scientific method also attempts to distance knowers from *places*, whether this is the place in which the object is situated, *with which* it is related, or from which knowers (can) know. In "[d]istancing themselves from the particularities of materiality, physicality, and all other circumstantial contingencies . . . autonomous practitioners" shield themselves "from any need to address the differences *difference makes*" (Code 2006, 133, my emphasis). Code continues: "This suppression of affect, thence of sociality, and of affective connections with other people and with the differences that the diversity of human embodiment entails is a significant cost" (134).

As a diffractive methodology, ecological thinking enables differences that matter to matter otherwise (discursively and materially) through its particular attention to (care for) the unique yet all-too-often overlooked (or looked down upon) knowledge and knowledge practices that emerge from anecdotal evidence and testimonies in case studies (Code 2006, 51). This evidence, Code argues, serves to activate or reimagine the instituted social imaginary. Specifically, it enables a movement from an "instituted imaginary" toward an "instituting imaginary" (Code 2006, 61). The renewal of our social imaginary is a practice that participates in reconfiguring a variety of relationships (e.g., epistemological, ethical, scientific, political) "between and among living beings and the inanimate parts of the world" (Code 2006, 47).

Code's (2006, 176) exploration of responsible and responsive knowledge leads her to posit that advocacy, at times, can be the sole means through which particular knowledge can emerge: "Advocacy practices work to get at truths operating imperceptibly, implicitly, below the surface of the assumed self-transparency of evidence." They do so by either "recognizing or discounting the experiences of certain would-be knowers as knowledgeable, granting or refusing their testimony a fair hearing, facilitating or blocking their participation in authoritative, emancipatory epistemic practices" (Code 2006, 170). For those without a voice, those unheard, those who do not yet *matter* or *matter* inequitably, or for those deterred from developing or using their epistemic abilities, knowing through advocacy can help make differences *matter*; it can enable the emergence—the *configuration*—of unique knowledge by providing the tools and resources they need to make themselves known. Rather than erasing and/or discounting the differences (anomalies that do not fit the "picture" the sciences aim to draw), imaginative/ecological thinking is about "contribut[ing] to the construction of knowledge" by "presuppos[ing] a certain human commonality . . ." (Code 2006, 206–7) all the while acknowledging the possibility of radical differences.

Toward a Conclusion

By reading Barad through Code, I hope to have shown how agential realism is an ethico-onto-epistemology of *care*. Whereas Barad explains that some mattering practices have ethical consequences, Code argues that the very act of knowing has an ethical dimension because the relationship between the knower and the known is similar to one that develops through the process of knowing a person. Indeed, the objects of observation in agential realism are inherently complex and only exist entangled in a web of relations; unlike simple cats and mats, they are more like persons in their complexity. It is through this *subjectivization* of matter that Code shows just how this ethico-onto-epistemology is ethical. Although FNM presents itself in distinction to object-oriented-ontologies (Haraway and Barad, notably, see as quite real and nonnegligible [or innocent] the risk to produce flat ontology, whereby all is equalized), I argue that retaining the concept of the person, as Code does, provides posthumanist ethics such as FNM the language and tools to justify how and why how one knows matters. Agential realism reveals a deep care by listening to its objects, inviting them to let themselves be touched, or for the knowers be touched, or to be transformed (made and unmade) in contact to them, *intra-actively*. FNM admits no other way to know, meaning that any act of knowing has ethical implications that reflect our social responsibility. Proponents of FNM care, come to care, and reveal deep care for their objects of investigation. In *Meeting the Universe Halfway*, for example, Barad cares about the difficult, complex "matter" of quantum physics as agential. All too often, perhaps because of the complex "objects of observation" with which it deals, FNM remains somewhat at a distance from the everyday political struggles of people and their communities, where "epistemologies of mastery" continue to deny some knowledges and capacities to know and to respond.

Ecological thinking centers ethical considerations in ontological matters by acknowledging the *community* involved or emerging for any knowing to take place; it assigns knowers/would-be knowers a responsibility ("response-ability," understood as the ability to respond and the responsibility to enable others to respond in their own capacity) toward community members to create openings for the emergence of other knowledges or bridges between knowledges that already exist but that *matter* differently or unequally. Knowing responsibly, which requires renewed imaginary practices, is necessary for encouraging more ethical ways of cohabitating. We need these new ethical ways and these renewed imaginary practices; they are needed in this world-in-the-making that is shared globally. With Code's ecological thinking, other knowledges/forms of knowledge *matter*, and *how* they matter matters.

Notes

1. Barad uses "re-member-ring" to illustrate how matter can be valued or understood differently when it takes a different material form, but this process occurs only through *remembering*, of matter being marked at its core by past enactments.

2. Space quantization is the name that was given to a phenomenon whereby "orientation of the place of the electron orbit [being] is limited to discrete values" (Barad 2007, 162). As Barad writes, this means "that only particular orientation in space are allowed" (162). At the beginning of the twentieth century, Otto Stern worked with Walther Gerlach to do an experiment on space quantization. Stern's argument was that once this experiment took place—that is, once the phenomenon was observed *in the real*—worldviews would have to accept quantum theoretical views in favor of classical physics. Bohr's model, and its extension by Sommerfeld and Debeye, shows "an atom [as] a 'tiny solar system' with a central nucleus surrounded by a discrete set of concentric electron 'orbitals'" (Barad 2007, 162). Barad explains: "[t]he observed hydrogen spectrum can be explained by taking account of all possible electron 'jumps'—that is, 'quantum leaps'—from one discrete orbital (i.e. energy level) to another" (162). While the model was accepted, without concrete, *real* evidence, physicists remain reticent to "give up" on classical physics (162). This is what sparked Stern (and Gerlach) to attempt the experiment, and how gender, race, nationalism, politics, nation, came to be part of the "agencies of (scientific) observation."

3. Agencies of observation are complex because they can encompass material objects that already and always exceed their "materiality" and come charged with layers of discursive effects, such as those related to race, class, and gender (Barad 2007, 165). In addition to complicating the former concept of the "subject" of sciences with the location of "agencies of observation," Barad conveys that scientists bring much more than their minds and knowledge to their scientific endeavors. What counts for the "agencies of observation" (formerly "subjects of knowledge") are the complex entanglements of the instruments of measure used to understand them, including scientific tools and concepts and the histories of both instruments, concepts, and agencies of observation. As such, it is not just the mind and the microscope but the bodies involved, including their modes of embodiment and their sex, gender, race, class, and ability, as well as their cultural, national, and political identities that compose agencies of observation and enable knowing.

4. The reference is to Cornelius Castoriadis's concepts of "instituted" and "instituting" social imaginaries, on which Code relies to develop her own ecological

practice as a renewed imaginary. He conceives the social imaginary as the instituted socialization process for individuals whereby "individuals [are given] access to a world of social imaginary significations whose instauration as well as incredible coherence goes unimaginably beyond everything that 'one or many individuals' could ever produce" (Castoriadis, as cited in Code 2006, 17). By contrast, the *instituting* imaginary, in Code's (2006, 18) words, is a "critical-creative activity of a society that exhibits its autonomy in its capacity to put itself in question." She adds: "Imaginatively initiated counter possibilities interrogate the social structure to destabilize its pretensions to naturalness and wholeness, to initiate a new making" (19).

5. Epistemologies of mastery are necessarily situated and embodied, but they manage to veil the features of their contexts to universalize their specific embodiment (see Code 2006, 21).

Works Cited

Barad, Karen. 2007. *Meeting the Universe Halfway: Quantum Physics and the Entanglement of Matter and Meaning*. Durham, NC: Duke University Press.

Code, Lorraine. 1987. "Second Persons." *Canadian Journal of Philosophy* 17, no. 1: 357–382.

———. 1991. *What Can She Know? Feminist Theory and the Construction of Knowledge*. Ithaca, NY: Cornell University Press.

———. 2006. *Ecological Thinking: The Politics of Epistemic Location*. New York: Oxford University Press.

———. 2010. "Quantum Entanglements and Hauntological Relations of Inheritance: Dis/continuities, Spacetime Enfoldings, and Justice-to-come." *Derrida Today* 3, no. 2:240–268.

Godard, Barbara. 1989. "Theorizing Feminist Discourse/Translation." *Tessera* 4: 41–53.

Haraway, Donna. 1997. *Simians, Cyborgs, and Women: The Reinvention of Nature*. London: Free Association.

Latour, Bruno. 2009. *Politics of Nature: How to Bring the Sciences into Democracy*. Cambridge, MA: Harvard University Press.

Maloney, Catherine. 2016. "From Epistemic Responsibility to Ecological Thinking: The Importance of Advocacy for Epistemic Community." *Feminist Philosophy Quarterly* 2, no. 2: 7.

Chapter 9

An Ecological Application to Service-Users in Psychiatry

The Social Imaginary and Ethical, Political, and Epistemological Relationships

NANCY NYQUIST POTTER

Introduction

One night, a 30-year old person of color (male to female) whom I'll call "Eleanor" visited emergency psychiatry where she previously had been seen a number of times before. The file identified the patient as male; however, she requested that she be referred to by the female pronoun, as she is transgender. She reported feelings of depression and anxiety, and presented to emergency psychiatry with suicidal ideation. This patient repeatedly expressed that she feared for her safety in the shelters, while the attending and the resident continued to refer to the patient by male pronouns even though she had asked to be addressed as female. The health care team believed that the patient thought hospitalization was a way to avoid spending another night in a shelter; they assessed her as not being a danger to herself and not to need crisis intervention. Therefore, she was discharged.[1]

Eleanor simultaneously is a victim of epistemic, political, and ethical harm, and Lorraine Code's work provides a framework for analyzing such cases. In my prior work regarding diagnosis and treatment in mental health, I have examined epistemic authority on the part of clinicians—and psychiatry as an institution—and identified important contexts where such authority distorts epistemic and ethical responsibility (Potter 2016). This especially can be seen in the silencing of patient/service-users' voices and experiences as knowers. Understanding the *episteme* of psychiatry is crucial both to the identification of ethico-politico-epistemic failures and to engagement with change; much of psychiatric practice rigorously attempts to maintain such distinctions as expert doctor/sick patient through an ontological and epistemological commitment to a faith in the objectivity of DSMs, evidence-based medicine (EBM), and a biological explanation for mental distress (Potter 2016). I apply Code's ideas of ecological thinking to the psychiatric clinic as a way to show the suggestive power that her work offers to ethico-politico-epistemic change. I will end with the worry that even some of the more progressive movements within psychiatry can be incorporated into this powerful epistemic, social, and political field—thus giving us all the more reason to take seriously Code's vision of ecological thinking and change.

This chapter focuses on three issues: Code's shift in the thinking about the relationship between epistemology and ethics; the significance of knowing other persons as it pertains to psychiatry; and how rethinking these issues in the context of the social imaginary can be transformative to the care of persons in distress. The example of Eleanor will be used throughout the paper in order to draw out particular points of relation between Code's work and persons experiencing mental distress, but the remarks I make also are applicable in many other contexts.

Shifting Ground

In *Epistemic Responsibility* (1987), Code treats ethics and epistemology as analogous. In discussing what is involved in assessing a knowledge claim, she writes, "That person's intellectual integrity counts as a significant part of the evidence in much the same way as, in moral matters, a person's moral integrity is a determining factor in decisions as to whether she or he should be trusted" (1987, 39). In a similar vein, she writes,

> Just as a person's actions can, to a significant extent, be judged with reference to his/her moral reliability, so cognitive activity

and its products might be able to be judged with reference to the epistemic reliability of would-be knowers. Implicit in this approach is a recognition of the extent to which knowledge-seeking situations and situations where claims to knowledge are assessed invoke questions about whom one is prepared to trust, and why. (Code 1987, 43)

Using words such as "analogous to," "akin to," and "just as" to note an affiliation between epistemology and ethics, Code simultaneously marks a boundary between epistemology and ethics and at the same time calls attention to the relationship between the two. Her position vis-à-vis what the precise relationship is between ethics and epistemology thus appears a bit murky. Most clearly, she distinguishes Lewis's claim that *"cognitive rightness is itself a moral concern* . . . in the broad sense of moral" (Lewis 1969, as quoted by Code 1987; emphasis added) by remarking that "this is the sense I would prefer to call analogical, to indicate that the reasoning, too, is analogous to, but not identical with, moral reasoning" (Code 1987, 49). The murkiness is in the claim that right reasoning and right or good conduct are analogical. Since arguments by analogy rest on the strength of the similarities in the comparison, readers want to know *how* similar Code takes epistemology and ethics to be and why, if she endorses Lewis's claim above, she still holds them as distinct rather than integrally connected. I agree that the two are not identical. Yet Code's commitment in her early work to holding the two as distinct had left a question in my mind as to *why* these two branches of thinking, knowing, and orienting ourselves in the world are not seen as integrally bound up with one another.

In fact, in *Ecological Thinking* (2006) and in "Advocacy, Negotiation and the Politics of Unknowing" (2008), Code brings the ethical and epistemological much closer together and offers a clearer picture of how she views the relationship between the two. She describes ecological thinking as "a frame for reconfiguring knowledge, sociality, and subjectivity and for reexamining the potential of epistemic and ethico-political practices to produce habitats where people can live well together and respectfully with and within the physical/natural world" (Code 2006, 19). Indeed, in her challenge to mainstream globalizing epistemology, she says that conventional epistemic norms and practices believe it is necessary to maintain a sharp distinction between the ethico-political and the epistemological, and she makes clear that she disagrees with a rigid dichotomy between these different fields.

> It is at the level of processes, practices, and particularities . . . that questions of equality, ethics, power, identity, voice, and social change arise and epistemic injustice is enacted and condoned, if often tacitly and with no ill intent. (Code 2008, 33)

Understood at more local levels, epistemology, politics, and ethics are experienced as interwoven, actively at play with one another between and among the players who bring into the foreground or background various issues and practices as they work out the conflicts, commonalities, mistakes, meanings, and import of daily living together. These later ideas have echoed and enriched the direction of much feminist writing about the integral relationship between ethics and epistemology, and I will argue that understanding the epistemic-ethico-political as integrally related is crucial in doing good clinical work. But first, let me address the epistemological frameworks that Code brings to the foreground. In this section, I defend the idea that these epistemic values are inseparable from both political and ethical responsibility for good psychiatric care.

Knowing Other Persons and Ecological Thinking

In her critique of mainstream epistemology, Code argues that knowing other persons is at least as great a contender for the paradigm for knowledge as are observational simples (Code 1991). Knowing other people, however, notably is distinct in that it requires us to engage with another intersubjectively as epistemic agents, a view that fundamentally challenges the status of knowledge and knowers as objective, disinterested, and rational. This highlights the centrality of second-person relationships and employs an epistemic methodology that is quite fundamentally different from third-person knowing. For one thing, third-person knowing treats knowers as independent agents who assess evidence for and against beliefs from a disinterested and detached perspective. That practice and ideology ignore the ways that epistemology is a collective, communal endeavor. Additionally, recognition that knowledge production is a communal practice, a concept introduced in *Epistemic Responsibility* (1996), brings to the forefront the ways that we bring different experiences, perspectives, and values to knowledge production.[2]

Yet it is inimical to knowing well to assume that certain views should get privileged just because they are the dominant ones, or that knowledge primarily is an *individual* project of ensuring that one's beliefs track the truth. The mastery assumed to be attainable through epistemic autonomy has some appeal in its aim to transcend the confusion of emotion, senses, and social particularity, Code explains, but it disqualifies more frankly situated contenders for knower status from being recognized. Because of this way of conceiving epistemic practices, it fails to recognize many people who are differently situated from the mainstream and also are knowers (Code 2006, 172). Ecological thinking disrupts and disturbs the scientific ideal of knowledge production by calling attention to the dynamic, live aspects of knowing that are found in the instability of ecology—a model that Code applies both literally and metaphorically. As she explains, ecological thinking is not intended to substitute one unified discourse with another; it is "both conflicted and unstable . . . capable of infiltrating gaps in the discourse of mastery" found in science and in humans' relations with the broader ecological world (Code 2006, 7). This approach "generates more responsible knowings" than mainstream knowing can—where "responsibility" is understood to be both epistemic and ethical (Code 2006, 9). Responsible knowing includes developing the capacity for perception, attentiveness to evidence, and openness to others' perspectives and differing experiences. Thus, the way we offer and respond to others' testimony is crucial. It also includes contestability, meaning that concepts such as "evidence" may need to be challenged, rethought, or refined, and that the norms for knowing well themselves are open to contestation. We cannot be epistemically responsible while be closed off to others' knowings, so inclusivity also is central to knowing well. Epistemic interdependence is a much more the on-the-ground reality for knowers, and it is more productive to recognize the ways that our different social situatedness places us as necessarily epistemically dependent on one another. Furthermore, it heightens the value of second-person and intersubjective knowledge production. Heidi Grasswick emphasizes the "unelimitable role of the social in shaping knowledge," while at the same time upholding a commitment to knowledge that is oriented toward truths about the world (Grasswick 2014, 8). "We need to be able to *perceive how things are with other people*, becoming aware of the relevant moral details of the situation so that we will be able to respond appropriately" (Grasswick 2012, 315; emphasis added). Attunement to other people is emphasized in Code's suggestion that knowing other people is an everyday basic necessity (Code 1991). To be clear, second-person knowing is not an individualistic way of knowing; it is social and has institutional shape and limitations. I return to this point later in the chapter.

These ideas are directly relevant to psychiatric practice. First, it is clear that clinician and patient/service-user encounters are best engaged in when we conceptualize the relationship as a second-person one. This is especially important when we consider the liability some clinicians have toward interpreting patient/service-user's reports of experience as well as their embodied communications from a strictly clinical (i.e., third person, DSM-driven, biologically based) perspective. I want to make three points here. First, second-person relations require us not to impose meanings on others' experience or lives. The removed and detached position in impersonal relations reinforces ignorance and indifference and pretends to neutrality, thus imposing interpretations on persons and whole classes of people that align with patterns of domination and subordination. When our knowings arise out of second-person relations, we are more likely to be attuned, informed, and sensitive to the others' communications—and theirs to ours—thus opening up possibilities for understanding that impersonal knowing impedes (see, for instance, Walker 2008).

Secondly, then, taking seriously the value of second-person knowing in clinical practice might involve the clinician deferring to the patient/service-user's reports. Consider the case of Eleanor in the introduction: rather than the health-care team in emergency psychiatry thinking that it knows best what Eleanor needs and "what she is up to," good psychiatric practice might give deference to her experiences as a trans person of color in this context where nearly everyone present was ignorant of the dangers and risks of being trans in a transphobic world. Thirdly, clinicians would better serve their patient/service users if trained in the arts of ecological thinking. Code notes that advocacy especially is needed to counteract silencing and epistemic injustice in the clinic (see § 5). Code writes:

> Negotiations designed to issue in effective advocacy require a minimal presumption of trust—something like a principle of charity—from the outset, for they commonly start from and generate vulnerability not only for the patient, but often also for nurses or doctors who may have to put their own professional credibility on the line in order to participate effectively in advocacy projects. (Code 2006, 191)

Deference need not amount to granting someone a privileged standpoint about their knowledge, but it does involve granting their testimony prima facie credibility in order to counteract the tendency to reject patient/service-user claims that do not fit within an epistemic schema of normal functioning brain/thought/behavior patterns.

An epistemology that takes seriously the experiences of those whose voices have been marginalized, whose local knowledges have been discredited, and those who are patients/service users, is one founded in social, political, and ethical change. Code's explication and application of the social imaginary found in both *Ecology Thinking* (2006) and in "Advocacy" (2008) demonstrate ways that social change requires a reconceptualization of "human locations and relations all the way down" (2006, 198). In the next section, I enrich the first argument on knowing other persons as tied to ecological thinking by explaining how responsible knowings are impeded by an instituted social imaginary. I will show that Code's work offers a rich field for identifying mechanisms of the instituted social imaginary that operate within clinical fields to suppress, distort, silence, and otherwise do epistemic and ethical violence to people living in distress or in distressing situations such as being homeless and trans—or voice-hearing. The social imaginary, as Code explicates it, has the potential to effect liberatory changes in institutions such as clinical practices that pave the way for more advocative intersubjective healing to occur—and for avoiding unnecessary medicalizing of social problems and the creation of "patients." Thus, the next sections illustrate one way that epistemic responsibility can be either impeded or enhanced by the social imaginary.

The Social Imaginary

The institutional structures of medicine and the epistemic commitments in psychiatry and psychology can impede clinicians' ability and will to challenge the social structures that shape experiences of service-users (Potter 2016). One way to understand both the impediments and potentialities for psychiatrists working with patients/service users is through the concept of the social imaginary. This concept, proposed by Code as more explicitly attentive to power and politics than is Miranda Fricker's "Social Imagination" (2007), is used to capture a matrix of operations that tend to bolster and reproduce hegemonic groups. It consists of discourses, representations, attitudes, values, affect, and legitimized knowledge that provide schemas of interpretations of reality. These schemas and interpretations are distributed primarily through school, media, and other social institutions, such as medicine and law (Cegarra 2012).

The social imaginary shapes and limits race and gender relations, as in the case of Eleanor in section 1. The #MeToo movement, for example, highlights how unimaginable it has been—and may still be—for working women to be unable to say *no* effectively to sexual advances from their employers or coworkers. The new immigration laws and efforts to rescind DACA illustrate how rare it is in the social imaginary that Mexicans are depicted as law-abiding productive citizens.

The social imaginary, as José Medina explains, is a system of social relations that shapes the character and possibilities of what is imaginable (Medina 2013, 67–68). Fricker analyzes the trial of *To Kill a Mockingbird* in terms of individuals' testimonial injustice, arguing that a prejudiced credibility deficit renders a verdict of Tom's guilt. Medina argues that testimonial injustice is not solely individual because of the social imaginary in which the racial ideology makes it unthinkable for a white girl (Mayella) to desire a Black man.

Code characterizes the instituted social imaginary as "implicit but effective systems of images, meanings, metaphors, and interlocking explanations and expectations woven through a social-political order, within which people, in specific time periods and cultural-geographical climates enact their knowledge and subjectivities and craft their self-understandings" (Code 2008, 34). The instituted social imaginary is naturalized and appears to many people as given and unquestionable—although who questions and who wants to hold fast to the instituted social imaginary depends on ethico-political commitments intersecting with social location. For example, Alice Pechriggl analyzes three aspects of the gender imaginary—the material body; the effective imaginary, which includes the normative man and woman; and the transcendent or social imaginary (Pechriggl 2005). She describes the mechanisms of the social imaginary as a "projection screen imaginary" wherein male hegemony is reproduced through its significations: "The female body imaginary—which has been and still is instrumentalized nearly exclusively for the representation of male institutions—is detached from real women. It is a screen of projections" (Pechriggl 2005, 104).

Pechriggl only analyzes a gender imaginary and a dichotomous one at that. Trans people, however, can attest to the fact that an instituted social imaginary reifies and reproduces limiting and confining social, scientific, and ethical mores that do not map onto some people's experiences. Additionally, it is clear that the instituted social imaginary circulates intersecting representations of race, gender, and class. Patricia Hill Collins calls these representations in the social imaginary "controlling images" and argues that they serve to naturalize racism, sexism, and poverty and make them appear to be an inevitable part of everyday life (Collins 2000, 69).[3] Thomas King remarks that, in film, three Indian types circulate: the bloody savage, the noble savage, and the dying savage (King 2012, 34). On television, the image of the Indian became that of Tonto, who was "trustworthy, loyal, helpful, friendly, courteous, kind, obedient, cheerful, thrifty, brave, clean, and reverent" (King 2012, 42); however, there is also the Indian-as-product as represented by Crazy Horse Malt Liquor, which turned "a great Oglala leader into a bottle of booze" (2012, 57). King argues that North Americans no longer see Indians; what we see are "war bonnets, beaded shirts, fringed deerskin dresses, loincloths, headbands, feathered lanced tomahawks, moccasins, face paint, and bone chokers" (54). Latino characters in media are three times more likely to be cast as criminals, are "least articulate, have the heaviest accent, dress less professionally, and talk more about crime and violence than other ethnic groups" (Rivadeneyra 2006, 394). They are viewed as lazy, shiftless, lawless, thieving, immoral, or violent. These images translate into social policy practices. For example, in the United States in 2018, plans appear to be underway to deport Latinos to Mexico, as if all Latinos are here illegally, and as if all Latinos are Mexican—more stereotypes with real-world repercussions.

Stereotypes also circulate about the mentally ill and play a central role in how people conceptualize and respond to those living with mental illness or distress. These include the assumption that people with mental illnesses are dangerous and violent, incapable of paid work or of taking care of themselves, and responsible for becoming and staying ill. The assumption behind this last stereotype includes the idea that those with strong characters will themselves to stay mentally healthy and so those who "succumb" to mental illness are to blame for their condition (Corrigan 2004). This is, then, a moral judgment on the character of certain people. The instituted social imaginary includes such evaluative assumptions such as that people with schizophrenia are dangerous, those with depression just need to pull themselves up by the bootstraps, people with borderline personality disorder are manipulative and attention seeking, and so on. Such stereotypes are part of the instituted social imaginary that legitimizes poor treatment options—especially for the incarcerated mentally ill—and high costs of medications that frequently are unavailable to the poor. They also feed stigma and shame that attend being mentally ill. What clinicians (and laypeople) think we know about the mentally ill is intertwined with ethical judgments as well as subpar ethical treatment of people who appear to have mental disorders. The instituted social imaginary even influences diagnoses. For example, stereotypes of women as manipulative and inappropriately or excessively angry may result in some of them receiving the diagnosis of borderline personality disorder (Potter 2009).

Returning to the opening case of Eleanor, I suggest that the instituted social imaginary the health-care team tapped into in emergency psychiatry operated to entrench Eleanor's lived experiences of gendered, racialized, and class-based oppression. (I say "class-based" because of her homelessness.) Nevertheless, her emergency psychiatry experience differed from that of many trans people. As Arlene Lev explains, for trans people who seek surgical treatment for transitioning, there is only one narrative available for them to present: that they are suffering from some version of gender dysphoria disorder (GDD). Eleanor is not seeking surgery and thus is not concerned with a diagnosis of GDD. Her trans identity may even leave open the possibility of a narrative of gender-nonconformist fluidity. What she *is* seeking in EPS is safety from the attacks and bullying by others for her nonconformity. Other narratives are silenced or erased because if alternative stories are told, one becomes ineligible for treatment. Anyone telling an alternative narrative is thus a gender outlaw (Arlene Istar Lev 2005, 45). Furthermore, Eleanor was refusing gender determination, the process of following legal and medical protocols to receive gender validation. Such validation requires genital reconstruction so that the trans person is repatriated from one side of the gender binary to the other (Westbrook and Schilt 2013). Eleanor was thus not quite even seen as a gender outlaw because she resisted the process required to change genders. Instead, she has only a "ghostly agency," to use a phrase from Jacob Hale's work (2009). I believe Eleanor was genuinely depressed and desperate to be understood as a person at risk because of stereotyping of gender and the stigma attached to being genderqueer. Gender policing occurred even in the emergency room, where the narrative she was trying to tell was ignored, and her voice was silenced. She was interpreted, it would seem, as not really trans but instead as someone who was exploiting racial and sexual identity politics in an attempt to manipulate the health-care system. To be clear, cisgendered Black women are also accused of exploiting and manipulating the health-care system through identity politicking, so one need not be trans to be accused of manipulativity. Returning to Eleanor, I suggest that the epistemic judgment that she was malingering was, at the same time, an ethical judgment that she was not deserving of treatment. Eleanor's encounter with emergency psychiatry, then, was likely to leave her feeling silenced, misunderstood, not credible when speaking about her own experiences, and very much alone. In the next section, I develop these ideas of credibility prejudice and silences and bring in the voices of patients/service users to illustrate how the social imaginary works in clinical environments. This will set up a discussion of what epistemic responsibility might look like in this field.

Silence and Voice

In §4, I explained that the instituted social imaginary reproduces representations, values, stereotypes, and epistemic authority that keep oppressive systems in place. One effect of the power of the social imaginary is that communication is embedded in patterns of structural injustice (see Kukla 2014; Potter 2000). Effective communication depends on active participation of both speakers and listeners. For instance, speakers depend on audiences' understanding of an illocutionary act in order for their communication to be successful (see Kukla 2014; Langton 1993), and listeners depend on speakers to give them good information and to be trustworthy (see Grasswick 2012). Yet as noted in section 3, communicative exchanges are not merely individualistic but patterns at play in social institutions and the imaginary. In this section, I highlight the ways in which epistemic injustice and credibility excesses and deficits are embedded in social institutions. Epistemic responsibility, as Elizabeth Anderson argues, often calls for structural remedies—and not just individual virtues, as Fricker argues—in order to correct for cumulative effects of an oppressive and systemically unequal instituted social imaginary.

Medina argues that epistemic vices that show up in a systematic pattern are arrogance, close-mindedness, and laziness and that epistemic virtues of humility, open mindedness, and curiosity/diligence are necessary in order for resistance to an instituted social imaginary to occur (Medina 2013). Epistemic laziness, for example, is expressed through active ignorance about what others' lives are like and how patterns of domination and subordination are propped up and fueled by an instituted social imaginary, including institutionalized ignorance (see Alcoff 2007; Mills 2007). Communication thus is intertwined with epistemic power and systemic inequalities in the distribution of knowers and not-knowers.

Recent work in epistemology has analyzed ways that issues of credibility, voice, and silencing/silence correlate with hegemonic relations.[4] Indeed, reliance on others' testimony is so basic to everyday life that we often overlook the ways it operates. As Fricker (2007) argues, assessments of credibility follow social patterns of systemic domination and subordination, whereby people in disadvantaged groups are considered to be less credible both because they are viewed as incapable of being knowers and because their character is untrustworthy. Their testimony is considered un-credible and is discounted.

This is a mechanism of silencing. Rae Langton explains it this way:

> If you are powerful, you sometimes have the ability to silence the speech of the powerless. One way might be to stop the powerless from speaking at all. Gag them, threaten them, condemn them to solitary confinement. But there is another, less dramatic but equally effective, way. Let them speak. Let them say whatever they like to whomever they like, but stop that speech from counting as an action. . . . Some kinds of speech acts are unspeakable for women in some contexts; although the appropriate words can be uttered, those utterances fail to count as the actions they were intended to be. (Langton 1993, 299)

Eleanor was silenced in that the meaning she was trying to convey with her utterances was dismissed, discounted, and treated with suspicion. Treating her as an un-credible witness to her own needs and experiences arises out of an instituted social imaginary where ontological commitments in psychiatry collide with stereotypes of gendered and racialized people. In what follows, I will try to make sense of some of the ontological, epistemological, sociopolitical, and ethical values and beliefs that prop up psychiatry in ways that reproduce damage to certain groups of people. In other words, I will be talking about the instituted social imaginary. I'll start with the tensions in epistemology within psychiatry.

As noted in §3, Code argues that knowing other persons is a central project of knowing well (Code 1991, 40). Since genuinely knowing other persons involves a rejection of stereotypes, biases, and close-mindedness, it implicates ethical intersubjective relations at every level. This clearly is the case in clinical fields such as psychiatry, where intersubjective knowing is vital to diagnosis and treatment. Mona Gupta, Simon Goyer, and I have argued that one of the characteristics of psychiatry that makes it different from many other branches of medicine is its dependence on second-person knowing (Gupta, Potter, and Goyer, forthcoming). In making psychiatric diagnoses, it is necessary to grasp the role that this kind of knowing plays in the epistemological process. We argue that the process of belief formation through second-person knowing is not only what psychiatrists *do* but that it is *necessary* to diagnostic reasoning in psychiatry. Second-person knowing, as Code suggests (1991), is paradigmatically an I-you process of knowing where various forms of evidence for beliefs about the other and oneself are explored, responded to, evaluated, discarded, clarified, and so on—by both parties. Communication is directed at a particular person instead of a generic being who instantiates a theory, and its two-way structure in the clinical encounter is a kind of invitation for each to respond to the other and for new shared knowledge to emerge (see Gupta, Potter, and Goyer forthcoming). This epistemic dyadic structure in most clinical encounters involves noticing, acknowledging, and understanding the signifying gestures, body language, comportment, and voice of the patients/service users and invites the psychiatrist to respond.[5] In this way, communicative interaction between the psychiatrist and her particular patient develops.

Third-person EBM can only be one strategy in psychiatric diagnosing because the primary task in psychiatry is not to understand a disease state or a bodily organ but rather to know a person.[6] As Code writes, "The crucial and intriguing fact about knowing people—and the reason it affords insights into problems of knowledge—is that even if one could know all the facts about someone, one would not know her as the person she is" (1991, 40). Code explains that to know another as more than just a collection of facts involves learning about how she perceives the role that various identifications—such as race, ethnicity, politics, class, age, and linguistic abilities—play in her everyday lives, how she experiences the possibilities for freedom and the kinds of responsibilities and burdens she bears, and how she communicates, lives with, and modifies her emotions, commitments, enthusiasms, desires, and interests (Code 1991, 46). Relevant to this point is the work of Devora Shapiro, who writes that "unlike propositional knowledge, one cannot merely read a set of sentences, memorize or even reflect on such statements, and suddenly come to understand and know 'what it's like' to be Latina in the academy, a woman walking down a dark alley, or black in the South" [of the United States] (Shapiro 2012, 69; see also Ben-Yami 1997). Code writes that

> entrenched social power structures generate and sustain certain 'kinds' of knowledge, knowers, and objectification, consigning others to the domain of the unknown, unknowable, constructing reality to fit received knowledge . . . there are real consequences for the ethics and politics of knowing. (Code 2008, 44)

Thus, the norm of intersubjective second-person knowing between clinician and patients/service users is only part of the story. Those very norms for clinician and patient/service-user interactions can be undermined by an ontological commitment to the status of mental disorder as a scientific and ultimately biological dysfunction in the brain. EBM drives much of psychiatric epistemology and reasoning, even though there currently are no diagnostic tests for determining whether or not a person has a particular mental disorder. Many psychiatrists at some point in the diagnostic process draw upon DSM criteria for diagnosing individuals. And although the DSM claims to take into consideration the social context in which a person's mental distress or unusual behavior arises, in practice the instituted social imaginary conceives of mental disorders as individual dysfunctions. For all of these reasons, I suggest that the epistemic commitments that fuel the structure of psychiatry are co-constitutive of an ethics that can harm or help patient/service-users. Anderson's argument that attention needs to be directed not only at individual local injustices but also at the social systems in which they occur is relevant here. Our epistemic system of evaluating the merits and demerits of differently situated knowers may elicit, evaluate, and connect countless communicative interactions in ways that can be unjust even if no particular epistemic interaction is unjust. This occurs, for example, in the larger systematic ways that we train certain people to be inquirers and give uptake and incorporation of some individuals' but not others' contributions to the construction of knowledge (Anderson 2012, 165).[7]

I will lend support for this position by bringing in additional voices of patients/service users. "Because psychiatry deals specifically with "mental suffering," its efforts are always centrally involved with the meaningful world of human reality" (Bracken and Thomas 2010, 219). And while in one sense this is true—psychiatry must engage in meaning making—it is much less clear that the users/survivors themselves are able to control what meaning *they* make of their suffering, distress, or disorder. Interpretation is slanted toward dominant epistemologies, in the clinic as elsewhere within an instituted social imaginary. Jijian Voronka emphasizes the importance of patient/service-user critiques of current practices in psychiatry.

> Those who had hitherto been objects of study (subaltern, disabled, queer, racialized, diasporic) critiqued the ways in which scholarship had historically been produced *on* them rather than *with* or *from* them and in this way sustained Western hegemonic epistemologies. (Voronka 2017, 190; emphasis added)

This need for change is as true for patient/service-user voices as it has been in feminist, anticolonialist, and critical race theory's scholarship. As Jayasree Kalathil and Nev Jones point out, "Service users and survivors continue to represent a tiny fraction of the overall research and evaluation workforce in academia, service delivery, organizations, and the community" (Kalathil and Jones 2017, 183). Few patients/service users are involved in knowledge production and, when they are, typically they are not treated as full participants. By this I mean that despite the idea in some areas of psychiatry of the value of democratic reform and co-participation in knowledge production, patients/service users are hardly ever treated as knowers without qualification. Knowing agents, by definition and by tradition, are objective, rational, and value neutral, whereas long-standing assumptions and stereotypes about mental capacity in service-users tend to reproduce what Kristie Dotson calls "epistemic violence."

Dotson introduced the concept of epistemic violence to describe various ways that oppressed people's testimony can be silenced. Epistemic violence is one of the outcomes of epistemic oppression, which Dotson defines as "persistent epistemic exclusion that hinders one's contribution to knowledge production" (Dotson 2014, 115). Epistemic exclusion occurs when there is an "unwarranted infringement on the epistemic agency of knowers" (115). By "epistemic agency," Dotson means the ability to be persuasive in using shared epistemic resources in a way that participates in knowledge production and revision (115). Epistemic violence occurs when local knowledges of oppressed people are suppressed, discounted, or lost, or when listeners refused to reciprocate in communicative exchanges (Dotson 2011). One form of epistemic violence that Dotson discusses is testimonial quieting, which occurs when the speaker's credibility as a knower is undervalued due to controlling images such as Patricia Hill Collins describes (1991). (On controlling images, see §4.)

We sometimes see this silencing in psychiatry. Eleanor in emergency psychiatry wants to be safe from harm and to find refuge for the night. She does not want to be understood as having a psychiatric illness, as many trans people claim in order to obtain surgery; instead, she seems to be crying out not only to be safe but also to be understood from the perspective of *her* experience and not from the perspective of either a diagnostic gaze or from that of a suspicious health-care team that views some visitors to emergency psychiatry as trying to game the system. Yet she is likely to feel silenced by the encounter.

Epistemic violence may not be done intentionally. Dotson explains that it arises out of "pernicious ignorance," a "maladjusted sensitivity to the truth with respect to some domain of knowledge" (Dotson 2011, 241–242). It is a kind of *situated* ignorance, meaning that it follows from one's social position and/or epistemic location and fosters significant epistemic gaps between different worldviews and knowledges. Eleanor, for example, knows what it is like to be a homeless trans person in fear of bullying and attack from others, while the trained and well-intended health-care team fails to grasp what life would be like for her or others in similar circumstances, largely because their epistemological system is so different. What Eleanor knows about the local world and what the health-care team knows about their patients/service users seem an unbridgeable gap. In other words, epistemic violence is partly explained by the social location of the advantaged and privileged individual or group, where the listener's failure to give uptake to the speaker is done out of ignorance when one could have (and should have) known better. Hence, the ignorance is pernicious even when it is unintentional. Yet as Anderson points out, even epistemic injustices with nonprejudicial causes may require structural remedies because cognitive biases are much more pervasive than we may realize and are difficult to detect in ourselves (Anderson 2012, 169).

These points are important because they highlight the connection between epistemic and ethical responsibility. Pernicious ignorance is bad both because it is epistemically irresponsible and because it is morally wrong—because it occurs as a pattern of violence. It is a form of structural violence and thus harmful because it damages members of a group's ability to speak and be heard. More specifically, it damages one's confidence in her beliefs and her confidence in herself as a knower; it undermines her sense of herself as an epistemic agent (and, hence, her humanity), hinders the development of intellectual courage, and "excludes the subject from trustful conversation" (Dotson 2011; Fricker 2007, 54). Additionally, it causes or contributes to ethical loneliness, a severe sense of isolation one feels when abandoned by humanity, or by those who have power over one's life possibilities (Stauffer 2015, 1). Ethical loneliness and epistemic violence can co-occur: when others are not listening or cannot properly hear one's testimony, when one has difficulty telling the story she most wants to tell in a way that can be heard, one can end up getting pinned to the wrong story or no story at all—and this might make recovery impossible (Stauffer 2015, 32). The failure to listen well—to hear both what another says and to pay attention to what is not said—can dramatically affect how the past impacts the present, because "it affects the human processes of revision" (Stauffer 2015, 2). And being able to revise one's stories is crucial not only to healing (for instance, when one is pinned to the wrong story or no story at all) but to effecting changes in the instituting social imaginary. Returning to Dotson, I suggest that when epistemic violence and ethical loneliness are features of patient/service users' experiences in the clinic, a third-order magnitude of change must occur within our epistemological systems (Dotson 2014). Epistemological systems include

> operative, instituted social imaginaries, habits of cognition, attitudes towards knowers and/or any relevant sensibilities that encourage or hinder the production of knowledge. An epistemological system is a holistic concept that refers to all the conditions for the possibility of knowledge production and possession. As such, epistemological systems are highly resilient. Resilience concerns "the magnitude of disturbance that can be absorbed before the system redefines its structure" (Gunderson 2000, 426, as quoted in Dotson 2014). To say that a given epistemological system is highly resilient is to say that it can absorb extraordinarily large disturbances without redefining its structure. (Dotson 2014, 121)

A third-order change—one of great magnitude—is one that enables individuals and communities to be aware and to reflect on current cultural beliefs and values *and* to challenge the instituted social imaginary in ways that change it collectively. Such changes in the instituted social imaginary are necessary in order not to reproduce damaging and oppressive ignorance.

Anderson suggests that "it would be better to reconfigure epistemic institutions so as to prevent epistemic injustice from arising" than to try to remedy credibility deficits and excesses solely by individualist approaches (Anderson 2012, 171). It would be more productive, she argues, to develop virtues of social institutions themselves rather than only virtues of individual character. While this seems right, it also presents one of the biggest challenges in enacting an instituting social imaginary. To emphasize the difficulties in overcoming epistemic resilience in psychiatry and shifting our ways of thinking regarding patients/service users, I will discuss experiences of voice-hearers—people who are most often treated as psychotic—I will suggest that despite directions of positive change I do not think a third-order change is likely. I close with some remarks on the importance of grasping the co-constitutive properties of the epistemic and the ethical within the clinic.

Jamal, a brown-skinned male in his early twenties, was brought into emergency psychiatry services by his father. The father was becoming increasingly alarmed at Jamal's reports that he could not sleep at night. The reason, Jamal said, is that he was hearing voices that were frightening to him. After interviewing the patient, the attending psychiatrist gave Jamal a diagnosis of psychosis. Jamal strongly protested the diagnosis and explained that, in anticipating that the psychiatrist might say this, he had researched "hearing voices" online and decided that just because he was hearing voices, this did not mean he was ill. Jamal refused medications. The psychiatrist then talked with the father in the presence of Jamal, explaining that first-onset psychosis indicated anti-psychotic medications and that the trajectory of Jamal's illness was likely to be grim.

A critical reading of Jamal's encounters with psychiatry suggests that his voice and his meaning making of voice-hearing experiences is met with epistemic violence and may engender ethical loneliness. Furthermore, it may make him worse—an outcome that seems clearly ethically as well as clinically undesirable if not wrong. Researcher Roz Austin and her team have studied the experiences of voice-hearing individuals. She reports that "a central finding has been the tendency of voice-hearers to suppress, deny or downplay their emotions" (Austin 2015). Yet, for those who have experienced complex trauma, Austin found that "talking about their emotions helps to reduce the frequency and intensity of voice-hearing experiences" (Austin 2015).[8] Because voice-hearing stigmatizes and medicalizes those whose experiences are outside the mainstream, people who are voice-hearing engage in testimonial quieting. This is not to blame those who quiet their own testimony but to recognize the power of the instituted social imaginary as it works in psychiatry to impede rather than to foster healing and recovery. Voice-hearers also may be met with a climate in which testimonial smothering is the only way to protect oneself from belittling epistemic violence when they come to suspect that listeners are not able to receive their testimony on its own grounds.

One strategy to initiate changes in epistemological systems that limit and constrain the experiences of patient/service users through an instituting social imaginary in psychiatry is to normalize the experience of voice-hearing. The assistant manager with whom Austin worked reported that Austin had changed her own understanding of voice-hearing. Austin had said that most people could relate to the experience of hearing their name being called in the absence of an external source. This is itself a voice-hearing experience. The Assistant Manager said that this helped her to place voice-hearing on a spectrum of common human experience, so that this was more normalized. (Austin 2015)

One blogger on hearing psychoses writes that "deep transformative growth could be the norm, if those claiming to be healers" actually understood what was involved in a healing journey from the service user's perspective (anonymous, blogspot, n.d.). And Suzanne Beachy, who lost a son who experienced periods of psychosis, writes that "in a 2005 interview for MedScape, former schizophrenia patient Daniel B. Fisher MD, PhD, was asked about his own journey of recovery from schizophrenia." He replied,

I was lucky—I was able to find a psychiatrist who was able to provide me with many of the principles we find have worked in recovery. He believed in me. When I told him, several months after coming out of the hospital the second time with a diagnosis of schizophrenia, that I wanted to go to medical school and become a psychiatrist, he said he would be at my medical school graduation. And about 7 years later, he was there. (as quoted by Beachy 2012)

Beachy comments that far too much is left to luck: the luck of patients/service users to find a psychiatrist who will help them learn strategies for reducing hearing voices or for healing without drawing on the DSM diagnoses and conventional psychiatric treatments for those who live with mental distress, the repercussions of trauma, or neurological differences.

However, I suspect that strategies like normalizing voice-hearing can be absorbed into psychiatry without substantial challenge. I worry, too, that efforts to include patients/service users in knowledge production—including in research and not just as objects of study—may be undermined by a general will not to hear and not to give uptake to the speakers as knowers in their own right, especially when such knowledge may threaten to undermine a powerful epistemological system. That is, I am skeptical that such strategies are sufficient for *third-order instituting socio-politico-ethico-epistemic changes* in psychiatry. My primary concern is that such measures, in psychiatry, are *removed from ecological thinking*. An engaged instituting social imaginary is a way to challenge psychiatry beyond the efforts of the critical psychiatry movement in that it requires a full contestation of material, ethical, social, political, and legal assumptions, stereotypes, and value systems that influence our responses to others' mental anguish, neurological difference, or experiences of otherness. Movements are underway, but the ethico-epistemological system of psychiatry is highly resistant.

We need ecological thinking if the world is going to be a better place. We cannot be understood independently of our habitat including our complex social, epistemic, ethical, and political systems and disciplinary technologies, and knowing and acting responsibly requires that we engage critically with the "given"—the instituted imaginary—at every level. As Code says, "The guiding image of epistemic normativity is an ecological model of reciprocally informing and sustaining, critically interrogating practices of engaged inquiry" (Code 2006, 90). We are, as Code writes, embodied, intersubjective, intersubjectively connected, and always engaged with our habitat; therefore, epistemic and ethical responsibilities call for us to be in the world in ways that are nonexploitative of either our fellow human beings or of our habitat. Such praxis is as applicable to the field of psychiatry as to any other area of our lives.

Notes

1. Eleanor's story appears in Potter and El-Mallakh (2018) and Potter (2018).

2. The claim that we produce knowledge in epistemic communities does not reduce to relativism, however, as Code's corpus argues.

3. One significant effect of the social imaginary is that it circulates representations and perceptions of groups that tend toward stereotyping and bias. The application and reproduction of stereotypes in our attitudes and treatment of one another can result in significant injustice to individuals and groups. Ann Cudd says that the injustice done through stereotyping suggests that stereotyping activity is immoral (Cudd 2006, 69). It is, thus, crucial to understand that the social imaginary is ethical and political as well as epistemological.

4. See, for example, Larson (2018); Potter (2016, 2017); McGowan, Walder-Biesanz, Rezaian, and Emerson (2016); Laugier (2015); Sanati and Kyratsous (2015); Medina (2013); Gendler (2011); Maitra (2009); Norval (2009); Batchelor (2006); Hornsby and Langton (1998); Collins (1990).

5. Not all clinical encounters are dyadic, of course. Group therapy, for instance, is a more complex sort of intersubjective communication, interpretation and giving uptake to patients/service-users.

6. The important issues about EBM and questions about even what should count as evidence are significant but beyond the scope of this paper. See Gupta, Potter, and Goyer (2018); Gupta (2014); and Tonelli (2006). Biological psychiatry, which increasingly dominates the field, does tend to pay more attention to brain dysfunction and mental disorders. However, this is only one model of psychiatry, and many psychiatrists resist what looks like a reductive approach to caring for people in distress.

7. An example of this is found in the training of people to be psychiatrists (see Potter 2016).

8. It is important to note that not all voice-hearers have experienced trauma.

Works Cited

Alcoff, Linda. 2007. "Epistemologies of Ignorance: Three Types." In *Race and Epistemologies of Ignorance*, edited by Shannon Sullivan and Nancy Tuana, 39–57. Albany: State University of New York Press.

Anderson, Elizabeth. 2012. "Epistemic Justice As a Virtue of Social Institutions." *Social Epistemology: A Journal of Knowledge, Culture and Policy* 26, no. 2:163–173.

Austin, Roz. 2015. "Voice-Hearing and Trauma: Considering the Impact of Stigma." In *The Hearing Voice*, June 9, http://hearingthevoice.org/2015/06/09/voice-hearing-and-trauma-considering-the-impact-of-stigma-by-roz-austin/.

Batchelor, Denise Claire. 2006. "Vulnerable Voices: An Examination of the Concept of Vulnerability in Relation to Student Voice. *Educational Philosophy and Theory* 38, no. 6: 787–800.

Beachy, Suzanne. 2012. "What Happened to Jake?" In *Everything Matters: Beyond Meds*. https://beyondmeds.com/2012/04/23/recoverschizophrenia/.

Bracken, Patrick, and Philip Thomas. 2010. "From Szasz to Foucault: On the Role of Critical Psychiatry." *Philosophy, Psychiatry, and Psychology* 17, no. 3: 219–228.

Code, Lorraine. 2008. "Advocacy, Negotiation, and the Politics of Unknowing." *Southern Journal of Philosophy* 66: 32–51.

Code, Lorraine. 2006. *Ecological Thinking: The Politics of Epistemic Location*. Oxford: Oxford University Press.

Code, Lorraine. 1991. *What Can She Know? Feminist Theory and the Construction of Knowledge*. Ithaca, NY: Cornell University Press.

Code, Lorraine. 1987. *Epistemic Responsibility*. Hanover, NH: University Press of New England.

Hill Collins, Patricia. 1990. *Black Feminist Thought: Knowledge, Consciousness, and the Politics of Empowerment*. Boston: Unwin Hyman.

Corrigan, Patrick. 2004. "How Stigma Interferes with Mental Health Care." In *American Psychologist* 59, no. 7: 614–625.

Cudd, Ann. *Analyzing Oppression*. 2006. Oxford: Oxford University Press.

Dotson, Kristie. 2011. "Tracking Silence, Tracking Epistemic Violence." *Hypatia* 26, no. 2: 236–257.
Dotson, Kristie. 2014. "Conceptualizing Epistemic Oppression." *Social Epistemology* 28, no. 2: 115–138.
Fricker, Miranda. 2009. *Epistemic Injustice: Power and the Ethics of Knowing.* Oxford: Oxford University Press.
Gendler, Tamar. 2011. "On the Epistemic Costs of Implicit Bias." *Philosophical Studies* 156: 33–63.
Grasswick, Heidi. 2014. "Understanding Epistemic Normativity in Feminist Epistemology." In *The Ethics of Belief*, edited by Jonathan Matheson and Rico Vitz, 1–29. Oxford Scholarship Online. Oxford: Oxford University Press.
Grasswick, Heidi. 2012. "Knowing Moral Agents: Epistemic Dependence and the Moral Realm." In *Out from the Shadows: Analytical Feminist Contributions to Traditional Philosophy*, edited by S. Crasnow and A. Superson, 307–338. Oxford: Oxford University Press.
Gupta, M., Potter, N. N., and Goyer, S. 2018. Diagnostic reasoning in psychiatry: Acknowledging an explicit role for intersubjective knowing. *Philosophy, Psychiatry, and Psychology*, forthcoming.
Gupta, Mona. 2014. *Is Evidence-Based Psychiatry Ethical?* Oxford: Oxford University Press.
Hale, C. J. 2009. "Tracing a Ghostly Memory in My Throat." In *"You've Changed" Sex Reassignment and Personal Identity*, edited by Laurie J. Shrage, 43–65. Oxford: Oxford University Press.
Hornsby, Jennifer, and Langton, Rae. 1998. "Free Speech and Illocution." *Legal Theory* 4: 21–37.
Kalathil, Jayasree, and Jones, Nev. 2017. "Unsettling Disciplines: Madness, Identity, Research, Knowledge." *Philosophy, Psychiatry, and Psychology* 23, no. 3/4: 183–188.
Kukla, Rebecca. 2014. "Performative Force, Convention, and Discursive Injustice. *Hypatia* 29, no. 2: 440–457.
Langton, Rae. 1993. "Speech Acts and Unspeakable acts." *Philosophy and Public Affairs*, 22, no. 4:293–330.
Laugier, Sandra. 2015. Voice as Form of Life and Life Form. *Nordic Wittgenstein Review Special Issue: Wittgenstein and Forms of Life* (October): 63–81.
Larson, S. R. 2018. "Survivors, Liars, and Unfit Minds: Rhetorical Impossibility and Rape Trauma Disclosure." *Hypatia* 33, no. 4 (November): 681–699.
Levy, Arlene Istar. 2005. "Disordering Gender Identity: Gender Identity Disorder in the DSM-IV-TR." http://www.haworthpress.com/web/JPHS.
Lewis, Clarence Irving. 1969. *Values and Imperatives: Studies in Ethics.* Stanford, CA: Stanford University Press.
Maitra. Ishani. 2009. "Silencing Speech." *Canadian Journal of Philosophy* 39, no. 2: 309–338.

McGowan, Mary Kate, Llana Walder-Biesanz, Morvareed Rezaian, and Chloe Emerson. 2016. "On Silencing and Systematicity: The Challenge of the Drowning Case. *Hypatia* 31, no. 1: 74–90.

Medina, José. 2013. *The Epistemology of Resistance: Gender and Racial Oppression, Epistemic Injustice, and Resistant Imaginations*. Oxford: Oxford University Press.

Mignolo, Walter. 2012. "Decolonizing Western Epistemology/Building Decolonial Epistemologies." In *Decolonizing Epistemologies: Latina/o Theology and Philosophy*, edited by Isasi-Diaz and Eduardo Mendieta, 19–43. New York: Fordham University Press.

Mills, Charles. 2007. "White Ignorance." In *Race and Epistemologies of Ignorance*, edited by Shannon Sullivan and Nancy Tuana, 11–38. Albany: State University of New York Press.

Norval, Aletta. 2009. "Democracy, Pluralization, and Voice." *Ethics and Global Politics* 2, no. 4: 297–320.

Potter, N. N., and El-Mallakh, R. 2018. "The Interface of Ethics and Psychiatry: A Philosophical Case Consultation on Psychiatric Ethics on the Ground." *Philosophy, Psychiatry, and Psychology* 25, no. 4.

Potter, N. N. 2018. "Voice, Silencing, and Listening Well: Socially Located Patients, Oppressive Structures, and an Invitation to Shift the Epistemic Terrain." In *The Bloomsbury Companion to Philosophy of Psychiatry*, edited by Robyn Bluhm and Şerife Tekin. London: Bloomsbury.

Potter, N. N. 2017. "Epistemic Friction, Affect and Learning to Know Patients Well: Setting New Norms for Medical Education." *European Journal for Person Centered Healthcare* 5, no. 1: 53–63.

Potter, N. N. 2016. *The Virtue of Defiance and Psychiatric Engagement*. Oxford: Oxford University Press.

Potter, N. N. 2009. *Mapping the Edges and the In-Between: A Critical Analysis of Borderline Personality Disorder*. Oxford: Oxford University Press.

Sanati, Abdi, and Kyratsous, Michalis. 2015. Epistemic Injustice in Assessment of Delusions. *Journal of Evaluation in Clinical Practice* 21: 479–485.

Shapiro, D. 2012. "'Objectivity' and the Arbitration of Experiential Knowledge." *Social Philosophy Today* 28, 67–82.

Stauffer, Jill. 2015. *Ethical Loneliness: The Injustice of Not Being Heard*. New York: Columbia University Press.

Voronka, Jijian. 2017. "The Politics of 'People with Lived Experience': Experiential Authority and the Risks of Strategic Essentialism." *Philosophy, Psychiatry, and Psychology* 23, no. 3/4: 189–201.

Tonelli, M. R. 2006. "Integrating Evidence into Clinical Practice: An Alternative to Evidence-based Approaches." *Journal of Evaluation in Clinical Practice* 12, no. 3:248–56.

Walker, Margaret Urban. 2008. *Moral Understandings: A Feminist Study in Ethics*. Oxford: Oxford University Press.

Westbrook, Laurel, and Schilt, Kristen. 2013. "Doing Gender, Determining Gender: Transgender People, Gender Panics, and the Maintenance of the Sex/Gender/Sexuality System." *Gender and Society* 28, no. 1: 32–57.

PART 4

"Human and Nonhuman Life (and) the Complexity of Interrelationships"

Environmental Justice, Climate Change, and Ecological Responsibility

Chapter 10

Rethinking Code's Approach of Ecological Thinking from an Indigenous Relational Perspective

RANJAN DATTA

Although Western[1] research has made significant progress acquiring scientific knowledge using the scientific method in both scientific and social-scientific research, some important questions remain unanswered for me as a participatory community-based action researcher (Datta 2017). These questions include: What does it mean to consider the responsibilities of a researcher to turn research into action in order to protect participants' needs, honor their knowledge and practices, respect and center their perspectives, and empower participants? How are we as researchers positioned in relation to the field of environmental practice? What moves us to take up this particular area of responsibility? What does it mean to understand our responsibilities in environmental practice as a system of reciprocal social relations and ethical practices and as a framework for environmental and social justice? What are a researcher's epistemic responsibilities? How do we create gateways between Western and Indigenous perspectives that are responsible and respectful to the environment and to people (Wilson 2008; Battiste 2013; Kovach 2010; Dei 2011; Smith 2008)? By answering these questions, this chapter brings together Lorraine Code's *ecological thinking* approach and Indigenous perspectives into a relational framework that results in a new worldview that blends Indigenous and Western worldviews, rather than making changes within the Western worldviews: a relational framework that can transform our research through responsible actions. The main aim of this chapter is to develop an epistemological framework for research that can build on and respect relationships with Indigenous people and Indigenous ways of knowing and that endorses responsible action to protect Indigenous people, their culture, and their land-water rights.

Lorraine Code's ecological thinking approach offers us an example of how to take responsibility in the form of a reimagined epistemology that provides physical, natural, and social scientists alike the practical and conceptual tools to engage more constructively with social and ethical considerations and to improve the quality of their scientific methods. Drawing on both feminist philosophies of science and the science of ecology, Code encourages a movement toward ecological thinking, a contextually situated, imaginative, and socially aware way of building knowledge that defies the traditional Western *epistemological monoculture*, which characterizes knowledge making as a form of mastery over the natural world.

In this chapter, I discuss how and why Indigenous relational perspectives on Code's work in ecological thinking *help us redefine our understanding of environmental knowledge and* take responsibility to protect our environment (Datta 2017). The first section of this chapter is on theory and organized into a three-part discussion, including: 1) an Indigenous relational framework, 2) Code's ecological thinking as a relational framework, and 3) connections between the two frameworks, focusing on how an Indigenous relational framework widens and deepens ecological thinking. In the second section of the chapter, I discuss a case study with a Laitu Khyeng Indigenous Community in Chittagong Hill Tracts (CHT), Bangladesh, that employs relational participatory action research (PAR) as research methodology. I reflect on how and why an ecological thinking approach is useful for rethinking our positioning as researchers, and I discuss how this inspires us to take responsibility in our practices and research for incorporating participatory ways of thinking, acting, and protecting our environment.

Rethinking Code's ecological thinking from a relational theoretical perspective could be useful in several ways, including helping to reshape researchers' positionality in the research, to unite theory with participatory inquiry, and to help us take responsibility for environmental justice. For instance, I learned from this case study that relational approaches to research are also helpful for situating the researcher as a participant in the research process. This case study's research participants inspired me as a researcher to learn the six core values for research within Indigenous communities: (1) to understand and follow traditional protocols and integrity, (2) to engage in learning how to honor Indigenous knowledge and practice, (3) to show respect, (4) to follow equity, (5) to contribute to Indigenous survival and protection, and (6) to take responsibility. Thus, depending on the views of the particular community, it may be critical that Indigenous ways of knowing are fully integrated into the research design and that the research is both participatory and beneficial to the community. Code's long-standing call for researchers to take epistemic responsibility "to engage in ways that put his/her subjectivity also on the line; to assume responsibility for what and how he/she claims to know" (Code 2001, 275) connects with my decision to choose PAR. It is a methodology that unites theory, participatory inquiry, and social justice through researcher collaboration with community members. PAR uses participatory engagement to decolonize and provide diverse solutions for resolving problems from a relational perspective (Datta et al. 2015; Wilson 2008). As an approach, PAR appears particularly well suited to environmental justice, so I used this case study to put theories of environmental action research into practice and to consider the implications of their continued development. I show how an exclusively Western perspective is problematic for an Indigenous community and how local Indigenous people see their everyday actions as an epistemic responsibility for protecting the environment in their community. Finally, this chapter relies on this case study to help us better understand and critique Code's work.

Indigenous Perspectives in a Relational Framework

What is the meaning of relationality from Indigenous perspectives? How can one imagine a relational framework within Indigenous worldviews, where everything is relational and everything has agency (Little Bear 2016; Wilson 2008), where nothing exists outside of relationships, and humans and nonhumans (both living and nonliving things) are mutually interconnected (Rice, Riewe, and Oakes 2005)? For many Indigenous communities in North America and South Asia, ongoing relationships create a person's identities, and tending to them is a person's responsibility (Roy 2000; Wilson 2008). North American Indigenous scholars Gregory Cajete (2005) and Leroy Little Bear (2016) describe how a foundation of relationships guides not only knowing and doing but also philosophy and ethics in communities. Little Bear (2016) notes that North American Indigenous peoples' metaphysics is about flux and similar to quantum physics, contrary to the reductionist, material-based ideas of Western enlightenment; Indigenous metaphysics is about energy and therefore about relationships rather than particles. Energy is found in everything, and this means everything is animate—plants, animals, rocks, stars, and so on.

Indigenous worldviews emphasize the relationality in the saying, "All my relations human, animal, plant, spiritual and elemental" (Lovern 2008, 4). In the past, Indigenous children were raised to respect and care for the land in situ (Bowers 2001, 2010; Deloria 2001; Ritchie 2015; Wildcat 2001). As Deloria (2001, 2) notes, "The best description of Indian metaphysics was the realization that the world, and all its possible experience, contributed a social reality, a fabric of life in which everything had the possibility of intimate knowing relationships because, ultimately, everything was related."[2] Cajete (2005, 70) articulates a similar argument about how the notion of relationality is at the heart of Indigenous teaching and learning: "*Mitakuye Oyasin* (we are all related) is a Lakota phrase that captures the essence of tribal education because it reflects the understanding that our lives are truly and profoundly connected to other people and the physical world." Cajete frames learning as a process of coming into resonance with the interconnection of oneself, the community, and the natural world in order to support the axiological principle of pursuing life and holding it sacred. Scholars from sub-Saharan Africa (see Musopole 1994; Sindima 1990; Tutu 1999) discuss relationality in terms of the traditional and enduring concept of *ubuntu/ umunthu*: the relational rationality weaves future, past, present, nature, and culture together with mutual dependency on each other.

What Is Lorraine Code's Ecological Thinking Approach?

Lorraine Code's concept of ecological thinking is situational, relational, complex, and multidimensional. Ecological thinking "does not reduce to a set of rules or methods; it may play out differently from location to location; but it is sufficiently coherent to be interpreted and enacted across widely diverse situations" (Code 2006, 5). Code begins by constructing the approach of ecological thinking as an epistemology born of anecdotal evidence, testimonials, and case studies in situ rather than limited by controls or a laboratory setting. Code's (2015, 5) approach of epistemic responsibility, which is connected with ecological thinking, leads to a fundamental question: "*Who do we think we are?*" This question makes us rethink our responsibilities toward ourselves, our community, and our community's ethics, values, and cultural practices. Considering our epistemic responsibilities helps us to restore, renew, and preserve the world for others who come after us and for those who live alongside us. The question "*Who* do we think we are?" is a political-ontological challenge to the Western self-oriented ontology. It invites an important debate about the concept of *we*: "Whoever we are, [we] know quite well who we are and, by extension, know the scope and limits of the rights, needs, and entitlements consequent upon claiming, and living, such identities" (Code 2016, 46). Code's (2006, 24) ecological thinking approach endows epistemic practices with "a large measure of responsibility" in that they are "about imagining, crafting, articulating, and endeavoring to enact principles of ideal cohabitation." As she explains, ecological thinking "is not simply thinking about ecology" or about "the environment" but rather a "revisioned mode of engagement with knowledge, subjectivity, politics, ethics, science, citizenship, and agency that pervades and reconfigures theory and practice" (Code 2006, 5). Code aims for not merely reconfiguring the approach of ecological thinking, but for a re-imagining of the "whole way of thinking about the diverse positionings and responsibilities of knowing subjects, the 'nature' of knowledge" (Code 2006, 61).

Ecological thinking is not only knowing differently but also behaving differently by switching from *they* thinking to *we* thinking. It is a call for a reconceived ontology and an ethics of place sufficiently sensitive to address specificities and particularities in ways that respect and honor Indigenous people. Australian Indigenous people's *respect for the sacredness of Uluru* compels us to rethink our sense of self, place, and ownership. Code's *Ecological Thinking: The Politics of Epistemic Location* provides a road map for ecologists who are looking for ways to situate their research ethically and politically, as well as scientifically. It offers multiple openings for thinking about collaborative interdisciplinary research or theoretical conversations across disciplines. Ecological thinking in everyday relational practice is about moving away from self-owning to collective owning.

Code's (2016) question *Who do we think we are?* aims to displace self-promotion, self-thinking, and self-doing through *ecological thinking*. She agrees that it is easy to imagine it and to think and speak about it but hard to understand and difficult to practice. She argues that thinking about *who* we think we are can help us to consider how best to live, take responsibility, and critically view the concepts of human and more-than-human as part of *we*; it can unsettle many of the self-oriented expectations that inform the "our" in our everyday thoughts and actions: if the self is relational, the individual becomes part of *we*. One of the benefits of ecological thinking is its foundation in the process of scientific inquiry. Rather than focusing on ways to explain the everyday relational practices and social significance of research retroactively, Code demonstrates ways to include social considerations in empirically based scientific methodologies and in the definition of problems. Ecological thinking addresses everyday relational practices and relational ways of doing that are important for Indigenous ways of knowing and doing.

If we approach ecological thinking relationally, it means that we cannot separate our actions from our thoughts and practices (Code 2015). Relationality in ecological thinking considers how everything relates to each other, to the natural environment, and to the spiritual world, and these relationships bring about interdependencies. For instance, Code (2015, 58) says that understanding the meaning of *we* requires "resisting the pride of undue self-promoting, requires standing back and finding no lessening of 'self' in acknowledging places or areas of not knowing, even of ignorance." Ecological thinking as a relational epistemological approach, then, does not adopt a specific standpoint according to Code. Rather, our epistemology should be relationally situated, flexible, and becoming (Code 2015). Feminist scholar Andrea Doucet (2018, 75), writing about Code, further argues that "meanings and practices of epistemic responsibilities, as well as situated knowledges, have shifted across time." Thus, applying ecological thinking to everyday practices can enlighten our understanding of how to work together to "[re-]shape and govern possibilities of being, thinking, acting; how they [our] legitimate or preclude certain epistemic and other human relations, to one another and to the physical/national/conceptual world; how philosophical systems reflect and reinforce these imaginaries" (Code 2006, 7). In the following section, I explain why Code's ecological thinking approach needs to be rethought from an Indigenous relational approach.

Bridging Lorraine Code's Ecological Thinking with an Indigenous Relational Framework

Imagining a relational framework built from Indigenous and non-Indigenous worldviews, in this case the pairing of Indigenous perspectives on relationality and Lorraine Code's *ecological thinking approach*, can transform our thoughts and actions into responsibilities (Rice, Riewe, and Oakes 2005; Wilson 2008) and have a substantial influence on our actions and our understanding of environmental issues.

Rethinking Code's ecological thinking through a wider relational framework can strengthen this groundbreaking work, which significantly shifted epistemologies and research practices through its call for knowledge-making practices that emphasize the inherent sociality of knowers. Code's work on ecological thinking challenges long-standing assumptions about the subjects and objects of knowledge, undoing orthodox epistemic ontologies of knowers, knowledge, and knowing relationships. I explore Code's ecological thinking in this section as a relational, critical, and collaborative approach to understand Indigenous epistemologies (i.e., how knowledge can be known).

Relational. A relational perspective is important for understanding Code's notion of epistemic responsibility. She argues that ethics not only studies how we live, how we construct and apply moral rules, and how we examine ethical choices, but it also centers on relational understandings of how and what we think. Code (1987, 95) strongly connects epistemic responsibility with ethical responsibility, writing that "ethical responsibility is founded upon epistemic responsibility, even if it is not identifiable with it. One who has not been scrupulous in knowing cannot be scrupulous in doing." She thus expands the scope of relational understanding and widens the discussion of relational practices.

Learning. Learning in *ecological thinking,* is relationally interdependent. Code's approach of epistemic responsibility connects people with each other. She writes, "One of the most important ways in which people come to know is by learning from others" (Code 1987, 168), inviting us to understand relationships by asking questions such as: Do I really know what I think I know? Do I know enough to act (as I do)? What don't I know? What are the moral consequences of my knowing/ignorance? Ecological thinking offers a model of knowing at once situated in and in relation to diverse aspects of the human and other-than-human world, interwoven with moral, sociopolitical, and epistemological issues and committed to exposing and critiquing the effects of power–knowledge intersections, be they benign, malign, or equivocal (Code 2006, 21).

Critical. Code's ecological thinking highlights how relational ways of thinking and acting represent a continuous critical process that helps to liberate the self. This critical perspective of our epistemic responsibilities challenges individualist Western understandings of self-liberation, separation, selfhood, and ownership that separate the individual from their social responsibilities—the Western "way of relating to the world which corresponds to a certain model of selfhood . . . conceived as that of the individual who stands apart from an alien other and denies his own relationship to and dependency upon this other" (Code 1993, 142).

Collaborative. With ecological thinking and its repudiation of individualism in favor of collaborative, interactive, engaged deliberative knowing, it need not be thus fraught, precisely because of an ongoing openness to a "counter sentence," discussion, and negotiated processes of listening and responding. Code's (2015, 46) recent work illuminates how ecological thinking *is* also a collaborative learning process that encourages knowledge making. For example, "Philosophers, social theorists, climate scientists, ecological activists, and teachers and educators in school and universities, who are committed to promoting ecological and social justice across diverse populations, and engaging knowledgeably with ecological questions." Code cautions us that a collaborative space is not, however, a one-size-fits-all concept; collaborative learning is multiple, complex, and situational, balancing analyses of the human and other-than-human.

Collaborative approaches potentially promote deep engagement between researchers and participants (Datta 2015). They serve to invite diverse groups to continually learn from one another about how each approaches the very question of knowledge in the first place and how these different approaches can work together to better steward and manage the environment and natural resources. Collaborative approaches to knowledge creation can and should be engaged in collaboration with Western and intersectional approaches.

The collaborative aspect of ecological thinking can be connected with Indigenous and non-Indigenous scholars' relational perspectives. For instance, Indigenous scholars Wilson (2008) and Kovach (2010) and non-Indigenous scholars Murdoch (2006) and Whatmore (2006, 2013) all suggest that the actions of humans and nonhumans are political and not merely relational and collaborative. Therefore, through relational ways of thinking and doing, we can take a strong political stand and opportunities to take responsibility for our actions.

Why Do We Need Bridging?

Bridging Lorraine Code's ecological thinking with an Indigenous relational framework opens up many possibilities for environmental research and practices, including those related to biodiversity, human and nonhuman relationships, spirituality, conservation, and local community empowerment.

An Indigenous relational framework provides a tentative manifesto of today's environmental thinking in action (Datta 2015). In particular, it challenges the idea that we are facing the end of uniquely Western ways of looking at the environment and, rather, suggests that new relational framework practices are already growing worldwide (Rice, Riewe, and Oakes 2005). North American Indigenous scholars Rice, Riewe, and Oakes (2005) discuss why we need a relational framework to bridge Western and Indigenous research methodologies. They argue that in a relational framework, "the acceptance of Aboriginal knowledge on the part of the dominant cultures makes it possible for Aboriginal and Euro-Western knowledge systems to work together to maintain a harmonious relationship between humans and the environment" (33). Rice and colleagues note that Western scientists conducting environmental research must understand wildlife movements and accept traditional environmental knowledge based on Indigenous culture and practices as valid. Western research can benefit from Indigenous ways of knowing, he explains, because "Aboriginal people understand a Euro-western scientific method of evaluating environmental knowledge because our [Aboriginal] philosophy embodies scientific knowledge plus moral and spiritual realms of knowledge; however, Euro-Western scientists find difficulties in incorporating Aboriginal philosophy with their science" (33). Rice and colleagues argue that Indigenous perspectives in a relational framework integrate spiritual beliefs for both humans and the environment. They therefore suggest that we (both Indigenous and Western populations) need to be more conscious of our environmental issues; we need to work together to develop a harmonious relationship between our two ways of knowing, "which is needed for both cultures to work together to protect the environment" (33).

Western environmental research and its scientific goals are challenged by a relational framework (Datta 2017), which invites a chorus of critiques about the reliability of scientific research methods; the politics inherent in the *recognition* of Indigenous scholarship; the disconnection of research from practice; the prioritization of Western research over Indigenous research; the murkiness of researcher responsibilities; historical and ongoing racism toward Indigenous people; the misinterpretation of Indigenous environmental practices; and the hierarchical ranking of supposed binaries such as disciplinary/interdisciplinary research, nature/culture, and human/nonhuman (Datta 2015, 2016).

Rejecting the objective of reaching a consensus on one solution for all environmental problems, a relational framework makes it evident that multiple local solutions are necessary for different places and people and that we must take a political stand for community knowledges and practices.

A relational framework also decolonizes Western ways of thinking and doing (Latour 2005; Rice, Riewe, and Oakes 2005) through unlearning and relearning processes (Battiste 2000). Relearning processes advance multiple ways of knowing, such as the nonrepresentational, nondiscursive, and material-oriented views of environmental thinking and practices performed in local communities. The benefits of decolonization are numerous, as they can

- advance multiple alternative, nonrepresentational views of environmental thinking and practice in local spaces;
- offer a political bridge between Western and Indigenous/local ways of solving problems with Indigenous/local people's knowledge and practices at the center when exploring solutions;
- offer a standpoint for revealing the entanglement between local knowledge, practices, and solutions. These processes are continuously changing based on local people's needs and expectations;
- engage socio-natural-technological networks in solving environmental problems by adopting multiple means and processes;
- move from universal understanding and actions when solving environmental problems to relational and purpose-oriented solutions; and
- build continuous, multiple, practical, and material negotiations between different networks of peoples.

In sum, ecological thinking with a relational framework demonstrates how new ways of thinking and doing are increasingly significant for the local community and their environment (Datta 2015). Relational frameworks interrogate, analyze, and support local people and their everyday practices; they constitute a process of becoming in order to reasonably and practicably achieve the goals of local people and their interest in protecting the environment. A relational framework does not seek universal and/or fixed solutions. Rather, it seeks the transformation of research approaches and practices into vibrant, committed, challenging, and inventive practices that will unveil new possibilities for, with, and by local people. In the following case study (the Laitu Khyeng Indigenous Community in Chittagong Hill Tracts (CHT), Bangladesh), I explain how rethinking ecological thinking from everyday relational practice can help us to be more responsible in both understanding and acting.

Case Study: Ecological Thinking and Everyday Relational Practice in the Laitu Khyeng Indigenous Community in Chittagong Hill Tracts (CHT), Bangladesh

I learned from a PAR methodology how to foster change through community-based participation, building from participants' everyday local practices, culture, and relational and spiritual knowledge (Datta et al., 2015). Although connections between ecological Indigenous perspectives were only made after my field research (i.e., 2006 to 2016), I then learned that there are many similarities between Indigenous and ecological thinking approaches to methodology and epistemology. Both draw on and advocate rethinking epistemic responsibilities and offer new possibilities for both Western-situated (i.e., Code's ecological thinking) and Indigenous epistemologies. Both also explore how a relational framework widens and deepens ecological thinking. Using PAR, this study explains why and where environmental issues become a matter of concern and how to rebuild environmental sustainability recognizing their situatedness focusing on the everyday practices that connect humans and nonhumans (Datta 2015). Although a relational framework represents a transformation of Western and Indigenous perspectives, it does not propose substantive epistemological or political theories, nor does it provide a list of "must-do things" or values to be adopted, and it does not define any ethical norms for humans to enact in dealing with nonhumans (Datta 2017; Wilson 2008). Rather it reveals the reasons why environmental disputes emerge.

The case study I will discuss in the next section presents findings from part of a larger study that explored Indigenous perspectives on land-water management and sustainability in the Laitu Khyeng Indigenous Community in CHT, Bangladesh, using PAR. The researcher, research topic, research questions, data analysis, and report writing were chosen or undertaken collaboratively by four Indigenous community participant researchers and a university researcher, in accordance with ongoing guidance from Indigenous elders and knowledge holders. The research was considered part of the collective responsibility of the researchers to prioritize Indigenous knowledge and everyday practices as authentic and scientific knowledge for the Indigenous community, which has been living sustainably on their land for centuries (Datta et al. 2015, 2016). The study used five data collection methods, including traditional sharing circles, individual story sharing, photovoice, participant observation, and commonplace books.

Western Meanings of Management

The study's research data analysis addressed issues directly corresponding to the question, *To what extent were the community members affected by introduced environmental practices*,[3] such as those promoted by the government, NGOs, commercial companies, and multinational corporations? This question reveals how the research team endeavored to explore the community's perceptions of outsider environmental practices, rather than directly examining outsiders' environmental ideas and policies. In addition to the use of sharing circles and individual story sharing, data were drawn from photovoice pieces and individual stories shared by elders. The results illuminate the community's perceptions of different outsiders' (Bangladeshi government and nongovernmental agencies) environmental practices enacted within the community. Participants often recounted that rather than contributing to the community's practices, the Bangladeshi government and nongovernment agencies' environmental management projects engendered feelings of exploitation, frustration, fear, and danger, thereby posing a formidable challenge to the community.

We wanted to know: why did the Bangladeshi government and nongovernment land, water, and forest management projects become painful for the community? In exploring this question, we heard many compelling stories from elders, knowledge holders, leaders, and youth participants; these stories, discussed below, express the community's views on particular management projects, along with the consequences suffered by the community. The projects most commonly referenced in the data include the government administrative structure, the brickfields, the tobacco plantations, the profitable lumber plantations, and the reserve forest projects.

The Imposition of the Bangladeshi Administrative Structure

This section answers a question that is vital to ecological thinking: why are everyday relational practices significant for understanding environmental injustice? For instance, the imposition of the current state administrative structure on the community's traditional administrative structure is described by participants as a form of oppression. One leader explained that while the Chittagong Hill Tracts (CHT) traditional Indigenous administrative structure started to weaken during British colonial rule, they have been more aggressively undermined during the Bangladeshi governance period (1971–present). It is clear from conversations with community elders and knowledge holders that the Bangladeshi government, through the state administrators, has helped outsiders to appropriate and control Indigenous communities' natural resources, management rights, and decision-making power.

LUMBER PLANTATION

The Bangladeshi government's second-largest environmental management project discussed by the participants consists of a group of for-profit lumber plantations. Driven by government forest management agendas, the plantation project was introduced primarily to appropriate Indigenous natural forestland to generate profits for outside interests. An elder explained that the plantation owners and supporters participated directly in the forced seizure of the community's forest and its recultivation. As one community knowledge holder explained:

> We had hundreds of hilly mountains, we used to cultivate *jhum* on these lands and we did not have a food crisis in our community. The outsider Bangali people came to our land and took ownership of our Mother-Land because of our lack of knowledge of the Bangladesh land laws. The Bangali administrators are not interested in knowing the Indigenous peoples' relationships with our Mother-forestland.

TOBACCO PLANTATION

The production of tobacco was discussed by participants as the third-largest cash crop introduced into the community. A number of national and multinational companies have established operations within the community, including the British American Tobacco Company, Abul Tobacco Company, and Virginia Tobacco Company. Elders said that the national and multinational tobacco companies have forcibly taken over the community's fertile plain lands in order to produce tobacco for export. Participants explained that most of the tobacco companies played an active role in not only destroying the fertile, cultivated land but also in spreading disease and increasing deforestation in the community. According to Elder and *Karbary*[4] Kosomo Prue Khyeng, tobacco plantations in the community have created significant poverty through their destructive practices. He explained how some community members got involved with the tobacco plantation projects and became impoverished as a result: "Most of the families obtained loans in a crisis moment, and/or sometimes tobacco companies have forcibly given loans with high interest." These are loans they cannot repay every year because the tobacco harvest gets less plentiful for lack of high fertilizers; and there are health hazards during the tobacco preparation process.

Brickfield

The private Brickfield Project is identified in the data as one of the major and most pernicious projects in the community. The community identified it as one of the largest wood-burning brickfield manufacturers within the Bandarban district. Knowledge holder Ching Shao Khyeng detailed the significant consequences of this land appropriation in the following statement:

> Sixty percent of our community plain lands food sources came from the Brickfield area prior to the Brickfield Company. We used to cultivate paddy crops, vegetables, and fish in this area. Most of us did not have a food crisis in our family. Now we have lost both our land and our forest for this project, and we cannot use our water as the water is now polluted as a result of using the water in the Brickfield.

The Brickfield Project has led to considerable poverty in the community. The research team observed that the community's livestock grazing areas have significantly diminished through the development of the brickfield industry. One account of this loss, provided by schoolteacher Mongla Prue Khyeng, highlights the decline of domestic animals, such as cattle, pigs, sheep, ducks, and chickens.

Impacts of Western Management and Indigenous Responsibilities

These Western (i.e., state government) environmental practices affected different forms of community and environmental colonization, including land grabbing, displacement, poverty, environmental destruction, and a water crisis. For instance, Elder Basa Khyeng, as well as other Elders and community leaders outlined how various agencies' management projects diminishing the community members' ability to sustainably provide for themselves and lead full lives. The elders and knowledge holders emphasized that forced migration and invisible displacement contributed especially to women's disempowerment, and traditional species extraction resulted in the loss of traditional species diversity.

Traditional Meanings of Management

Elder Kosomo Prue Khyeng stated that the purpose of sustainability was "to protect our traditional cultivation culture," which exemplifies why it is the most important issue to address when discussing the community's concept of responsibilities. According to the elder, the community's traditional cultivation culture serves several roles: to protect nature, encourage everyday relational and spiritual practices, preserve ancestors' stories, and fulfill everyday needs. After having talked to the community's elders and knowledge holders, Indigenous coresearcher Mathui Ching Khyang explained in her book why their traditional cultivation culture is fundamental to environmental sustainability. She wrote,

> Our traditional cultivation is our relationship with mountain, sun (i.e., it rises every day in our Mother mountain's lap. It delights and inspires us like an ongoing flame), land, culture, history, and traditions. Our traditional cultivation is not only for our people, but also for our relationships. (2013, 10)

In addition to acknowledging traditional cultivation culture as a community's responsibility, participants in the study grounded their perceptions of sustainability in a number of interrelated responsibilities: spiritual practices, ancestor stories, voicing community needs, and dreams, hopes, sounds, and smells. During the data-gathering process, participants advanced recommendations to help alleviate problems, specifically advocating particular actions and interventions (both collective and individual).

Although the Laitu Khyeng Indigenous Community's land-water management practices have been sustainable for centuries, the Bangladeshi state government does not recognize these Indigenous environmental practices, seeing them as unscientific and unprofitable to those outside to the Indigenous community. As such, the government introduced various unwanted development projects in the community, mostly for non-Indigenous outsiders' profit and interest, without the people's consent and engagement (Adana 2004; Chapola 2009; Datta 2015, 2016, 2017).

The data revealed that youth in the community were active and hopeful, driven by a dream of achieving sustainability goals by fulfilling a series of key responsibilities. They believe that now it is a critical moment for reclaiming their voices and rights and that if they are unsuccessful, then the youth of future generations will soon lose their identity as well as the possibility for a sustainable livelihood in their community.

This case study illuminates how exclusively Western (i.e., the Bangladeshi government and nongovernmental agencies') meanings of environmental management led to exploitation, frustration, fear, and danger for the Indigenous community and thereby posed a formidable challenge to the community. The Indigenous worldviews, by contrast, see all management entities in a relational context and stress interdependency and justice for all life-forms. Responsible environmental management aims to respect, preserve, and maintain knowledge, innovations, and practices of Indigenous and local communities embodying traditional lifestyles relevant for the conservation and sustainable use of biological diversity. Indigenous ways of approaching environmental management are oriented according to Indigenous traditional ways of knowing, practicing, and informing cultivation culture.

Discussion

The case study in the previous section explicitly shows why and how we need to rethink Code's ecological thinking approach from an Indigenous relational perspective, which is complex and diverse (Datta et al. 2015). This relational form of epistemic responsibility challenges Western/current forms of colonization. This research shows that our relational responsibilities extend beyond our human interests, perspectives, and well-being. Through respect, preservation, and maintenance of knowledge, innovations and practices of Indigenous and local communities, our elders, and knowledge holders explained why Laitu Khyeng youth consider relational responsibilities part of caring, respecting, and honoring both humans and the environment. From a relational perspective, responsibility includes different forms of accountability. Altman (2004) suggests that a relational approach is a holistic approach to how people address local and regional development and, in the thoroughness of their approach, ensure environmental justice. During the analysis part of the study, three themes emerged that resonate with ecological thinking: researcher responsibilities, Indigenous epistemic responsibilities, and recognizing and challenging Western perspectives. I understand the themes through the concept of relationality and the process of achieving resonance between oneself, one's community, and the surrounding ecosystem. The guiding quality of this resonance, as Cajete (2005) emphasizes, is the pursuit and enrichment of life.

Researcher Responsibilities

As a community-based scholar, activist, and researcher, responsibility for me means being relationally accountable (Datta 2015; Wilson 2008), which a number of Indigenous studies (Datta 2016; Kovach 2010; Smith 2008; Wilson 2008) argue entails being accountable as a researcher alongside participants, honoring and respecting participants' knowledge and practice, empowering tools, and centering the participants' voices. Indigenous scholar Shawn Wilson (2008, 8) clearly states the importance of relational accountabilities in our research, maintaining that "idea[s] cannot be taken out of this relational context and still maintain its shape." A number of non-Indigenous scholars have also focused on relational responsibilities. For instance, John Law states, "Nothing has reality or form outside the enactment of . . . relations" (Law 2007, 1). Relationships between humans and nonhumans are regarded as capable of motivated action. Whatmore (2013) explains that relationships have action and agency. Agency not only comes from our everyday relationships but also from our responsibility to rethink our actions (Wilson 2008). As a researcher, I took a strong political position in favor of the participants' needs, knowledge, and culture: elders and knowledge holders counted as researchers, and community knowledge about their environment and cultural practices was included as scientific knowledge.

Learning about responsibility from the Indigenous community helped to transform and inspire me to decolonize my position as a researcher and an educator. As researchers, we need to undergo a significant transformation and fully adopt the range of new antiracism and participant-oriented research approaches (Dei 2013, 2011; Smith 2005; Wilson 2008). This decolonizing process empowered me to develop a collective research model incorporating action for, within, and by the participant's community. Within this collaborative framework, participants and researchers cannot be separated. They are politically and spiritually related. Similarly Code's ecological thinking approach offers important and timely suggestions on the aspects of responsibilities by saying that

> I am suggesting that the precepts, principles, practices and ideologies of orthodox epistemology are not merely reconfigured but reimagined, rethought all the way through, when they are thought ecologically. It is not that some pieces of an epistemological system are rejigged, some cast-offs reclaimed, and some rejects recycled from a misremembered romantic and symbiotic era, but a whole way of thinking about the diverse positionings and responsibilities of knowing subjects. (2006, 61)

Redefining researcher responsibilities in research, Code's ecological thinking calls for a new epistemology to be taken up by good empiricist thinkers.

These mutual relationships between participants and researchers helped me to develop care and respect for the participants' knowledge and practices. The research project showed me that building a trusting relationship with participants is a researcher's first and most important responsibility.

Indigenous Responsibilities in Ecological Thinking

Environmental justice has become an important aspect of understanding many Indigenous communities' battles over environmental conditions and sacred sites (Korteweg, Gonzalez, and Guillet 2010). A number of studies argue that indigenizing environmental justice means actively taking responsibility for recognizing, centering, validating, and honoring the Indigenous rights, values, epistemologies or worldviews, knowledges, languages, and stories of the people of the Land (Korteweg, Gonzalez, and Guillet 2010; Simpson 2008). Although current forms of Western environmental practices have a negative impact on Indigenous culture, knowledge, and spirituality, as well as environmental sustainability and species diversity, the Laitu Khyeng Indigenous Community is not without hope. They understand their responsibility to protect Indigenous culture, environments, and traditions of sustainability. The research results illuminate why and how community youth wish to protect traditional land and water management practices in order to achieve environmental justice.

Indigenous people have a broad knowledge of how to live and sustainably manage their environment (Baker 2003). Many participants said that their responsibilities involved collective actions, expectations, and inspirations, which are interconnected with their traditional land and water practices, their identities, and their lives. Elders suggested taking responsibility for protecting Indigenous cultivation culture, knowledge, and practice.

Relational ways of thinking and working with land and water can enrich environmental justice initiatives for the local community (Escobar 2010). While relational community activities are important for celebrating cultural rituals, they also offer a significant bridge across cultures. My Indigenous coresearcher participants and I have seen that children's and youth's relational land activities can encourage mutual sustainability processes such as intergenerational responsibility (learning between children and youth; children, youth, and adults; adults and elders; and elders and children), and cross-cultural responsibility (learning from and within different cultures). We also observed that children and youth learned from their land-based activities and traditional stories from their elders and knowledge keepers.

In defining environmental sustainability, Code's ecological thinking approach offers a similar responsibility for what and how we know, on an understanding of responsibility that is as epistemological as it is ethical and political. In this study, participants also explained and suggested how to understand their environment and take responsibility. For instance, participants explained their perceptions of environmental sustainability from everyday practices, including traditional cultivation, spiritual practices, and ancestor stories.

Recognizing and Protesting Colonization

A number of Indigenous and non-Indigenous studies (Adnan 2004; Smith 2008; Nadasdy 2011; Simpson 2010) claim that recognizing and protesting ongoing colonization is a significant responsibility of Indigenous research. This research project took a bold step in that direction by showing how current environmental practices and colonization are interconnected. For instance, valuing outsider (i.e., non-Indigenous) knowledge over Indigenous knowledge was viewed as having a significant colonial impact on the Laitu Khyeng Indigenous Community's traditional land management practices.

Indigenous scholars Tuck and Yang (2012) from North America and Roy (2001) from South Asia, show how a colonial-settler framework privileges settler knowledge over Indigenous knowledge. Other researchers have argued (Berkes 1999, 2009; Roy 2000) that outsider management practices on Indigenous land can be a significant barrier to sustainable Indigenous practices because the perspective that land is profitable, static, and exploitable justifies its disembodiment from the community's social life and from local connections. Participants in this research project argued that Indigenous understandings and practices were significantly undermined by outsider (governmental and nongovernmental) land policies and projects. For example, Elder Basa Khyeng characterized these different environmental practices as indisputably profit driven, detached, and sure in their methods. Adnan (2004, 72) draws similar conclusions, stating that in the CHT, the Laitu Khyeng Indigenous people were "clearly exploited and dominated by Bengali [non-Indigenous people] while also being neglected by the state government and agencies of the state." The results of this study also show that current governmental and nongovernmental environmental practices enacted within the Laitu Khyeng Indigenous Community are the means through which poverty, health problems, land appropriation, and environmental degradation have become endemic in the region.

Code's ecological thinking approach also suggests a contextually situated, imaginative, and socially aware way of building knowledge that defies the traditional Western "epistemological monoculture" (2006). Similarly in this study I learned that the traditional management practices disrupt the binary opposition between Western (outsider) and Indigenous subject—or the colonizers and the colonized (Amoamo and Thompson 2010; Escobar 2008). The Indigenous elders and knowledge holders in this study repeatedly argued that it is oppressive to change Indigenous cultures for the benefit of outsider resource extraction. In other words, current governmental environmental management promotes a colonial perspective and results in decreasing species diversity, declining water availability, soil degradation, and deforestation. In order to get to the root of the problem of colonialism for the Laitu Khyeng Indigenous in CHT, researchers must be responsible for understanding and acknowledging that colonial oppression is ongoing and is enacted via non-Indigenous, outsider profiteers, state administrators, and imposed management projects.

Conclusion

Indigenous relational perspectives are based on connection, reciprocity, and ethical relationships show what is missing in the mainstream doctrine of environmental sustainability. Indigenous relational perspectives deeply challenge the foundations of environmental sustainability and the colonizing power structures that underlie it; these perspectives also invite further thought about posthuman and relational ontologies. Indigenous relational perspectives and ways of being in sacred, ethical, and reciprocal relationships with "nature" are enhancing and developing more sustainable approaches to living in what Code calls *ecological thinking*.

While a relational framework is not new to Indigenous research, bridging Lorraine Code's ecological thinking with environmental justice from an Indigenous perspective results in new ways of protecting the environment in many Indigenous communities, particularly from deforestation, pollution, displacement, and poverty. Code's ecological thinking approach provides a road map for bridging traditional and Western worldviews ethically and politically, as well as scientifically. It offers multiple openings for thinking about collaborative responsive conversations and actions. This chapter shows how a relational framework provides a way to rethink our research responsibilities for producing knowledge, protecting participants' needs, honoring their knowledges and practices, respecting and centering their perspectives, and empowering them. This chapter also provides direction for how we (as researchers) need to reposition ourselves in relation to the field of environmental practice and how we need to understand our responsibilities in environmental practice as a system of reciprocal social relations and ethical practices and as a framework for environmental and social justice. Therefore, as a researcher, one of my epistemic responsibilities is to learn from participants' cultural environmental practices. I have learned from the Laitu Khyeng Indigenous Community that a relational framework provides insight into the complexity of Indigenous ways of knowing, contributes multiple practical solutions, and provides opportunities to bridge Western research and Indigenous ways of knowing that are responsible and respectful of both the environment and people.

Notes

1. Numerous Indigenous communities experience the Western perspective as a form of violence, exploitation, and discrimination toward their land, culture, and knowledge (Datta 2015, 2016; Kovach 2010; Smith 2008). Studies show that researchers with only Western scientific training have become a challenge for many Indigenous communities (Datta 2017; Smith 2008; Wilson 2008), and this Western training has been implicated in the "worst excesses of colonialism" (Smith 2008, 1).

2. Deloria here refers to the peoples now called "American Natives." In Canada, these people have chosen to name themselves "First Nations, Métis," and Inuit peoples; in showing a relationship with First Peoples globally, the term "Indigenous" is often used.

3. According to elders and knowledge holders, the word "outsider" refers to non-Indigenous Bengali: those who do not live in the community. In other words, this encompasses Bangladeshi state administrators who are mostly from outside the CHT (Adnan 2004).

4. *Karbary* means "village leader."

Works Cited

Adnan, Shapan. 2004. *Migration Land Alienation and Ethnic Conflict: Causes of Poverty in the Chittagong Hill Tracts of Bangladesh*. Dhaka: Research & Advisory Services.

Altman, Jon. 2004. "Indigenous Affairs at a Crossroads." *Australian Journal of Anthropology* 15, no. 3: 306–8.

Battiste, Marie. 2000. "Maintaining Aboriginal Identity, Language, and Culture in Modern Society." In *Reclaiming Indigenous Voice and Vision*, edited by Marie Battiste, 192–208. Toronto, ON: UBC.

Battiste, Marie. 2013. *Decolonizing Education: Nourishing the Learning Spirit*. Saskatoon: Purich.

Battiste, Marie. 2008. "Research Ethics for Protecting Indigenous Knowledge and Heritage: Institutional and Researcher Responsibilities." In *Handbook of Critical and Indigenous Methodologies*, edited by N. K. Denzin, Y. S. Lincoln, and L. Tuhiwai Smith, 497–509. Berkeley, CA: SAGE.

Berkes, Fikret. 1999. *Sacred Ecology: Traditional Ecological Knowledge and Resource Management*. Philadelphia: Taylor and Francis.

Berkes, Fikret. 2009. "Indigenous Ways of Knowing and the Study of Environmental Change." *Journal of the Royal Society of New Zealand* 39, no. 4: 151–156.

Bowers, C. A. 2001. "Addressing the Double Binds in Educating for an Ecologically Sustainable Future." *International Journal of Leadership in Education* 4, no. 1: 87–96.

Bowers, C. A. 2010. "Educational Reforms that Foster Ecological Intelligence." *Teacher Education Quarterly* 37, no. 4 (Fall): 9–31.

Cajete, Gregory A. 2005. "American Indian Epistemologies." *New Directions for Student Services* 109 (Spring): 69–78.

Chapola, Jebunnessa. 2008. "Labour Migration, Inter-ethnic Relations and Empowerment: A Study of Khyang Indigenous Garments Workers, Chittagong Hill Tracts, Bangladesh." MA thesis, University of Bergen.

Code, Lorraine. 2016. "Who Do We Think We Are?" *Social Philosophy Today* 32: 29–44.

Code, Lorraine. 2015. "Care, Concern, and Advocacy: Is There a Place for Epistemic Responsibility"? *Feminist Philosophy Quarterly* 1, no. 1: 1–20.

Code, Lorraine. 2006. *Ecological Thinking: The Politics of Epistemic Location*. Oxford, UK: Oxford University Press.

Code, Lorraine. 1993. *Taking Subjectivity into Account Feminist Epistemologies*. New York: Routledge.

Code, Lorraine. 1987. *Epistemic Responsibility*. Hanover, NH: University Press of New England.

Cooper, Thomas W. 1993. "Review Essay: Lorraine Code's Epistemic Responsibility, Journalism, and the Charles Stuart Case." *Business & Professional Ethics Journal* 12, no. 3 (Fall): 83–106.

Datta, Ranjan. 2017. "Decolonizing Both Research and Researcher, and its Effectiveness in Indigenous Research." *Research Ethics* 14, no. 2: 1–24.

Datta, Ranjan. 2016. "How to Practice Posthumanism in Environmental Learning: Experiences with North American and South Asian Indigenous Communities." *The IAFOR Journal of Education* 4, no. 1: 52–67.

Datta, Ranjan, Khyang, Nyojy U., Khyang, Hla Kray Prue, Khyang, Hla Kray Prue, Khyang, Mathui Ching, and Chapola, Jebunnessa. 2015. "Understanding

Indigenous Sustainability: A Community-Based Participatory Experience." *Revista Brasileira de Pesquisa em Educação em Ciências* 14, no. 2: 99–108.

Dei, George J. S. 2011. "The Possibilities of Research, Educational Programming and Training in Indigenous Knowledges in the Academy." Invited Address, First International Conference Endogenous Development and Trans-Disciplinarity in Higher Education: Challenges for the Co-evolution of Mainstream and Endogenous Knowledge Traditions. Cochabamba, Bolivia.

Deloria, Vine, Jr. 2001. "American Indian Metaphysics." In *Power and Place: Indian Education in America*, edited by Vine Deloria & Daniel Wildcat, 1–6. Golden, CO: Fulcrum.

Doucet, Andrea. 2018. "Feminist Epistemologies and Ethics: Ecological Thinking, Situated Knowledges, Epistemic Responsibilities." In *Sage Handbook of Qualitative Research Ethics*, edited by R. Iphofen and M. Tolich, 73–88. London: SAGE.

Escobar, Arturo. 2010. "Latin America at a Crossroads." *Cultural Studies* 24, no. 1: 1–65.

Korteweg, Lisa, Ismel Gonzalez, and Jojo Guillet. 2010. "The Stories are the People and the Land: Three Educators Respond to Environmental Teachings in Indigenous Children's Literature." *Environmental Education Research* 16, no. 3: 227–246.

Kovach, Margaret. 2010. *Indigenous Methodologies*. Toronto: University of Toronto Press.

Latour, Bruno. 2004. *Polities of Nature: How to Bring the Sciences into Democracy*. Translated by Catherine Porter. Cambridge, MA: Harvard University Press.

Law, John. 2007. *Actor Network Theory and Material Semiotics*. Lancaster, UK: Lancaster University Centre for Science Studies. http://www.lancaster.ac.uk/fass/centres/css/ant/ant.htm.

Little Bear, Leroy. 2016. "Big Thinking and Rethinking: Blackfoot Metaphysics: Waiting in the Wings." Congress Event, Federation of the Humanities and Social Sciences.

Lovern, Lavonna. 2008. "Native American Worldview and the Discourse on Disability." *Essays in Philosophy* 9, no. 1: 1–8.

Murdoch, Jonathan. 2006. *Post-Structuralist Geography*. London: SAGE.

Musopole, Augustine C. 1994. *Being Human in Africa: Toward an African Christian Anthropology*. New York: Peter Lang.

Nadasy, Paul. 2011. "We Don't Harvest Animals; We Kill Them: Agricultural Metaphors and the Politics of Wildlife Management in the Yukon." In *Knowing Management*, edited by M. Goldman, P. Nadasdy, and M. D. Turner, 135–151. Chicago: University of Chicago Press.

Rice, Brian, Roderick R. Riewe, Jill E. Oakes. 2005. *Seeing the World with Aboriginal Eyes*. Winnipeg: University of Manitoba Press.

Ritchie, Jenny. 2015. "Food Reciprocity and Sustainability in Early Childhood Care and Education in Aotearoa New Zealand." *Australian Journal of Environmental Education* 31, no. 1: 74–85.

Root, Emily. 2010. "This Land Is Our Land? This Land is Your Land: The Decolonizing Journeys of White Outdoor Environmental Educators." *Canadian Journal of Environmental Education* 15: 103–119.

Roy, Rajkumari Chandra. *Land Rights of the Indigenous Peoples of the Chittagong Hill Tracts, Bangladesh*. Copenhagen, Denmark: IWGIA Document No. 99, 2000.

Schlosberg, David, and David Carruthers. 2010. "Indigenous Struggles, Environmental Justice, and Community Capabilities." *Global Environmental Politics* 10, no. 4:12–35.

Simpson, Leanne. 2008. *Lighting the Eighth Fire: The Liberation, Resurgence, and Protection of Indigenous Nations*. Winnipeg: Arbeiter Ring.

Sindima, Harvey. 1990. "Liberalism and African Culture." *Journal of Black Studies* 21, no. 2: 90–209.

Smith, Linda Tuhiwai. 2008. "On Tricky Ground: Researching the Native in the Age of Uncertainty." In *The Sage Handbook of Qualitative Research*, edited by N. K. Denzin and Y. S. Lincoln. Thousand Oaks, CA: SAGE.

Tuck, Eve, and Marcia McKenzie. *Place in Research: Theory, Methodology, Methods*. New York: Routledge, 2016.

Tuck, Eve, and K. Wayne Yang. "Decolonization is not a Metaphor." *Decolonization: Indigeneity, Education & Society* 1, no. 1 (2012): 1–40.

Tuck, Eve, and K. Wayne Yang. 2014. "R-Words: Refusing Research." In *Humanizing Research: Decolonizing Qualitative Inquiry with Youth and Communities*, edited by D. Paris and M. T. Winn, 223–247. Los Angeles, CA: SAGE.

Tutu, Desmond. 1999. *No Future Without Forgiveness*. New York: Doubleday.

Whatmore, Sarah. 2006. "Materialist Returns: Practising Culture Geography in and for a More-than-Human World." *Cultural Geographies* 13, no. 4: 600–609.

Whatmore, Sarah. 2013. Practicing More-Than-Human Geographies: Thinking with/through Materials (lecture). https://www.youtube.com/watch?v=FVxfHV4Vl6Y.

Wildcat, Daniel. 2001. "Indigenizing Education: Playing to our Strengths." In *Power and Place: Indian Education in America*, edited by V. Deloria and D. Wildcat, 7–19. Golden, CO: Fulcrum.

Wilson, Shawn, and Alexandria Wilson. 2013. "Nayo Way in Ik Issi: A Family Practice of Indigenist Research Informed by Land." In *Indigenous Pathways into Social Research: Voices of a New Generation*, edited by D. M. Martens, F. Cram, and B. Chilisa. Walnut Hills, CA: Left Coast.

Wilson, Shawn. 2008. *Research is Ceremony: Indigenous Research Methods*. Winnipeg: Fernwood.

Chapter 11

How Does the Monoculture Grow?

A Temporal Critique of Code's *Ecological Thinking*

ESME G. MURDOCK

Throughout Lorraine Code's development of epistemological frameworks, she has stressed the necessity of broadening conceptions and spaces of knowledge beyond the rigid confines of Anglo-American philosophical traditions. She has done this through articulating the importance and necessity of contextualizing knowledge claims, projects, and conditions as well as by examining the centrality of subjectivity and positionality to ways of knowing. In "Taking Subjectivity into Account," Code analyzes the particularly socially located conditions and assumptions that accompany "*S*-knows-that-*p*" propositional models of knowledge (Code 2008). A key assumption in this dominant propositional model is the idea that S and p are always already clearly identifiable and distinct in ways that matter for the predictive capacity and success conditions of knowledge. She focuses on how S and p are constructed as subject and object but totalized in ways that assign fixity as well as differential value. She carries and fleshes out this critique further in *Ecological Thinking* where she works with ideas of mastery dualisms present in dominant Western traditions of thinking about humans and environments. These mastery dualisms also construct humans and environments as fundamentally and unproblematically distinct as well as differentially positioned in relation to power (Code 2006). Code's emphasis on learning *how* to know through relationality extends beyond the parameters of the Anglo-American philosophical tradition's ideas about agency stopping at the bounds of the "properly" human. Code also offers an argument for the relevance and importance of incorporating and examining the standpoint and positionality of both knowers and objects of knowledge. In this way, she asserts that the evasion of the particularity of knowers' subjectivity, as well as standpoint or positionality, leads to problematic conclusions as to what we can know and who is considered a knower.

Relatedly, refusal to inspect the "fingerprints" on our knowledge projects, as Sandra Harding puts it, has serious implications for how our understandings and relations to the natural world are always already fraught with ideological assumptions (Harding 1993). These assumptions can be various, but perhaps we can say that they are never inert; they constitute our knowledge of the object in ways that disallow the strict demarcation of S and p that mainstream epistemological projects assert and, in many ways, depend on (Longino 1995). Code goes further in *Ecological Thinking* to identify the mainstream Anglo-American epistemological tradition as one that also participates in epistemic projects of domination and mastery or dominant thinking. She offers "ecological thinking" as an alternative and "new" epistemological framework that avoids many of the problems of dominant thinking as the normative way to know. Thus she emphasizes, once again, the importance and centrality of epistemic *location* to processes of knowing. While Code invokes the alternative of "ecological thinking" in contrast to dominant thinking, constructing it as both "new" and nondominant, she makes these assertions from a positionality that looms large and relatively unexamined in the background.

This construction of "ecological thinking" as both a "new" and nondominant epistemological framework belies a problematic residue of the dominant thinking Code hopes to overcome: the inattention to a Western construct of time as linear. The fashioning and creation of Code's argument imports temporal aspects that are critical to projects of epistemological domination, namely the exclusion of epistemological systems, frameworks, and traditions that preexist, emerge, and are classified as both outside of and necessary for the landscape of dominant epistemological projects. Thus, through the description of "ecological thinking" as both temporally or chronologically later and also as progressive in the Western linear sense of time, the roots and influences of nondominant epistemological frameworks are obscured. In this way, Code's argument, even if it does so inadvertently, participates in the tradition of a temporal master narrative that still confers uncritical preference and normativity to the Euro-Anglo tradition of dominant epistemology she purports to overcome.

This chapter will argue that Code's "ecological thinking" is inattentive to the role of linear time and linear progress narratives in ways that position her "new" epistemological framework in a dominant master narrative. The construction of "ecological thinking" as "new" while also being only attributed to white Western knowers, betrays a chronotope of knowledge and knowledge traditions that confers centrality and value to a reified epistemological tradition as *the* tradition: a master narrative. This consequently also conflicts with Code's critique of the objectification of knowledge as this "new" epistemological framework is narrated in such a way that it excludes, obscures, and does not credit diverse epistemological traditions that already articulate "ecological thinking" and downplays the real-world conditions of oppression that make the Western epistemological tradition/narrative and this "new" epistemological framework, qualified as progressive, possible.

The first section provides an overview of Code's argument of what "ecological thinking" is and how it functions as a worthy alternative to dominant thinking found in the Anglo-American epistemological tradition. This section examines how "ecological thinking" is not only constructed as distinct from dominant thinking but also how it is constructed as temporally progressive through its ascription as "new" and nondominant. The next section argues that attention must be given to the particular concept and construction of time that accompanies analysis of the locational context of knowledge projects. Epistemologies are not just ways of knowing but are also particular narrative constructions. The ways epistemological traditions are narrated matters not only for how we understand the context of knowledge but also the conditions that make epistemic domination and epistemic liberation possible. This section analyzes how the linear progress narrative Code provides participates in practices of dominant thinking by articulating Western epistemology as progressive: as a fixed continuum that is merely added to. The third and fourth sections examine how the novelty of "ecological thinking" for Code involves a critique of dominant thinking, constructed from a slightly expanded epistemic location and community: namely, that of white women. These sections elucidate the limitations of this epistemic location through analyzing passages of *Ecological Thinking* where knowledge attribution is functioning problematically through the lack of engagement with the epistemic communities and traditions of women of color, specifically Black women and Indigenous peoples.

"Ecological Thinking"

In *Ecological Thinking: The Politics of Epistemic Location*, Lorraine Code endeavors to own and overcome self-observed limitations of her previous work, particularly her construction of knowers and epistemic communities in *Epistemic Responsibility* (Code 1987) as sanitized, of what she calls, the "politics of knowledge" (Code 2006, viii). Through this confession, Code recognizes the challenges of critiquing a dominant epistemological framework from an epistemic location steeped in the language and cosmological purview of a particular epistemological tradition, in this case in particular the pervasive baggage of liberal constructions of undifferentiated access to the universal "stuff" of knowledge. In this way, Code reflects on the ease of dominant positionality slipping into the background of epistemic practices and emerging as normative practice or as just the ways things are or have "always" been.

In Code's explication of "ecological thinking" she hopes to offer an alternative to epistemologies of mastery she identifies in the Western tradition that underwrite particular modes of human-environmental prescription such as the environmental degradation and domination of late capitalism (Code 2006, 4). In this way, part of Code's argument as to the saliency of "ecological thinking" is its ability to serve as an alternative to the dominant Western epistemological framework that proffers distinct epistemic subjects and objects mediated by domination as the primary way of knowing, where different value is ascribed to knower and known. She suggests that a reorientation toward the entanglement of knowledge with the world, and place more particularly, disrupts the dominant epistemological frameworks that prescribe mastery as the only or best way to know. Code, therefore, hopes to offer "ecological thinking" as a way of knowing grounded in the epistemic significance of place and its role/entanglement with knowledge.

Code draws out the metaphorical power of ecology further by analogizing epistemologies of domination to monocrop systems of agriculture that assert mastery through the destruction of other entangled and relational plurocrop systems. In this way, one can understand the domination enacted upon nature and the environment as something reproduced or co-present in epistemological projects bound up in those worlded practices. She hopes that "ecological thinking" is also an alternative to a dominative monocropped epistemological system or epistemological monoculture (Code 2006, 8–10; Shiva 1991, 2010). These metaphors emphasize "ecological thinking" as a practice that recognizes and prioritizes how our knowing is always already worlded or bound up with the world.

Code's argument for the significance of epistemic location, however, is complicated by the qualifications she gives to it: namely, the way she describes "ecological thinking" as not only "new" but also "revolutionary" to the Western epistemological tradition (Code 2006, 1). Code's description of "ecological thinking" as a "new" epistemology matters for at least two reasons: (1) it positions "ecological thinking" as an epistemology distinct from the dominant Anglo-American tradition, and (2) it positions "ecological thinking" as a temporally progressive epistemology in a linear narrative, a development subsequent to the dominant Anglo-American epistemological tradition.[1] That these assumptions travel with the qualifications of new as temporally progressive is further supported by the way in which she describes the emergence of "ecological thinking" as something Western and revolutionary in the choice of analogizing its emergence to the "Kantian turn" or Copernican Revolution for Western philosophy. The Kantian turn, for Code, refers to the centering of or reinsertion of "man" into philosophical investigations, and she likens the emergence of "ecological thinking" as a framework that could manifest a similar kind of revolutionary reorientation for Western philosophy (Code 2006, 3). However, critical attention to the importance of time, in particular linear conceptions of time, is absent from Code's analysis, which has important consequences for understanding how we can read the "discovery" of "ecological thinking," emerging from a Western context, as a practice of ongoing epistemic domination. In this way, I will argue that while Code is right to assign epistemic significance to place, she asserts it in a temporal narrative of dominance that obscures the epistemologies and epistemic traditions outside its crafted purview: a temporal narrative that still uncritically ascribes centrality and higher value to the West.

Time and Epistemic Domination

First, a clarification of what I understand Western to mean and how I am using Western when I refer to Western-dominant epistemological frameworks. Martinican theorist Édouard Glissant wrote: "The West is not in the West. It is a project, not a place" (Glissant 1999, 2). By this, Glissant meant that the power of the West as an ideology and apparatus of empire is not something exhausted by the location of the literal Occident. This is how I understand Western, not always as a literal place (though it can coincide with the literal geography of the Occident) but as an ideology that does and will travel. The term "will travel" refers to portability and traveling nature of ideology, in this case particularly Western ideology, that can be transported quite literally through projects of domination such as imperialism, colonialism, and war. The internalization of these traveling foreign ideologies often accompanies naturalizing processes that can obscure the origins of the ideologies in question as well as how they arrived in different geospatial locations and how they persist in different places. Indeed, one of the primary features of Western domination, especially in the form of colonialism and imperialism, is that epistemological frameworks developed and grounded in a literal place are picked up and taken, as it were, to a distinct place to dominate (through violence and displacement, both literal and epistemological) those colonized (Quijano 2008; Mignolo 2008; Tuck and Yang 2012; Whyte 2016). However, this place-based epistemology of domination so characteristic of the Western tradition is ascribed superiority, normativity, and universality such that this place-based epistemology *should* supersede all others and also obscure its particular positionality: in other words, it should be placeless. In this way, we can identify colonialism as a project and profound structure of epistemic domination. Further we can question dominant Western epistemological narratives, forged in the praxis of domination, which simultaneously exclude or obscure the place of domination as a literal condition of the knowledge produced therein, as suspect.

By Code's own argument both the dominant thinking characteristic of the Western epistemological tradition and the "ecological thinking" she characterizes as "new" have an epistemically significant location and place. However, what Code fails to adequately address is how place is also constituted through temporal narratives that can and do confer superiority and dominant status to the erasure and obfuscation of *other* epistemologies. In this way, Code's introduction and "discovery" of ecological thinking, without straying far from the dominant Western—and importantly for the purposes of this chapter, white—epistemological tradition, participate in a linear progress narrative that is epistemically irresponsible at least and epistemically dominative at worst.

In *Physics of Blackness: Beyond the Middle Passage Epistemology*, Michelle Wright explores conflicts that arise around the metaphysical status of Blackness and Black identity due to contradictory conceptions of time that are presented as equivalent. She argues that spacetime is often fitted to a linear progress narrative that conflicts with the interpretative moment of the "now" as experienced. As such, she distinguishes between linear progressive constructions of time and epiphenomenal time; time both as it is constructed to fix spacetime in a linear narrative and time as excessive of this construct as it is experienced in the now (Wright 2015, 4). Throughout her argument, Wright provides compelling ways of understanding how dominant discourses operate through linear progress narratives. Wright understands epistemologies not only as ways of knowing but also (and importantly) as the concurrent narrative we tell about that knowing. Stressing epistemologies as narrative knowledges, there is room to conceive of epistemologies as sites of both domination and liberation. In this way, a dominant discourse not only tells a particular story but also "expresses the will of a center of political, social, or economic power within a given social structure, in effect constructing within that structure the identities of social classes based on presumed degrees of freedom to exercise agency" (Wright 2015, 5). Think of how the Anglo-American tradition of epistemology Code critiques enacts a narrative of a universal, placeless, accessible, and normative knowledge, while also expressing the will and perspective of a small, privileged group: Western white men. In this way, the Anglo-American tradition of epistemology tells a particular story at the same time that it ignores or denies its own social location that contradicts that same narrative. Those who craft the knowledge and secure its verification procedures are able to universalize, de-place, and normativize this epistemology precisely through the material and contingent power of their sociopolitical position steeped in race, class, and gender privilege achieved through domination.

For the purposes of this chapter, we can understand the construction of linear progress narratives accompanying dominant discourses as ways of bounding, fixing, or reifying both knowledge and knowers as particular entities, with both linear spatial *and* temporal implications. The narrative expressed is bounded (qualified as having strict, clear boundaries) and mapped to capture a particular sequence and arrangement of events as well as agents and participants. Within a particular enclosed structure of dominant discourse that relies on a linear progress narrative, epistemological projects are seen to follow previous ones sequentially in ways that not only imply chronological succession but that also arc toward a value-laden "progress." Chronologically "new" ideas in a linear progressive narrative also connote a sense of improvement in relation to the past or chronologically prior epistemological projects. In this way, part of how dominant discourse understands itself is to impose a linear progress narrative onto its framework that orders the succession of knowings as an ever-accumulative progress of knowledge, where value can be assigned and temporalized in a backward- and forward-looking nature. Colloquially we might understand this by the positive association and meaning ascribed to phrases like "We know more now" or "We know better now," the latter sometimes implied by the former. (We rarely say we know "differently," for instance.)[2] However, this progress narrative is not a straightforward construction free from power pathologies because a particular temporal construction of time as linear *progress* necessarily excludes other narratives and, hence, other knowers, to constitute, reference, and understand itself. This is because epistemologies as narratives that impose particular dominant linear progressive constructions also provide a relatively fixed and homogenous representation of knowers *and* knowledge.

> While the problem of holistic representations is understandable, its effects are hard to swallow: as certain bodies crowd the foreground of our representations, we begin to assume and look only for similar bodies, producing an inaccurate history of which peoples, groups, movements, or individuals were part of which events, much less of the (interpretative) effect of those moments on their lives. In other words, we run the risk that our mistakes will only be compounded in future generations: raised on histories that primarily feature men, we grow up to assume that women didn't accomplish anything and same-sex desire and relationships rarely if ever occurred. (Wright 2015, 13)

In this way, the temporal logic of the linear progress narrative tells a story that overdetermines the contributions and presence of particular actors that are seen and centered again and again in previous iterations of the story. The decentering of these dominant, overrepresented actors is often met with resistance, especially by those who are part of the dominant group historically and continuously overrepresented. This happens even when the contributions of the dominant actors are made entirely possible by labor and subordination of nondominant groups. For example, think of the marginalization and absence of Black women and Black women's labor from the historical success narratives of US history. This absence can and often does translate to a hermeneutic interpretation of Black women as nonintegral historical actors or a presence or population that contributed anything to "national progress." Thus, temporal constructs that attempt to fix a linear progressive narrative in dominant discourses can create epistemological horizons that historically exclude and continue to exclude particular knowledges, epistemological traditions, and knowers. This is true even when the traditional scope of dominant discourse is expanded for *other* knowers but remains bounded in the context of domination, specifically for the purposes of this chapter when the narrative remains bounded in the dominative praxis of whiteness. This is important to the meaning making that accompanies Western knowers only referencing a particularly constructed Western tradition and qualifying epistemologies as "new" that are actually already well established in the epistemological traditions and terrains *excluded from* but crucial to the construction of Western dominant knowledge within the dominant Western narrative and purview. Nondominant epistemological traditions and terrains become background for the high relief of the main event, the foreground: the white dominant narratives (Plumwood 2002).

The Politics of Epistemic (Dis)location

The temporal qualification of Code's "ecological thinking" as "new" represents a particular understanding of the thrust of "ecological thinking" as arising from a particular time and place, by particular knowers. While Code is right to understand the follies of Anglo-American mainstream epistemology's evasion of its particular homogenous positionality, through its metamorphosis of dominant positionality into objective universality, she fails to adequately critique the similarly narrow positionality she credits as the productive sites of "ecological thinking." In this way, Code participates in the construction of another monocropped or monoculture epistemology that bypasses the nondominant epistemologies that have been articulating knowledges foundational to "ecological thinking" for a long time. I am thinking generally of traditional ecological knowledges (TEK), found the world over, but more specifically the thought traditions coming out of western Africa that traveled and transformed through diaspora to different places throughout the Americas. I am also thinking of Indigenous knowledge systems that were/are both relied upon for Euro-American settler survival and colonization but are rarely if ever included in the narrative of the Euro-American epistemological tradition (hooks 2014; Lewis 1995; Glave 2010; Kimmerer 2015a; Cajete 2016; Finney 2014). Euro-centric epistemological traditions are actually very late to the scene of ecological thinking and have worked quite diligently to destroy and suppress knowledge traditions that they now espouse as saying something quite useful for the purposes of hemorrhaging the damage of domination. This absence of knowledge attribution to these knowledges and knowers flies in the face of notions of epistemic responsibility as well as ideas about "ecological thinking" as a praxis that moves us toward more liberatory epistemic practices. This particular construction of "ecological thinking" as attributed primarily to whiteness, specifically white women, also participates in a well-established tradition of domination that reads women of color out of epistemological traditions and attempts to fix strict demarcations of noncontact between diverse epistemological systems. As Wright explicates, linear progress narratives have the potential for distortion when the "chronotope" or spacetime is "rigidly monologic, reflecting only the spacetime of the hero even when it produces contradictions (such as minor characters whose imminent peril is forgotten in the course of the story or who fail to age or change in the absence of the hero even though the hero does so or vice versa)" (Wright 2015, 21–22). In this way, we can understand part of the narrative Code gives "ecological thinking" as a temporal distortion of the conditions of domination that allow certain epistemological frameworks or concepts to emerge as novel. Thus, Code's "ecological thinking" represents a monocrop or monoculture in following ways: (1) it relies on a linear spatial/temporal form and narrative and (2) it suppresses or removes other epistemological traditions, plurocultures, and systems for the expression of the singularity: the monoculture. To address the first point, a monoculture is distinctive in that it imposes a particular order onto the land to express itself. A monoculture is most physically and visibly distinct in the practice of row cropping or lines. Monocultures literally impose linearity onto and within the landscape. This can be applied epistemologically to the limited linear narrative imposed upon Code's version of "ecological thinking." Secondly, in order for a plot to be formed into a monoculture through row cropping, other plurocultures and ecological systems must be uprooted and continuously suppressed, usually through removal and then applications of pesticides and herbicides. This can be applied epistemologically to Code's narrow citational practice and history of knowledge production referenced as integral to the emergence and growth of "ecological thinking." Put another way, Code's "ecological thinking" participates in the monocrop epistemologically by telling an overly simplified, singular, and incomplete story that evades ownership of the conditions for its own possibility. Evasion of the less savory aspects of epistemic location is integral to the production of the Western white epistemological tradition's understanding and telling of itself as not only superior but self-sufficient in its genesis, namely the politics and epistemic location of white supremacist domination. In this way a nonlinear understanding and narrative of time is necessary for understanding the sites of entanglement and nonneutral contact between diverse epistemological traditions' relationships to the maintained centrality of dominant narratives, and as such this nonlinear understanding and narrative of time must be read *back into* the story of ecological thinking.

Understandings of nonlinear conceptions of time can be found throughout multiple nondominant cultural and epistemological traditions. An example would be to think of time as cyclical, which is an understanding, wedded quite deeply with observations, interactions, and attention to the natural world and environment (LaDuke 1993). We can use Code's example of monocrop farming itself in distinction to mound farming to illustrate this distinction. Mound farming is a style of farming used throughout the world and was a primary form of cultivation employed by Indigenous peoples, especially in the Americas. Mound farming looks quite different from row cropping and was perceived by many settlers in the Americas as disorder and evidence of the absence of cultivation practices on the part of Indigenous peoples (Lewis 1995; Dunbar-Ortiz 2014). This misunderstanding comes in part from a conception of order that invokes both spatial and temporal linearity, or linear spatial and temporal relationships. Mound farming is a successful mode of cultivation that relies on and gives space to the cyclical and entangled temporal agency of earth. It does not ascribe to a linear temporal narrative of discrete and discernible cause and effect but rather makes space for understanding the co-constituted cyclical temporality of ecological cooperation emerging within the mound (Kimmerer 2015b). While sequence and repetition are present in nonlinear conceptions of time, they are conceived in ways that are quite different from a linear narrative (Cajete 2016).

In many ways, Code is building on a well-documented tradition of knowledge as embedded in and entangled with the world. However, the particular language she uses to describe "ecological thinking" in various passages invokes important non-Western and nondominant epistemological traditions without naming or referencing them. To bound the genesis, formation, and importance of "ecological thinking" to the white West contributes to the accumulative narrative and reproduction of Western white dominant thinking. I turn now to some textual analyses of particular passages of note. In describing the merits of "ecological thinking" Code writes:

> Practicing a methodological pluralism that stems from a respect for particularity, both ecological thinking and feminisms of the late twentieth and early twenty-first century draw, often similarly, on studies of (linked) oppressions to generate multiple coalitions and forms of activism. Their task is to develop liberatory strategies to counter the myriad, mutually reinforcing oppressions endemic to white patriarchal capitalist societies. In contrast to single-issue defined and enacted theories and activism, ecological feminism yields multi-issue theories and practices: it engages with multiple oppressions. (Code 2006, 19)

It is interesting that here Code references theories of intersectionality without naming them as such. Code references theories of oppression formed and understood, not as she states "on studies of (linked oppressions)" but through the interstitial analyses of the lived realities of their authors, namely women of color, specifically Black women (Cooper 1995; Combahee River Collective 1983; Beale 1995; Spillers 1984; Crenshaw 1989). This general reference to intersectionality, unnamed, is also accompanied by reference only to the work of white women (Noel Sturgeon and Donna Haraway). While no one is held to the standard of awareness of or engagement with all the knowledge produced on a particular topic, this absence of the thoroughly documented and long history of women of color and Black women's knowledge production informed by the situation and positionality of their lives as oppressed persons in a power-imbalanced world points to a more systematic, pervasive exclusion of certain knowledge and knowers from the annals of Western epistemology. The dearth of knowers of color in general (but women of color in particular) from the narrative of Code's *Ecological Thinking* as a project concerned with the importance of epistemic location and place-based knowledge indicates a narrative with a dominant spacetime or monologic "chronotope" problem. That an entire tradition and continuous site of indispensable knowledge that has been articulating the importance of epistemic location for decades, centuries even, should remain unengaged in a project aimed at epistemic liberation demonstrates the pervasiveness and deep roots of epistemic domination. What's worse is that the dislocation of intersectional theory from its particular context, with the accompanying erasure of its knowledge producers' positions, appropriates this knowledge as not only "new" but, just as importantly, as white (Alexander-Floyd 2012; Bilge 2013; Nash 2016). This dislocates knowledge from its context and objectifies it in ways Code's project in *Ecological Thinking* seeks explicitly to avoid. To echo Wright's earlier statement, these exclusions maintain and reproduce inaccurate histories that dislocate certain peoples' presence and contributions to discourse over and over again (Wright 2015).

Intersectionality as a term is attributed to Kimberlé Crenshaw (Crenshaw 1989), but interstitial and intersectional analysis can be read and understood as a foundational tenet of Black feminist thought (Cooper 1995; Combahee River Collective 1983; Beale 1995; King 1995; Collins 1986, 2008; Hull, Bell-Scott, and Smith 1993; Crenshaw 1989, 1991). The concept of the interstitial or intersectional nature of oppression is grounded in the lives and work of Black women because it was/is their own lived experiences as oppressed peoples in the vice of multiple reinforcing oppressions that guided their understanding of their experiences, the world, and their own position in it. In this way, beginning from the positionality of Black women and their own experiences, Black women articulate sophisticated analyses of how domination functions. However, the domination and intersecting oppressions Black women face are furthered and compounded by their exclusion and erasure as knowers and knowledge producers in dominant discourse. If part of what feminist epistemology aims to do is demonstrate the limitations and particularity of white male dominant discourse, it must also pay attention to the ways in which expansion of the positionality of knowers to include white women and not women of color is an ongoing act of epistemological domination. If part of Code's critique of dominant thinking is that it divorces its content from the positionality of the world, then we must question why ideas of intersectionality and "ecological thinking" are divorced from their context as the knowledge production of women of color and positioned as "new." Put another way, why are nondominant knowers of color positioned as beyond the scope of the linear progress narrative of "ecological thinking"? One answer this chapter offers is to think of the epistemic locatability and legibility as mediated through both spatial *and* temporal modes of domination. This again reinforces the necessity of awareness of the ways in which dominant narratives' attention to particular events is accompanied by an inattention, erasure, or denial of the conditions that make it possible in many ways: namely, historical and ongoing practices of domination.

The appropriation of concepts, methods, and analyses of nondominant knowers accompanied by a lack of reference to their contribution as knowers and knowledge producers is a well-worn tradition of dominant discourse (Dotson 2014; Medina 2012). The qualification and presentation of these knowledges or aspects of knowledge as "new" is not only harmful in the continuous erasure of nondominant knowers' existence, presence, and contribution but also importantly because this appropriation has unequal, privileged consequences and results when disseminated and received by/for dominant (white) knowers. In this way, we can understand part of the harm of this exclusion in the ways in which the knowledge traditions of the nondominant are used to further the dominant discourse's narrative of progress and how the knowledge of nondominant knowers is presented as a solution by the dominant discourse to problems domination itself and dominantly positioned actors created. Hence, this is why the spacetime of domination matters for the narratives we tell, the knowers we cite, and the qualifications we give to our solutions.

Land-Based Epistemologies as Indigenous Knowledges

Another conspicuous absence from Code's analysis of "ecological thinking" is reference to the deep, complex, land-based epistemologies from non-Western traditions. In describing ecological naturalism, Code states:

> Ecological naturalism builds on the relations of organisms with one another and with their habitat, which comprises not just the physical habitat or the present one, but the complex network of locations and relations, whether social, historical, material, geographical, cultural, racial, sexual, institutional, or other, where organisms—human or non-human—try to live well, singly and collectively. . . . Ecological analyses work to understand the implications for organisms, of living where and as they do while constructing strategies for knowing well that are exploitative neither of the habitat nor of other inhabitants. The ecological subject, then, is materially situated: embodied location and interdependence are integral to its possibilities for knowledge and action. (Code 2006, 91)

Here, Code is describing a way of knowing advocated and articulated quite extensively in nondominant epistemological traditions. Sophisticated philosophies of entangled agencies pervade nondominant traditions as seen before in the collaborative, nonlinear temporal understandings of cultivation referred to in Indigenous mound-farming systems. The attention to the web of relations and the interdependence of the natural world, humans included, is a fundamental tenet of Indigenous philosophies worldwide (LaDuke 1993; Kimmerer 2015a; Cajete 2016). Code situates this description of ecological naturalism in the text as, again, a progressive move away (in linear temporal distance) from "a science of the individual subject whose epistemic processes are flattened in a mechanical, input-output modeling" (Code 2006, 90). However, nondominant knowers are, again, not referenced as important contributors and knowers in this understanding of "ecological thinking" or ecological naturalism. The ecological naturalism that Code describes is grounded in tenets of relationality, interdependence, and embodiment in the world for both knower and known. These are core principles of Indigenous epistemologies and TEK (Maracle 2002; Geniusz 2009; Cajete 2016; Kimmerer 2015a; McGregor 2008; Figueroa 2011; Whyte 2017). Again, this is not to say that dominant epistemic practitioners can or should be all knowing when it comes to epistemological histories but that an entire epistemic project such as *Ecological Thinking*—about the importance of epistemic location *and* responsibility—would not engage outside of a dominant (white) tradition is troubling in its maintenance and reproduction of sanitized epistemological narratives. Also, that dominant Anglo-American epistemological discourse, especially in the North American context, sits in nonneutral contact with Indigenous peoples, namely in the context of continuous settler colonial violence.

The histories of how the science of isolated, indifferent knowers and their epistemologies gain traction are also important ones that include colonization, attempted epistemicide, and the subjugation of Indigenous ways of knowing (to name a few) (Tuck and Yang 2012; Whyte 2017; Simpson 2017). These histories matter especially for the qualification of the return to and evocation of principles foundational to Indigenous epistemologies, without credit or reference, as both "new" and liberatory for Western science and Western epistemology. To contextualize, examine a description of native science by Gregory Cajete:

> Native science reflects the unfolding story of a creative universe in which human beings are active, creative participants. When viewed from this perspective, science is evolutionary—its expression unfolds through the general scheme of the creative process of first insight, immersion, creation, and reflection. Native science is a reflection of the metaphoric mind and is embedded in creative participation with nature. It reflects the sensual capacities of humans. (2016, 14)

Again, we must ask why such a rich epistemological tradition that has said (and continues to say) so much about "ecological thinking" should be omitted from a project concerned with the politics of epistemic location. I would argue that the linear progress narrative combined an ingrained dominant positionality to see whiteness, as a backgrounded condition of knowing is an important dimension. Otherwise, the temporal and citational narrative of "ecological thinking" would be quite different. Part of understanding the epistemic irresponsibility and continuous domination of linear progress narratives that exclude nondominant epistemological traditions and knowers means turning the logic of Code's argument for the importance of place to epistemology on itself; to examine what the seemingly innocuous (to some) omissions of traditions and narratives says about the positionality of Western epistemology itself as presented in *Ecological Thinking*. That "ecological thinking" should remain the exclusive purview of Western epistemology and also that it should be understood through the qualification of "newness" reveals that the conditions of a dominant Western epistemological tradition have not been sufficiently addressed.

The dominative nature of certain epistemological traditions is backgrounded into normativity; a dominant discourse that only references itself or knowers sufficiently similar to its constitution. This involves a lack of reckoning with the literal temporal-spatial positionality of dominant discourse: in this case, dominant Western epistemologies. Which is to say that the question of how the dominant discourse became/becomes dominant is not a question posed or answered through the self-reflexivity of Code's critique of the Anglo-American epistemological tradition. Dominant discourses become and remain dominant (and normative) through the historical and continuous domination, suppression, and oppression of other epistemologies and epistemological traditions. We are not just embedded in the world; we are embedded in a world of unequal power relations compounded by histories and systems of domination and oppression. The object of knowledge is not lodged in a neutral context ripe for anyone's picking, but rather knowledge is constituted collectively in a world where only some knowledges gain traction in relation to power. "Ecological thinking" makes the mistake and does the harm of "discovering" nondominant knowledge only to dominate it all over again and read out the constitution of that knowledge from spacetimes largely and continuously ignored within the Western dominant epistemological purview. Thus the narrative of "ecological thinking" is temporally compromised in the way it dislocates and detemporalizes the nondominant contexts out of which it arises.

In this chapter, I have offered a temporal critique of the rendering of "ecological thinking" Code offers in *Ecological Thinking*. By situating, both spatially and temporally, the sites of genesis of "ecological thinking" within the Western (white) epistemological tradition Code fails to locate the particularity of the Western epistemological tradition in a continuous linear progress narrative grounded in the domination and incorporation of other epistemological systems. This leads to Code's contribution to a similarly sanitized dominant narrative that reads out the epistemological systems and knowledges of nondominant knowers. I explored two particular exclusions in the lack of reference to Black women's theorization about intersectional theories of oppression grounded in contextualized and lived relationality as well as the lack of reference to Indigenous land-based epistemologies and TEK. In this way, I have noted how Code's dissatisfaction with monoculture epistemologies is not accompanied by a temporal attention to the conditions by which the monoculture grows. The monoculture grows by practices that ensure the viability and sustainability of a singularity to the domination and suppression of other pluralities and systems. Dominant discourse grows and continues to grow by practices that nurture the dominant knowers and traditions irrespective of its rootedness in the domination and suppression of other nondominant traditions and knowers. If we care to truly think ecologically and to know responsibly, it is time to locate the knowledges and contributions dominant discourse continuously buries, which grow powerfully all the while.

Notes

1. Here, it is important to note that I am not equivocating Code's iteration or formation of "ecological thinking" as representative of all ecological thinking or ecological thinking per se. Forms of ecological thinking exist both within and outside of the narrow confines of the Anglo-American and Euro-descendent epistemological traditions. The broader notion of ecological thinking can and does articulate itself as nonlinear, relational, and systematic or weblike. However, Code's particular form of "ecological thinking" (which I always reference by putting it into quotes) notes a certain genesis, origin, and progression which I argue is very much a part of Western dominant conceptions of time as both linear and narratively progressive.

2. Here, I am not arguing for or supporting relativism but rather attempting to make space for a diversity of perspectives informed by different social locations that produce differing vantage points that more holistically or objectively both shape and represent our knowledges and their attendant narratives. Of course, we can (and should be able to) make comparative judgments between different knowledge claims and projects as better or worse, more problematic or less problematic. What I want to trouble, however, is the acquisitive logic that can be found within dominant thinking that equates simply assigning a knowledge a place of privilege in linear progressive chronotope (ascribed to a particular origin within dominant knowing) with the status of better or more progressive. In this way, I am more aligned with a realist or strong objectivity view grounded in the contributions of feminist standpoint theory (Lewis 1995; Kimmerer 2015b; Cajete 2016; Dunbar-Ortiz 2014; hooks 2014; Finney 2014).

Works Cited

Alexander-Floyd, N. G. 2012. "Disappearing Acts: Reclaiming Intersectionality in the Social Sciences in a Post-Black Feminist Era." *Feminist Formations; Baltimore* 24, no. 1: 1–25.

Beale, F. 1995. "Double Jeopardy: To Be Black and Female." In *Words of Fire: An Anthology of African-American Feminist Thought*, edited by B. Guy-Sheftall. New York: New Press.

Bilge, S. 2013. "Intersectionality Undone: Saving Intersectionality from Feminist Intersectionality Studies." *Du Bois Review; Cambridge* 10, no. 2: 405–24. https://doi.org/http://dx.doi.org.ezproxy.auctr.edu:2051/10.1017/S1742058X13000283.

Cajete, G. 2016. *Native Science: Natural Laws of Interdependence*. 1st ed. Santa Fe, NM: Clear Light.

Code, L. 1987. *Epistemic Responsibility*. 1st ed. Hanover, NH: Brown.

———. 2006. *Ecological Thinking: The Politics of Epistemic Location*. New York: Oxford University Press.

———. 2008. "Taking Subjectivity into Account." In *The Feminist Philosophy Reader*, edited by A. Bailey and C. Cuomo. New York: McGraw-Hill.

Collins, P. H. 1986. "Learning from the Outsider Within: The Sociological Significance of Black Feminist Thought." *Social Problems* 33, no. 6: S14–32. https://doi.org/10.2307/800672.

———. 2008. *Black Feminist Thought: Knowledge, Consciousness, and the Politics of Empowerment*. 1st ed. New York: Routledge.

Combahee River Collective. 1983. "A Black Feminist Statement." In *Home Girls: A Black Feminist Anthology*, edited by Barbara Smith. New York: Kitchen Table: Women of Color Press.

Cooper, A. J. 1995. "The Status of Woman in America." In *Words of Fire: An Anthology of African-American Feminist Thought*, edited by B. Guy-Sheftall. New York: New Press.

Crenshaw, K. 1989. "Demarginalizing the Intersection of Race and Sex: A Black Feminist Critique of Antidiscrimination Doctrine, Feminist Theory and Antiracist Politics." *University of Chicago Legal Forum*, no. 1: 139–67.

———. 1991. "Mapping the Margins: Intersectionality, Identity Politics, and Violence against Women of Color." *Stanford Law Review* 43, no. 6: 1241–99. https://doi.org/10.2307/1229039.

Dotson, K. 2014. "Conceptualizing Epistemic Oppression." *Social Epistemology* 28, no. 2: 115–38. https://doi.org/10.1080/02691728.2013.782585.

Dunbar-Ortiz, R. 2014. *An Indigenous Peoples' History of the United States*. Boston: Beacon.

Figueroa, Robert. 2011. "Indigenous Peoples and Cultural Losses." In *The Oxford Handbook of Climate Change and Society*, edited by John S. Dryzek, Richard B. Norgaard, and David Schlosberg, 232–47. Oxford: Oxford University Press.

Finney, C. 2014. *Black Faces, White Spaces: Reimagining the Relationship of African Americans to the Great Outdoors*. Chapel Hill: University of North Carolina Press.

Geniusz, W. 2009. *Our Knowledge Is Not Primitive: Decolonizing Botanical Anishinaabe Teachings*. Syracuse, NY: Syracuse University Press.

Glave, Dianne D. 2010. *Rooted in the Earth: Reclaiming the African American Environmental Heritage.* Chicago: Chicago Review.

Glissant, E. 1999. "Introductions: From a 'Dead-End' Situation." In *Caribbean Discourse: Selected Essays.* Charlottesville: University of Virginia Press.

Harding, S. 1993. "Rethinking Standpoint Epistemology: What is 'Strong Objectivity'?" In *Feminist Epistemologies*, edited by L. M. Alcoff and E. Potter. New York: Routledge.

hooks, b. 2014. *Black Looks: Race and Representation.* 2nd ed. New York: Routledge.

Hull, A., P. Bell-Scott, and B. Smith, eds. 1993. *But Some Of Us Are Brave: All the Women Are White, All the Blacks Are Men: Black Women's Studies.* Old Westbury, NY: Feminist Press at CUNY.

Kimmerer, R.W. 2015a. *Braiding Sweetgrass: Indigenous Wisdom, Scientific Knowledge and the Teachings of Plants.* Minneapolis: Milkweed Editions.

———. 2015b. "The Three Sisters." In *Braiding Sweetgrass: Indigenous Wisdom, Scientific Knowledge and the Teachings of Plants*, 128–40. Minneapolis: Milkweed Editions.

King, D.K. 1995. "Multiple Jeopardy, Multiple Consciousness: The Context of Black Feminist Ideology." In *Words of Fire: An Anthology of African-American Feminist Thought*, edited by B. Guy-Sheftall. New York: New Press.

LaDuke, W. 1993. "Voices from White Earth: Gaa-Waabaabiganikaag." Presented at the Thirteenth Annual E. F. Schumacher Lectures, New Haven, October. https://centerforneweconomics.org/publications/voices-from-white-earth-gaa-waabaabiganikaag/.

Lewis, D. R. 1995. "Native Americans and the Environment: A Survey of Twentieth-Century Issues." *American Indian Quarterly* 19, no. 3: 423–50. https://doi.org/10.2307/1185599.

Longino, H. 1995. "Gender, Politics, and the Theoretical Virtues." *Springer* 104, no. 3: 383–97.

Maracle, L. 2002. *I Am Woman: A Native Perspective on Sociology and Feminism.* Reprint ed. Vancouver: Press Gang.

McGregor, D. 2008. "Linking Traditional Ecological Knowledge and Western Science: Aboriginal Perspectives from the 2000 State of the Lakes Ecosystem Conference." *The Canadian Journal of Native Studies* 28, no. 1: 139–58.

Medina, J. 2012. *The Epistemology of Resistance: Gender and Racial Oppression, Epistemic Injustice, and Resistant Imaginations.* 1st ed. New York: Oxford University Press.

Mignolo, W. D. 2008. "The Geopolitics of Knowledge and Colonial Difference." In *Coloniality at Large: Latin America and the Postcolonial Debate*, edited by M. Moraña, E. Dussel, and C. A. Jáuregui, 225–58. Durham, NC: Duke University Press.

Moya, P. M. L. 2002. *Learning from Experience: Minority Identities, Multicultural Struggles.* Berkeley: University of California Press.

Nash, J. C. 2016. "Feminist Originalism: Intersectionality and the Politics of Reading." *Feminist Theory* 17, no. 1: 3–20. https://doi.org/10.1177/1464700115620864.

Plumwood, V. 2002. *Feminism and the Mastery of Nature*. London: Taylor & Francis.

Quijano, A. 2008. "Coloniality of Power, Eurocentrism, and Latin America." In *Coloniality at Large: Latin America and the Postcolonial Debate*. Durham, NC: Duke University Press.

Shiva, V. 1991. "Biotechnology Development and Conservation of Biodiversity." *Economic and Political Weekly* 26, no. 48: 2740–46.

———. 2010. *Staying Alive: Women, Ecology, and Development*. Brooklyn, NY: South End.

Simpson, L. B. 2017. *As We Have Always Done: Indigenous Freedom through Radical Resistance*. 1st ed. Minneapolis: University of Minnesota Press.

Spillers, H. 1984. "Interstices: A Small Drama of Words." In *Pleasure and Danger: Exploring Female Sexuality*, edited by Carole S. Vance. Boston: Routledge.

Tuck, E., and K. Wayne Yang. 2012. "Decolonization Is Not a Metaphor." *Decolonization: Indigeneity, Education & Society* 1, no. 1: 1–40.

Whyte, K. P. 2016. "Indigenous Experience, Environmental Justice and Settler Colonialism." In *Nature and Experience: Phenomenology and the Environment*, edited by B. Bannon. Rowman and Littlefield.

———. 2017. "Food Sovereignty, Justice, and Indigenous Peoples: An Essay on Settler Colonialism and Collective Continuance." In *Oxford Handbook on Food Ethics*, edited by A. Barnhill, T. Doggett, and M. Budolfson. Oxford: Oxford University Press.

Wright, M. M. 2015. *Physics of Blackness: Beyond the Middle Passage Epistemology*. 1st ed. Minneapolis: University of Minnesota Press.

Chapter 12

Taking Code to Sea

Susan Reid

Introduction

The ocean[1] soaks into our being. In barely discernible, quotidian ways they[2] provide almost half the oxygen we breathe and regulate the planetary hydrological cycle that irrigates our cells and crops. The ocean is a sight of beauty, stormy spectacle, and sensual, watery pleasure in which to dive, surf, or swim. For many, they are an entity to worship. One of the largest moving entities any of us will ever witness, the ocean is the dynamic carrier of canoes and cargo ships. Around three billion humans rely on the ocean's fish for protein (WWF 2019). In contrast to the ocean's generosities, intensifying industrial human activities and appetites are responsible for declining biodiversity, untrammeled mineral and fossil fuel extractions, warming and acidifying waters, toxic pollution, and now a global material flow of plastics that speckle planetary currents. Although differently entangled, responsible, and affected, we humans are dependent on the very oceanic systems, lifeways, and materials that our ongoing relations and actions unjustly imperil. We are thoroughly implicated in these material transitions.

Our knowledge of previously unknown, wondrous marine life, and complex dynamic systems is mostly thanks to the exploratory research and incredible advances across the sciences. Discovery's troubled connection with exploitation, however, implicates particular scientific knowledge with capitalism's impatient appetite for commercialization and extraction. This is more evident in the remote depths of the ocean where discovery of a marine species or geomorphic feature is frequently accompanied by proposals for their exploitation. Neither is more science alone necessarily going to fix the parlous state of the ocean or institute more just relations—the past fifty years have seen human industrial impacts intensify despite significant growth in marine scientific activity. International and national governance regimes are also failing the ocean, as they prioritize development over conservation. Rather, there is a need to look beneath governance regimes and orthodox science to the foundational imaginaries driving the expansion of industrialized, extractivist frontiers.

Crafted by Western ideologies of mastery and fueled by the Cartesian values still in their holds, Western science and law enact hierarchical relational approaches that envisage a disembodied and instrumentalized nature. How then might alternative, less harmful, and more relationally considered epistemologies and imaginaries be cultivated? How might justice be advanced for the seas? What forms of ocean testimony can we rely on to guide justice when the high seas and their remote abyssal depths are beyond reach for most of us, predominantly without sunlight, and with places, inhabitants, and phenomena not yet encountered? How, too, might we understand and balance the different and transitioning conditions of ocean habitability on which humans and others depend? These are some of the questions that arise as I begin to explore the contours of my conception of ocean justice.

To navigate the challenges of building ocean epistemologies that are generative for transitioning justice approaches, I propose taking the epistemological framework developed by Lorraine Code to sea. At a time when attending to oceanic relations couldn't be more urgent, Code's "ecological thinking" framework offers an attentive, situated, ethico-political model of knowledge making toward more respectful, relational cohabitation in the world (Code 2006, 280). This is a robust, activist approach for countering social imaginaries at odds with responsible ecological living, which are tacitly enacted through dominant legal and scientific formulations. Steeped in feminist theoretical inheritances, ecological thinking intends to "denaturalize the instituted imaginary of mastery" and exclusionary claims to being and knowing that underpin hegemonic knowledge structures (Code 2006, 51). It provides a dynamic, epistemic scaffold for envisioning ocean justice.

This chapter navigates some of the watery onto-epistemic terrain immanent to ocean-inclusive approaches to justice. It analyzes selected tenets of Code's ecologically modeled thinking that are relevant to negotiating the associated physical, epistemological, and conceptual challenges. One of these tenets is the deliberative practice of epistemological diversity and "methodological pluralism" (Code 2006, 199) to counter the epistemic monocultures dominating how the ocean is governed. Another tenet is imagination, which is critical to conceptually reach the inaccessible realms and temporal materialities of the deep ocean. Justice processes that respond to the vulnerabilities of deep ocean lifeways also require an amplified imagining of ontological possibilities beyond human modes of being and time scales. Imagination, in this sense, needs to be rigorous by responsibly drawing on wide knowledge traditions and creating pathways for new knowledges and oceanic relations. Rigorous imagination is a powerful conceptual tool for identifying the testimonies critical to ocean justice, and the forms that will enable their circulation, as advocacy. Code argues that knowledge is made possible through testimony (Code 2006, 165–69) and that testimony is "the epistemic core of advocacy" (Code 2006, 175). Testimony is also at the heart of justice. As a tenet of ecological thinking, it is broadly conceived in this chapter to include the ocean as source and maker of particular types of knowing. I also introduce into a framework of ocean justice epistemology, the figuration of "sea-truthing" as a methodology to test the ocean's agentic materialities and relations against the exclusionary claims of orthodox legal and scientific formulations.

Though explicated within a philosophical context, Code's ecological thinking provides a practical epistemological approach for examining the obstruction to and constituent knowledges of ocean justice. Justice for the ocean is complicated—its ongoing formulations will need to necessarily build from knowledges across multiple, interconnecting disciplines, knowledge traditions, and imaginative approaches. As Code writes, "Activists, both singly and collectively, have to know a lot just to see what might be possible and may have to develop strategic compromises to be able to work toward sometimes distant and often unstable goals" (Code 2008, 201). Code's consciously activist proposal is committed to overthrowing epistemic monocultures but also considers how the intra-actions, to use Karen Barad's neologism (Barad 2003, 829), of multiple epistemes and enactments create certain habitats that intervene to make "knowledgeable living possible" (Code 2006, 172–73).

A "Carrier Bag" Not a Catch-All

Ecological thinking is not just "thinking about the ecology or about 'the environment'"(Code 2006, 24), but is an epistemological approach to developing knowledge itself; a "revisioned mode of engagement with knowledge, subjectivity, politics, ethics, science, citizenship and agency that pervades and reconfigures theory and practice" (Code 2006, 5). The appeal to ecology is both literal and metaphoric. It literally involves the science of ecology as a source of knowledge making, though Code cautions against unquestioned claims to truth (Code 2006, 51, 68). Ecology also functions metaphorically (51) in the relational process of ecological thinking. The changing nature and situations of knowledge-making models the "multiply contested character" and instability of ecology (Code 2013, 7). Flowing and upwelling with the ocean's continual transitions, knowledge making emerges through processes of ongoing contestation, reflection, reexamination, and renewal.

The capaciousness of ecological thinking enables complexities and interconnections of actual oceanic ecologies to be brought into the knowledge-making field. In addition, a host of theoretical, aesthetic, and affective approaches to knowledge making may be held at once in its broad epistemic weave. This is important for emerging reckonings with ocean justice, given the paucity of knowledge that exists about the ocean realm and their more-than-human communities. However, Code advocates not simply for a multiplicity of knowledges but for "multi-vocal thinking together" (Code 2017, 214) and "engaged, interpretative deliberations" (Code 2017, 206; see also Code 2013, 851).

The broad epistemic weave of Code's model corresponds with Ursula Le Guin's "carrier bag" figuration (Le Guin 1989) in which a bag is understood as a collective, relational device. Such relational scaffolding is needed for developing broadly inclusive ocean epistemologies that are constitutive of multiple views, knowledge makers, testimonies, and rigorous, generative imaginings. By acknowledging a wider field of knowledge makers, knowledges, and testimonial forms, ecological thinking serves to discredit claims inherent "in epistemology and the politics of knowledge [that] insist on and reinforce an imagined cognitive autonomy" (Code 2006, 172). In an ecological model, beings and the knowledges they make together continually transition through the intra-actions of their (and others') constituent elements. For ocean justice this means considering marine communities, environments and systems, diverse knowledges, governance frameworks, corporate interests, consumer commodity demands, and their intra-actions on the same plane.

Ocean justice is contingent on stretching imaginatively beyond the hegemonic knowledge structures and legal regimes that control how the ocean is made available for development. It needs knowledge-making processes that "denaturalize the instituted imaginary of mastery," as Code prescribes (Code

2006, 51), and unsettle "the self-certainties of western capitalism" (Code 2006, 8). Given the scale of not yet known and potentially unknowable deep ocean lives, relations, and communities, justice entails more than recognition of suppressed knowledge systems and deliberative strategies and practices to ensure their inclusion, though this is critical. It insists on recognizing the literal and metaphoric habitats produced by Western epistemic traditions of mastery and their devastating impacts on ocean lifeways.

In its diagnostic function, Code's model insists on challenging claims of universalization or objectivity. It questions the ethical and political dimensions of how knowledges are created and perpetuated, as well as the knowledge habitats they create. In the context of the expanding seabed mining frontier, ocean advocacy asks why certain knowledge contributions and relational perspectives are legitimated by the United Nations Convention on the Law of the Sea (UNCLOS) and not others? Who are the beneficiaries of such exclusions? For example, putative claims of "responsible" deep seabed mining performed in self-regulating, sunless environments—beyond auditable scrutiny or public observation—need to be interrogated to expose the adequacy of knowledge claims and to make visible the discursive efforts to disappear associated ecological harms. If UNCLOS's legal foundations are purportedly built on detached objectivity, why are the voices of industrialists so prominent? And why should conservation principles be observed only where they are economically viable? Why should the ocean's preservation itself be trumped by development? In this view, knowledge ecologies create habitats conducive to certain ways of understanding the world and not others.

Habitats and Habitability

Habitability is a recurring theme for Code. As a quality of knowledge-making environments, its significance for ocean justice is to signal pathways for considering the very real, physical interventions of particular epistemologies and actions on ocean communities. In her analysis "Ecological Thinking, The Politics of Epistemic Location," Phyllis Rooney notes Code's interest in how the interactions of the terms "habitat" and "habitability" imbue ecology with significant moral, political, and epistemological dimensions (Rooney 2008, 170). Code gained these insights by observing how the relationship between habitat and habitability informed Rachel Carson's understanding of ecological (Rooney 2008, 170). Thinking about epistemology and ecology from the perspective of habitat and habitability, as well as the implications of their interaction, is also generative for understanding how the enactments of master models intervene in physical ecologies.

Rooney also queries whether epistemologies of mastery could be considered as forms of ecological thinking (173). I am grateful for the clarification this question makes possible. Ecological thinking can be thought of as a carrier-bag epistemological approach for examining how the intra-action or exclusion of particular knowledge contributions, value systems, and ethos creates knowledge habitats and conditions of habitability. Further, such knowledge habitats have real material, physical impacts on the worlds in which they intervene. In this context, epistemologies of mastery are "not very habitable (still) for many who do not find their epistemic authority reflected in them and for many who want to think in new ways about knowledge and about epistemology" (Rooney 2008, 174). In a metaphoric sense, epistemologies of mastery cultivate exclusionary knowledge habitats. The interrogatory approach of ecological thinking can reveal the limitations of these practices and their impacts on human and more-than-human worlds.

UNCLOS is one of international law's largest framework conventions and instruments of mastery. Applying ecological thinking to the Convention's knowledge ecologies can identify how its intra-acting elements produce conditions of habitability both metaphorically and literally. This includes its legal discursivities, enactments and subjugated conservation measures, extractivist enabling imaginaries, and the unprepared seafloor communities extinguished and intervened upon. Thinking ecologically then about UNCLOS's ocean governance framework makes explicit the collective consequences and ethico-political dimensions of decisions made by jurists, policymakers, consumers, transnational resource corporations, company directors, company scientists on ocean habitats. Non-Western knowledge systems that recognize human interconnectedness with the ocean are absent in UNCLOS; the voices of their proponents and communities of practice are silent. Absent, too, are forms of advocacy that acknowledge the situatedness and partiality of their creation or that bring forward testimonies of the complex conditions of livability for other-than-human marine entities. We can see how the knowledge ecology and imaginary driving UNCLOS's seabed mining mandate physically intervene to create thinner conditions of habitability for particular deep ocean lives. In these changed conditions it is not clear which lives, if any, will replace those that are extinguished. Epistemologies, enactments and social imaginaries collectively sustain habitats, change, or end them.

The ecology of (Western) ocean governance, including its real-world interventions, are not very habitable for present ocean communities. As ecological elements, the conservation measures in UNCLOS are simply insufficient to the needs of a habitable, biodiverse ocean world. UNCLOS legitimates the intervention of seabed mining in some of the least understood ecosystems on the planet (Earle 2016; International Seabed Authority 2011). Knowledge environments buttressing UNCLOS rally behind extractivist rhetoric and enactments that emphasize economic growth and business-as-usual development of the ocean as a material reservoir. Through its knowledge habitats and discursive enactments UNCLOS contributes ecologically to real physical ocean ecologies, demonstrating that knowledge is not passive—it has consequences. As Santos argues, knowledge intervenes on reality: "Knowledge is not representation; it is intervention" (Santos 2014, 207). Particular ways of knowing and acting intervene in the ocean and change habitats both for marine entities and the planet's habitability more generally.

Gathering and Building Epistemologies for Ocean Justice

There are of course myriad alternative ways of knowing the ocean than through the constraints of Western epistemology alone. However, the intrinsic coloniality of Western epistemologies of mastery privileges and attempts to universalize particular ways of knowing while subordinating and denying the contributions of alternative, relational knowledges and perspectives from different cultures. Under the inherent binarisms of the master model, the human/nature divide separates humans from nature. Within this conception, the ocean is a "shadow place," to use Val Plumwood's apt figuration (Plumwood 2008), where the contributions of other-than-human entities to knowledge and earthly habitability are "backgrounded" (Plumwood 1993, 153).

Guided by instrumentalizing imaginaries, development-focused governance instruments such as UNCLOS, put nature to work in the service of human enterprise. Their reductive, discursive strategies enable marine environmental exploitations by spatializing and territorializing the ocean as a background place where human actions are enacted: marine creatures are harvested, commercial species protected, cables laid, bombs tested, waste and bilge waters dumped, bedrock drilled, fossil fuels extracted (see also Anna Grear 2015; and Klaus Bosselmann 2010). As I have written elsewhere,

"In this imaginary the ocean is instrumentalised as quarry, pantry, sink and sump" (Reid 2018).

Rattling the stronghold of extractive imaginaries by building alternative epistemologies for ocean justice is not without its challenges. For a start, the ocean constitutes 99 percent of the earth's biosphere, and 80 percent of this is without sunlight. They are also not comprehensively explored nor are their marine life forms and interconnectivities fully understood; many are yet to be encountered. Until recently humans did not know of the existence of thermophilic or chemosynthetic life forms, the material temporalities and complex dynamics of hydrological cycles and dynamic ocean systems, or the chemistry of climate-changing ocean waters. In these places, communities are bonded through voluminous, fluid pressures, chemical exchanges and photic socialities, their relationalities still unchartered. Thinking beyond human-oriented experiences to reimagine the ocean outside the hegemony of extractivist imaginaries requires "coming terms with ambiguity" (Code 2006, 204). It also means being open and ontologically adaptive to the ocean's unknown physical, relational, and temporal complexities.

As with Donna Haraway's comparable invocation of "staying with the trouble" (Haraway 2016), Code's proposition urges against the need for premature and partial knowledge closures. Code drew insight from Rachel Carson's extensive, patient fieldwork and observations of long-range impacts of anthropogenic chemical influences. Carson was averse to the urgency with which corporations tried to find quick solutions, urging patience while sufficient ecological evidence could be found to justify remedial actions—to wait "an extra season or two" (Code 2006, 42). What would Carson think of the corporate pressures to advance seabed mining when so little is known of the deep ocean and so much is already known of our other impact?

Carson's practice of mapping patterns and relationships in often unchartered environmental events (see Code 2006, 62) informs Code's methodological approach. However, Carson had the advantage of visiting agricultural and coastal ecotone sites to closely observe their ecologies and the impacts of agricultural practices and government policies. How do we map patterns and relationships in the deep ocean where they are unlike any that may compare to our own lived experiences; or where intra-actions materially and temporally transition beyond human time scales? In these times of climate-changing oceans and expanding resource frontiers, it is precisely because our empirical knowledge of deep ocean realms is so limited that for ocean justice to develop, there is a need to amplify scientific research while simultaneously incorporating diverse other knowledges. This includes legitimating ocean testimonies and those of diverse others, such as an expanded field of creative, intellectual, and cultural contributions.

Exceeding the Thinkable with Rigorous Imagination

Ecological thinking invites an "imaginative-interpretative attentiveness" (Code 2006, 211) to "imagine into the unknown" (229). This is crucial for providing the conceptual reach into deep ocean realms that are physically unreachable to all but a handful of research aquanauts. Seeking out ocean testimony requires us to "exceed the thinkable," as Code invokes (Code 2006, 224), and to keep open to the onto-epistemic possibilities of ways of knowing, relating, and being that are unimaginable within the strictures of habitus and sedimented imaginaries. "It takes seriously the high probability—of radical difference" (206).

Rigorous imagination is needed in order to rummage deep into creative and affective reservoirs of innovation and inspiration and to synthesize insights across diverse epistemic contributions and testimonies from diverse and always renewing new forms: lyrical theoretical approaches, artistic engagement, literature, and other aesthetic approaches as valid, critical tools for discerning unseen connections and implications of ocean relations. Rigor is also needed to stay mindful of the limitations of the imaginaries in which imagining functions (Code 2006, 206) and, as Code urges, to attempt "to think one's way," as openly as possible, "into the situations of differently situated Others" (207).

Reimagining Ocean Knowing

Reliance on marine scientific accounts is understandable given their insights provide a vital knowledge portal to the deep and remote ocean realms. The point here is not to discard science but to interrogate and potentially contest its claims of neutrality while identifying unasked questions and patterns that obstruct progress toward ocean justice. What types of questions are (or are not) being asked of the ocean and who is benefiting from scientific research commissioned by transnational resource corporations? For example, putatively independent scientific studies provide institutional justifications for issuing seabed mining licenses in an era of unprecedented ocean industrialization, anthropogenic climate change, and their intersecting impacts. They might also be used to determine the degree of precaution that qualifies for observance of the precautionary principle. Claims to "objective," "independent" knowledge fail to reveal their situatedness and the implications and interests of human subjects behind the "veil of neutrality" (Code 2013, 842).

As the following paragraph demonstrates, even something as relatively minor as the disposition of researchers can tilt the scope and type of knowledge garnered. Code makes the salient feminist point that knowledge claims come from somewhere, from people "inculcated into a form of life—a habitus and ethos—where conditions for their articulation and acknowledgement are already in place" (Code 2006, ix). If the habitus that informs epistemic knowledge is not trained to acknowledge certain forms of knowledge or certain subjects—but merely the hegemonic knowledge systems it is familiar with—then it will not see (or it will unsee) or exclude evidence of other beings, relations, and vulnerabilities that do not fit the frame. As Code says, "discovery requires a mind prepared" (Code 2014, 674).

One of the world's leading and highly respected marine ecologists, Cindy Van Dover, comments that scientists do not want to advocate for or against deep seabed mining, but rather their role is to gather information that will ensure the best possible mining (TED Archive 2015). In an earlier *Wired* interview, Van Dover remarks that "deep-sea conservation is something I never thought I'd have to deal with in my career" (Van Dover, interview; Marlow 2012). During her early career, Van Dover did not foresee the rapid expansion of ocean industrialization, imagining that "human activities and impacts in the deep sea were decades, if not centuries into the future" (Van Dover, interview; Marlow 2012). If this was Van Dover's experience, it is entirely possible that this was also the situation for other scientists producing research for environmental assessments of the deep seabed during the late 1990s and early 2000s. Scientists accumulated knowledge of the deep ocean based on discoveries of wondrous lifeforms that had never been seen before but without conservation at the forefront of their concern or knowledge practices. They made taxonomic find after find without realizing their role in preparing the ground for extractive industries.

Sea-Truthing

Code situates the circumstances of knowledge making and makers by "relocating inquiry down on the ground" (Code 2006, 6). Locating knowledge down on the seabed (to contextualize the ocean) invites respectful interrogation of the claims of neutrality accompanying scientific research to show the various ways that authored partiality steers particular knowledge and occludes others. Sea-truthing is an ecological approach that seeks to tack across the accounts of siloed disciplines to synthesize knowledge and rigorously imagine ways to know the ocean more expansively—on their terms. Code's counsel for engaging with such epistemic material is to do so "imaginatively, respectfully and with an intellectual moral humility" (Code 2006, 231). Where the nexus of knowledge claims and law implicate deep ocean ecological communities, sea-truthing necessarily involves bringing testimony of ocean lives, ecological communities, and relations onto the same plane. The simultaneous consideration of law, science, extractivist activities, and the ocean themselves generates flashpoints for the radically violent, habitat-changing practices of current ocean governance to be acknowledged and contested. Sea-truthing recognizes the living real of ocean inhabitants in negotiations for seabed mining expansions by foregrounding their indescribable, mysterious, temporal, and vulnerable qualities and co-constituencies. It is a process of sea-truthing: iterative readings and imaginings between diverse testimonials and claims.

Through my concept of sea-truthing I propose a methodology that tests the seaworthiness of ocean governance and relations by foregrounding the living reality of marine communities, the ocean's lively depths, sediments, and their interconnecting flows. While ocean testimonies give evidence of the conditions of habitability and vulnerability for different life cycles and forms, sea-truthing draws on testimonies to interrogate the representations and interventions of legal instruments and particular uses of orthodox science.

As this chapter noted earlier, because humans are unable to physically dwell in the deep ocean or witness their habitats, relations, and intra-actions firsthand, we are significantly reliant on marine scientific accounts. Creating alternative ocean imaginaries, therefore, requires reading such accounts deeply and imagining with "epistemic humility," as Code suggests (Code 2006, 207). Lively transitional materialities, creatures, and relations coalescing as ocean nature are poorly represented in development-focused environmental reports and governance instruments. Sea-truthing them into visibility requires stretching epistemic texts beyond taxonomic and scientifically framed inquiries or representations. Sea-truthing what's missing might be a matter of reading these accounts closely to discern vested interests and unasked questions. Which elements in legislation or policy keep the living ocean beyond view, beyond legitimacy? What are the operative ideas that underwrite "patterns of legitimacy and credibility and their opposites" (29)? In the self-regulating seabed mining environment, sea-truthing seeks to discern absences in the facts or methodologies of environmental impact assessments. Different, situated sea-truthings may emerge through iterative processes that take seriously yet challenge the representations and accounts of legislators, miners, scientists, and consumers (2018).

Testimony and Advocacy

While sea-truthing tests the seaworthiness of such accounts, building knowledges for ocean justice requires widening the epistemic sea-nets to make space for suppressed and new forms of testimony. This means decolonizing scientific and governance epistemologies in order to recognize knowledges destructively ignored or suppressed through ongoing colonization. Testimonies of nondominant humans and of the ocean and their constituencies will also need to be recognized, gathered, and foregrounded in ways that transform how the ocean is known and governed for responsible cohabitation. To not proceed in this way is to perpetuate ongoing epistemic violence toward nondominant human populations and the ocean. Code describes as "epistemic violence" the process by which knowledges shaped by experiences and conditions specific to women "disappear into putatively global, generalised analyses" (Code 2017, 215). Drawing on the silencing experiences of women of color, Kirstie Dotson also examines epistemic violence but focuses on the harm resulting when audiences fail to meet their speakers' communicative needs (Dotson 2011). Dotson writes that successful testimonial exchange requires audiences to competently understand speakers in reciprocal communicative events within specific domains of knowledge. Ongoing failure to do so, due to what Dotson describes as "pernicious ignorance," institutes harmful acts of silencing that perpetuates epistemic violence (238).

Relatedly, Dotson, following Code, discusses the "situated ignorance" that arises from one's social position and worldview (Code1993, 39 cited in Dotson 2011, 248). Locating knowledge makes it possible to apprehend how particular understandings of reality arise from different epistemic positionings, which can both enable epistemic advantages and present epistemic limitations (Dotson 2011, 248).

The concept of epistemic violence has significant bearings on ocean justice processes. Ongoing harmful impacts of human activities on the ocean are a direct result of the failure to recognize the ocean as a knower nor their testimonies as valid knowledge contributions. Profound dissonance exists between UNCLOS as the international governance order for the ocean and the domain and ecological communities over which it seeks to exerts control. Situated as an instrument of epistemological mastery, the knowledge habitats it creates enable global capitalism, extractivism, corporate commodity accumulations, and geopolitical advancements of certain nation-states. Within these habitats, scientific knowledge of the ocean is instrumentalized in the service of ocean "resource" development. As a governance framework though, UNCLOS lacks the wider knowledge competencies and sea-truthing sensitivities to understand the ocean and their testimonies in ways that recognize the vulnerabilities and habitability needs of marine ecologies and planetary systems.

There is violence, too, in abstract representations. Consider UNCLOS's reductive definition of the international seabed jurisdiction, called the Area, which makes up almost forty percent of the surface of our planet: "For the purposes of this Convention: (1) 'Area' means the seabed and ocean floor and subsoil thereof, beyond the limits of national jurisdiction;" (UNCLOS, article 1, para. 1). Abstractions are of course invaluable as they enable us to think and communicate but, as Moore cautions, such representations "abstract too much reality in the interests of conceptual clarity" (Moore 2015, 27), as UNCLOS's erasure and silencing of the ocean floor's marine life demonstrates.

Countering the epistemological incompetence of UNCLOS and the lifeless world of its juridical representations, ocean justice recruits testimonies from the seabed communities: the spectacular long red-lipped tube worms of the East Pacific Ridge; ghost crabs that scamper up hydrothermal vent turrets in water hot enough to melt lead; micro-sponges living atop millennia-old manganese nodules; giant yellow sponges of the Southern Ocean; purple feathery topped polycheate worms, ribboned ascidians, orange brittle stars, and translucent holothurians. And what of the crowds of marine lives traveling nightly from the floor to feed under the moonlit surface? Ecological thinking lays the groundwork for ocean justice by acknowledging and recruiting testimonies from these lively worlds, bringing them in to the epistemological weave and on the same plane for consideration as a resource corporation's bid for mining licenses.

Following other feminist examples of "citing the natural world" (see Daly 1978 and Haraway 2016; Neimanis and Walker 2014; Neimanis 2017), ocean justice admits the ocean as a legitimate, conceptual, knowledge-making source for developing new relational imaginaries. However, what does testimony mean in relation to understanding the different life stages and livability conditions of vent and seep organisms, hagfish, and humpback whales? What does it mean to the gaseous surface exchanges and the carbon and chemicals that sink with propagules, eggs, feces, and the dead to rest on the seabed and in sediment? What does it mean in relation to the vulnerability of massive water transport systems that circulate across ocean basins, eddying off to massage continental edges and replenished by upwelled nutrients? Thinking with and through these complex relationalities including those interconnecting and implicated with law, resource frontiers, and science is thinking ecologically with Code, "reconfiguring, relationships all the way down" (Code 2006).

Sourcing ocean testimony involves imagining beyond human and terrestrial centric paradigms to conceive different conditions of livability in deep ocean. It suggests turning down the human register a little to discern ocean differences with sensitivity. Code poignantly observes that "imagining, too, occurs within an imaginary" (Code 2006). This goes to the tangled challenge of how to sink imaginatively into the ocean, open to the ambiguities and radical differences, in order to discern signals of testimony. For example, absence of sunlight, or the dense pressure caused by cubic kilometers of moving seawater, are seen from a human, terrestrial perspective as conditions to which deep-sea creatures have had to adapt. Through a different, oceanic lens, those same elements enable life—as conditions of livability. Pressure functions like a great muscle around each organism, providing containment of organs, holding bodies together. Moving up through the water column to escape mining plumes is no option for slow-growing, slow-moving deep-sea creatures whose only escape is sideward across the ocean floor and bottom layer of seawater. Sea-truthing recognizes that darkness, too, enables life in the benthos. Rather than a state that creatures have had to adapt to, creaturely existence depends on darkness to provide camouflage from predators, cool temperatures, and the conditions for bioluminescent communication between creatures. Alaimo's description of life at this depth as a "violet black ecology," unmoors heliocentric models of human sovereignty by situating creaturely livability in a vast aphotic realm (2014, 235).

Code's epistemological project seeks to create epistemic habitats in which the contributions of previously marginalized voices may come forward. "The other is already speaking. It is a matter of listening, and not from here but from as close to there as responsible imaginings can go" (Code 2006, 235). Developments toward ocean justice will need the silencing practices of ocean governance and dominant scientific epistemologies to be deinstituted in order to bring forward other voices and knowledges. Where "other" are remote, deep ocean life worlds, how might we listen well and what form might responsible imaginings take? Imagining ocean justice for a predominantly aphotic realm needs knowledge-making methodologies for reaching beyond human ocular-centric modes of understanding; to recognize complex, polysonic relations and intra-actions. This involves working across materials such as scientific accounts and acoustic recordings of remote ocean worlds to evidence nonhuman acoustic conditions for livability, for example: how the crackling sound of sessile feeders guide a fish around deep ocean ridge contours; whale moans, clicks, and songs used to communicate across family pods; or the need to hear the rain at the surface as a signal of intensifying storms at sea. Testimony for ocean justice will need to hear evidence of how human-made noises: the sonic booms, rattles, and chugging associated with resource exploration, 24/7 extractive activities, war games, and ship traffic, alter acoustic habitability, forcing marine communities to migrate, dwell deeper, and lose their bearings. In addition to sound, bioluminescent, spatial, chemical, and other ways of knowing can be foregrounded as testimony by reading deeply across and between scientific accounts and through video documentation of deep ocean ROV expeditions. Ocean testimony can also include the associated commentary and affective responses of scientists at their ROV consoles as they see a creature for the first time and then subsequent comments as efforts are made to quickly corral their discovery into known taxa.

Testimony of the ocean's temporal complexities can be read into seemingly banal images such as recent photographs of the still-crisp tracks left by a research vessel that had explored the abyssal plains thirty years earlier (Chin and Hari 2020, 23). The image attests to the slow movement of abyssal currents and the slow trickle of marine snow from the surface to the floor. By analogy, how long would it take to disperse sediment plumes stirred by mining activities? And how likely is it that micro communities of coral and sponges would endure in this changed habitat? Testimony can take the form of absences, where the limited presence of large animal carcasses on the seafloor speaks volumes about voracious overfishing. Absence of announcements from resource corporations about their major investments in conservation measures and technologies designed to alleviate the damage is evidence of the prioritization of extraction over conservation. The word biodiversity is absent from the text of UNCLOS, which indicates an absence of concern for the ocean's biodiverse communities in the drafting of UNCLOS.

The examples of oceanic testimony described in this chapter are not novel but much of them lie buried in siloed research reports that rarely make it into public knowledge. As previously indicated, there is ocean testimony that can be found in the interstices of scientific reports, or in the affective and phenomenological dimensions of ocean relations; or the testimonies of marginalized non-Western epistemologies. Astrida Neimanis's feminist posthumanist phenomenology siphons and stirs through the same epistemological and ontological challenges extrapolated through this chapter, which is how to reach "actual but ungraspable events" (Neimanis 2017, 53). Neimanis offers the notion of "proxy stories" where access to knowledge and direct experience is physically impossible. Human/ocean phenomenological connections can take the form of the "proxy stories": artistic and literary accounts that work to "amplify and sensitise embodied experiences and desediment human-scaled perspectives" (55).

Neimanis's posthumanist phenomenological approach offers yet another testimonial formulation, one that activates practices of "deep description" (25) to connect the ocean with the myriad fluids streaming, trickling, dripping, evaporating, and discharging from human bodies. The figuration of "bodies of water" is a feminist, embodied, ethical orientation of human bodies with the hydrosphere in which all our fluids cycle. "Getting back to the ocean body, accessing that which we cannot inhabit through the resource of our bodies and their various kinds of experiential knowledge" (43).

Artistic or philosophical forms that evoke feelings such as awe, curiosity, empathy, horror, intrigue, shame, bewilderment can offer valid, affective testimony toward building relational knowledge for ocean justice. Aesthetics, too, has testimonial value through the experiences of wonder and beauty by portraying complexity and as indicative of a desire for relationality, even simply at the level of care. "Jellyfish Science, Jellyfish Aesthetics: Posthuman Reconfigurations of the Sensible" (Alaimo 2013) examined the photographic documentation collected as part of the Census of Marine Life, and the hyper-aesthetic photographs of jellyfish produced by artist Claire Nouvian in her book *The Deep: The Extraordinary Creatures of the Abyss* (Nouvian cited in Alaimo 2013, 141). Just as the artist reveled in the beauty of her subjects, Alaimo also reveled in the beauty of the photographs although conscious of them having been cleansed of background marine snow. "To be astounded or astonished is to be unmoored, cut loose from an established order of things, to find oneself floating somewhere as yet unmapped, where unexpected, unrecognizable forms of life seem to demand some sort of recognition and response" (151). Alaimo argues that these aesthetic presentations could be understood as "manifestations of care, wonder and concern" (141). A subject ordinarily invisible in their ocean domain was rendered sumptuously visible. The time and consideration given to assemble the photograph, and the lighting and production treatment, together signal both an acknowledgment of the subject and also that they were worthy of aesthetic care.

In recruiting conceptually imaginative testimonials for ecological thinking, how might the resulting speculations, aesthetic forms, synthesizing of lyrical theories, imagery, and stories contribute responsibly? Code's simple but practical suggestion is that for testimonial evidence to perform as advocacy, it "requires epistemically responsible, on-going investigation to inform it. It has to be kept open to justification or contestation at various levels" (Code 2013, 851). Careful deliberations are needed to establish when certain material is evidence and which testimony can be trusted toward knowledge making (Code 2006, ix). It is when testimony circulates through science, literary, philosophical, artistic, and other imaginative speculative approaches that it becomes advocacy (176).

Making Visible Our Material Connections to Ocean Extractions

In "Doubt and Denial: Epistemic Responsibility Meets Climate Change Skepticism," Code makes a case for 'critically renewed conceptions and enactments of subjectivity at a social and collective level (Code 2013, 846). The subject of her essay is climate change skepticism and advocacy, however, epistemic responsibility to account for subjectivity reverberates through Code's wider framework of ecological thinking. It is a call to "re-think and re-enact assumptions about who we think we are—a radical unsettling of the tacit, instituted social-political-epistemic imaginaries with which we live and think" (846–47). This is a salient point for the purposes of ocean justice, which needs knowledge projects and imaginaries that implicate subjectivity with extraction by emplacing our material dependencies, and the places we take our materials from, into the visible frame of who we think "we" are.

Extractive development imaginaries continue to swing wrecking balls through the ocean, while failing to adequately account for the species extinguishments resulting from their enactments. Transnational resource corporations and their shareholders may have the most to gain from such activity; however, this is something that implicates us all, albeit by different degrees. Ocean justice seeks not just the liquefaction of the development-tilted legal order but also of disassociated, exploitative, relational approaches to the ocean as well. For as long as individual desires for consumer goods such as laptops, cement, copper pipes, and batteries drive the demand, consumers are also the beneficiaries and patrons of mining. Our material dependencies and flows profoundly connect and differently implicate us in the ocean. Through the lens of dominant Western imaginaries and global capitalism, these connections are "dematerialized" (Plumwood 2008, 141) through myriad disconnecting increments of processing, manufacture, and market. The productive epistemological task toward ocean justice is to build knowledges that make more visible the connection between consumerist accumulations, the earthly materials from which they are manufactured, and the spent marine life that is consequent on obtaining such materials.

Tracing the deep ocean connections of our material dependencies and accumulations is not easy. A degree of detail and particularity is necessary to follow seabed minerals from their extraction into commodity products and to begin to recognize how extractive processes impact the specific material and social conditions of livability and vulnerability experienced by marine dwellers. This is significant for ocean justice because, as Code argues "people need to know enough to think and act well," toward "respectful cohabitation." Developing justice-centered epistemological processes for the ocean requires knowledge contributions from the ocean and their constituent lifeways, materialities, and temporalities. New materialism provides the analytical and conceptual tools to engage with the deep ocean across the detail of marine scientific sources and contributions from an expanded field of constituencies and testimonial forms, to simultaneously engage with the ocean's transitioning materialities and embodiments, as well as the intervening discursivities and imaginaries. For example, Stacey Alaimo's "transcorporeality" provides an important figuration for thinking through the ethical implications of materialities such as the transition of microplastics across porous, saltwater bodies (Alaimo 2010, 2014) and ocean ecologies. Such material flows result from and disrupt the enactments and discursive partitioning of law.

As a counter to the oversimplifications of legal abstractions and compartmentalized perspective of nature, new materialist approaches facilitate thinking and imagining with ocean complexities such as luminescent communications and chemical and other material exchanges and their intra-actions. Taking a new materialist approach to the deep ocean, for example, Alaimo contends that "a violet-back ecology would attempt to understand the water of the *abyssal zone* as something rather than nothing, as substance rather than background" (Alaimo 2014, 235). Astrida Neimanis's new materialist phenomenology offers a beautifully enlivening approach to think with the archival, thick time agencies of water (not exclusively oceanic) and the present and long-range material implications as it flows from body to body (Neimanis and Walker 2014).

Conclusion

Ocean justice is speculative as it entails casting ethical relations toward deep ocean communities and beings that have yet to be discovered and complex relationalities that we are yet to understand. Neither can ocean justice always be static or evenly negotiated for all. The ocean that existed at the time of the drafting of UNCLOS, for example, is not the same ocean as they are today. Neither will the ecological conditions of the near future ocean be what they are now. Conditions for justice will inevitably change as the planet's material transitions present new challenges for habitability for some, or thriving for others. Human population growth will also further increase demands on the ocean for protein and other materials, which will likely force justice triage situations.

This chapter has gone some way in explicating the complexities of developing epistemological approaches for my concept of ocean justice. Code's ecological thinking provides an important epistemic framework and practical activist approach for bringing together the multiple and diverse knowledges needed to build broadly constitutive ocean epistemologies. Its capaciousness allows for the interactions of different methodologies, theoretical approaches, and epistemologies. Notably, ecological thinking is productive for examining scientific and legal epistemologies as knowledge habitats whose enactments physically intervene to sustain, change, or end habitable conditions for humans and marine others. Rigorous imagination is central to these knowledge-building practices and to resisting the dominant narratives of mastery and extractivism. Through imagination we can also find and feel the minute and planetary, materially-embodied connections with the ocean that justice demands.

Epilogue

Follow the light as it disappears, falling with the detritus rain and whales. Squeeze through fish gills and weave thick gelatinous kelp groves. Flow beneath ice shelves and along tropical reef edges dotted with brightly colored ascidians. Be the salt that dilutes in the flush of fresh rain. Rotate slowly with the offshore eddies and upwell to travel the currents, basin to basin.

Acknowledgments

I acknowledge the ocean, which continues to nurture and inspire. I am also grateful to my supervisor Astrida Neimanis and editors of this edition, Andrea Doucet and Nancy McHugh, whose feedback on earlier drafts has been so helpful, and to Lorraine Code, whose incredible contributions to feminist epistemology are a continuing ballast for my research. This chapter was written on the unceded Gadigal lands of the Eora Nation.

Notes

1. This chapter conceives "ocean" to mean the undivided ocean body, more-than-human others, lifeways, materialities, and phenomenological systems.
2. The pronouns "they/their/them" are deliberately used to recognize the ocean as not an object but as a gender-neutral, collective planetary entity.

Works Cited

Alaimo, Stacey. 2010. *Bodily Natures: Science, Environment and the Material Self.* Bloomington: Indiana University Press.
———. 2013. "Jellyfish Science, Jellyfish Aesthetics: Posthuman Reconfigurations of the Sensible." In *Thinking with Water Edited by Cecilia Chen, Janine Macleod and Astrida Neimanis McGill.* Montreal: McGill-Queens University Press.
———. 2014. "Violet-Black." In *Prismatic Ecology: Ecotheory beyond Green*, edited by Jeffrey Jerome Cohen Editor, 233–51. Minneapolis: University of Minnesota Press.
Barad, Karen. 2003. "Posthumanist Performativity: Toward an Understanding of How Matter Comes to Matter." *Signs: Journal of Women in Western Culture and Society* 28, no. 3: 801–31.
Bosselmann, Klaus. 2010. "Losing the Forest for the Trees: Environmental Reductionism in the Law." *Sustainability* 2, no. 8: 2424–48. https://doi.org/10.3390/su2082424.
Chin, A., and K. Hari. 2020. Predicting the Impacts of Mining of Deep Sea Polymetallic Nodules in the Pacific Ocean: A Review of Scientific Literature,

Deep Sea Mining Campaign and Mining Watch Canada (website). http://www.deepseaminingoutofourdepth.org/wp-content/uploads/Nodule-Mining-in-the-Pacific-Ocean-1.pdf.

Code, Lorraine. 1998. "How to Think Globally: Stretching the Limits of Imagination." *Hypatia* 13, no. 2: 73–85. http://www.jstor.org.ezproxy1.library.usyd.edu.au/stable/3810638?pq-origsite=summon.

———. 2006. *Ecological Thinking; the Politics of Epistemic Location.* New York: Oxford University Press.

———. 2007 "Thinking about Ecological Thinking." *Hypatia* 23, no. 1: 187–203. https://muse-jhu-edu.ezproxy1.library.usyd.edu.au/article/228156.

———. 2013. "Doubt and Denial: Epistemic Responsibility Meets Climate Change Scepticism." *Social Science Research Network*, Human Rights and the Environment: In Search of a New Relationship 3, no. 5: 838–53. https://papers.ssrn.com/abstract=2247830.

———. 2014. "Culpable Ignorance?" *Hypatia* 29, no. 3: 670–76. https://doi.org/10.1111/hypa.12071.

———. 2017. "The Tyranny of Certainty." *Symposium: Canadian Journal of Continental Philosophy* 21, no. 1: 206–18.

Daly, Mary. 1978. *Gyn/Ecology: The Metaethics of Radical Feminism.* Boston: Beacon. http://www.feministes-radicales.org/wp-content/uploads/2010/11/mary-daly-gyn-ecology-the-metaethics-of-radical-feminism.pdf.

Dotson, Kristie. 2011. "Tracking Epistemic Violence, Tracking Practices of Silencing." *Hypatia* 26, no. 2: 236–257.

Earle, Sylvia. 2016. "Deep Sea Mining: An Invisible Land Grab—Mission Blue." Mission Blue. https://www.mission-blue.org/2016/07/deep-sea-mining-an-invisible-land-grab/.

Environmental Humanities 9, no. 1: 149–66. https://doi.org/10.1215/22011919-3829172.

Grear, Anna. 2015. "Towards New Legal Foundations? In Search of Renewing Foundations." In *Thought, Law, Rights and Action in the Age of Environmental Crisis*, 283–313. Cheltenham, UK: Edward Elgar.

Haraway, Donna J. 2016. *Staying with the Trouble: Making Kin in the Chthulucene.* Experimental Futures: Technological Lives, Scientific Arts, Anthropological Voices. Durham, NC: Duke University Press.

International Seabed Authority. 2011. "Environmental Management of Deep-Sea Chemosynthetic Ecosystems: Justification of and Considerations for a Spatially-Based Approach." 9. ISA Technical Study Series. Kingston, Jamaica: International Seabed Authority. https://www.isa.org.jm/sites/default/files/files/documents/tstudy9.pdf.

Marlow, Jeffrey. 2012. "Deep-Sea Mining Is Closer Than You Think." *Wired*, December 2012. https://www.wired.com/2012/12/deep-sea-mining-is-closer-than-you-think/.

Moore, Jason W. 2015. *Capitalism in the Web of Life: Ecology and the Accumulation of Capital*. London: Verso.

Neimanis, Astrida. 2017. *Bodies of Water: Posthuman Feminist Phenomenology*. Environmental Cultures Series. London: Bloomsbury.

Neimanis, Astrida, Cecilia Åsberg, and Suzi Hayes. 2015. "Post-Humanist Imaginaries." In *Research Handbook on Climate Governance*, 480–90. Cheltenham, UK: Edward Elgar. https://www-elgaronline-com.ezproxy1.library.usyd.edu.au/view/9781783470594.00055.xml.

Neimanis, Astrida, Loen Walker, Rachel. 2014. "Weathering: Climate Change and the 'Thick Time' of Transcorporeality." *Hypatia* 29, no. 3: 558–575. https://onlinelibrary.wiley.com/doi/abs/10.1111/hypa.12064.

Plumwood, Val. 1993. *Feminism and the Mastery of Nature*. New York: Routledge.

———. 2008. "Shadow Places and the Politics of Dwelling." *Australian Humanities Review*, no. 44: 139–150. http://www.australianhumanitiesreview.org/archive/Issue-March-2008/plumwood.html.

Reid, Susan. 2018. "Science and Culture: Transitioning Currents in Times of Climate Change." In *Living with the Sea*, 114–28. London: Routledge.

———. 2020. "Solwara 1 and the Sessile Ones." In *Blue Legalities, The Life and Law of the Sea*, edited by Irus Braverman and Elizabeth Johnson. Durham, NC: Duke University Press.

Rooney, Phyllis. 2008. "Epistemic Responsibility and Ecological Thinking." *Hypatia* 23, no. 1: 170–176. https://www-jstor-org.ezproxy1.library.usyd.edu.au/stable/25483156?pq-origsite=summon&seq=1#metadata_info_tab_contents.

Santos, Boaventura de Sousa. 2014. *Epistemologies of the South: Justice against Epistemicide*. Herndon, UK: Routledge.

TED Archive. 2015. *Beyond the Edge of the Sea*. Mission Blue. https://www.youtube.com/watch?v=XevZCOiBNAs.

United Nations Convention on the Law of the Sea, December 10, 1982, UN Doc. A/CONF.62/122 (1982), 21 I.L.M. 1261 (1982) [UNCLOS].

World Wildlife Fund (WWF). 2019, May 10. "Sustainable Seafood." World Wildlife Fund. https://www.worldwildlife.org/industries/sustainable-seafood.

Chapter 13

Climate Advocacy as a Form of Epistemic Responsibility

A Case Study

Codi Stevens

Introduction

In 2013, while the Fifth Assessment Report of the Intergovernmental Panel on Climate Change (IPCC) was soon to be finalized, Lorraine Code wrote about climate change skepticism and the political and cultural atmosphere within which such skepticism exists. Code argues that the high value placed on unfettered individual freedom (especially in the United States) fuels what elsewhere she calls "culturally sanctioned ignorance" (Code 2007, 216). If the frightening predictions of climate scientists are credible, then a variety of regulatory measures are warranted; the threat such regulatory measures might pose to individual liberty provides a reason to dismiss the scientific findings. Nevertheless, Code concluded her essay with cautious optimism, remarking, "Whether the denials can continue in the face of the 2013 IPCC report remains to be seen; deniers will have to work relentlessly to manufacture levels of uncertainty sufficient to counter the force of these findings" (2013, 852).

In 2015, psychologist and economist Per Espen Stoknes took a paradox as his point of departure in the book *What We Think about When We Try Not to Think about Global Warming*. The paradox—one that prima facie suggests that even cautious optimism about the impact of IPCC reports and the like may be too sanguine—is this: over the past few decades, evidence of climate change has mounted, and yet, when surveyed, laypeople at the time of the book's publication were *less* likely to believe that climate change is happening than they had been in the past (Stoknes 2015, 3–4). Stoknes interprets this as a failure of conventional approaches to climate science communication. The go-to strategy of many science communicators and climate advocates has usually consisted of attempts to highlight the mounting evidence, offering ever more charts, graphs, and experimental data in the hope that the nth datum offered will be convincing. He argues that such strategies fail to convince because they ignore many of the realities about the ways in which people commonly think, behave, and form beliefs. Stoknes's goal is to generate alternative, more effective climate communication strategies, and his approach is informed by his training as a psychologist. What emerges from the text is an approach to climate advocacy that is responsive to the realities of our ordinary and imperfect epistemic practices.

The broad aim of this essay is to bring Code and Stoknes in conversation with each other. Code's work provides a powerful and valuable lens through which to analyze advocacy projects with clear epistemological components, like the one proposed by Stoknes. Code's work on epistemic responsibility, which evolves from *Epistemic Responsibility* (1987) through *Ecological Thinking* (2006) and beyond, provides a framework within which to recognize the importance of the relationship between advocacy and knowing well. Code and Stoknes have in common a deep concern about climate change denial. Although Stoknes does not use the language of epistemic responsibility to describe his own work (nor does he cite any texts on the subject), the concept of epistemic responsibility is eminently applicable to his climate communication proposals, and there are compelling connections to be made between his approach to advocacy and Code's philosophical work.

Informed by Code's accounts of responsible knowing and ecological thinking, I will show that Stoknes's project can be understood as a case study in the sort of advocacy work that is a form of epistemic responsibility. While there are many ways to understand what it means to conduct a case study, I have in mind John Gerring's description of the case study as "an intensive study of a single unit for the purpose of understanding a larger class of (similar) units" (2004, 342). In this case, Stoknes's climate advocacy project is the "single unit," and my purpose in examining that project is to deepen understanding of Code's concepts of epistemic responsibility and ecological thinking. The concepts themselves do not, I think, constitute a "larger class of units," to be understood. Rather, I contend that understanding them *will* make it easier to recognize other instances of epistemic responsibility in action, and it is instances of epistemic responsibility that make up the "larger class."

Why should we want a case study to help us understand how to identify epistemic responsibility and ecological thinking? Code does not offer precise technical definitions of epistemic responsibility or ecological thinking; she provides no necessary and sufficient conditions with which to determine which advocacy projects qualify as either. Indeed, she has good reason not to attempt to rigidly define these concepts. In "Responsibility and Rhetoric," Code responds to a criticism from Paul Moser, who complains that even if the line separating epistemic responsibility from irresponsibility is fuzzy, "we might still provide necessary and sufficient conditions for the wide range of typical instances, and then handle the wayward cases independently" (quoted in Code 1994, 7). Code explains, "The demands of epistemic responsibility are more wide-ranging, and the places where they arise do not divide easily into the 'typical' and the 'wayward.' They do, I think, more often than not bear family resemblances to one another" (1994, 17).

Since instances of epistemic responsibility and ecological thinking are best identified by family resemblance, our understanding of them increases as our set of recognized examples increases. To understand the family resemblances, we must "see a complicated network of similarities overlapping and criss-crossing" (Wittgenstein 2009, 66). The more examples we have available to consider, the easier it becomes to see the network of similarities. Code herself highlights some important examples that we might treat as case studies in her work, most notably the ecological thinking of Rachel Carson (2006). Recognizing that knowing responsibly and thinking ecologically are open-ended, unfolding projects realized in myriad contexts and locations, she invites us to imagine and articulate additional examples of these concepts in action (Code 2006).

The numerous and varied climate communication strategies Stoknes considers in his book (and the parallels to Code associated with each) outrun what I can reasonably detail within the purview of this essay. I will begin with an explanation of the phenomenon Stoknes calls "the global warming paradox" before narrowing my focus to two of the major categories of strategies Stoknes offers: the first comprises efforts aimed at making environmentally responsible behaviors effort*less*; the second includes climate communication strategies inspired by the thoroughly social context in which we come to know and choose to act (or not) based on our knowledge.

Paradoxes of Denial

Stoknes presents polling data showing that citizens of both the United States and Norway expressed greater concern about climate change in the late 1980s and early 1990s than they did circa 2014. Those polled in the United States responded to the question, "How much do you personally worry about the greenhouse effect or global warming?" Norwegians polled were asked, "How concerned are you about greenhouse effects and climate change?" The group of US respondents who answered, "Not worried," or, "A little," grew from about 37 percent in 1989 to roughly 44 percent in 2014. Norwegians' concern plunged even more dramatically: from approximately 31 percent "Not," or "A little," worried in 1989 to an outrageous 53 percent in 2013 (Stoknes 2015, 4–5). Though these questions are not direct inquiries about the doxastic attitudes of those polled, Stoknes reasons that lower levels of concern about climate change indicate lower likelihood of believing that the predictions of climate scientists are accurate, which often accompanies the belief that climate change is not happening.

To Stoknes, the global warming paradox is a clear sign that something about the conventional approaches to climate communication has gone awry. He characterizes the conventional approaches as basically repetitive attempts to push data on a chronically unimpressed public, as though the only possible explanation for each unsuccessful attempt was a dearth of graphs and tables. The subsequent advocacy campaigns will resemble the previous ones because the underlying assumptions that inform the climate communicators' efforts will remain unchanged (Stoknes 2015, xix). The often unarticulated (read: often unchallenged) axiom underwriting these communication strategies is that *belief formation is essentially a function of the amount and quality of evidence one is shown.* This axiom leads us to suppose that since scientific findings establishing the extent of human-caused climate change are more abundant in the present decade than in decades past, and because the consensus among climate scientists has only grown over time, belief among members of the lay public in human-caused climate change would only increase as the evidence mounts.

The results of the polls Stoknes cites appear paradoxical because the data flies in the face of this frequently made assumption. The disconcerting discovery of the global warming paradox serves as but one reason among many to reject the idea that evidence is the decisive factor in belief formation. A rudimentary reflection on human psychology reveals how very common it is that we believe things for which we lack evidence, or fail to believe things for which evidence abounds. Our beliefs are routinely the products of emotions, cognitive biases, and other factors exerting influence in tandem with (and shaping our perceptions of what counts as) the evidence we possess. Isolating any single belief-influencing factor and declaring it to be decisive in most cases paints an unrealistically simplistic picture of belief formation.

Code rejects such simplistic pictures of belief formation. She has repeatedly demonstrated an acute sensitivity to the (often messy) realities of our actual doxastic and epistemic practices in her work. Addressing the problem of climate change skeptics, she identifies a crucial contributing factor to the skeptics' beliefs:

> A systemic prejudice against disrupting the complacency of the status quo is embedded in charges that climate change scientists are promulgating irrational fears. . . . For members of a social-economic elite, acknowledging and acting to minimize the injustices climate change skepticism condones would entail significant personal "losses," not only of physical comfort, but of the myriad privileges and self-certainties that structure their entire ways of being. (2013, 843)

The fear that one's way of life may be threatened (indeed, the fear that the very systems that make possible that way of life could be subverted) does not provide justifiable grounds upon which to object to the quality of the body of scientific evidence of climate change. Nevertheless, fears of this kind affect peoples' willingness to accept the body of evidence as credible. Perhaps more worryingly, it is possible to assent to the scientific findings on some level and simultaneously fail to appreciate the extent of the problem. A person may, for instance, read in *Scientific American* that atmospheric carbon dioxide has exceeded four hundred parts per million, accept this as fact, noting the article's alarmed tone—and yet, her adjacent beliefs about the urgency of the situation and the importance of acting to mitigate environmental damage may be unaffected (Kahn 2016). This is an example of what Stoknes refers to as "passive denial" (2015, 17).

Passive denial is arguably the greatest challenge currently facing climate science communicators. There is reason to believe that active denial of climate change is waning. At the time of this writing, the most recent Gallup data reveal public belief in global warming to be at an all-time high in the United States. Gallup acknowledges that American belief in climate change has had a volatile history but states that 62 percent of Americans polled in 2017 reported believing that the effects of climate change have indeed begun, and 68 percent reported belief that human activities have caused temperature increases (Saad 2017). All the same, at the time of this writing, there is no substantial global solution on the horizon. A global tax on carbon seems an outlandish proposition. I write this essay only months after President Donald Trump announced to the United Nations that the United States was withdrawing from the Paris climate agreement. And even with the Paris agreement in place, no major industrialized nation is currently meeting the CO_2 reduction it pledges (Victor et al. 2017, 25–27).[1] While we may no longer face the particular paradox Stoknes identified circa 2015, there is still a pressing need for effective climate advocacy.

Both active and passive denial of climate change involve ignorance, but the difference lies in what these two types of denialists are ignorant *of*. For those in active denial, the failure to know stems from a failure to believe. One who does not, for whatever reason, believe the climate facts she hears and reads will not claim to know those facts: by extension, knowledge of the severity of the climate crisis is made impossible for her. For those in passive denial, however, the failure to know seems only partial. According to something like an *S*-knows-that-*p* rubric, the passive denialist appears to know the climate facts. In the context of a discussion of epistemologies of ignorance, Code points out that *S*-knows-that-*p* epistemology "holds a straightforward ignorance/knowledge opposition in place, together with an equally straightforward assumption that knowledge achieved can erase ignorance with one stroke" (2007, 221). The passive denialist's willingness to assent to climate facts, paired with her failure to demonstrate an understanding of the ramifications of those facts, indicates that her epistemic position relative to the facts lies somewhere in between knowledge and ignorance. Code provides an explanation of this kind of partial ignorance (or quasi-knowledge) in *Epistemic Responsibility*. Code's insights are particularly prescient, considering the latest results of polls on Americans' beliefs about climate change.

> It is, theoretically, possible to know everything yet understand nothing. Those who seem to know a great deal, having collected a great number of facts, yet who give no evidence of understanding these assembled items of information, of seeing their significance and interconnections, must still be regarded as knowers. . . . Knowing *well* is much more than accumulating facts (1987, 149–50).

A person in passive denial may well have accumulated facts, but the goal of climate communicators has never been merely to peddle facts to be collected. Climate communicators want policymakers and the lay public alike to believe the facts *and* understand their significance—and therefore be moved to act. In the case of global warming, it seems that giving "evidence of understanding these assembled items of information" is constituted by taking action, which is precisely what the passive denialist does not do. For Code, knowing well and action are entwined. As Christine Koggel observes, describing Code's account of ecological thinking, "Responsible knowing emerges through engagement in and interaction with the world. . . . [Code's] is an account that is as much about being and doing as it is about thinking" (2008, 180). Since action that might serve as evidence of their understanding appears to be lacking, those in passive denial may *know*, insofar as they do not explicitly judge certain climate facts to be false, but they do not know responsibly (in Code's sense), and therefore do not *know well*.

Acting on Knowledge and Knowledge Based on Acting

One type of approach to climate advocacy proposed by Stoknes demonstrates especially clearly that he shares Code's appreciation of the close connection between knowing and acting, doing and thinking. For Stoknes, there is no bright line dividing strategies for influencing belief from strategies for influencing behavior. He distances himself from any approach underwritten by the assumption that people will come to appreciate climate facts by passively absorbing information. Stoknes calls for strategies that promote direct engagement by simply making direct engagement *easy*. He argues that the circumstances in which people make certain mundane decisions should be intentionally shaped to facilitate environmentally sound choices; he uses the term "green nudging" to refer to such interventions (Stoknes 2015, 124–125). Green nudges can take myriad forms, some of which are astonishing in their simplicity. For instance, Stoknes points out that the default setting on most printers is single-sided printing. When the default is changed to double-sided printing, however, people use less paper: according to one study, introducing this simple green nudge at a large Swedish university resulted in a 15 percent reduction in paper use (Stoknes 2015, 125). Of the many specific green nudges Stoknes shares, examples of some of the least demanding include utility services making green energy programs opt out rather than opt in by enrolling customers in such programs by default, dining halls and cafeterias eschewing trays to curb food waste, and restaurants selecting meatless dishes as daily specials more frequently (without conspicuously flagging them as the "vegetarian option") to promote a reduction in meat consumption (2015, 126–128).

Green nudges are designed to lead to reductions in resource consumption, but no green nudge alone, nor all green nudges collectively, can bring about reductions sufficient to offset the effects of global warming. Stoknes presents the green nudge not as a definitive solution to the problem of global warming but as one tool climate advocates might use in combination with many others. Although climate communicators will rarely be directly responsible for putting green nudges into effect, introducing these measures to those who *are* positioned to implement them could be an especially fruitful strategy. It may be easier and more effective, for instance, to persuade the kitchen manager of a cafeteria to eliminate trays than it is to persuade large numbers of people to individually make a conscious effort to decrease the amount of food they consume in that same cafeteria.

What is crucial to note is that, to Stoknes, green nudges are not an auxiliary to climate communication; rather, they are themselves *forms* of climate communication. The greatest benefit of implementing green nudges may not be the immediate resource conservation they bring about but rather the long-term effects they may have on people's attitudes and beliefs. It is often assumed that we act in accordance with our beliefs (e.g., one recycles because she believes that caring for the environment is important), yet it is not uncommon for actions to inspire corresponding beliefs (e.g., one believes that caring for the environment is important because she recycles). Stoknes explains, "The idea that change happens in the direction from behavior to belief, versus the opposite, may seem surprising. But it is a quite well-established finding in social psychology" (2015, 130–131). The proposal to implement green nudges is not novel. What *is* novel about Stoknes's treatment of green nudges is that he proposes they be implemented in recognition of their didactic value. The hypothesis that we sometimes act first and form beliefs that cohere with our actions second, though somewhat counterintuitive, has been supported by psychology research for decades.[2] Those who have not studied psychology might not be aware of this idea, which may explain its absence from most discussions on climate communication. Green nudges may be seen purely as practical means of, say, reducing emissions, while the green nudge's potential as a component of campaigns to *teach* climate information goes unrecognized. While being nudged does not itself directly teach any particular fact, individuals and communities who are nudged become more receptive to facts that indicate the value of environmentally responsible action by virtue of having already participated in environmentally responsible activity.

The suggestion that climate communication projects incorporate behavioral nudges strikes me as a sagacious application of facts about human psychology to climate advocacy. Consider Code's advice in *Epistemic Responsibility*:

> Theory of knowledge is well advised to proceed in close connection with cognitive psychology in efforts to understand specifically human methods of constructing knowledge out of experiences of the world. Such methods are dependent, for their successful functioning, upon being exercised within a social, communal context (1987, 115–116).

Even if climate communicators might not describe their work as engagement with theory of knowledge, their projects are decidedly epistemological in nature. Climate communication must proceed from some hypothesis about "human methods of constructing knowledge" (which may be mainly correct or incorrect; explicitly articulated or unarticulated). The success of the methods climate communicators use to educate policymakers and the public depends significantly on whether those methods were selected in accordance with an accurate picture of our ordinary epistemic practices. Code's advice to epistemologists, then, seems equally applicable to climate communicators—and Stoknes's approach to climate communication and advocacy resonates with Code's advice.

Climate Communication for Social Knowers

Code offers an especially important insight: "Human methods of constructing knowledge . . . are dependent, for their successful functioning, upon being exercised within a social, communal context" (1987, 115). Rejection of the focus on individual knowers and propositional knowledge claims so pervasive in analytic epistemology—and appreciation of the consummately *social* nature of knowledge—have long been defining characteristics of Code's work. She rightly asserts, "Human beings are cognitively interdependent in a fundamental sense. . . . When we look at cognitive practice, it is clear . . . that one of the most important ways in which people come to know is by learning from others" (1987, 167–168). This cognitive interdependence ought to be readily apparent upon even a cursory reflection. As Richard Moran points out, even such basic facts about ourselves as the time and place of our birth are only known to us (and *can* only be known to us) on the basis of our acceptance of facts others have communicated to us (2005, 1). Indeed, as Lynn Hankinson Nelson argues, "The knowing we do as individuals is derivative . . . your knowing or mine depends on *our* knowing, for some 'we' " (1993, 124).

Like Code, Stoknes takes seriously the social nature of knowledge. He understands that the ordinary epistemic practice of learning from others has meaningful implications for climate communication, which he argues would do well to appreciate how strongly our beliefs are influenced by others within our social networks. Stoknes laments what he takes to be a failure to apply this insight:

> Conventional climate information, however, has targeted the individual mind as if it is not swayed by colleagues and friends. NGOs and public agencies publish countless what-you-can-do lists, all heaping the full weight of climate disruption onto the shoulders of lone individuals. . . . The approach is well intended, but underlying the push lies an individual-by-individual assumption of behavior change. (2015, 95)

The problem Stoknes identifies with climate communication directed at individuals lies in a tendency to ignore the broader social context within which the individuals it targets are embedded. The kind of approach described above establishes climate communication as an organization-to-individual (or perhaps journalist-to-individual) message. Information coming from a familiar organization or writer may lend the message some epistemic credibility, but when, say, an NGO or a journalist publishes a recommendation that *you* switch to "green energy," the message comes either from a nebulous entity or a person from whom you are socially disconnected. This is not in itself problematic; of course, we routinely rely on information published by organizations and individuals personally unknown to us. The problem here arises because, in addition to coming from somewhat abstract sources, the messages tend to portray individual actions as solitary sacrifices. The role of individual actions is not effectively explained as part of a greater collective effort, which may foster a sense of helplessness that can ultimately discourage individuals from acting.

The contents of two recent "what-you-can-do" lists illustrate Stoknes's point well. A contributor to *Forbes* presents readers with four onerous suggestions: refrain from having children, owning a car, flying, and eating meat (McMahon 2017). The *New York Times* includes more attainable articulations of some of these suggestions in its list: reduce driving speed and distance, invest in a fuel-efficient vehicle, take 10 percent fewer flights, consume 7 percent less meat, and be mindful of food waste (Sivak and Schoettle 2017). These and similar articles include estimates of individual emission reductions associated with taking their suggested actions. They sometimes gesture at these actions as contributions to a larger effort with estimates of the reductions possible in a counterfactual scenario featuring universal participation. Knowing what would happen *if* everyone adopted some environmentally friendly habit, however, is not the same as knowing how many people have *actually* adopted the suggested habit, and the difference is crucial. Making a (perhaps significant) change to one's lifestyle on the basis of lists of recommendations authored by people with whom one will never interact—without having any sense of whether others are making similar changes—seems a dubious proposition and is therefore easily dismissed.

Stoknes points out that when such publications *do* include data about actual rates of participation in green habits, these figures are often included to bemoan the relative unpopularity of these habits (e.g., articles sharing the mind-boggling number of plastic bottles unrecycled and currently adrift in the ocean). This, he cautions, does more harm than good. Stoknes argues that since human behavior is strongly influenced by social norms, highlighting a widespread failure to take environmentally responsible action reaffirms the acceptability of acting in an environmentally *ir*responsible way ("Since nobody else does it, why should I bother?") (2015, 95–97). Code, referring to those in wealthy nations who balk at the prospect of sacrificing anything of value for the good of the environment, asks: "Why would people whose lives are constructed around the illusions such unsustainable practices uphold be prepared to relinquish these privileges that have long been theirs?" (2013, 843). Why, indeed, if compounding their attachment to the status quo is the expectation that their individual efforts would be undertaken alone? Relinquishing privileges is rendered all the more unappealing when one imagines doing so in a context where others decline to do the same.

Yet, Stoknes argues, the same tendency that inclines us to persist in environmentally irresponsible habits when we perceive our peers to be doing so can be harnessed to promote environmentally sound choices. It behooves us to "model our best behaviors," he says, since those who believe their peers are making environmentally sound choices are likely to follow suit (Stoknes 2015, 100). Climate communication strategies appealing to our situatedness within communities and social networks, and our responsiveness to the social norms promulgated by these groups, can be successful. Consider Code's remark: "It is crucial that individuals be recognized as social beings, as members of communities with all the obligations membership entails" (1987, 44). Stoknes appears to be making a case for sharing knowledge with our peers as one responsibility entailed by community membership. To this end, Stoknes urges us to ourselves become climate communicators in our own peer groups. "[Peers are]," he claims, "the most credible spokespeople for an idea" (2015, 100–101). This is consonant with Code's observation that epistemic communities are sustained by "intricate networks of shared trust" (1987, 173). Indeed, it is our trust in our peers that makes them appear credible.

Simply initiating conversations with friends and family is meaningful: one of the most reliable predictors of a person's environmentally minded behavior is the environmentally minded behavior of her peers (Stoknes 2015, 96). Such conversations—and even conspicuous performance of "green" habits absent a conversation—avoid the pitfalls associated with the popular climate communication approaches described previously. Peer-to-peer communication is radically unlike reading a published what-you-can-do list; Stoknes emphasizes, "People yearn for personal interaction and face-to-face communication to help them process and embody the information" (2015, 101). If we can demonstrate to other members of our social networks that we recycle, conserve water, or bike in lieu of driving, this serves as one step toward establishing these behaviors as group norms. When it is clear that such behaviors are norms of one's social group, worries about the thankless burden of making solitary sacrifices dissolve.

There is a valid concern to be raised about the potential reach of such peer-to-peer communication. Those who would be willing to initiate conversations about carbon emissions with their peers may be already ensconced in social networks whose norms skew toward environmentally friendly behavior. Fortunately, there are other subtler and wider-reaching methods for distinctly social climate communication. To take just one example, Stoknes points out that when people are shown a monthly comparison of their electricity or water usage against the neighborhood average and the average of "efficient" neighbors on their bills, the community's average usage tends to decline (2015, 98–99). Though Stoknes largely attributes this effect to the enjoyment individuals derive from "competing" with their neighbors, this is also partially a product of the tendency to follow social norms. Seeing the average water or power usage for one's community clues one into a norm that would not otherwise be salient. Communicating this sort of information, whether it appeals to desires to compete or conform, is an effective way to inspire action. As with the actions engendered by green nudges, the behavioral changes provoked when climate advocacy takes our situatedness within social networks seriously can ultimately change attitudes and beliefs about the significance of caring for the environment. According to Stoknes, "Dispassionate statistics are relinked with social meaning particular to place" when climate communication is aimed at communities rather than individuals (2015, 107).

Conclusion

The specific climate communication strategies Stoknes proposes in his book are manifold; the examples I have discussed in this essay represent only a meager portion of the whole. This is important to note because, taken in isolation, these strategies and recommendations may seem gimmicky or shallow as responses to the problem of global warming. Stoknes's recommendations, however, are intended to be taken together as guidelines that can be variously selected and combined as local circumstances require. In aggregate, they constitute a climate advocacy characterized by sensitivity to the psychological needs and limitations that make human beings the imperfect epistemic agents we are. Stoknes is willing to countenance our actual doxastic and epistemic practices because he aims, above all, to offer an *effective* approach to climate communication. He understands climate communication to be effective when it not only convinces people of the veracity of certain facts but also inspires action—therefore he prioritizes considerations of what it is that *actually* convinces people and moves them to act over idealized notions of what ought to. Stoknes's advocacy project, in its concerns and goals, coheres with recommendations Code makes for epistemologists and descriptions she provides of what it means to know well.

Stoknes's approach to climate advocacy provides an informative case study of epistemic responsibility. In *Ecological Thinking*, Code emphasizes the epistemological importance of advocacy, even as she acknowledges that advocacy has a reputation for aiming "to win rather than to know" (2006, 179). Later, writing on advocacy in "Doubt and Denial," she characterizes epistemic responsibility as "the responsibility to know well in order to advocate honorably" (2013, 845). That Stoknes has indeed assumed such a responsibility is clear when one considers the great care he has taken to combine his own professional expertise with a thorough investigation of relevant empirical data to support his advocacy strategies. As one requirement of epistemic responsibility, Code explains, "Knowledge claimants whose claims merit respect will have taken pains to become familiar with the currently available information that pertains to the claims they wish to make" (1987, 62).

Some aspects of the advocacy project Stoknes pursues fit especially well within the philosophical framework of Code's account of ecological thinking. Consider the description Code provides:

> In ecological thinking, knowers are repositioned as self-consciously part of nature, while anthropocentric projects of mastery are superseded by projects of displacing Enlightenment "man" from the center of the universe and developing radical critiques of the single-minded mastery claimed for "human reason." Ecological thinking works against the imaginary of God-given human dominion over all the earth and, more precisely, of dominion arrogated to certain chosen members of the human race, not just over the earth but over other human Others as well. (2006, 32)

This passage contains a variation of a critique Code has expressed many times about the ingrained effects that the Enlightenment construct of the "man of reason" has had on epistemology. Compare her remarks to Stoknes's criticisms of the same construct's influence on psychology:

> Built into mainstream psychology's self-understanding as a discipline is the idea that the psyche is somehow inside the individual, while the science of ecology is about what happens outside the individual, in forests or oceans or other natural spaces. . . . This exposes psychology's own denial. Conventional psychology has studied the human mind and emotion as if the climate, the air we're breathing, and the food we're eating don't really matter. . . . Ever since the Enlightenment, the air has been viewed as nothing more than inert dead gases. But in climate symptoms, we may eye the breakdown of a world whose depth and agency have been ignored by the prejudices of our climate science and psychology. (2015, 199–200)

Stoknes is emphatically committed to reaffirming the status of humans as immersed in and existing within—rather than "above"—nature. In addition to particular facts about the climate and the impact of human activities on it, he hopes climate communication can ultimately teach a new self-understanding that reflects our status as part of nature.

Despite this, Stoknes's project is arguably an imperfect instantiation of ecological thinking. In one respect, his project is informed by assumptions more closely resembling Code's views at the time of *Epistemic Responsibility* than those she expresses in *Ecological Thinking*. Describing her older treatment of knowers, Code writes, "Implicitly, in the 1987 book, I assume their unmediated access to the 'stuff' of which knowledge is made . . . and [that] the acknowledgment upon which knowledge depends is unfettered by constraints consequent upon asymmetrical distributions of power and privilege" (2006, viii). Stoknes realizes that inequitable distributions of power among and within communities are relevant to the issue of global warming, acknowledging that the brunt of climate change impacts will be borne by marginalized people (2015, 174). Yet, as he discusses climate communication strategies, and especially how communicators might take seriously the social contexts in which information is exchanged, he does not appear to consider the significance of these power dynamics. Code observes in her later work that "in white western societies, the freedoms abstractly invoked and zealously defended by the climate change deniers are not equally distributed across the sex/gender—or any other—social-political order," and advocates "exposing the sources and power-infused social-political effects of tacit yet entrenched assumptions about whose knowledge matters and can claim acknowledgement" (2013, 845–846). Stoknes's text seems to ignore the ways in which such assumptions come to bear on the issue of climate communication. However, referring to the book *Merchants of Doubt*, Code remarks, "It is not unusual in [tacitly assuming the irrelevance of gender, race, etc.], and its political motivations are nonetheless laudable for ecological thinking" (2013, 845).[3] This comment seems equally applicable to Stoknes's work.

Code's epistemological work contributes useful concepts to knowers whose practical real-life concerns bear little resemblance to "the cups on tables or cats on mats beloved of classical empiricist inquiry" (2013, 846). Climate change denial, in both its active and passive forms, is a strikingly apt site for the application of her work. In the pursuit of more effective strategies for climate advocacy, Code's philosophical framework, along with a wide variety of responsible advocacy projects like Stoknes's that fit within it, will be extraordinary assets.

Notes

1. To climate advocates, the withdrawal of the United States from the Paris agreement is nevertheless a disturbing gesture, as it symbolizes the Trump administration's refusal to take seriously the relevant climate science, as well as its denial of responsibility for the country's outsized share of CO_2 emissions.

2. For examples, see Davis and Jones (1960); Eiser and Harding (1983); Klaas (1978).

3. In *Merchants of Doubt*, Naomi Oreskes and Eric Conway present an illuminating account of the ways in which scientists hired by private corporations have challenged the scientific consensus on climate change, thereby fueling public doubt and impeding measures to address the causes of climate change.

Works Cited

Code, Lorraine. 1987. *Epistemic Responsibility*. Hanover, NH: University Press of New England.

———. 1994. "Responsibility and Rhetoric." *Hypatia* 9, no. 1. http://www.jstor.org/stable/3810434.

———. 2006. *Ecological Thinking*. New York: Oxford University Press.

———. 2007. "The Power of Ignorance." In *Race and Epistemologies of Ignorance*, edited by Shannon Sullivan and Nancy Tuana, 213–229. Albany: State University of New York Press.

———. 2013. "Doubt and Denial: Epistemic Responsibility Meets Climate Change Skepticism." *Oñati Socio-Legal Series* 3, no. 5. https://papers.ssrn.com/sol3/papers.cfm?abstract_id=2247830.

Davis, Keith E., and Edward E. Jones. 1960. "Changes in Interpersonal Perception as a Means of Reducing Cognitive Dissonance." *Journal of Abnormal and Social Psychology* 61, no. 3 http://dx.doi.org/10.1037/h0044214.

Eiser, J. Richard, and Christina M. Harding. 1983. "Smoking, Seat-Belt Use and Perception of Health Risks." *Addictive Behaviors* 8, no. 1. https://doi.org/10.1016/0306-4603(83)90060-6.

Gerring, John. 2004. "What Is a Case Study and What Is It Good for?" *American Political Science Review* 98, no. 2. http://www.jstor.org.ezp1.lib.umn.edu/stable/4145316.

Kahn, Brian. 2016. "Earth's CO_2 Passes the 400 PPM Threshold—Maybe Permanently." *Scientific American*, September 27. https://www.scientificamerican.com/article/earth-s-co2-passes-the-400-ppm-threshold-maybe-permanently/.

Klaas, E. T. 1978. "Psychological Effects of Immoral Actions: the Experimental Evidence." *Psychological Bulletin* 85, no. 4. http://dx.doi.org/10.1037/0033-2909.85.4.756.

Koggel, Christine M. 2008. "Ecological Thinking and Epistemic Location: The Local and the Global." *Hypatia* 23, no. 1. http://www.jstor.org/stable/25483157.

McMahon, Jeff. 2017. "The Four Most Effective Things You Can Do about Climate Change, According to Science." *Forbes*, July 13. https://www.forbes.com/sites/jeffmcmahon/2017/07/13/the-four-most-effective-things-you-can-do-about-climate-change-according-to-science/.

Moran, Richard. 2005. "Getting Told and Being Believed." *Philosophers' Imprint* 5, no. 5: 1–29.

Moser, Paul. 1988. "Review of *Epistemic Responsibility*." *Philosophical Books* 29, no. 3: 154–56.

Nelson, Lynn Hankinson. 1993. "Epistemological Communities." In *Feminist Epistemologies*, edited by Linda Alcoff and Elizabeth Potter, 121–159. New York: Routledge.

Saad, Lydia. 2017. "Global Warming Concern at Three-Decade High in U.S." March 14. http://news.gallup.com/poll/206030/global-warming-concern-three-decade-high.aspx.

Sivak, Michael, and Brandon Schoettle. 2017. "What You Can Do About Climate Change." *New York Times*, March 25. https://www.nytimes.com/2017/03/25/opinion/sunday/what-you-can-do-about-climate-change.html.

Stoknes, Per Espen. 2015. *What We Think about When We Try Not to Think about Global Warming*. White River Junction, VT: Chelsea Green.

Victor, David G., Keigo Akimoto, Yoichi Kaya, Mitsutsune Yanaguchi, Danny Cullenward, and Cameron Hepburn. 2017. "Prove Paris Was More Than Paper Promises." *Nature*, 548: 25–27. http://dx.doi.org/10.1038/548025a.

Wittgenstein, Ludwig. 2009. *Philosophical Investigations*, edited by P.M.S. Hacker and Joachim Schulte. 4th ed. Oxford: Wiley-Blackwell.

Appendix

"I Am a Part of All That I Have Met"

A Conversation with Lorraine Code on "Knowledge Processes and the Responsibilities of Knowing"

LORRAINE CODE, WITH ANDREA DOUCET
AND NANCY ARDEN MCHUGH

This interview with Lorraine Code began with a set of questions developed by Andrea Doucet and Nancy McHugh and then unfolded into a conversation that wove together selected threads from Code's life, her writing, and her thinking across a half century.

The interview was conducted through an in-person interview and a follow up phone call. Andrea visited Lorraine at her home in Toronto, on February 25, 2020. She had planned to return on March 13, but this visit was canceled due to the COVID-19 pandemic. A follow-up call occurred on April 7, 2020. These conversations were recorded, transcribed, and edited for clarity.

Early Career and Influences: "I Didn't See Myself as a Philosopher at All . . . and Then My Thinking Started to Move in Odd Ways"

AD: Let's start by looking back on your career. You have really played a key role in mapping out a place for—and the field of—feminist philosophy. You've been one of the leaders and cocreators of the field of feminist epistemologies and have also been one of the very few explicitly feminist epistemologists of your generation who was able to spend her career in a philosophy department. What were the conditions that led to this?

LC: So much of what I did was by pure accident. I had done an undergraduate degree in philosophy, from which I graduated many decades ago, in 1958. I did philosophy only because Queen's was much smaller in the 1950s. At that time (and I think it's partly because of Queen's Scottish and European connections), first-year students in arts at Queen's had to do an Introduction to Philosophy course.

I had no idea at all what philosophy was, and I actually didn't like it very much. Partly because analytic philosophy was just coming into its own. We read this well-known two-volume thing called *Language, Truth and Logic* (Ayer 1952), but it was when folks began by doing analyses of boring texts. I didn't like *Language, Truth and Logic*, so I didn't think I liked philosophy that much. In my first year at Queen's, and maybe even my second year, I did a couple of courses with a man in the French department who was teaching some of the French literature of the Enlightenment—and that merges with philosophy in a way. He was a real thinker—in ways that I previously hadn't really caught on to. There was also a man in the philosophy department who taught a little bit about continental German philosophy. These were all fragmented.

I didn't see myself as a philosopher at all. I saw myself as a Kingston kid, a university town kid (i.e., I lived in the same town where Queen's University was). I probably would have even found my university experience "ho-hum-ish" and boring, apart from the fact that I had (and still have) a very close friend there. And I persuaded my economically strapped father to give me permission and financial support to move out of my family home to live in an apartment near campus with her and three other people. I think if he hadn't been willing to do that . . . and it was tough for him. He had four children, and I was the eldest and the girl. I don't think he carried with him that "it's only the girl" thing, but I think if I hadn't been able to move out of my parents' house, which needless to say shocked Kingston, I would not have gone on studying. It made me become a person. So, I moved out and I lived in a flat with four other women. It was great. And that one friend, most significantly, is still my closest friend.

So, I did those courses at Queen's, but I didn't identify particularly as a philosopher. There wasn't much European philosophy being taught. It was mainly analytical philosophy, *Language, Truth and Knowledge* stuff, that was in its absolute ascendency. People were really excited about it.

AD: What was your major then?

LC: French and German. I think that so many things for me happened by chance. Most people have their lives mapped out. I had no idea, no idea what I wanted to do after Queen's. But I applied for and got the Queen's German exchange scholarship and went to Germany for a year. And Murray Code (my partner) decided that he would come over also, and we kind of drifted around Europe fairly aimlessly. Although I did take courses at the University of Cologne, mostly philosophy courses. And Merleau-Ponty's work had just come out—it was really controversial. We had it in preprint, and they were reading it in French and talking about it in French and partly in German. I was floundering about, but it was fun. Totally challenging. So, we went to Berlin driving an old wreck through the East Zone, and we spent some time there.

AD: What year would that have been?

LC: 1959. I graduated in 1958. I mean, everything I did was by chance. None of it was the carefully mapped out career that many people have. Murray and I had traveled together all year, and my parents had been very unhappy about it. They couldn't have known that we would still be together more than fifty years later. Murray had become an engineer at Queen's, and he didn't want to be an engineer. He had no idea what to do. I had no idea what to do. We were all adrift, and then we sort of drifted over to London.

Those were the years when lots of colonial kids in their early twenties were drifting to London because it was fun and cheap. I couldn't figure out how to earn money at all. But then I ended up teaching French at a secondary modern school for two or three years. The first and second forms did French and for some reason, I got appointed to teach French. I wasn't thinking about philosophy at that point at all.

But I loved living in London. We had what we thought was the most wonderful apartment in the world. When my mother visited, she wrote home and said to my family, "You should see what they have to live in!" So, we lived in London and Murray started doing a degree at one of the technical colleges. He wanted to do a degree in mathematics. He was tired of being an engineer.

Part of this was enabled by the fact that I had a really good friend, who was probably older than my mother—a really wild, bohemian, artistic woman who knew a lot about London and introduced us to art exhibitions and things. London in those days was something you could afford. We could afford to go to the theater. We traveled by subway. We used to hitchhike, too. But I had not thought at all about going back to university. I had not thought at all about what I was going to do next. There I was, teaching French.

So, we came back to Canada in 1965 with a six-month-old baby, and Murray had somehow gotten a place at Queen's as a graduate student. I don't know how those intricacies worked themselves out, but he had a job. That filled my mother with joy because they were still living in Kingston. We arrived with this little baby daughter and no money. I decided to go to the philosophy department because that's where I had graduated from. Nobody ever praised people in those days, and they certainly never praised women, but I somehow recognized that I had been reasonably highly thought of by my professors at Queen's. We were desperate for money, and I managed to get hired as a marker/grader for a couple of philosophy courses at Queen's, which sort of moved me back toward philosophy. But that was after several years away, and it was out of desperation rather than enthusiasm. We just needed the money. And we had another child in the middle of that confusion as well. Then, when Murray was finishing his master's and starting his PhD, he got hired by the newly growing math department at the University of Guelph. And that's why we ended up at Guelph.

And I still didn't know what I wanted to do. And, again, I went to the philosophy department, this time at the University of Guelph, to see if they had any marker/grader positions. And by pure chance—and this was a turning point—one of the young faculty at Guelph said, "Well, why would you want to be a marker/grader? Why don't you register as a graduate student? And take on a TA position?" And I didn't realize that they saw me like manna from heaven because they were trying to establish a department, and they weren't getting much registration. So, I started being a TA and a graduate student. And I became the first PhD graduate of that philosophy department. And I did well. And then my thinking started to move in odd ways. I don't know exactly how it came about. The term "epistemic responsibility" probably didn't exist as a mode of inquiry at that time, although someone may have used it talking about what's involved in knowing: "Well, you have to be epistemically responsible." Maybe something like that.

AD: But had you seen that anywhere? That word "responsibility" and how it could be linked to epistemic practices? It's a very provocative coupling.

LC: No. Well, there was a really nice, kind man at Brown University, Ernest Sosa, who had done some work in that general line. And there are a couple of people who read my manuscript, "Epistemic Responsibility," as if it had a place in the conceptual repertoire of philosophy, but so much of what I did (in contrast to what people do now) was kind of cobbled together out of happenstance. I didn't intend it to be a mess. Partly I was having too many babies because there was one more child born by then.

Feminist Epistemologies and Becoming a Feminist Philosopher: "It's Not a Linear Story" and "Not Even Like a Patchwork Quilt"

AD: So, where was feminist epistemology at that time? Who else was working on these issues alongside you or with you?

LC: One person who had a lot of influence in making a feminist turn was Sue Sherwin. She was a real influence in how she conducted herself in philosophical circles. From her, I had a sense that I could do it, too, without being one of these fast-tongued, flashy, quasi-American people. Sue was a very thoughtful person. I will not use the term "role model." I won't use it at all. I just don't think it captures anything about the kinds of influence people have on other people.

I was in Halifax at that time (at Mount Saint Vincent for my first sabbatical), and I was writing all those chapters for my book *What Can She Know?* (Code 1991). And there was so much to manage: the children, Murray, and my work. It all sort of blended into confusion. I have no idea how I managed to come out at the end with something kind of coherent.

AD: Thinking back still, how did you get a tenure track position in philosophy at York University?

LC: There just weren't jobs. And I think there was also a pretty serious residual misogyny. "If we get a real job, we'll give it to a man, and women can always do a few teaching courses on the side the way the older generations used to do their embroidery." Well, seriously, that's not a bad analogy. I was aware of it. My mother said to me at one point, "You're never going to call yourself doctor, are you?" And I never had, but I could have. And all the men around there were doing it, of course.

The thing about you getting a story from me is that my own story, in my own head, is quite a muddled story. I was never able to keep up with myself because there were lots of children, there was Murray, there were conferences, there were papers to write. And I was just never able to keep up with myself.

AD: But you were obviously doing this kind of deep thinking, even with the children. Do you know what I mean? Everything was percolating.

LC: Oh, for sure.

AD: I remember reading that you'd put the kids down for their naps (and I read that with interest because I also juggled the early years of my career with three young children). So, the children would nap and that is when you would write. I remember reading that you'd become really efficient with your writing.

LC: I wasn't exactly efficient, but I had to do it!

AD: You stayed up late?

LC: I stayed up later than I could now, or even than I could have ten years later. I was tired all the time! And at the start of that time, I was living in Kingston with my mother nearby. Which was not necessarily the joy that people think it would be. She didn't want to babysit because she'd already raised four children. And she had not had anything of her own outside of that.

I had three children. The youngest was born in Guelph. Those were the years when the universities were really hiring. So, Murray and I were part of a huge influx of new faculty when we were hired at Guelph, '67 or '68. He was hired and I was finishing my PhD. And there was a group of women—faculty wives—who did lots of sharing of childcare. I was the only one who was trying to study, I think. And the rest of them thought I was a bit round the bend.

AD: And your PhD was titled "Knowledge and Subjectivity"? In the quite new Guelph-McMaster program.

LC: Yes. I was their first. And one of the joyous things that happened that year at Guelph was that Gadamer was teaching at McMaster for a year.

And a good friend of mine who was doing his PhD in philosophy: he and I used to drive down from Guelph to McMaster once a week to sit at the feet of Gadamer.

AD: Oh, I didn't know you studied with him. I knew you edited that collection, *Feminist Interpretations of Hans-Georg Gadamer* (Code 2003).

LC: Well, that's why I edited the book. Because it was so interesting. It was quite amazing because for his course, there was just one requirement: one thirteen-page essay.

AD: Was it a seminar or a lecture?

LC: It was a seminar.

AD: And how many people in the seminar?

LC: Probably seven or eight. It was paradise. It really was.

AD: What was he like?

LC: He was an elderly European gentleman. Soft-spoken, slow spoken. Somehow the mood of the class just flowed. He was some kind of god-figure. Very gentle. The whole requirement for the class was one essay for the grades, but he expected you to attend.

And all of these things had a lot of personal dimensions. Halfway between Guelph and McMaster there's a little village called Freelton, where my father's eldest sister lived. She was much older than my mother. She was a wizened little old lady—and deaf. She was one of the people I loved best in the entire world. And so, on my way down to see Gadamer, I'd see her.

AD: So, we're still thinking about your journey toward becoming a philosopher.

LC: It's really not a linear story.

AD: But that's okay.

LC: Most people do have a linear story. Actually, I don't think most women have a linear story because I don't think philosophy was always welcoming women with open arms. I think about Carol Stewart, the one female philosopher on faculty at Guelph, whom I very much liked and admired. She was the only woman on faculty. Her husband was also on faculty. And I think she was earning less than he was, and I think she was always fighting for legitimacy even though she was much smarter than he was and much more academically accomplished.

But if one goes to university looking for role models, I didn't find them.

So, I think if you were writing about a male philosopher from my generation who had made his mark, and maybe even the next level, you'd find that most of them have a straighter trajectory. Mine's a mess. Not even like a patchwork quilt because that holds together—and mine really doesn't hold together. It's a messy life.

Epistemic Responsibility (Code 1987): "There Was No Way of Bridging the Epistemology and Ethics Divide"

AD: Did the concept of epistemic responsibility come out of your MA work? I remember reading that your MA was on Wittgenstein, Heidegger, and Merleau-Ponty (Code 2015a).

LC: I can't figure out how I ever came across that! Epistemic responsibility certainly is a large thought. It wasn't easy. I wrote papers and I felt like I was fighting for legitimacy all the time. And part of that had to do with me because I didn't know how to survive in the adversarial atmosphere of North American philosophy. If people criticized me, I'd immediately think "Oh, I'm wrong." I wouldn't stand up for my work and say, "This is really important."

AD: When people criticized your work on epistemic responsibility, what did you do?

LC: Well, if I'm being honest, if I'd been at home, I would have sat down and wept. But philosophy, at that time, was a male social environment. It still is—but not to that extent. And some branches of philosophy are still as adversarial as they were then. I don't see it as an adversarial discipline anymore, but that's because I sort of walked my way through the brambles. But the brambles were really tough. I didn't know how to affirm my own legitimacy in philosophy for a long time.

AD: You have written about how your book *Epistemic Responsibility* was initially badly reviewed and a "sleeper" (Code 2015a). But, clearly, with the passing of time, more and more thinkers are taking on similar issues of researcher and epistemic responsibilities (e.g., Karen Barad, Annemarie Mol, Helen Verran). Why do you think that scholars who write about epistemologies, ontologies, and ethics are so interested in epistemic responsibilities?

LC: There wasn't much interest back then, when the book was published in 1989. It fell fairly flat. Indeed, it was something of a sleeper, but not entirely so. And partly my own diffidence made it difficult to recognize that it was claiming a place, albeit slowly. And one of the problems, I think, is that there was no way of bridging the epistemology and ethics divide. Which is what it was trying to do. It seemed to me that this was a fairly simple move, but it wasn't a simple move. Because at that time, the philosophical disciplines were more distinct and "disciplined." "You can't say that that's ethics when we're doing epistemology."

AD: So, that was one of the big problems?

LC: Well, I think it's part of the legacy of logical positivism as well. How can you talk about ethics when you're talking about epistemology? Ethics also didn't seem to have a very strong epistemological foundation at that time. So, it seemed as if it was jumping over a chasm that was dangerous when it really, really wasn't. And the two—ethics and epistemology—were dealing with the same matters with different approaches. You really can't have epistemology without epistemic responsibility—because you can't do epistemology without a knowing subject. Part of the aim of the positivist epistemologist was to get an epistemology without a knowing subject, but there's no place to put the responsibility if you don't have a knowing subject. I think that was a huge divide that I didn't even recognize I was violating. It seemed to me it was kind of obvious.

I couldn't accept that, basically, epistemic responsibility is an oxymoron in the traditional vocabulary. I couldn't accept its oxymoronic character. I wouldn't have put it that way. I couldn't see why it would be an issue. I think there was a real positivist drive for cleanliness and purity, and that gets muddled if you're doing epistemic responsibility because responsibility is already such a muddled structure.

AD: With the ontological turn and some of the arguments you're making in *Manufactured Uncertainty*, including the question "Who do we think we are?"—and issues of ontology, do you think it's wider than epistemic responsibility now?

LC: Oh, yes.

AD: Would you call it ethico-onto-epistemic responsibilities?

LC: Probably now, yes.

AD: I think it sort of is that now.

LC: I'm not sure why it seemed such a violation to cross those borders. But positivism had a very strong hold, and people were really afraid of the kind of excesses of the pre-Kantian culture, which seemed to be kind of overblown, I think, with the rise of a certain amount of scientism.

AD: Postmodern threat?

LC: Well, I'm not thinking that yet, but with a rise of positivism, which really got tighter and tighter before it got softer, there was a sense that you couldn't put something as fluid as epistemological . . . it wasn't supposed to be as fluid either, but it could only be called legitimate philosophy if it could be shown to be quite rigorous. So, it was reduced to subject-object for propositions and was a very strange period. It was partly because the rise of logical positivism promised so much, particularly postwar, when the world was in chaos. The rise of positivism promised a routine of rigor and control.

AD: It's interesting how you came to see it. Do you remember when you had the "aha" moment?

LC: I don't.

AD: Interesting . . .

LC: It's partly a personal thing with me. I was always on the defensive going into things.

AD: Perhaps some of these insights came from being on the margins of the discipline. I am thinking of the argument that Phyllis Rooney (2011) makes about feminist epistemologies consistently developing its key insights from the margins.

LC: I couldn't endorse that kind of austere rigor (of logical positivism). I couldn't do it. It seemed to me fake and artificial. And if we're talking about the kind of knowledge that people need to have, even if we're only going to regard scientific knowledge as the "real" knowledge, even then, if you read some of the biographies of some of the scientists working at that time, they'd often talk about the "lure of the technically sweet." They'll talk about the lure of certainty. And after World War II, and the mess that the world was in, it's understandable. They needed certainty really badly. They needed something to hang on to, which they didn't get. But there was a time when epistemologists really wanted that. And that's why epistemic responsibility looked a little bit flaky.

AD: Did you develop the concept of epistemic responsibility after you completed your PhD?

LC: Yes.

AD: Was the groundwork in your doctoral dissertation, *Knowledge and Subjectivity*?

LC: Probably. It must have been, although I wouldn't have seen it. And I probably haven't looked back at my PhD at all.

Anyway, I don't know how I made that transition. I think I always felt that some of those things were missing. And I think I felt that my own precarity as somebody trying to be an epistemologist who didn't fit—it didn't quite allow me to move toward the things I moved toward in the later works and more full-blown affirmations of epistemic responsibility.

I think part of epistemic responsibility not being as widely known as I think it should have been had to do with a sheer accident. I don't know who the person was, but someone at the press was going to be assigned *Epistemic Responsibility* as a book to read. I don't remember what press or how this happened, but that person left and the book moved, then, to University Press of New England, where Ernest Sosa saw that it should be published. And he's the person who invited me to come to Brown for a semester after the book was published. He's a lovely man. Ernest Sosa is the person who got the book published. And the book won the Brown University Press Book Prize Award, which included a term teaching at Brown. A splendid experience.

AD: And so, *Epistemic Responsibility* is being released again by SUNY Press (Code 2020b). What are you hoping? What conversations do you think it will generate?

LC: I did write the new preface, and I'm hoping it will situate the book more explicitly. I don't know if I've done justice to the concept. Even though I keep coming back to it. Because I think it's a profoundly important concept.

AD: What do you mean you haven't done it justice? What would do justice to the concept?

LC: I think the main point that I want to make keeps eluding me, but I can't tell you what that main point is *because* it's eluding me. I think it's absolutely crucial. I think it's a crucial philosophical value. I think it's a crucial moral value. I think it's a crucial epistemic value. I think it's a crucial value of society. And if you look at society, it's an epistemically irresponsible society now, almost all the way through. It's one of the problems, it seems to me, with modern Western society.

What Can She Know? (Code 1991): "I Think It's One of My Most Important Books"

LC: The one thing we haven't mentioned is *What Can She Know?* It seems to me that that's the question I've been trying to answer all my life.

AD: Tell me more about that.

LC: What can *she* know? With a negative inflection on the "she."

AD: That's what you also called the "outrageous question" (Code 1991).

LC: That's how I meant it to sound. I wanted to get something a little more bitter. But I was so pleased that Cornell University Press wanted to publish *What Can She Know?* (Code 1991) (and working with Cornell was such a pleasure). I would have liked it to be a little more acerbic. I like that book, although it's dated now. It's lost its initial punch because so many other people have done the same thing, but I think it was important in its time. And it was important to me.

AD: I think it was ahead of its time.

LC: That's the question I was asking myself all the time, as well, when I had time to stand back and look in the mirror. I was asking myself, "What can *she* know?"

And it didn't always go over well because at the American Philosophical Association meetings I was very, very diffident. I didn't have the strength to speak with conviction about my own work. And I thought people were critiquing it all the time. Even when they weren't. So many of my performances at the APA—the APA always scared me to death anyway—were less than ideal.

AD: And there were probably few feminist, female philosophers speaking, right?

LC: I wasn't even self-identifying as a feminist philosopher at that time when I began writing *What Can She Know?* I was just identifying as a philosopher who was a woman. And I didn't want to make that distinction for a long time. I don't think I agreed to own the title "feminist philosopher" for a very long time. Part of it is not commendable. I didn't want to be part of "the boys" because I realized I didn't like them very much at that point. Probably because they were so territorial. I do think that Sue Sherwin made a difference. She made a difference to my being able to approach philosophy with some conviction. There were some occasions I was being ganged up on in ways I couldn't handle and Sue, even though she was in Halifax and I was elsewhere, she was able to be there and help me get past them. I think she did that for a lot of women. She was really a pioneer, a total pioneer. There wasn't anyone else. She was superb with faculty and students.

What Can She Know? is an explicitly feminist book, which I like. I think it connects to my other books very closely. It was after I started thinking about epistemic responsibility that I started doing feminist work. And certainly, the fact that women have not been regarded or held as great knowers—doesn't suggest that they can't know, that they can't know well and ethically. I think that's crucially important in *What Can She Know?* I don't mean to minimize that. I think it's one of my most important books.

Ecological Thinking (Code 2006): "Rachel Carson . . . Is Probably the Pivotal Thinker in My Thinking"

AD: With *Ecological Thinking*, you have so many rich influences because you bring together the phenomenological-hermeneutic resources (Gadamer, Wittgenstein, Ricoeur, and others) as well as many other epistemological traditions (social epistemology, feminist epistemologies, and others).

LC: I've never been able to trace for myself a linear path through any of this stuff. I think I've been something of a scavenger philosopher!

AD: But maybe that's how you came to work with ecological theories?

AD: And you do say some of that in your new book, *Manufacturing Uncertainty*.

LC: Maybe I had enough courage by then to say it. I mean, some people can't be epistemically responsible because of the social-political systems that block them. Epistemic responsibility affects everything. It affects everything.

AD: It changes everything.

LC: I think it should be the fundamental value of human life. But it's not. And it might be if one could say it in non-philosophical terms.

AD: In your book *Ecological Thinking*, I'm interested in how you found yourself in ecological theories and how you came to the writing of Rachel Carson. I think that your move into ecological theories is very unique and innovative. And I think you're the only person who has brought ecological theories so centrally into—

LC: I'm using it metaphorically and literally.

AD: But how did you come to it? Where did that come from?

LC: You know, so often, I can't figure out where my ideas come from.

AD: Your ecological metaphors seemed to have started in 1996. With your piece on naturalized epistemologies (Code 1996)?

LC: Yes, I suppose.

AD: I can see some of the roots of ecological thinking are in that piece.

LC: I haven't looked at that piece in years! I'm trying to think of how unnatural it is for philosophers to try to isolate thoughts and moments of experience and ontological moments . . . how unnatural that seems to be, in a sort of loose sense of natural, and how we—whoever we are—would know much better if we could recognize our knowing endeavors as being so complicatedly intertwined. In order to say anything meaningful, one has to pull the threads apart a little bit. But it's difficult to do. And it doesn't make sense doing that: losing a sense of where the ends of the threads might come together. That's a badly spelled-out metaphor because there are some places where that's not going to work, but it's that kind of thing. With ecological thinking, I want to do something like that old "Ozymandias." "Look down upon my writing and despair." Something like that. Also, that "I am part of all that I have met." That seems to be the fundamental truth. Even in a newborn baby. "I am a part of all that I have met." (Tennyson 1891).

AD: Where is that from?

LC: It's simply something I picked up while I was at Queen's.

AD: Is this something like Donna Haraway's phrase, "Nothing comes without its world" (Haraway 1997, 137)?

LC: It's perhaps the same kind of thing.

AD: And Rachel Carson's "Nothing exists alone . . ." (Carson 1962).

LC: Rachel Carson. I wouldn't like to go through a lot of the pain she went through. But she is probably the pivotal thinker in my thinking now.

AD: In *Manufactured Uncertainty* you say she's "iconic" in your thinking. For me, she grounds ecological thinking.

LC: There's a really powerful film about her.

AD: *The Power of One Voice* (Dixon 2014). Yes, you mentioned the film in *Manufactured Uncertainty* (Code forthcoming).

LC: One of the things that always made me think about ecological thinking is that those boundaries are so inhibiting. In ecological thinking, if it were to work well, there's a fluidity that doesn't block the possibility of definitive knowing. But it also doesn't make the possibility of definitive knowing so exclusive that it excludes things that we ought to have been thinking about. That's sort of what I mean by epistemic responsibility as well. So, it all kind of clusters together around these thoughts.

Epistemologies, Literary Resources, and Feminist Methodologies: "Human Experience Isn't so Compartmentalized and Divided Up"

AD: You're one of the few philosophers that really works with literature as an important epistemological resource for developing epistemological and ethico-onto-epistemological frameworks. What moved you in this direction, and what do you see as the benefits of using literature as an epistemic device?

LC: I think because I never really learned how to compartmentalize—and this could be a strength and a failure. And this goes right back to the beginning of everything we talked about. Because it seemed to me that things and events are so incredibly interrelated. The things analytical philosophy wanted to make never captured human experience because human experience isn't so compartmentalized and divided up. Which is both its strength and its weakness. So, I'm also reaching for things that don't really belong there because they really strike a chord. And that's how we got to Nadine Gordimer (1981). I've been in a reading group for years, and often the novels we read connect with what I'm thinking about. And I can't seem to see why the novels I'm reading shouldn't have bearing on what I'm thinking about.

It's not that something moved me to see the benefits of literature as an epistemic device as often as I was trying to wrestle with these philosophical thoughts while I would, at the same time, be reading novels.

AD: How was it that you got into feminist methodology when you wrote a book about it with Sandra Burt? When I read it in the late nineties, I was looking for epistemological work that was actually grounded in methodology, so I cowrote a chapter called "Responsible Knowing" (Doucet and Mauthner 2002/2012). And I came to your work because you were the only philosopher who was working with feminist methodological work. Which is where I located myself. So, where did that come from? Because that was unusual: to see a feminist philosopher connect so directly to feminist methodologies and to participatory methodologies.

LC: Well, almost everything is an accident. When I needed to locate my fellowship somewhere, and we were living in Guelph, I decided on Waterloo, where there was a center for feminist research. Sandra was in sociology. We became friends before we became academic colleagues. And went on to do some work together.

It seems to me that it may not be just a feminist point, but if you're thinking about knowing as a thing people do, as opposed to a mechanical operation (which is what positivism thought of it as being), and it somehow shapes lives and decisions and so on, at some point, it becomes imperative to ask who these people are. That's really simple. That's where *What Can She Know?* comes from.

AD: And that's what you're doing in *Manufactured Uncertainty*.

LC: Exactly. But traditional theories of knowledge didn't do that. And you can see why. Because the fear was—particularly under the influence of positivism—that if you started analyzing individual events and circumstances and situations and so on, you'd just have a totally relativistic model. At the time, particularly in the strongest readings of logical positivism, the idea that things could be sort of soft and fluid, the idea that things are circumstance dependent, seemed to be a recipe for chaos. And at that point, chaos was the opposite of knowing. Knowing was supposed to put chaos at bay, it seems to me. Probably some of that has to do with two postwar eras. Positivism even takes its title to say: "We can do all this stuff, and we don't have to have chaos." The fear of chaos was huge.

Manufactured Uncertainty

AD: In *Manufactured Uncertainty* (Code 2020a) it seems to me, there is a more urgent sense of the politics of knowledge making.

LC: Yes. And maybe it's more possible to say it now.

AD: So, the Oreskes and Conway (2010) book, *Merchants of Doubt,* which you've drawn on before in your writing bolsters that urgency of the politics of knowledge making and deepens that point you make in the preface to *Ecological Thinking* that epistemic communities are not "benign" (Code 2006, vii). You now add they are also "credentialled." So, it feels to me that in *Manufactured Uncertainty,* ecological imaginaries are even more political. Indeed, you refer much more explicitly to questions of social justice.

LC: I think it's almost all political, but I agree that it's overt in more recent developments. And maybe that makes it bad, and maybe it makes it good. I mean, I'm so far removed from standard epistemology right now.

AD: But do you think ecological imaginaries lends itself more to political projects? You do say that ecological imaginaries are informed by or resonate with postcolonial and antiracist theories, Indigenous epistemologies—the big questions of the day that are social justice–oriented, or they're about suffering or trauma. I view your work as moving on that difficult terrain.

LC: I hope it is informed well enough to move securely on that terrain because it really seems to move there, albeit cautiously.

Connections between and across Code's Writing (Code 1987, 1991, 1995, 2006, 2020a): "It's All About Responsible Epistemic Practices"

AD: Would you like to say anything about the connections between your books?

LC: They are sort of connected in the sense that each builds on something from the previous one, sometimes explicitly and sometimes not. They are written more in response to a certain situation. Well, *Epistemic Responsibility* probably was not written that way, obviously, because it was the first book, but it captured an idea that had been absolutely frustrating me all along and still does. I am glad to know the press is reissuing *Epistemic Responsibility* with my new preface and together with my new book because I think that basically all my books are about epistemic responsibility in various ways, even though it's not always articulated that way.

AD: Can you say a bit more about that?

LC: I couldn't make the relationships/connections absolutely explicitly. I think the question that runs through all of my books, either overtly or covertly, is how responsible epistemic practice can be possible in quite different areas of inquiry. So, even asking "What can she know?" or questions about ecological thinking are all different aspects of responsible practice, but I don't say it in every book.

My books don't build on each other in that they are written at different points in time. Philosophy has gone on developing, and I'm drawing on things that weren't necessarily explicit in my previous books, but perhaps they were present in all of them? I mean, who says "every philosopher has only one thought" and everything he/she writes about builds on that one thought? Well, that might be true for me. I wouldn't be anywhere if it weren't true. So, it reappears in different guises, but it's the same thought. And I think each book addresses the same question.

AD: So how would you articulate that question?

LC: Well, it's all about responsible epistemic practices across the social, political, geographic, and temporal circumstances. I think it's a huge question.

Selected Key Contemporary Influences and Relationships: "A Gathering" . . . and "If I Had 10 or 20 More Years"

AD: Who are the feminist philosophers or epistemologists that have had the most influence on your work and/or were important colleagues to you?

LC: I would like to start with the significance of my friendship with Jenny—Genevieve—Lloyd in the making of my academic life. Without her friendship and collegiality, I would not have accomplished half of what I have done. So, Jenny's influence on me is probably the most significant, both philosophically and personally. I've worked with her in Australia and North America quite a lot. I wouldn't credit her with having contributed directly to my work and, certainly, I have not contributed to hers because she is, I think, one of the most outstanding female-feminist philosophers alive. That may be an exaggerated comment, but her work is so thoughtful and deep and life-changing.

I have also had a connection with Australia, to a lesser extent, through Peta Bowden, who taught at Perth, and who died last year. I want to acknowledge these Australian relationships.

As for people whose work I very much admire—Naomi Scheman, Donna Haraway, Sonia Kruks, Sandry Bartky, Karen Barad—I have worked with and know some of them personally, and for others, I've worked a lot with their work. I don't usually start by working from someone else's work. I start with kind of random ideas and chase them in various weird ways. I would also mention Iris Marian Young and lots of recent philosophers. Sue Sherwin for sure; her influence on Canadian philosophy is profound. Shannon Sullivan, including her book with Nancy Tuana on epistemologies of ignorance.

Rachel Carson is a big influence, even though she's not a philosopher. She's a huge influence in the way that she approached the world and life. Val Palmwood, whose philosophy I much admire, and whose death I deeply mourn. Cornelius Castoriadis, Lewis Gordon, Adrianna Cavarero, Linda Alcoff, Allison Bailey, Adrienne Rich, and Ludwig Wittgenstein. And R. G. Collingwood. I read him as an undergraduate; he was an eclectic thinker and, mostly, I admire a little eclecticism in thinkers.

I would also say Heidegger, who seems not to fit, but he does. Heidegger somehow struck a chord with me. I found that both his treatment of questions about technology and his book *Being, Dwelling, Thinking* (1971) captured a kind of approach that was missing from a typical stand-back analytical approach. I read Heidegger in Germany and in German, and I found it deeply rewarding.

It's important to add that I pick up problems and start working on them and find contributions to thinking about them from various people, kind of randomly. I draw on other people to help me develop my ideas rather than starting the other way around. It's not as careless and thoughtless as a scavenger hunt; it's a process of gathering more than hunting or scavenging, I suppose.

I would be working and writing and thinking and so on, and it would occur to me that there were some thoughts I'd want to pursue further. But my philosophical life is much less purposeful than most people's. As I said, it's kind of a gathering, a picking up and getting excited about something and pursuing it, rather than saying I really need to write something about ethics . . . I don't do that. I tend to see an idea that grabs me and makes me think, and I will want to learn more about that, so I fiddle away with it. Things sort of randomly come up and I'll think, "Oh, well there's something to pursue there."

And it has always been the ethical dimension of knowledge and epistemologies that has drawn my attention, rather than the epistemic dimension of ethics. That's what gave me the idea of epistemic responsibility, which, to me, is still a most important topic.

If I had ten or twenty more years, I'd probably keep writing things that were unintentionally about epistemic responsibility. The knowledge process and the responsibilities of knowing—that is what is important to me. Presenting oneself as a knower is a huge responsibility that people often don't acknowledge.

Works Cited

Ayer, A. 1952. *Language, Truth, and Logic*. New York: Dover.

Carson, R. 1962. *Silent Spring*. Boston: Houghton Mifflin.

Code, L. 1987. *Epistemic Responsibility*. Providence, RI: Brown University Press.

———. 1991. *What Can She Know? Feminist Theory and the Construction of Knowledge*. Ithaca, NY: Cornell University Press.

———. 1995. *Rhetorical Spaces: Essays on Gendered Locations*. New York: Routledge.

———. 1996. "What is Natural about Epistemology Naturalized? (Feminism and Ecological Model for Naturalized Epistemology). *American Philosophical Quarterly* 33, no. 1, 1–22.

———. ed. 2003. *Feminist Interpretations of Hans-Georg Gadamer*. University Park: Pennsylvania State University Press

———. 2006. *Ecological Thinking: The Politics of Epistemic Location*. Oxford: Oxford University Press.

———. 2010. "Testimony, Advocacy, Ignorance: Thinking Ecologically About Social Knowledge." In *Social Epistemology*, edited by A. Haddock, A. Millar, and D. Pritchard. Oxford: Oxford University Press.

———. 2015. "Care, Concern, and Advocacy: Is There a Place for Epistemic Responsibility?" *Feminist Philosophy Quarterly* 1, no. 1:1–20.

———. 2020a. *Manufactured Uncertainty: New Challenges to Epistemic Responsibility*. Albany: State University of New York Press.

———. 2020b. *Epistemic Responsibility*. 2nd ed. Albany: State University of New York Press.

Dixon, M., dir. 2014. *The Power of One Voice: A 50-Year Perspective on the Life of Rachel Carson*. Pittsburgh: Steeltown Entertainment Project.

Doucet, A., and N. Mauthner. 2002. "Knowing Responsibly: Ethics, Feminist Epistemologies and Methodologies." In *Ethics in Qualitative Research*, edited by M. Mauthner, M. Birch, J. Jessop, and T. Miller, 123–145. London: SAGE.

Doucet, A., and N. Mauthner. 2012. "Knowing Responsibly: Ethics, Feminist Epistemologies and Methodologies." In *Ethics in Qualitative Research*, edited by T. Miller, M. Birch, M. Mauthner, and J. Jessop, 122–139. London: SAGE.

Gordimer, N. 1981. *July's People*. New York: Viking.

Haraway, D. 1997. *Modest_Witness@ Second_Millennium. FemaleMan©_Meets_Onco Mouse™: Feminism and Technoscience*. New York: Routledge.

Heidegger, M. 1971. "Building Dwelling Thinking." In *Poetry, Language, Thought*. Translated by A. Hofstader. New York: Harper Colophon.

Oreskes, N., and Conway, E. 2010. *Merchants of Doubt: How a Handful of Scientists Obscured the Truth on Issues From Tobacco Smoke to Global Warming*. 1st ed. New York: Bloomsbury.

Rooney, P. 2011. "The Marginalization of Feminist Epistemology and What That Reveals about Epistemology 'Proper.'" In *Feminist Epistemology and Philosophy of Science: Power in Knowledge*, edited by H. Grasswick, 3–24. New York: Springer.

Tennyson, A. L. 1891. *Works*. London: Macmillan.

Lorraine Code's Body of Work

Key Works, 1973–2021

Books

Code, Lorraine. 2020. *Epistemic Responsibility.* 2nd ed. Albany: State University of New York Press.

Code, Lorraine. 2020. *Manufactured Uncertainty New Challenges to Epistemic Responsibility.* Albany: State University of New York Press.

Code, Lorraine. 2006. *Ecological Thinking: The Politics of Epistemic Location.* New York: Oxford University Press.

Code, Lorraine. 1995. *Rhetorical Spaces: Essays on Gendered Locations.* New York and London: Routledge.

Code, Lorraine. 1991. *What Can She Know? Feminist Theory and the Construction of Knowledge.* Ithaca, NY: Cornell University Press.

Code, Lorraine, Maureen Ford, Kathleen Martindale, Susan Sherwin, and Debra Shogan. 1991. *Is Feminist Ethics Possible?* Ottawa: Crlaw/lCreF.

Code, Lorraine. 1987. *Epistemic Responsibility.* Hanover, NH: University Press of New England.

Edited Volumes

Burt, Sandra D., and Lorraine Code. 1995. *Changing Methods: Feminists Transforming Practice.* Peterborough, ON: Broadview.

Burt, Sandra D., Lorraine Code, and Lindsay Dorney. 1993. *Changing Patterns: Women in Canada.* Toronto: McClelland & Stewart.

Code, Lorraine. 2003. *Feminist Interpretations of Hans-Georg Gadamer.* University Park: Pennsylvania State University Press.

Code, Lorraine. 2000. *Encyclopedia of Feminist Theories.* New York: Routledge.

Code, Lorraine, Sheila Mullett, and Christine Overall. 1988. *Feminist Perspectives: Philosophical Essays on Minds and Morals*. Toronto: University of Toronto Press.

Journal Articles

Code, Lorraine. 2017. "The Tyranny of Certainty." *Symposium: Canadian Journal of Continental Philosophy* 21: 206–18.
Code, Lorraine. 2016. "Who Do We Think We Are?" *Social Philosophy Today* 32: 29–44.
Code, Lorraine. 2016. "Knowing Responsibly, Thinking Ecologically: Response to Panelists." *Feminist Philosophy Quarterly* 2: 1–9.
Code, Lorraine. 2015. "Care, Concern, and Advocacy: Is There a Place for Epistemic Responsibility?" *Feminist Philosophy Quarterly* 1: 1–20.
Code, Lorraine. 2015. "Knowledge and Subjectivity." Guelph Philosophy at 50. Guelph: University of Guelph.
Code, Lorraine. 2014. "Culpable Ignorance?" *Hypatia* 29: 670–676.
Code, Lorraine. 2013. "Doubt and Denial: Epistemic Responsibility Meets Climate Change Skepticism." *Oñati Socio-Legal Series* 3: 838–853.
Code, Lorraine. 2012. "Ecological Responsibilities: Which Trees? Where? Why?" *Journal of Human Rights and the Environment* 3: 84–99.
Code, Lorraine. 2011. "An Ecology of Epistemic Authority." *Episteme: A Journal of Social Epistemology* 8: 25–37.
Code, Lorraine. 2010. "Particularity, Epistemic Responsibility, and the Ecological Imaginary." Philosophy of Education Archive, 23–34.
Code, Lorraine. 2010. "The Power of Social Imaginaries: Fact, Fiction, and the Politics of Knowledge." *Transhumanities: Journal of the Humanities Korea Project* 2: 9–31.
Code, Lorraine. 2009. "A New Epistemology of Rape?" *Philosophical Papers* 38: 327–345.
Code, Lorraine. 2008. "Rereading Ecological Thinking." *Ethics, Place & Environment* 11: 76–90.
Code, Lorraine. 2008. "Thinking Ecologically about Biology." *Insights* 1: 2–17.
Code, Lorraine. 2008. "Thinking about Ecological Thinking." *Hypatia* 23: 187–203.
Code, Lorraine. 2008. "Advocacy, Negotiation, and the Politics of Unknowing." *Southern Journal of Philosophy* 46: 32–51.
Code, Lorraine. 2006. "Skepticism and the Lure of Ambiguity." *Hypatia* 3: 222–228.
Code, Lorraine. 2005. "Ecological Naturalism: Epistemic Responsibility and the Politics of Knowledge." *Dialogue & Universalism* 15: 87–101.
Code, Lorraine. 2005. "Here and There: Reading Christopher Preston's Grounding Knowledge." *Ethics, Place and Environment* 8: 349–360.

Code, Lorraine, Kristi Malterud, and Lucy Candib. 2004. "Responsible and Responsive Knowing in Medical Diagnosis: The Medical Gaze Revisited." *Nora: Nordic Journal of Women's Studies* 12: 8–19.

Code, Lorraine. 2004. "The Power of Ignorance." *Philosophical Papers* 33: 291–308.

Code, Lorraine. 2002. "Narratives of Responsibility and Agency: Reading Margaret Walker's Moral Understandings (Symposium)." *Hypatia* 1: 156–173.

Code, Lorraine. 2001. "Statements of Fact: Whose? Where? When?" *Canadian Journal of Philosophy* 26: 175–208.

Code, Lorraine. 1999. "Flourishing." *Ethics and the Environment* 4: 63–72.

Code, Lorraine. 1998. "How to Think Globally: Stretching the Limits of Imagination." *Hypatia* 13: 73–85.

Code, Lorraine. 1998. "Feminists and Pragmatists: A Radical Future?" *Radical Philosophy* 87: 22–30.

Code, Lorraine. 1996. "What Is Natural about Epistemology Naturalized?" *American Philosophical Quarterly* 33: 1–22.

Code, Lorraine. 1994. "Responsibility and Rhetoric." *Hypatia* 9: 1–20.

Code, Lorraine. 1992. "Who Cares? The Poverty of Objectivism for a Moral Epistemology." *Annals of Scholarship* 9: 1–18.

Code, Lorraine. "The Impact of Feminism on Epistemology." Nancy Tuana, ed., *APA Newsletter on Feminism and Philosophy* 88: 25–29.

Code, Lorraine. 1989. "Collingwood's Epistemological Individualism." *The Monist* 72: 542–567.

Code, Lorraine. 1988. "Autonomy Reconsidered." *Atlantis* 13: 27–35.

Code, Lorraine. 1987. "Tokenism." *Resources for Feminist Research* 16: 46–48.

Code, Lorraine. 1986. "Stories People Tell." *New Mexico Law Review* 16: 599–606.

Code, Lorraine. 1986. "Simple Equality Is Not Enough." *Australasian Journal of Philosophy* 64: 48–65.

Code, Lorraine. 1986. "Collingwood: A Philosopher of Ambivalence." *History of Philosophy Quarterly* 3: 107–121.

Code, Lorraine. 1984. "Toward a 'Responsibilist' Epistemology." *Philosophy and Phenomenological Research* 45: 29–50.

Code, Lorraine. 1984. "The Knowing Subject." *Idealistic Studies* XIV.

Code, Lorraine. 1983. "Responsibility and the Epistemic Community: Women's Place." *Social Research* 50: 537–555.

Code, Lorraine. 1983. "Father and Son: A Case Study in Epistemic Responsibility." *Monist* 66: 268–2982.

Code, Lorraine. 1981. "Is the Sex of the Knower Epistemologically Significant?" *Metaphilosophy* 12: 267–276.

Code, Lorraine. 1982. "The Importance of Historicism for a Theory of Knowledge." *International Philosophical Quarterly* 22: 157–174.

Code, Lorraine. 1980. "Language and Knowledge." *Word: Journal of the International Linguistics Association* 31: 245–258.

Code, Lorraine, and John King-Farlow. 1973. "Bonne foi/mauvaise foi, sincérité et Espoir." *Dialogue* XII.

Book Chapters

Code, Lorraine. 2021. "The Power and Perils of Examples: 'Literizing is not Theorizing.'" In *Making the Case: Feminist and Critical Race Philosophers Engaging Case Studies*, edited by Heidi Grasswick and Nancy McHugh. Albany: State University of New York Press.

Code, Lorraine. 2014. "Feminist Epistemology and the Politics of Knowledge: Questions of Marginality." In *The SAGE Handbook of Feminist Theory*, edited by Mary Evans, Clare Hemmings, Marsha Henry, Hazel Johnstone, Sumi Madhok, Ania Plomien, and Sadie Wearing, 9–25. London: SAGE.

Code, Lorraine. 2013. "'Manufactured Uncertainty': Epistemologies of Mastery and the Ecological Imaginary." In *Relational Architectural Ecologies: Architecture, Nature and Subjectivity*, edited by Peg Rawes. London: Routledge.

Code, Lorraine. 2012. "Reason and Woman." In *Reason and Rationality*, edited by Nicla Vassallo and Cristina Amoretti, 71–91. Frankfurt: Ontos Verlag.

Code, Lorraine. 2012. "Feminism, Ecological Thinking and the Legacy of Rachel Carson." In *Reconsidering Knowledge: Feminism and the Academy*, edited by Meg Luxton and Mary Jane Mossman. Halifax and Winnipeg: Fernwood.

Code, Lorraine. 2012. "Thinking Ecologically: The Legacy of Rachel Carson." In *The Environment: Philosophy, Science, and Ethics.* Vol. 9: *Topics in Contemporary Philosophy*, edited by William P. Kabasenche, Michael O'Rourke, and Matthew H. Slater, 117–135. Cambridge, MA: MIT Press.

Code, Lorraine. 2011. "Ecological Thinking as Interdisciplinary Practice: Situation, Silence, and Scepticism." In *Valences of Interdisciplinarity: Theory, Practice, Pedagogy*, edited by Raphael Foshay, 191–211. Edmonton, Alberta: Athabasca University Press.

Code, Lorraine. 2011. "*Self, Subjectivity, and the Instituted Social Imaginary.*" In *The Oxford Handbook of the* Self, edited by Shaun Gallagher. Oxford: Oxford University Press.

Code, Lorraine. 2011. "'They Treated Him Well': Fact, Fiction, and the Politics of Knowledge." In *Feminist Epistemology and Philosophy of Science: Power in Knowledge*, edited by Heidi E. Grasswick, 205–222. New York: Springer.

Code, Lorraine. 2010. "Testimony, Advocacy, Ignorance: Thinking Ecologically about Social Knowledge." In *Social Epistemology*, edited by Adrian Haddock and Alan Millar, 29–50. Oxford: Oxford University Press.

Code, Lorraine. 2010. "Must a Feminist Be a Relativist After All"? In *Relativism: A Compendium*, edited by Michael Krausz. New York: Columbia University Press.

Code, Lorraine. 2010. "Feminist Interpretations of the Self." In *The Oxford Handbook of the Self*, edited by Shaun Gallagher, 713–735. Oxford: Oxford University Press.

Code, Lorraine. 2008. "Epistemology: 5 Questions." In *Epistemology: 5 Questions*, edited by Vincent F. Hendricks and Duncan Pritchard, 63–77. Copenhagen: Automatic.

Code, Lorraine. 2007. "The Power of Ignorance." In *Race and Epistemologies of Ignorance*, edited by Shannon Sullivan and Nancy Tuana. Albany: State University of New York Press.

Code, Lorraine. 2006. "Images of Expertise: Women, Science and the Politics of Representation." In *Figuring It Out: Science, Gender, and Visual Culture*, edited by Bernard Lightman and Ann B. Shteir. Hanover, NH: University Press of New England.

Code, Lorraine. 2003. "Introduction: Why Feminists Do Not Read Gadamer." In *Feminist Interpretations of Hans-Georg Gadamer*, edited by Lorraine Code. University Park: Pennsylvania State University Press.

Code, Lorraine. 2002. "Incongruities." In *The Philosophical I: Personal Reflections on Life in Philosophy*, edited by George Yancy. New York: Rowman & Littlefield.

Code, Lorraine. 2001. "Rational Imaginings, Responsible Knowings: How Far Can You See From Here?" In *Engendering Rationalities*, edited by Nancy Tuana and Sandra Morgen, 261–282. Albany: State University of New York Press.

Code, Lorraine. 2000. "Naming, Naturalizing, Normalizing: The Child as Fact and Artifact." In *Toward a Feminist Developmental Psychology*, edited by Patricia Miller and Ellin Scholnik. New York: Routledge.

Code, Lorraine. 2000. "The Perversion of Autonomy and the Subjection of Women: Discourses of Social Advocacy at Century's End." In *Relational Autonomy*, edited by Catriona Mackenzie and Natalie Stoljar. New York: Oxford University Press.

Code, Lorraine. 1998. "Voice and Voicelessness: A Modest Proposal?" In *Philosophy in a Different Voice*, edited by Janet Kourany. Princeton, NJ: Princeton University Press.

Code, Lorraine. 1995. "Taking Subjectivity into Account." In *Feminist Epistemologies*, edited by L. M. Alcoff and Elizabeth Potter, 15–48. New York: Routledge.

Code, Lorraine. 1995. "How Do We Know? Questions of Method in Feminist Practice." In *Changing Methods: Feminists Transforming Practice*, edited by Sandra D. Burt and Lorraine Code, 14–44. Peterborough, ON: Broadview.

Code, Lorraine. 1994. "Who Cares? The Poverty of Objectivism for a Moral Epistemology." In *Rethinking Objectivity*, edited by Alan Megill. Durham, NC: Duke University Press.

Code, Lorraine. 1994. "Gossip: A Plea for Chaos." In *Good Gossip*, edited by Robert F. Goodman and Aaron Ben-Ze'ev. Lawrence: University of Kansas Press.

Code, Lorraine. 1994. " 'I Know Just How You Feel': Empathy and the Problem of Epistemic Authority." In *The Empathic Practitioner: Essays on Empathy, Gender and Medicine*, edited by Ellen More and Maureen Milligan. New Brunswick, NJ: Rutgers University Press.

Code, Lorraine. 1993. "The Unicorn in the Garden." In *Women and Reason*, edited by Elizabeth Harvey and Kathleen Okruhlik. Ann Arbor: University of Michigan Press.

Code, Lorraine. 1993. "Taking Subjectivity into Account." In *Feminist Epistemologies*, edited by Linda Alcoff and Elizabeth Potter. New York: Routledge.

Code, Lorraine. 1988/1993. "Feminist Theory." In *Changing Patterns: Women in Canada*, edited by Sandra Burt, Lorraine Code and Lindsay Dorney. Toronto: McClelland & Stewart.

Code, Lorraine, Maureen Ford, Kathleen Martindale, Susan Sherwin, and Debra Shogan. 1991. *Is Feminist Ethics Possible?* Ottawa: Crlaw/lCreF.

Code, Lorraine. 1988. "Credibility: A Double Standard." In *Feminist Perspectives: Philosophical Essays on Method and Morals*, edited by Lorraine Code, Sheila Mullett, and Christine Overall. Toronto: University of Toronto Press.

Code, Lorraine. 1988. "Tokenism." In *Feminist Research: Prospect and Retrospect*, edited by Peta Tancred-Sheriff. Montreal: McGill-Queen's University Press.

Code, Lorraine. 1988. "Experience, Knowledge and Responsibility." In *Feminist Perspectives in Philosophy*, edited by Morwenna Griffiths and Margaret Whitford, 187–204. Bloomington: Indiana University Press.

Code, Lorraine. "Second Persons." In *Science, Morality and Feminist Theory*, edited by Marsha Hanen and Kai Nielson. Calgary: University of Calgary Press.

Code, Lorraine. 1987. "Persons and Others." In *Power, Gender, Value*, edited by Judith Genova. Edmonton: Academic Printing.

Code, Lorraine. 1987. "The Tyranny of Stereotypes." In *Women: Isolation and Bonding: Readings in the Ecology of Gender*, edited by Kathleen Storrie. Toronto: Methuen.

Code, Lorraine. 1986. "Est-ce l'égalité qu'il nous faut?" In *Égalité et différence des sexes*, edited by Louise Marcil-Lacoste. Montreal: Les Cahiers de l'ACFAS.

Contributors

Karen Adkins is professor of philosophy at Regis University in Denver, Colorado. She works primarily in feminist philosophy and social theory and has published *Gossip, Power, and Epistemology: Knowledge Underground* (2017), as well as articles in *Social Epistemology, Philosophy in the Contemporary World, Expositions, Teaching Philosophy*, and *Hypatia*.

Carolyn J. Craig is assistant director of Research Compliance Services at the University of Oregon. In that role, she supports responsible conduct of research training, human subject research protections, and conflict of interest management. Over the past fifteen years, Carolyn has taught political science, women's and gender studies, research methods, and writing courses at the University of Colorado at Denver, Rutgers University, Clark University, the University of Oregon, and Chemeketa Community College. Her own research includes analyses of immigration politics, trade politics, and environmental politics within the United States and from a comparative perspective.

Ranjan Datta is Canada research chair II in community disaster research in Indigenous studies in the Department of Humanities, Mount Royal University, Calgary, in Alberta, Canada. Ranjan's research interests include advocating for Indigenous environmental sustainability, Indigenous energy management, decolonization, Indigenous reconciliation, community-based research, and cross-cultural community empowerment.

Émilie Dionne is a researcher at VITAM—Research Centre for Sustainable Health and adjunct professor in the Department of Sociology, Université Laval, in Québec. She has a PhD in social and political thought from York University and a master's and bachelor's degree in political science. Her expertise is in new-feminist-materialist approaches, feminist sciences, feminist and open epistemologies, gender and critical disability studies, and critical qualitative methodology.

Andrea Doucet is a Canada research chair in gender, work, and care and professor of sociology and women's and gender studies at Brock University in the Niagara region of Canada. She has published widely on care, fathering, parental leave, feminist methodologies and epistemologies, reflexivity, and the politics and ethics of knowledge-making practices. She is the author of *Do Men Mother?*, which was awarded the 2007 John Porter Tradition of Excellence Book Award from the Canadian Sociological Association (second, updated edition, 2018) and coauthor of two editions of *Gender Relations in Canada: Intersectionality and Social Change* (2006, 2017). She is project director and principal investigator of a seven-year (2020–27) partnership grant entitled "Reimagining Care/Work Policies" from the Canadian Social Sciences and Humanities Research Council (SSHRC). Working with a cross-disciplinary and diverse group of scholars and community organizations, she plans to further develop ecological social imaginaries and methodological pluralism in this research program. Her website is: http://www.andreadoucet.com

Catherine Villanueva Gardner is professor of philosophy and women's and gender studies at the University of Massachusetts Dartmouth. Gardner's primary areas of interest are in the history of women philosophers and ethics. She has published two monographs that encompass these areas: *Women Philosophers: Genre and the Boundaries of Philosophy* (2004) and *Empowerment and Interconnectivity: Toward a Feminist History of Utilitarianism* (2013).

Catherine Maloney is a PhD candidate at York University. Her work focuses on the implications a dialogical model of understanding has for ethical and political action and suggests that dialogical approaches to understanding have the right *epistemic fit* for the kind of social understanding that is necessary to responsibly ground action. Her recent paper "From Epistemic Responsibility to Ecological Thinking: The Importance of Advocacy for Epistemic Community" was published in the fall 2016 issue of the *Feminist Philosophy Quarterly*. She currently works at the Centre for International Experience, University of Toronto, as the manager of intercultural initiatives and learning strategy.

Nancy Arden McHugh is professor of philosophy at the University of Dayton and executive director of the Fitz Center for Leadership in Community through which she partners with communities, students, and faculty to move forward community-identified needs. Nancy is the author of *The Limits of Knowledge: Generating Pragmatist Feminist Cases for Situated Knowing* (SUNY Press, 2015), the research for which was funded by the National Science Foundation, and *Feminist Philosophies A–Z* (2007). She is also the author of articles in feminist philosophy of science and epistemology, as well as the coeditor (with Heidi Grasswick) of *Making the Case: Feminist and Critical Race Philosophers Engaging Case Studies* (SUNY Press, 2020). Nancy teaches philosophy courses in juvenile detention centers and in adult prisons; she also partners with reentry programs for women who were incarcerated and with the Kettering Foundation on deliberative dialogue on reentry from prison. Her website is http://www.nancyamchugh.org.

Esme G. Murdock is assistant professor of American Indian studies at San Diego State University. Her research explores the intersections of social/political relations and environmental health, integrity, and agency. Specifically, her work troubles the purported stability of dominant, largely Eurodescendent and settler-colonial philosophies through centering conceptions of land and relating to land found within African American, Afro-diasporic, and Indigenous ecophilosophies. She has work forthcoming in *Environmental Values* and the *Journal of Global Ethics*.

Kamili Posey is assistant professor of philosophy at Kingsborough Community College, CUNY. Her research interests include social epistemology, feminist epistemology, and philosophy of race and gender. She is currently finishing a manuscript tentatively titled "Centering Epistemic Injustice."

Nancy Nyquist Potter is professor emeritus of philosophy and adjunct with the Department of Psychiatry and Behavioral Sciences at the University of Louisville. Her research interests are philosophy and psychiatry, feminist philosophy, virtue ethics, and understanding forms of violence. Her current work is on meanings and interplays between voice, silence, and giving uptake—in particular in clinical settings and with respect to patients/service users. Her most recent books are *The Virtue of Defiance and Psychiatric Engagement* (2016); *Mapping the Edges and the In-Between: A Critical Analysis of Borderline Personality Disorder* (2009); and the edited volume *Trauma, Truth, and Reconciliation: Healing Damaged Relationships* (2006).

Susan Reid is a PhD candidate in the Department of Gender and Cultural Studies at the University of Sydney where she is researching ocean and juridical imaginaries, relationalities, and justice. She is a writer, artist, curator, and lawyer, with a master's degree in design and a master's of international law.

Codi Stevens is a doctoral candidate in philosophy with a specialization in social epistemology at the University of Minnesota, Twin Cities. Epistemic responsibility is her primary research interest. Her current work combines this interest with her interdisciplinary interest in psychology to explore the ways in which theories of epistemic responsibility can be constructed with sensitivity to facts about human-belief formation processes.

Index

advocacy, 1, 4, 78–82, 89n6, 104, 108, 114–115, 142–143, 145, 145n3, 151, 156, 176, 185, 188, 198, 265, 279; climate, 286–288, 293, 297–299, 322
Alcoff, Linda Martín, 26, 33–35, 88
American Institutional Review Boards (IRBs), 149–157, 159–164, 167, 169, 170n5, 171n6
agency, 165–166, 202, 221, 235, 243, 253; epistemic, 8, 25, 47, 50, 52, 60, 185, 207

Bailey, Allison, 322
Bakhtin, Mikhail, 129–130, 133–145, 145n2
Bal, Mieke, 110, 115
Barad, Karen, 93–94, 98, 100, 175, 177–182, 186–187, 189, 190n1–n3, 265, 322
Bartky, Sandra Lee, 322
Bowden, Peta, 322
Burt, Sandra, 319

care, 182, 184, 186–189, 278–279
Cajete, Gregory, 221–222
Carson, Rachel, 105, 109, 119, 270, 316, 322
Castoriadis, Cornelius, 49, 99, 322

Cavarero, Adrianna, 116, 322
Chittagong Hill Tracts, Bangladesh, 220, 228–239. *See also* Laitu Khyeng Indigenous Community
Collingwood, Robin George, 322
climate change, 1–2, 4, 28–29, 288–290, 299; denial, 286, 299; skepticism, 279, 285, 288, 289, 300n3
Code, Lorraine, 1, 2, 4, 7–13, 16–21, 22n14, 25–33, 36–40, 41n2, 42n5, 48–50, 65, 67n14, 73–76, 78–87, 89, 89n4, 89n6, 90n12, 93, 95–100, 102–112, 114–120, 121n8, 121n9, 121n10, 129–136, 139, 141, 142, 144–145, 145n3, 149–151, 153, 166, 175–177, 181–190, 190n4, 193–199, 205, 212, 219–226, 235, 238, 243–248, 251–254, 256, 258, 259n1, 264–267, 270–274, 276, 279, 285–287, 290–291, 293, 296–299, 303–323; key works, 325–330
cohabitation, 49, 80, 118, 182–183, 189, 223, 264, 274, 280
colonial rule, 10–12, 21n6, 230
colonialism, 237–238, 247–248
colonization, 26, 32, 35, 232, 234, 238, 251, 257, 274; protesting, 30, 237

335

communication, 203, 212n5; climate science, 286–288, 292–294, 296–297
community(ies), 13, 16–19, 85–85, 131, 141–145, 149, 155, 163–164; African American, 42; epistemic 28–29, 137; research 152, 154–155
context: of knowledge, 33–34, 75–78, 83, 87, 89n4, 90n12, 119, 131, 141, 144, 178–179, 245, 254; of research, 152, 166, 168
Conway, Eric, 111, 112, 300n3, 320
courage: intellectual, 19, 208
credibility, 86, 115, 198, 203–204, 296
culpability, 18–19, 39–40, 41n2

Daniel Deronda, 10, 12, 30, 40
Diagnostic and Statistical Manual (DSM), 194, 198, 206, 211, 273
deadspace(s): epistemic, 48, 50, 51, 52, 57, 59, 61–64, 65n2; embodiment in, 61–64
decolonization, 227–228, 235
deference, 198
Deleuze, Gilles, 104, 106
dialogue, 143, 156, 161, 176
diffractive reading. *See* methodologies, diffractive

ecological thinking, 3–4, 48, 49, 50, 74, 81, 83, 84, 85, 86, 87, 103, 136–137, 141, 144–145, 149–150, 155, 159–160, 162–170, 176, 181–183, 185, 187–190, 195, 197, 212, 219–226, 228–229, 234–235, 238; shortcomings of, 244–248, 251–258, 259n1, 264–268, 279, 281, 286–287, 317–318
Ecological Thinking, 3–4, 48, 104, 106–108, 121n10, 131, 136, 139–142, 150, 175–176, 184, 187, 195, 223, 243–245 254, 257–258, 286, 297, 299, 316
ecology(ies), 82, 182–183, 265–267
efficacy: epistemic, 47, 60–61
Eliot, George, 8, 10, 30
environmental management strategies, 229, 237; indigenous, 233–234, 237; western, 230–232, 238
Epistemic Responsibility, 1, 3, 7–10, 19, 27–28, 194, 286, 290, 293, 311, 320
epistemic responsibility(ies), 7, 16–18, 20, 25–26, 28, 31–33, 38, 41, 102, 121n8, 130, 221, 225, 286–287, 297, 310–313, 315–316, 323
epistemology/epistemologies), 1–3, 8–11, 13, 16, 18, 21n2, 22n14, 25, 27, 65, 81, 83, 87, 98, 100, 103, 110, 121n9, 129, 141, 194, 204, 209, 220, 224–225, 229, 246, 264, 267, 275–276, 278, 293, 297, 304, 311, 314, 316–323; ableism in, 41n3; ethico-onto, 93, 100–101, 176, 179, 189; ethics and, 194–196; feminist, 9, 88, 100, 103, 120, 121n8, 175–176, 255, 303–304; historical, 95, 100; of ignorance, 10, 11, 16–17, 18, 20–21, 21n5, 41n1, 25–26, 33, 41n1, 41n3; of incarceration, 61; indigenous, 225, 229, 256–258; of mastery, 49, 184–185, 187, 191n5, 268; ocean, 264–266, 280–281; orthodox, 7, 11, 16–18, 21n2, 25, 35, 82, 83, 99, 101, 131–132, 141, 184, 206, 220, 244–252, 255, 257–258, 269; politico-ethico-onto, 13, 96, 97, 110, 117–118; social, 96, 103, 111
ethical loneliness, 208–210
ethics, 106, 118, 150, 175–176, 181–184, 189, 193–195, 199, 204, 208, 212, 225, 238–239, 311, 323;

in research, 152–154, 162, 169, 170n1
evidence, 58–60, 66n12, 80, 109–110, 188, 197, 279, 288–291
evidence-based medicine (EBM), 194

feminism, 1, 90n13, 175; black, 3, 254

gender, 33, 62, 199–200, 282n2; nonconformity, 54–56, 202
Glanville, Doug, 31–32, 39
Glaspell, Susan, 76, 81–82, 84, 87
Gluckman, Max, 75
Gordimer, Nadine, 9, 30
Gordon, Lewis, 322
gossip, 73–89, 89n11, 90n12

habitat(s), 50, 57, 75–77, 104–106, 112, 119, 268–269; epistemological, 48–50, 57, 59, 65, 267–269, 275–276, 261
habits, 49, 51, 61, 63, 65, 295–296; epistemological, 51, 65
Haraway, Donna, 120, 177, 181, 186, 322
Harper, Frances E. W., 8–13, 15–17, 20, 21n3, 21n10
Heidegger, Martin, 322
humility: epistemic, 40, 60, 203, 273

ignorance, 2, 10–13, 15–19, 25, 203, 290; epistemologies, of 21, 21n5, 25, 33, 41n1, 103–104; epistemic, 21, 25–27, 29–31, 33, 35–36, 39, 41n1; pernicious, 208; racialized, 12, 15–17, 22n11; situated, 15–19, 32, 39–40; "white," 16, 20; willful hermeneutical, 27, 36–40
imaginary(ies), 31–32, 96, 102, 108–109, 142, 181, 188, 190n, 264, 271, 279–280; dominant, 32, 36, 42n5; ecological, 96–97, 103–104, 111, 320; extractive, 270; gendered, 199–200; instituted, 49–50, 96, 98, 145n3, 204, 206, 209–210, instituting 9, 40, 49–50, 96, 99–101, 209–210; social, 31–33, 35–37, 40, 116, 137, 199–204, 212n3; of white supremacy, 8–10, 13, 16, 20, 22n10
imagination, 265, 271, 281
incarceration, 52–54, 60–65, 66n8, 67n13
injustice, 64, 203, 212n3; epistemic, 1–2, 38, 41n3, 67n14; testimonial, 200
institutional review boards (IRB), 149–170, 170n5, 171n6
Intergovernmental Panel on Climate Change (IPCC), 285
Iola Leroy, 8, 10, 12–20, 21n3–4, 22n12–13

"Jury of her Peers, A," 76–78, 79, 85, 87–88
July's People, 9, 12, 30
justice, 3, 18, 264; environmental, 220–221, 234, 236; ocean, 264–267, 270, 274–281; social, 35–36, 40

Kant, Immanuel, 130–136
knowers: marginalized, 27, 32, 35–36, 39–40
knowledge(s), 7–20, 22n9, 22n10, 25, 29, 33, 35, 41n2, 57, 74–78, 85, 88, 90n12, 93–104, 108–110; 131–132, 150–151, 157, 161, 165, 176–188, 190n3, 196–197, 205, 211, 212n2, 221, 223, 225, 226, 227–228, 234–238, 243–246, 249, 251, 254–255, 258, 259n2, 263–275, 278, 290, 293, 299, 313, 323;

knowledge(s) *(continued)*
  "black," 14, 16; holders/keepers, of 229–236, 238; marginalized, 38–41; responsible, 31; situated, 21n2; "white," 14–15
knowledge practices, 179–188
knowledge production, 21n2, 100–103, 108–109, 116, 118, 120, 150–151, 161, 163, 167, 169–170, 197, 207, 211, 212n2, 220, 226, 266–267, 272, 277, 319–320
Kruks, Sonia, 116–120, 322

Laitu Khyeng Indigenous Community, 220, 228–239
literary fiction, in epistemology, 8–9, 30, 318
Lloyd, Genevieve, 321
LoCI–Wittenberg University Writing Group, 53, 60, 61, 66n9
Lodge, Reni Eddo, 37, 41

Manufactured Uncertainty: New Challenges to Epistemic Responsibility, 1, 2, 4, 107, 110, 116, 312, 318–320
meaning making, 129, 137
Medina, José, 27, 37, 40, 50
methodology/methodologies, 36, 39–40, 94, 97, 111, 273–274; diffractive, 98, 186–188, 177, 186–188; feminist, 99, 319; narrative, 96–97; participatory action research, 220–221, 229; pluralism in, 109, 159, 265; social justice, 35–36, 40
Mills, Charles, 21n5, 21n6 25–26, 31, 37, 59
mining, 267–272
Mol, Annemarie, 311
monoculture(s): epistemological, 252, 258–259, 265

narratives, 2–3, 28–34, 36, 39, 42n5, 53, 76–89, 94–97, 103, 111–117, 119–120, 121n7, 121n11, 202, 258n2; dominant, 244–245, 249–255, 257–258, 259n1
narrative history, 26–34, 36, 38–40
Neimanis, Astrida, 278

ontology(ies), 61, 179, 187, 189, 223; multiple, 100–101, 119; relational, 94–95, 100, 104, 111–112, 119
Oreskes, Naomi, 107, 111, 300n3, 320

Philosophy, 22n14, 133–134, 247, 304–307, 309–310, 312, 315, 321; discipline of, 77–78, 89n5, 89n8; feminist, 72, 77, 89n5, 278, 304, 307, 315
Pohlhaus, Gaile, Jr., 36
Positionality, 26–27, 34, 244, 251, 255, 257
power relations, 9, 22n10, 31–32, 58–62, 87, 143–144, 150, 151, 153–154, 158, 160, 208, 210, 258; epistemic, 58, 60, 62
power structures, 29–30, 35–36, 41, 52–53, 59, 64, 83–84, 109–110, 139, 142, 160, 167, 186, 203, 238, 249, 299
"Power of Ignorance, The," 8, 10, 12–13, 18–19
Prison Rape Elimination Act (PREA), 54–57, 66n10
prisons, 51–56, 58, 62, 66n5, 66n6, 66n8. *See also* incarceration
prisoners: political 47–48; trans, of color, 54–56
privilege, 30, 65n2, 144, 150–151; black 17–18; epistemic, 16–17, 27, 36–39, 41; gender, 249; "white," 17, 30, 37

psychiatry, 194, 197–199, 204–207, 210–212, 213n6; emergency services, 198, 202, 207
patients/service users, 194, 197–199, 205–211
psychology: discipline of, 199, 298; human, 212, 293, 297

Racial Contract, The, 11, 25
racial passing, 10, 13, 17
racialization, 8–10, 12–18, 21n3, 21n4
realism, 177; agential, 100, 177–179, 187, 189
research, 107, 111, 151–170, 170n2,3,4, 171n6,9,10, 219, 223, 226–227, 229, 238, 271; communities, 107, 155, 169; environmental, 221, 226–227, 271–272; ethics of, 150, 152–153; feminist, 94; human subjects, with, 149–150, 152, 156, 161–166, 169; Indigenous, 227, 237–238; participatory action, 220, 237; practices, 109, 111, 152, 165, 167, 225, 228, 235. See also methodologies
responsibility(ies): indigenous, 232, 236; moral, 16; researcher, 227, 234–235. See also epistemic responsibility
Ricoeur, Paul, 316

Scheman, Naomi, 322
science(s), 99, 149, 179, 180–181, 257; climate, 28–29; ecological, 104, 266, 276; Western, 264, 273. See also epistemologies, orthodox
sea-truthing, 265, 272–276
second person knowing, 114–115, 185–186, 197–198, 204–206

sexism: in philosophy, 77, 88, 89n5, 89n8
sexual harassment, 88, 90n13; in philosophy, 77, 89n5, 89n8
Sherwin, Sue, 307, 315, 322
Silencing, 83, 88, 142–143, 194, 198–199, 202–204, 207, 274–276; epistemic, 35, 57, 185
Simpson, Leanne Betamosake, 113
slavery, 21n8, 22n9; epistemologies of, 12–20
social position, 26, 29–34, 36, 40, 200, 208, 249
Somers, Margaret, 97, 111–116
Sosa, Ernest, 41n2, 307, 313–314
Stewart, Carole, 310
Stoknes, Per Espen, 285–299
stories, 9, 26–27, 34–36, 38–40, 79–80, 94–97, 101, 104, 109–117, 119–120, 202, 208, 230, 233, 236, 257–258, 278–279
subjectivity, 2, 4, 26, 32–35, 93–97, 100, 102–103, 110–111, 113–114, 120, 140, 181–182, 279
Sullivan, Shannon, 41n1, 322
suspicion: epistemic, 31, 59–60, 63

testimony, 56, 59, 76, 81, 85, 89n10, 94–97, 110–115, 117, 119–120, 176, 188, 203–204, 210, 264–266, 271, 273–280; injustice, 76, 81, 200; silencing, 59, 63, 67n14, 207–208, 210
"They Treated Him Well," 8–10
time: nonlinear narratives, 248, 252–253, 280–281; western thought, in, 244–245, 247–248, 250, 259n1
traditional ecological knowledge (TEK), 251, 256, 258
trans people, 54–57, 66n11, 198–200, 202. See also prisoners, trans of color

trust, 76, 80–82, 86–87, 296
Tuana, Nancy, 41n1, 322

United Nations Convention on the Law of the Sea (UNCLOS), 267–269, 275, 277, 281

Van Dover, Cindy, 272
Verran, Helen, 311
Violence, 94–95; colonial, 239n1, 257; epistemic, 51, 57, 63, 67n14, 207, 208–210, 274; medical, 63; sexual, 62, 94; structural, 52, 208; systemic, 58
voice hearers, 209–210, 213n8

Waddington, Kathryn, 84
Wickham, Chris, 76–78
Wittgenstein, Ludwig, 22n14, 76, 322
worldviews: Indigenous, 219–222, 224, 234, 238; Western, 219, 224, 238
Wright, Michelle, 248–254

Young, Iris Marian, 322

www.ingramcontent.com/pod-product-compliance
Ingram Content Group UK Ltd.
Pitfield, Milton Keynes, MK11 3LW, UK
UKHW041922140426
5217IPUK00014B/276